Faith and Boundaries

It was indeed possible for Indians and Europeans to live together peace-fully in early America and for Indians to survive as distinct communities. *Faith and Boundaries* uses the story of Martha's Vineyard Wampanoags to examine how. On an island marked by centralized English author-ity, missionary commitment, and an Indian majority, the Wampanoags' adaptation to English culture, especially Christianity, checked violence while safeguarding their land, community, and, ironically, even cus-toms. Yet the colonists' exploitation of Indian land and labor exposed the limits of Christian fellowship and thus hardened racial division. The Wampanoags learned about race through this rising bar of civilization – every time they met demands to reform, colonists moved the bar higher until it rested on biological difference. Under the right circumstances, like those on Martha's Vineyard, religion could bridge the wide differ-ence between the peoples of early America, but its transcendent power was limited by the divisiveness of race.

David J. Silverman is Associate Professor of History at the George Washington University. His several articles include "Indians, Missionar-ies, and Religious Translation," which won the Lester J. Cappon award for best essay of 2005 in the *William and Mary Quarterly*. He com-pleted this book as a Mellon Post-Dissertation Fellow at the American Antiquarian Society.

Studies in North American Indian History

Editors

Frederick Hoxie, University of Illinois, Urbana-Champaign
Neal Salisbury, Smith College

This series is designed to exemplify new approaches to the Native American past. In recent years scholars have begun to appreciate the extent to which Indians, whose cultural roots extended back for thousands of years, shaped the North American landscape as encountered by successive waves of immigrants. In addition, because Native Americans continually adapted their cultural traditions to the realities of the Euro-American presence, their history adds a thread of non-Western experience to the tapestry of American culture. *Cambridge Studies in North American Indian History* brings outstanding examples of this new scholarship to a broad audience. Books in the series link Native Americans to broad themes in American history and place the Indian experience in the context of social and economic change over time.

Also in the series:

RICHARD WHITE *The Middle Ground: Indians, Empires, and Republics in the Great Lakes Regions, 1650–1815*
SIDNEY L. HARRING *Crow Dog's Case: American Indian Sovereignty, Tribal Law, and United States Law in the Nineteenth Century*
COLIN G. CALLOWAY *The American Revolution in Indian Country: Crisis and Diversity in Native American Communities*
FREDERICK E. HOXIE *Parading through History: The Making of the Crow Nation in America, 1805–1935*
JEAN M. O'BRIEN *Dispossession by Degrees: Indian Land and Identity in Natick, Massachusetts, 1650–1790*
CLAUDIO SAUNT *A New Order of Things: Property, Power, and the Transformation of the Creek Indians, 1733–1816*
JEFFREY OSTLER *The Plains Sioux and U.S. Colonialism from Lewis and Clark to Wounded Knee*

This book is published in association with the American Antiquarian Society (AAS), in Worcester, Massachusetts, which supported the author's research and writing through a Mellon Post-Dissertation Fellowship, funded by a grant to AAS by the Andrew W. Mellon Foundation.

Faith and Boundaries

Colonists, Christianity, and Community among the Wampanoag Indians of Martha's Vineyard, 1600–1871

DAVID J. SILVERMAN
George Washington University

To Sharon,

In appreciation of our renewed friendship.

David

CAMBRIDGE
UNIVERSITY PRESS

CAMBRIDGE UNIVERSITY PRESS
Cambridge, New York, Melbourne, Madrid, Cape Town, Singapore, São Paulo

Cambridge University Press
32 Avenue of the Americas, New York, NY 10013-2473, USA

www.cambridge.org
Information on this title: www.cambridge.org/9780521842808

First published 2005
First paperback edition 2007
Reprinted 2007

Printed in the United States of America

A catalog record for this publication is available from the British Library.

Library of Congress Cataloging in Publication Data
Silverman, David J., 1971–
Faith and boundaries : colonists, christianity, and community among the Wampanoag Indians
of Martha's Vineyard, 1600–1871 / David J. Silverman.
p. cm. – (Studies in North American Indian history)
Includes bibliographical references and index.
ISBN 0-521-84280-8
1. Wampanoag Indians – Religion. 2. Wampanoag Indians – Government relations.
3. Wampanoag Indians – History. 4. Christianity and culture – Massachusetts – Martha's
Vineyard. 5. Martha's Vineyard (Mass.) – History. 6. Martha's Vineyard (Mass.) – Social
life and customs. I. Title. II. Series: Cambridge studies in North American Indian history.
E99.W2S54 2005
305.897'348074494 – dc22 2004029138

ISBN 978-0-521-84280-8 hardback
ISBN 978-0-521-70695-7 paperback

To Linda, more than ever, with love

Contents

Maps, Tables, and Figures

Abbreviations

AAS	American Antiquarian Society, Worcester, Mass.
AICRJ	*American Indian Culture and Research Journal*
BPL	Boston Public Library, Rare Books and Manuscripts, Boston, Mass.
Conquests and Triumphs	Matthew Mayhew, *The Conquests and Triumphs of Grace: Being a Brief Narrative of the Success which the Gospel hath had among the Indians of Martha's Vineyard (and the Places adjacent) in New-England* (London, 1695).
Cotton Journal	"The Missionary Journal of John Cotton Jr., 1666–1678," Len Travers, ed., *Proceedings of the Massachusetts Historical Society* 109 (1998), 52–101.
CPGNE	Corporation for the Propagation of the Gospel in New England, Records, New England Historic Genealogical Society, Boston, Mass.
DCCF	Dukes County Court Files, Office of the Clerk of Courts, Dukes County Courthouse, Edgartown, Mass.
DCCP	Dukes County Court of Common Pleas, Records, Office of the Clerk of Courts, Dukes County Courthouse, Edgartown, Mass.
DCCR	Dukes County Court Records, Office of the Clerk of Courts, Dukes County Courthouse, Edgartown, Mass.
DCD	Dukes County Deeds, Dukes County Registry of Deeds, Dukes County Courthouse, Edgartown, Mass.
DCGSP	Dukes County General Sessions of the Peace, Records, Office of the Clerk of Courts, Dukes County Courthouse, Edgartown, Mass.

DCP   Dukes County Probate, Records, Dukes County
                             Registry of Probate, Dukes County Courthouse,
                             Edgartown, Mass.
Earle Report   John Milton Earle, *Report to the Governor and
                             Council, Concerning the Indians of the
                             Commonwealth, Under the Act of April 6, 1859*,
                             Senate Document No. 96 (Boston, 1861).
Edgartown Records   Edgartown Town Records, Edgartown Town Hall,
                             Office of the Town Clerk, Edgartown, Mass.
FNPR   Farm Neck Proprietors' Records, 2 vols., Office of
                             the Clerk of Courts, Dukes County Courthouse,
                             Edgartown, Mass.
Force Papers   Dukes County, Mass., Records, MS 79–1773,
                             1712–1812, 173 items. Part of the collection of Peter
                             Force Papers, Library of Congress, Washington,
                             D.C.
Gay Head Report   Richard L. Pease, *Report of the Commissioner
                             Appointed to Complete the Examination and
                             Determination of All Questions of Title to Land,
                             and of All Boundary Lines between the Individual
                             Owners, at Gay Head, on the Island of Martha's
                             Vineyard* (Boston, 1871).
GIP   Guardians of Indian Plantations, Records,
                             Massachusetts State Archives, Boston, Mass.
Glorious Progress   Edward Winslow, *The Glorious Progress of the
                             Gospel amongst the Indians in New-England*
                             (London, 1649), Massachusetts Historical Society,
                             Collections, 3d ser., 4 (1834), 69–98.
Good News   Edward Winslow, *Good News from New England:
                             or a true Relation of things very remarkable at the
                             Plantation of Plymouth in New England*, in Edward
                             Arber, ed., *The Story of the Pilgrim Fathers,
                             1616–1623, A.D., as Told by Themselves, Their
                             Friends, and Their Enemies* (1624; London, 1897),
                             509–98
Hawley Journal   Gideon Hawley Letters and Journal, 4 vols.,
                             1753–1806, Congregational Library, Boston, Mass.
"Historical   Daniel Gookin, "Historical Collections of the
Collections"   Indians in New England," Massachusetts Historical
                             Society, *Collections*, 1st ser., 1 (1792), 141–227.
"Indian Visitation"   Grindal Rawson and Samuel Danforth, "Account of
                             an Indian Visitation, A.D. 1698," Massachusetts
                             Historical Society, *Collections*, 1st ser., 10 (1809),
                             129–34.

Indian Converts	Experience Mayhew, *Indian Converts: Or, Some Account of the Lives and Speeches of a Considerable Number of the Christianized Indians of Martha's Vineyard* (London, 1727).
JAH	*Journal of American History*
JER	*Journal of the Early Republic*
JMEP	John Milton Earle, Papers, American Antiquarian Society, Worcester, Mass.
Light Appearing	Henry Whitfield, *The Light appearing more and more towards the perfect Day. Or, a farther Discovery of the present state of the Indians in New-England, Concerning the Progresse of the Gospel amongst them* (London, 1651), Massachusetts Historical Society, *Collections*, 3d ser., 4 (1834), 101–47.
Mass. Acts and Resolves	*The Acts and Resolves, Public and Private, of the Province of the Massachusetts-Bay*, 21 vols. (Boston, 1869–1922).
Mass. Archives	Massachusetts Archives Series, Massachusetts State Archives, Boston, Mass.
MHSC	Massachusetts Historical Society, *Collections*
Mass. House Journals	*Journals of the House of Representatives of Massachusetts, 1715–1766*, 43 vols. (Boston, 1919–73).
Mass. House Rept. No. 68	D. L. Child, H. Stebbins, and D. Fellows Jr., *Report on the Condition of the Native Indians and Descendants of Indians, in This Commonwealth*, Massachusetts House Report No. 68 (Boston, 1827).
Mayhew Papers	Mayhew Papers (1648–1774), Howard Gotlieb Archival Research Center at Boston University, Boston, Mass.
NBFPL	New Bedford Free Public Library, Special Collections, New Bedford, Mass.
NCD	Nantucket County Deeds, Registry of Deeds, Town and County Building, Nantucket, Mass.
NCR	Nantucket County, Records, Registry of Deeds, Town and County Building, Nantucket, Mass.
Native Writings	Ives Goddard and Kathleen J. Bragdon, eds., *Native Writings in Massachusett*, 2 vols. (Philadelphia: The American Philosophical Society, 1988).
NE Co. MSS	New England Company, Records, Guildhall Library, Corporation of London.
NEHGR	*New England Historic Genealogical Register*
NEQ	*New England Quarterly*

PLP	Passed Legislation Packets, Massachusetts State Archives, Boston, Mass.
Plymouth Records	Nathaniel B. Shurtleff and David Pulsifer, eds., *Records of the Colony of New Plymouth*, 12 vols. (Boston, 1855).
Report of the Commissioners	F. W. Bird, Whiting Griswold, and Cyrus Weekes, *Report of the Commissioners Relating to the Condition of the Indians*, Massachusetts House Document No. 46 (Boston, 1849).
RSCJ	Records of the Superior Court of Judicature, 1686–1700, Massachusetts State Archives, Boston, Mass.
Senate Doc. No. 14	*Report of the Committee of the Legislature of 1869, on the Condition of the Gay Head Indians*, Senate Doc. No. 14 (Boston, 1870).
Some Account of those English Ministers	Thomas Prince, *Some Account of those English Ministers who have Successfully Presided Over the Work of Gospelizing to the Indians on Martha's Vineyard and the Adjacent Islands* (London, 1727), appendix to Experience Mayhew, *Indian Converts*.
Some Correspondence	John W. Ford, ed., *Some Correspondence between the Governors and Treasurers of the New England Company in London and the Commissioners of the United Colonies in America, the Missionaries and Others between the Years 1657 and 1712* (London: Spottiswoode and Co., 1896).
SPGNA	Society for Propagating the Gospel in North America, Papers, Philip's Library of the Peabody Essex Museum, Salem, Mass.
Strength Out of Weaknesse	Henry Whitfield, *Strength Out of Weaknesse; Or, a Glorious Manifestation of the further Progresse of the Gospel among the Indians in New England* (London, 1652), Massachusetts Historical Society, *Collections*, 3d ser., 4 (1834), 149–96.
Suffolk Files	Suffolk Files, Massachusetts State Archives, Boston, Mass.
Tears of Repentance	John Eliot and Thomas Mayhew Jr., *Tears of Repentance: Or, a Further Narrative of the Progress of the Gospel Amongst the Indians in New England* (London, 1653). Massachusetts Historical Society, *Collections*, 3d ser., 4 (1834), 197–260.
ULRIA	Unpassed Legislation Relating to Indian Affairs, Massachusetts State Archives, Boston, Mass.

WMQ   *William and Mary Quarterly*, 3d ser.
ZHP   Zachariah Howwoswee Papers, MS America, John
                  Carter Brown Library at Brown University,
                  Providence, R.I.

Preface

Do Good Walls Make Good Neighbors?

The inspiration for this study came, innocently enough, with a walk along a stone wall. Linda, my fiancé (now my wife), and I were on a late May vacation after I had finished my first year of graduate school. Short of money and in desperate need of some time outside, we were lucky to have a week at a ramshackle timeshare on the island of Martha's Vineyard, just off Cape Cod in Massachusetts. I wanted this trip to be a diversion from my studies of early America, and when the island greeted us with glorious sun and lilac-perfumed sea air I knew it would not disappoint. No sooner had we set down our bags than we ventured out for a hike, unwilling to watch the day pass. An arbitrarily chosen trail led us winding through scrub pine and oak trees, past the weed-choked foundations of a colonial-era farmstead, and up a gradual peak, until it ended at a boulder split by a deep diagonal crack sitting atop a wooded hill. This landmark, our tourist literature explained, was called Waskosim's Rock and figured prominently in the oral tradition of the island's Indians, a group that I mistakenly assumed – as I soon discovered much to my embarrassment – had disappeared several generations ago, leaving whatever stories they once told about this monument to conjecture now.

A classic New England stone wall extending from the boulder into the forest added a poetic element to the scene. Although it was not until the nineteenth century that stone walls became a common feature of the New England landscape, in the popular imagination they symbolize the pluck, piety, and permanence of the region's colonial stock, and the supposedly inevitable demise of the Natives. The story goes that Puritans sailed to America's "howling wilderness" resolved to fulfill God's dictate in Genesis 1:28 to subdue the land, only to discover that New England's craggy ground made their new Israel not unlike the desert of old. No matter: a Protestant work ethic of legendary proportions impelled them to hitch up their oxen, plow the earth, and transform overturned rocks into sturdy farm walls. The stones, once barriers to cultivation, now demarcated private property and hemmed in domestic animals, clear signs of civilized living. Faced with

xix

generations of such stubborn rivals, Indians lost one tract of territory after another, until finally their unwillingness to discard beloved hunting ways for the dominant order led them either to put up a futile resistance or fade into the western woods. The Natives' destiny, in other words, was death or migration, a subtly sinister but pervasive myth that makes Indians who have adapted to their times invisible to the broader public or somehow inauthentic. They were not supposed to have a place in a land of stone walls.

My naiveté came to an abrupt end that afternoon. With the hilltop juncture of Indian and English symbols piquing my imagination, at first opportunity I asked a "Vineyarder" about the place, sparking a conversation that went something like this: "Oh, the wall," he answered, "that's the Middle Line." "The Middle Line?" "That's right. It divided whites and Indians in the old days. We built half," he said, referring to the colonists, "they," the Indians, "built the other. Before that, the rock divided two tribes." "You know," he digressed, "we never had an Indian war here on the island." Because this was as much news to me as the Middle Line, I followed up, "well, what happened to the Indians?" Clearly I was from the mainland, or as some Vineyarders call it, America. The man leaned forward in his chair, pointed down the road, and explained matter-of-factly, "most of them live at Gay Head." I was incredulous: "Now?" "Sure enough," he responded, trying not to look bemused, "and if you're interested in Indians, down the way follow the signs to Christiantown. That's where the Mayhews used to preach to them."

I had read a bit about the Mayhews from scholars of Christian missions, most of whom use the tolerant methods of this proselytizing Puritan family as a counterpoint to the more demanding "civilizing" program of a Boston-area evangelical named John Eliot. Curious, we followed the man's directions, parked, and then followed a narrow path leading to an overgrown graveyard of unmarked headstones and a replica of a tiny eighteenth-century meetinghouse. According to a plaque, these were the places of rest and worship for some of the Mayhews' "praying Indians," who, the surroundings implied, had found little refuge in their Christianity. However, another nearby sign crushed that old chestnut too, for *currently* maintaining the site was the Wampanoag Tribe of Aquinnah (or Gay Head). As it turned out, they boasted the oldest Protestant Indian congregation in continuous existence in North America.

Vacation or not, my mind was spinning: here, away from the centers of colonial population, power, and trade, were Indians who built stone walls, worshipped Jesus, and buried one another in marked graves; Natives and newcomers who erected boundaries rather than breastworks to address their differences; people who spoke about historical populations as "we" and "they"; a New England Indian community that refused to vanish. This was something special. So on the first rainy day I poked around the island's town and county archives and the local historical society. In these places I found a treasure trove of documents relating to and occasionally penned by Indians, sometimes in their own Wampanoag language. Many of these gems lay covered in dust, bound in twine, or in a few cases, hidden, having fallen untold years ago behind office filing cabinets. Historians of American Indians commonly bemoan the lack of source materials. Yet contained within the unassuming walls of Martha's Vineyard's institutions were piles of records that shed light on a supposedly inaccessible population. A story that *should* be told *could* be told.

This book is my attempt to explain the uneasy, often troubling, yet permanent Wampanoag–English coexistence on Martha's Vineyard, and to determine why some Wampanoag communities survived the colonial period and beyond, while others did not. Islands "are a catalogue of quirks and superlatives," one scholar has observed, which makes the relevance of their histories suspect.[1] Yet exceptions to the pattern of total Indian dispossession and removal in the face of Anglo-American expansion need to be studied in order to critique the widespread assumption that this outcome was inevitable. Telling isolated stories of a shared America provides a better understanding of lost opportunities in other times and places. As I learned from my encounter with an aging stone wall, tales from unexpected sources can breathe new life into places we think we already know.

Crafting a book is similar to building a stone wall. One must survey the historiographical ground one wants to enclose, dig up the source materials, and then carefully piece them together. Over the last several years, the gracious assistance I have received from others has made this enterprise less toil and more a labor of love.

Two mentors guided me through the landscape of early American history, inspired me with their own research, and offered sage advice at every turn. When I first returned from Martha's Vineyard flush with excitement about my latest research topic, James Axtell encouraged me to pursue the idea. Long after I finished my M.A. work under his tutelage, he continued to read my materials, applying his renowned sharp pen and puckish humor to make my prose into intelligible history. I count myself fortunate that he stayed with me to the end.

John Murrin has been an ideal advisor from the start. Beginning at Princeton through our time together at the American Antiquarian Society, he provided unequivocal moral support and helped me to see the larger context by asking questions rather than giving answers. Equally important, he has provided me with a model of historian, colleague, and friend, and passed

---

[1] Philip Morgan, "Encounters Between British and Indigenous Peoples," in Mary Daunton and Rick Halpern, eds., *Empire and Others: British Encounters with Indigenous Peoples, 1600–1850* (London: UCL Press, 1999), 55.

along several priceless tips about the arts of hitting a softball and delivering a bad, bad pun. I cannot thank you enough, John.

Several institutions opened their doors and coffers to make this book possible. The Center for the Study of New England History's W. B. H. Dowse Fellowship introduced me to the Massachusetts Historical Society's goldmine of manuscripts. In graduate school, I was able to focus on this study without distraction because of the consistent financial generosity of Princeton University. During the main stage of writing, the Woodrow Wilson National Fellowship Foundation provided me with a Charlotte W. Newcombe Doctoral Dissertation Fellowship and timely requests for progress reports. The American Antiquarian Society's Mellon Post-Dissertation Fellowship was a year of uninterrupted thinking, reading, and revising, aided by a magnificent staff and academic community. I extend special thanks to Wayne State University's Department of History and especially to its indefatigable department chair, Marc Kruman, for permitting me to indulge in this special opportunity, to Caroline Sloat for making my time in Worcester so productive, and to my fellow Fellows, including Pat Cohen, Benjamin Reis, Joanne Radner, Daniel Mandell, Robert Gross, Karsten Fitz, Bridget Ford, and Eliza Richards for serving as lunch-time sounding boards and good chums.

The munificence of the above organizations enabled me to indulge my fondness for archival research in some of early Americana's great repositories. Along the way, I received courteous assistance from the staffs of the Alexander Library of Rutgers University, American Antiquarian Society (Worcester), Boston Public Library, Congregational Library (Boston), Connecticut Historical Society (Hartford), Connecticut State Archives (Hartford), Chilmark Town Hall, Dukes County Superior Court, Edgartown Town Hall, Guildhall Library (London), Houghton and Pursey Libraries of Harvard University, John Carter Brown Library of Brown University, Massachusetts State Archives (Boston), Howard Gotlieb Archival Research Center at Boston University, Newberry Library (Chicago), Philips Library of the Peabody-Essex Museum (Salem), Edouard A. Stackpole Library and Research Center of the Nantucket Historical Association, Nantucket Registry of Deeds, Nantucket Superior Court, Rhode Island State Archives (Providence), and especially Princeton's Firestone Library. I extend warmest appreciation to the good people of the Dukes County Registry of Deeds, led by Jean Powers, and the Martha's Vineyard Historical Society, particularly Jill Bouck, who gave me more liberty to explore their rich collections than I had any right to expect. I will always warmly recall my time in their company. Thanks are also due to Michael Fickes, Holly Mitchell, Ann Marie Plane, and Daniel Mandell, who called my attention to manuscript collections and provided me with copies of items that I otherwise might have missed, and to Ives Goddard, who translated two Wampanoag language documents that I found in the archives. At a later stage of writing, genealogist Andrew Pierce's detailed memory saved me from a number of errors and steered me toward sources I had overlooked. Students of New England history will benefit handsomely from his painstakingly researched, co-authored genealogical study of the Vineyard Wampanoags. I only wish I had access to it from the start.

The input of scholarly audiences, colleagues, and friends has made this a better book. I presented draft chapters and related works-in-progress before the Colonial Society of Massachusetts, the annual meeting of the American Society of Ethnohistory, the 31st Algonquian Conference, the McNeil Center for Early American Studies, an Annual Meeting and Colloquium of the Omohundro Institute of Early American History and Culture, the New England Seminar at the American Antiquarian Society, and history department brown bags at Wayne State University and the George Washington University. Good citizens Barry O'Connell, Nancy Shoemaker, Len Travers, Pat Cohen, John Hench, and Caroline Sloat charted a clear path to revision by reading an early version of the manuscript and then trenchantly, but kindly, explaining what hard choices I had to make. Neal Salisbury and Fred Hoxie prodded me to extend my reach in later drafts and showed the way how. Daniel K. Richter gave an essay version of Chapter 5 his expert editorial critique, while Virginia Anderson, Christopher Grasso, Jenny Hale Pulsipher, Alden T. Vaughan, and Douglas Watson helped me fine-tune articles containing this book's theses. My thanks to *Explorations in Early American Culture* (now *Early American Studies*), *New England Quarterly*, and *William and Mary Quarterly* for permission to reprint portions of those articles that have appeared in their pages. Hans Hummer, Andrew Isenberg, Chris Johnson, Marc Kruman, Kenneth Mills, Jon Parmenter, Elizabeth Lewis Pardoe, Stanley Shapiro, Sandra Van Burkleo, and my perpetual partners in crime, Denver Brunsman and Jarbel Rodriguez, have also provided me with friendly, constructive criticism (some of which I have even accepted). Needless to say, I take all responsibility for errors of fact and interpretation.

The most penetrating exchanges have come in discussions with several members of the Wampanoag Tribe of Aquinnah, among them, Ryan Malonson, Helen Manning, June Manning, William Derwood Vanderhoop, Gladys Widdiss, Beverly Wright, and time and time again, Tobias Vanderhoop. My Wampanoag colleagues have taught me valuable lessons about how people's actual lives are influenced by family, community, cultural norms, historical and racial consciousness, and the universal challenge of making ends meet. They have also exposed the assumptions I brought to my research, raised numerous questions that would never have occurred to me, and reminded me that scholars of the Indian past carry an extra obligation to be sensitive in their writing and thorough in their research. I am grateful to the individuals listed above, as well as to others whom I might have forgotten, for taking the time to speak with me. I also appreciate Nan Doty for helping to arrange our meetings and for countless other contributions along the way.

My family has been a rock of support during the construction of this book. My parents, Richard and Julia Silverman, secured me a place to stay on Martha's Vineyard while I rummaged through the archives, and then kept me on track till completion by babysitting and hinting that even academics should have deadlines. My children, Aquinnah and Bela, just by being here, have taught me more than any work of history about the sacrifices people will make for the younger generations – If there is a humanistic tone to this book, I owe it to them.

Above all, I thank my wife, Linda. She has lived with this project since its inception, and even suggested an early version of the topic. As I've lugged book boxes and furniture during our several moves, I've often teased her that among Indians, women were responsible for carrying nearly all of the family's goods and children during their people's seasonal migrations, while the men went relatively unencumbered. Nevertheless, she has certainly shouldered her own burdens because of this study. She has never been anything but encouraging throughout my seemingly endless research trips and compulsive bouts of writing and rewriting, even though she has been overloaded with her own responsibilities of work, graduate school, and, now, motherhood. She has read every line of this book, often several times, and kept me ever mindful that I should be writing for an audience of educated nonhistorians. Her strength during the trying times has been a constant reminder to not lose sight of what drew me to historical scholarship in the first place – pursuit of the quiet drama of everyday lives. I will never be able to thank her enough for her loving devotion to me and our children. But as one small gesture of my enduring gratitude, admiration, and affection I dedicate this work to her.

Montgomery Village, Maryland
D.J.S.
March 2004

Introduction

Epenow's Lessons

E penow's pulse must have quickened when he caught the first scent of pine forest drifting eastward from a land still out of view but foremost on his mind. Just days later the vessel carrying him from England approached the Maine shoreline and then plied southward past Massachusetts Bay into waters that crashed against the sand dune frame of his Wampanoag people's territory. The power of the moment would have unleashed pent up heartache and fury in a weaker man, but mastering his emotions had brought Epenow this far and he was not about to abandon the course. Patiently, he endured the long last stage of his journey around Cape Cod and the treacherous Nantucket shoals, and finally toward the island of Noepe, his home. It had been three years since a fateful day in 1611 when Captain Edward Harlow abducted Epenow from the New England coast and carried him across the ocean into an adventure bordering on the surreal. Once in London, Epenow's captors shuttled him from place to place exhibiting him as "a wonder" before gawking crowds, a humiliation suffered by dozens and perhaps hundreds of other kidnapped Indians during the previous century.[1] For Epenow, however, the city was on show with its throngs of people and livestock jamming the streets, the abject poor begging at the heels of their ornately clad "betters," and a whirling commerce in goods from nearly every corner of the globe, all in the shadow of mighty architecture sponsored by England's church and state. The spectacle of wealth and poverty, power and population, was unlike anything Epenow had ever known in the Wampanoags' village world. Yet there was hardly enough

---

[1] Alden T. Vaughan, "Sir Walter Ralegh's Indian Interpreters, 1584–1618," *WMQ* 59 (2002), 341–76; Harald E. L. Prins, "To the Land of the Mistigoches: American Indians Traveling to Europe in the Age of Exploration," *AICRJ* 17 (1993), 175–95; Olive P. Dickason, *The Myth of the Savage and the Beginnings of French Colonialism in the Americas* (Edmonton: University of Alberta Press, 1984), 203–32; Carolyn Thomas Foreman, *Indians Abroad, 1493–1938* (Norman: University of Oklahoma Press, 1943).

time to get his bearings, for when audiences tired of gazing at a bona fide "savage," he was transferred some 200 miles westward to the port town of Plymouth and the custody of Sir Ferdinando Gorges, a prime mover in England's first colonization efforts and a collector of informative Indians.[2]

However disoriented Epenow might have become during the unfolding of these events, eventually he regained his footing and transformed himself from a puppet to puppet master. Somehow he gained a rudimentary command of the English language, perhaps enough to free his words from the strained translations and editorial comments of another captive Indian, a Wabenaki from Maine named Assacomoit, and certainly enough to learn something of his captors' strange behavior. The Englishmen's greatest motivation turned out to be so foreign yet simple that one imagines Epenow shaking his head and laughing in disbelief when he uncovered it. One also can picture the smile crossing Gorges' face as Epenow began to spin tall tales about Noepe's gold mines and offered to lead an expedition to them. The Wampanoag's stories attracted enough investors to outfit a 1614 voyage under the command of Nicholas Hobson. In a change of fortune nearly as incredible as his captivity, Epenow was heading home.[3]

Onboard, both the crew and their Indian passenger were excited by the promise of future rewards, but nervous that either party could destroy the other's plans. Consequently, when the ship anchored off Noepe, which the English called Martha's Vineyard, Hobson placed Epenow under close watch and clothed him in long garments, "fitly to be laid hold on, if occasion should require." Wampanoags canoeing out to investigate were equally suspicious, since violence had marred all their recent encounters with Europeans. Yet the astonishing reappearance of Epenow eased their caution and drew them to shipside. Reveling in the sound of his mother tongue, Epenow told his people to come back in the morning to trade, or so Hobson thought. Accordingly, the next day a flotilla of canoes approached the craft, and once they were within bowshot, Epenow threw off his guards, leapt into the water, and swam to safety while his tribesmen pinned down the sailors with a barrage of arrows. "[The Indians] carried him away in despight [despite] of all the Musquetteers aboard,"

---

[2] Vaughan, *New England Frontier: Puritans and Indians, 1620–1675*, 3d ed. (Norman: University of Oklahoma Press, 1995), 1–10; David B. Quinn, *North America from Earliest Discovery to First Settlements: The Norse Voyages to 1612* (New York: Harper and Row, 1977), 412–13; Neal Salisbury, *Manitou and Providence: Indians, Europeans, and the Making of New England, 1500–1643* (New York: Oxford, 1982), 95.

[3] Philip L. Barbour, ed., *The Complete Works of Captain John Smith (1580–1631), in Three Volumes* (Chapel Hill: University of North Carolina Press for the Institute of Early American History and Culture, 1986), 1:433, 2:403; James Phinney Baxter, ed., *Sir Ferdinando Gorges and His Province of Maine*, 3 vols. (Boston: The Prince Society, 1890), 1:209–11, 2:21–23. Prins, "To the Land of the Mistigoches," 185–6, tells the fascinating story of the Wabenaki captive, Assacomoit.

a stunned Gorges was told.[4] The English had sailed to Martha's Vineyard blinded by the prospective shine of gold. Instead, "they lost [Epenow]; and not knowing what to do, returned againe to England with nothing."[5]

Epenow exhibited his flair for dramatic reappearance again in 1619. That year Captain Thomas Dermer coasted southern New England at the request of a passenger named Squanto, another Wampanoag who had fallen into Gorges' possession after Thomas Hunt snatched him and twenty-six other Natives from the mainland in 1614.[6] While mooring at Martha's Vineyard, the crew was shocked to be greeted by none other than Epenow, who in "indifferent good English" recounted his earlier captivity with Gorges, Dermer's very sponsor, "laughed at his own escape, and reported the story of it." To the sailors' relief, he offered no sign of lingering hostility, but rather played the gracious host and even encouraged Dermer to return to the island on his way back north from Virginia, the captain's destination. Like Gorges chasing gold, Dermer took the bait, unaware that Wampanoags yearned for revenge against his nation for the repeated crimes of men like Harlow and Hunt.[7] The captain stopped again at the Vineyard and "going ashore amongst the Indians to trade, as he used to do, was betrayed and assaulted by them, and all his men slain, but one that kept the boat."[8] Gorges believed, "a war has now began between the inhabitants of those parts and us."[9]

[4] Baxter, ed., *Sir Ferdinando Gorges*, 2:25.

[5] Barbour, ed., *Complete Works of Captain John Smith*, 2:403. For another full account of Epenow's story, see Samuel Purchas, *Hakluytas Posthumus, or, Purchas His Pilgrimes: Contayning a History of the World in Sea Voyages and Land Travells by Englishmen and Others*, 20 vols. (Glasgow, 1907), 19:272–5.

[6] Neal Salisbury, "Squanto: Last of the Patuxets," in David G. Sweet and Gary B. Nash, eds., *Struggle and Survival in Colonial America* (Berkeley: University of California Press, 1981), 228–46.

[7] Accounts of these clashes are found in Quinn, *North America from Earliest Discovery to First Settlements*, 385–416; James Axtell, "At the Water's Edge: Trading in the Sixteenth Century," in his *After Columbus: Essays in the Ethnohistory of Colonial North America* (New York: Oxford University Press, 1988), 144–81; Axtell, "The Exploration of Norumbega: Native Perspectives," in his *Beyond 1492: Encounters in Colonial North America* (New York: Oxford University Press, 1988), 75–96; Prins, "To the Land of the Mistigoches"; and David J. Silverman, "Conditions for Coexistence, Climates for Collapse: The Challenges of Indian Life on Martha's Vineyard, 1524–1871" (Ph.D. diss., Princeton University, 2000), 10–11, 17–22.

[8] Dermer's story can be traced in George Parker Winship, ed., *Sailor's Narratives of Voyages along the New England Coast, 1524–1624* (Boston: Houghton, Mifflin, and Company, 1905), 251–7 ("indifferent good English" at 255); Barbour, ed., *Complete Works of Captain John Smith*, 2:441; William Bradford, *Of Plymouth Plantation, 1620–1647*, ed. Samuel Eliot Morison (New York: Alfred A. Knopf, 1979), 82–3 ("going ashore . . ."); Baxter, ed., *Sir Ferdinando Gorges*, 2:29 ("laughed . . ."). Gorges' account of these events should be read with care because he wrote it forty years after the fact and seems to have suffered from a clouded memory about certain details. See Salisbury, *Manitou and Providence*, 265–6, n. 15.

[9] Quoted in Vaughan, *New England Frontier*, 16. See also Dwight B. Heath, ed., *Mourt's Relation: A Journal of the Pilgrims at Plymouth* (1622; Bedford, Mass.: Applewood Books, 1963), 52; Bradford, *Of Plymouth Plantation*, 83; Purchas, *Hakluytus Posthumus*, 19:279.

FIGURE 1. The Wampanoags' Early Contacts with Europeans. The Wampanoags had steady contact with European explorers during the early seventeenth century. Usually they met in the context of trade, as depicted in Theodore de Bry's drawing of Bartholomew Gosnold's 1602 visit to Martha's Vineyard and the Elizabeth Islands. However, almost invariably these sessions degenerated into violence, as in a drawing of Samuel de Champlain's 1606 clash with Wampanoags at Monomoy on Cape Cod, and involved Europeans carrying Indians away into captivity. This pattern led the Vineyard Wampanoags to avoid English colonists until the 1640s, twenty years after the founding of Plymouth colony.

Island Wampanoags retained their belligerent reputation for years to come. In 1622, they were implicated in a regional Indian conspiracy to cut off the young Plymouth colony, and even after they signed a treaty of friendship, the settlers still considered them "mortal enemies to all other English."[10]

[10] Vaughan, *New England Frontier*, 82–8; Francis Jennings, *The Invasion of America: Indians, Colonialism, and the Cant of Conquest* (New York: W. W. Norton for the Institute of Early American History and Culture, 1975), 186–7; Salisbury, *Manitou and Providence*, 129; John Pory to the Earl of Southampton, January 13, 1622/23, in James, ed., *Three Visitors to Early Plymouth* (quote). See also John H. Humins, "Squanto and Massasoit: A Struggle for Power," *NEQ* 60 (1987), 54–70.

FIGURE 1 (*continued*)

Emmanuel Altham wrote in 1623 that since Dermer's murder at the Vineyard, "no English hath been there," although he intended to try "well armed."[11] When Thomas Lechford returned to England in 1641 after three years in Boston, he remembered "an Island called Martins Vineyard, uninhabited by any English, but Indians, which are very savage."[12] Lechford's contemporary, John Josselyn, heard that Vineyard Wampanoags once "seized upon a boat that put into a By-Cove, kill'd the men and eat them in a short time before they were discovered."[13] Fact or fiction, the point was clear: Englishmen were not welcome on Epenow's island.

Yet the early 1640s called for a new strategy. Epenow had disappeared from the historical stage, and although he left little record of his political career, undoubtedly his people's hostile isolationism had been influenced by him. But the island's saltwater moat struggled to contain the forces raging outside. Between 1616 and 1618 and then again in 1633, European epidemics tore into New England, dropping the Native population along the mainland coast and the Connecticut River Valley by some seventy-five percent or

[11] Emmanuel Altham to Sir Edward Altham (1623), in James, ed., *Three Visitors to Early Plymouth*, 27.
[12] Thomas Lechford, *Plain Dealing, or Newes from New-England* (London, 1642), MHSC 3d ser., 3 (1833), 100.
[13] John Josselyn, "The Second Voyage," in Paul J. Lindholdt, ed., *John Josselyn, Colonial Traveler: A Critical Edition of "Two Voyages to New-England"* (1674; Hanover, N.H.: University Press of New England, 1988), 91.

more, but apparently sparing the Vineyard.[14] Meanwhile, English numbers grew exponentially from a few hundred settlers in 1629 to over 15,000 a decade later, driven by streams of immigration to the Massachusetts Bay Colony.[15] If these trends were not enough to shift the balance of power to the English, the Pequot War of 1636–1637 certainly was. Even Indians hardened to forest warfare were shocked by the colonists' torching of a Pequot village and slaughter of hundreds of innocents who tried to escape the flames. Captain John Mason's order to his troops, "we must burn them," reverberated throughout Indian country.[16]

As colonist William Hubbard wrote, the Pequot War "struck such a terror into all the Indians in those parts (some of whom had been ill affected to the English before) that they sought our friendship and rendered themselves to be under our protection."[17] Wampanoag sachems on Cape Cod who had

---

[14] On the first outbreak, see Timothy Bratton, "The Identity of the New England Indian Epidemic of 1616–1619," *Bulletin of the History of Medicine* 62 (1988), 351–83; S. F. Cook, "The Significance of Disease in the Extinction of the New England Indians," *Human Biology* 45 (1973), 485–508; Dean Snow and Kim M. Lanphear, "European Contact and Indian Depopulation in the Northeast: The Timing of the First Epidemics," *Ethnohistory* 35 (1988), 15–33; Catherine C. Carlson, George L. Armelagos, and Ann Magennis, "Impact of Disease on the Precontact and Early Historic Populations of New England and the Maritimes," in John W. Verano and Douglas H. Ubelaker, eds., *Disease and Demography in the Americas* (Washington, D.C.: Smithsonian Institution Press, 1992), 141–52; and Brenda J. Baker, "Pilgrim's Progress and Praying Indians: The Biocultural Consequences of Contact in Southern New England," in Clark Spencer Larsen and Geroge R. Milner, eds., *In the Wake of Contact: Biological Responses to Conquest* (New York: Wiley-Liss, Inc., 1994), 35–44. On the second, see John Winthrop, *The Journal of John Winthrop, 1630–1649*, eds. Richard S. Dunn, James Savage, and Laeititia Yeandle (Cambridge, Mass.: Belknap Press of Harvard University Press, 1996), 101, 105–6, 108–10; Edward Johnson, *Johnson's Wonder-Working Providence, 1628–1651*, J. Franklin Jameson ed. (New York: Charles Scribner's Sons, 1910), 79–80; Salisbury, *Manitou and Providence*, 190–92; and William A. Starna, "The Pequots in the Early Seventeenth Century," in Hauptman and Wherry, eds., *The Pequots in Southern New England*, 46.

[15] Virginia DeJohn Anderson, *New England's Generation: The Great Migration and the Formation of Society and Culture in the Seventeenth Century* (New York: Cambridge University Press, 1991).

[16] The authoritative account of these events is Arthur A. Cave, *The Pequot War* (Amherst: University of Massachusetts Press, 1996). See also Vaughan, "Pequots and Puritans: The Causes of the War of 1637," in his *Roots of American Racism: Essays on the Colonial Experience* (New York: Oxford University Press, 1995), 277–321; and the recent debate over the English massacre of Pequots: Ronald Dale Karr, "'Why Should You Be So Furious?': The Violence of the Pequot War," *JAH* 85 (1998), 876–909; Adam J. Hirsch, "The Collision of Military Cultures in Seventeenth-Century New England," *JAH* 47 (1988), 1187–212; Steven T. Katz, "The Pequot War Reconsidered," *NEQ* 64 (1991), 206–24; Michael Freeman, "Puritans and Pequots: The Question of Genocide," *NEQ* 68 (1995), 278; Katz, "Pequots and the Question of Genocide: A Reply to Michael Freeman," *NEQ* 68 (1995), 641–9.

[17] William Hubbard, *A Narrative of the Indian Wars in New England, From the first Planting thereof in the Year 1607 to the Year 1677* (1677; Boston, 1775), 39. See also John Strong, *The Algonquian Peoples of Long Island from Earliest Times to 1700* (Interlaken, N.Y.: Empire State Books, 1997), 156–8.

previously rebuffed the English suddenly began to welcome them as neighbors, leading to the establishment of the towns of Sandwich (settled by the English in 1638), Yarmouth (1638), and Barnstable (1639).[18] As the colonists' newfound allies, these Indians could breathe easy even when Boston threatened in August of 1642 to "strike some terrour into the Indians" because of a rumor that "the Indians all over the country had combined themselves to cut off all the English."[19] But island Wampanoags shuddered at these words, since the English had long suspected them. They needed to make a peaceful gesture and fast. Just then, within months, if not weeks, of Boston's warning, a proverbial *deus ex machina* appeared in the form of a colonist named Thomas Mayhew, who had recently bought the previously worthless English title to Martha's Vineyard and Nantucket, and now wanted "to obtain the Indian right."[20] Tawanquatuck, sachem of the east-end territory, Nunnepog, took this opportunity to distance his people from the supposed conspiracy and sold Mayhew land for a settlement, believing that this concession was the price of peace.

Tawanquatuck's people were so opposed to this bargain that he was forced to divide his jurisdiction and grant the dissidents independence. However, even the Wampanoags' long and troubled history with the English could not have prepared them for the vast tumult about to enter their lives – epidemic diseases, a new religion, land loss, and political upheaval, followed by debt peonage, exogamous marriage, racial castigation, and much more. Mayhew's colonists were quite unlike the roughneck crews that the Wampanoags had confronted during Epenow's time, but they came with an agenda far more threatening, if also more subtle: they were not interested in seizing the Indians, but they did intend to subjugate them to English authority and religion; they had no plans to force the Indians into slavery, but they did want them as servants; they would not ship the Indians to distant lands, but they did encroach upon the Natives' very lands. And what was more, the colonists intended to stay, not to strike quick and sail off. Remarkably, the two parties never came to blows, but English good fortune was bought at the Wampanoags' expense, leading to the gradual disintegration of several Native communities over the course of two centuries and more.

Yet not all of them, and this book aims to explain why. Recent scholarship contends that during the opening years of colonization, and on the edges of empire where the fur trade thrived and Europeans were scarce, Natives

[18] Winthrop, *Journal of John Winthrop*, 245, 252, 299; Frederick Freeman, *The History of Cape Cod: The Annals of Barnstable County and Its Several towns, Including the District of Mashpee*, 2 vols. (1858; Yarmouth Port, Mass: Parnassus Imprints, 1965), 1:chap. 8; H. Roger King, *Cape Cod and Plymouth Colony* (Landham, Md.: University Press of America, 1994), 44–5, 53.

[19] Vaughan, *New England Frontier*, 157; Jennings, *Invasion of America*, 260–1 (quote).

[20] Charles Edward Banks, *The History of Martha's Vineyard, Dukes County, Massachusetts*, 3 vols. (Boston: George H. Dean, 1911), 1:84.

and newcomers were linked by economic interdependence, growing political ties, and in some cases, earnest missionary activity, producing exchanges of material culture, ritual behavior, and, to a lesser extent, even beliefs.[21] This was the case even in New England, long held to be a bastion of uncompromising colonial expansion, between the Pequot War of 1636–1637 and King Philip's War of 1675–1676. This interpretive emphasis on cooperation and negotiation, rather than just on exploitation and brutality, brilliantly modifies the long-standing view of an unbridgeable cultural gap between peoples that automatically degenerated into bloodshed. Nevertheless, in one case study after another, Indian–European communion implodes, often in a murderous orgy, usually within decades of inception – a track record that is especially grim for English regions. In this sense, the new scholarship has reinforced the narrative of inevitable warfare and Indian dispossession even though it has successfully complicated and delayed its trajectory. The history of Martha's Vineyard, where the two peoples managed to live in close proximity for hundreds of years without slaughtering one another, demands explanation in this context.

Along similar lines, current scholarship offers few positive assessments of Indian attempts to use Christianity to negotiate colonial systems over the long term. Historians of New England agree that Indians who gathered into the region's "praying towns," or Christian reserves, during the

---

[21] On New England, see Salisbury, "Social Relationships on a Moving Frontier: Natives and Settlers in Southern New England, 1638–1675," *MNE* 33 (1987), 89–98; Robert James Naeher, "Dialogue in the Wilderness: John Eliot and the Indians' Exploration of Puritanism as a Source of Meaning, Comfort, and Ethnic Survival," *NEQ* 62 (1989), 346–68; Harold W. Van Lonkhuyzen, "A Reappraisal of the Praying Indians: Acculturation, Conversion, and Identity at Natick, Massachusetts, 1646–1730," *NEQ* 63 (1990), 396–428; Richard Cogley, *John Eliot's Mission to the Indians before King Philip's War* (Cambridge, Mass.: Harvard University Press, 1999); James D. Drake, *King Philip's War: Civil War in New England, 1675–1676* (Amherst: University of Massachusetts Press, 1999).

Among many works on other colonial regions, see Richard White, *The Middle Ground: Indians, Empires, and Republics in the Great Lakes Region, 1650–1815* (New York: Cambridge University Press, 1991); Daniel H. Usner Jr., *Indians, Settlers, and Slaves in a Frontier Exchange Economy: The Lower Mississippi Valley before 1783* (Chapel Hill, N.C.: University of North Carolina Press for the Institute of Early American History and Culture, 1992); Axtell, *The European and the Indian: Essays in the Ethnohistory of Colonial North America* (New York: Oxford University Press, 1981); Axtell, *The Invasion Within: The Contest of Cultures in Colonial North America* (New York: Oxford University Press, 1985); Peter C. Mancall, *Valley of Opportunity: Economic Culture along the Upper Susquehanna, 1700–1800* (Ithaca, N.Y.: Cornell University Press, 1991); Colin G. Calloway, *Indians, Europeans, and the Remaking of Early America* (Baltimore: The Johns Hopkins University Press, 1997); Andrew R. L. Cayton and Fredrika Teute, eds., *Contact Points: American Frontiers from the Mohawk Valley to the Mississippi, 1750–1830* (Chapel Hill: University of North Carolina Press for the Omohundro Institute of Early American History and Culture, 1998); Jane T. Merritt, *At the Crossroads: Indians and Empires on a Mid-Atlantic Frontier, 1700–1763* (Chapel Hill: University of North Carolina Press for the Omohundro Institute of Early American History and Culture, 2003).

mid-seventeenth century were trying to cloister portions of their land from insatiable Massachusetts, and that this strategy worked, although only for a time.[22] The "praying Indians'" status as Christians enabled most of them to sustain a fragile peace with the English during King Philip's War and to emerge from the conflict with some territory intact. Yet the war and subsequent frontier conflicts permanently heightened the colonists' suspicion and hatred of all Indians, Christian or not, which, combined with their lust for Indian resources, sapped their enthusiasm for missionary work and encouraged them to violate the Indians' land and jurisdiction at every turn. The praying Indians could hardly muster a defense, supposedly because acculturation had weakened their social institutions and sense of collective identity, and the empty promises of Christianity demoralized them. Thus, throughout the eighteenth century, Englishmen steadily chipped away at praying town boundaries, exploited the Indians economically, and eventually drove most of the Natives west or into the company of the wandering poor. Given this telling, it would appear that Christianity failed New England's Indians just as it failed the Indians of so many other times and places throughout the colonial saga: Hurons who hosted Jesuit missionaries during the 1630s and 40s to secure French military assistance and trade advantages, only to become so hopelessly factionalized by Christianity that they disintegrated under Iroquois attack; Florida Indians who became easy targets for European diseases and South Carolina's slave raids by gathering into Christian settlements after the Spanish promised their leadership military and material support; Moravian Delawares in the Ohio mission town of Gnadenhutten, who, having embraced Christianity as a means of revitalizing their communities after rampant land loss and despondency, were mercilessly bludgeoned to death by frontier settlers, their fellow Christians, toward the end of the Revolution.[23] Counterexamples exist among the Pueblo Indians of New Mexico and

[22] Elise M. Brenner, "To Pray or to be Prey: That is the Question: Strategies for Cultural Autonomy of Massachusetts Praying Town Indians," *Ethnohistory* 27 (1980), 135–52; James P. Ronda, "Generations of Faith: The Christian Indians of Martha's Vineyard," *WMQ* 38 (1981), 369–94; Axtell, "Were Indian Conversion Bona Fide?" in *After Columbus*, 100–24; Naeher, "Dialogue in the Wilderness"; Van Lonkhuyzen, "A Reappraisal of the Praying Indians"; Daniel Mandell, "'To Live More Like my Christian English Neighbors': Natick Indians in the Eighteenth Century," *WMQ* 48 (1991), 552–79; Mandell, *Behind the Frontier: Indians in Eighteenth-Century Eastern Massachusetts* (Lincoln: University of Nebraska Press, 1996); Dane Morrison, *A Praying People: Massachusett Acculturation and the Failure of the Puritan Mission, 1600–1690* (New York: Peter Land, 1995); Jean M. O'Brien, *Dispossession by Degrees: Indian Land and Identity in Natick, Massachusetts, 1650–1790* (New York: Cambridge University Press, 1997); Cogley, *John Eliot's Mission to the Indians*.
[23] On the Hurons, see Bruce G. Trigger, *The Children of Aataentsic: A History of the Huron People to 1660*, 2d ed. (Montreal: McGill-Queen's University Press, 1985); Denys Delâge, *Bitter Feast: Amerindians and Europeans in Northeastern North America, 1600–1664*, Jane Brierley, trans. (Vancouver: University of British Columbia Press, 1993). On Florida, see Jerald T. Milanich, *Laboring in the Fields of the Lord: Spanish Missions and Southeastern*

the various tribes of the Saint Lawrence River Valley, who used Catholicism to secure permanent safe havens, but histories of the Southwest are more likely to emphasize how missions sparked the Pueblo Revolt of 1680, while those of Canada tend to sublimate Christianity to imperial politics, trade, and war.[24] Students of the period are left with the overwhelming impression that adopting Christianity could, at best, only postpone the Indians' dispossession, not halt it.

The Indians' Christianity appears no stronger than their defenses in most studies. Generally, historians portray Indian Christianity as a diplomatic cloak under which to maintain traditional beliefs and customs, or a minor syncretic addition to a fundamentally unchanged Indian religion.[25] Some add that the cultural and linguistic barriers between peoples were so high that it was nearly impossible for Indians to gain a solid command of Christian doctrine, especially the heady Calvinism of New England Puritans, even for those few who pursued it. If one also accepts that the mission was an essential component of colonial expansion, and that it was at best a short-lived and imperfect means to come to grips with colonial society for Natives barely knowledgeable about the faith's basic tenets, it is no wonder that Christian Indians tended to fare so badly.

Indians (Washington, D.C.: Smithsonian Institution Press, 1999); David J. Weber, *The Spanish Frontier in North America* (New Haven: Yale University Press, 1992); Amy Turner Bushnell, "Ruling 'the Republic of Indians' in Seventeenth-Century Florida," in Peter Wood, Gregory A. Waselkov, and M. Thomas Hatley, eds., *Powhatan's Mantle: Indians in the Colonial Southeast* (Lincoln: University of Nebraska Press, 1989), 134–50; Alan Gallay, *The Indian Slave Trade: The Rise of the English Empire in the American South, 1670–1717* (New Haven: Yale University Press, 2002). On Moravian Indians and Gnadenhutten, see Merritt, *At the Crossroads*; White, *Middle Ground*, 389–90; Gregory Evans Dowd, *A Spirited Resistance: The North American Indian Struggle for Unity, 1745–1815* (Baltimore: The Johns Hopkins University Press, 1992), 83–9.

[24] Daniel K. Richter, *The Ordeal of the Longhouse: The Peoples of the Iroquois League in the Era of European Colonization* (Chapel Hill: University of North Carolina Press for the Institute of Early American History and Culture); Colin G. Calloway, *The Western Abenakis of Vermont, 1600–1800: War, Migration, and the Survival of an Indian People* (Norman: University of Oklahoma Press, 1990); Ramón Gutiérrez, *When Jesus Came, the Corn Mothers Went Away: Marriage, Sex, and Power in New Mexico, 1500–1846* (Stanford: Stanford University Press, 1991); Weber, *Spanish Frontier*; Andrew L. Knaut, *The Pueblo Revolt of 1680: Conquest and Resistance in Seventeenth-Century New Mexico* (Norman: University of Oklahoma Press, 1995).

[25] For skeptics of the quality of Christianity among southern New England Indians, see Salisbury, "Red Puritans: The 'Praying Indians' of Massachusetts Bay and John Eliot," *WMQ* 31 (1974), 29–31; O'Brien, *Dispossession by Degrees*, 54–5, 57; Jennings, "Goals and Functions of Puritan Missions"; Elise M. Brenner, "Strategies for Autonomy: An Analysis of Ethnic Mobilization in Seventeenth Century Southern New England" (Ph.D. diss., University of Massachusetts at Amherst, 1984), 115; and Kenneth M. Morrison, "'That Art of Coyning Christians': John Eliot and the Praying Indians of Massachusetts," *Ethnohistory* 21 (1974), 77–92. For a rare dissenting position, see Axtell, "Were Indian Conversions Bona Fide?"

In this light, it would seem to be no coincidence that most of the eastern tribes who still retain portions (however miniscule) of their ancestral lands, such as the Mohegans and Pequots of Connecticut, the Narragansetts of Rhode Island, the Mattaponis, Pamunkeys, and Rappahannocks of Virginia, and the Catawbas of South Carolina, were latecomers to Christianity. The aforementioned New England tribes held out until the mid-eighteenth century and most of the southern tribes until the late eighteenth and even the nineteenth centuries. Historians have identified several factors that enabled these peoples to survive the unyielding hazards of the colonial era while rejecting the colonizers' religion: the Natives' willingness to make themselves valuable to Englishmen as military allies, slave catchers, and laborers; acceptance of diminished territory in exchange for clear title to reservations; cultivation of powerful colonial patrons; and numerous socioeconomic adjustments, which often contained spiritual undertones, but not on the scale of systematic religious change. Long after the Indians of Martha's Vineyard had become Christians, the above groups were still using the faith mainly as a negative reference, with their resistance providing a source of Native cohesion and vitality.[26] How, then, to explain the Vineyard Wampanoags' marriage of Christianity and community survival?

This study uses two questions to explore the problematics of peaceful Indian–colonist coexistence and the role of Christianity in intercultural relations and Native community life. First, why was bloodshed conspicuously absent from colonial Martha's Vineyard even though the Wampanoags there suffered many of the same tensions, such as evangelization and English encroachment, that burst into war on the continent? Secondly, how did certain Wampanoag communities on Martha's Vineyard, such as Chappaquiddick, Christiantown, and especially Aquinnah, manage to survive as distinct geographical, social, and cultural units into the nineteenth century and beyond, while others, such as Nunnepog, Sengekontacket, and Nashuakemuck, did not? In pursuit of answers to these queries, each of the seven chapters in this book focuses upon a particular challenge, or a series of interrelated challenges, that confronted the Indians from their violent contacts with European

[26] Eric S. Johnson, "Uncas and the Politics of Contact," in Robert S. Grumet, ed., *Northeastern Indian Lives, 1632–1816* (Amherst: University of Massachusetts Press, 1996), 29–48; Wendy B. St. Jean, "Inventing Guardianship: The Mohegan Indians and Their 'Protectors'," *NEQ* 72 (1999), 362–87; Michael Leroy Oberg, *Uncas: First of the Mohegans* (Ithaca: Cornell University Press, 2003); Paul R. Campbell and Glenn W. LaFantasie, "'Scattered to the Winds of Heaven': Narragansett Indians, 1676–1880," *Rhode Island History* 47 (1978), 66–83; William S. Simmons, "Red Yankees: Narragansett Conversion in the Great Awakening," *American Ethnologist* 10 (1983), 253–71; Helen C. Rountree, *Pocahontas's People: The Powhatan Indians of Virginia through Four Centuries* (Norman: University of Oklahoma Press, 1990); James H. Merrell, *The Indians' New World: Catawbas and Their Neighbors from European Contact Through the Era of Removal* (New York: W. W. Norton for the Institute of Early American History and Culture, 1991).

explorers in the early seventeenth century until they became formally incorporated into the Commonwealth of Massachusetts in 1871. Chapters 1
and 2 discuss Thomas Mayhew Jr.'s Congregationalist mission with the special priority of placing Wampanoag Christianity within the contexts of the
Indians' religious, political, and social worlds. The great test posed by King
Philip's War to the Gospel of Peace is the subject of Chapter 3. Chapters 4
and 5 begin after hostilities ceased and explore the relationship between
shrinking Indian territory, Native political leadership, and the increasing importance of landed communalism as a component of Wampanoag identity.
The final two chapters scrutinize the central challenges to Indian community life and identity during the late eighteenth and nineteenth centuries. The
causes, scope, and deep cultural consequences of Indian indentured service
under English masters are examined in Chapter 6. Chapter 7 chronicles marriages between Natives and non-Natives, the recasting of Indians as "people
of color" by outsiders, and debates over whether the Wampanoags should
drop their official "Indian" status and become full citizens of Massachusetts.
This book ends in 1871, not because that year closed the story of the Vineyard
Wampanoags, but because afterwards the Natives' main concerns and the
solutions they devised were so qualitatively different from the ones discussed
here, that to do them justice would require more pages than is desirable for
a single volume. In any case, a number of studies, including one directed
by the Wampanoag Tribe of Aquinnah itself, ably pick up where this book
leaves off, and oral accounts of the late-nineteenth and twentieth centuries
vibrantly circulate through the contemporary Wampanoag community, full
of more subtle truths and engaging stories than any work of history could
ever hope to capture.[27] Wampanoag tribal elders are the best tellers of their
people's modern history.

   The argument that emerges from these chapters is that Vineyard
Wampanoags who fared best during their centuries' long trial drew upon
Epenow's lesson that seemingly powerless people could chart space between
a suicidal violent resistance and an unthinkable total surrender by combining
resourcefulness, resilience, adaptability, and carefully picked battles. Along
the way, they, like Epenow, were forced into hard choices and sometimes humiliating concessions dictated by circumstances rarely of their own making.

[27] See Jack Campisi, James D. Wherry, Christine Gabrowski, Bettina Malonson, et al., "Sub-
    mission of the Historical Narrative and Supportive Documentation in Support of a Petition
    Requesting the Acknowledgement of the Gay Head Wampanoag Tribe" (1983), MS in the
    possession of the Aquinnah Wampanoag Tribal Council, Aquinnah, Mass. My thanks to He-
    len Manning for allowing me to have access to this document; Gloria Levitas, "No Boundary
    is a Boundary: Conflict and Change in a New England Indian Community" (Ph.D. diss.,
    Rutgers University, 1980); William A. Starna, " 'We'll All Be Together Again': The Federal
    Acknowledgement of the Wampanoag Tribe of Gay Head," *Northeast Anthropology* 51
    (1996), 3–12; Christine Tracey Gabrowski, "Coiled Intentions: Federal Acknowledgement
    Policy and the Gay Head Wampanoags" (Ph.D. diss., City University of New York, 1994).

However, whereas several mainland peoples, including Wampanoags, responded to English provocations with violence that ultimately achieved little more than their own death and dispossession, the islanders saw no recourse in war. Recognizing the futility of bloodshed, they swallowed hard on their pride to compromise several times over, and in the process adopted many of the social and cultural behaviors of the colonists who pressed upon them. Yet in a deeply ironic development, the Wampanoags' acculturative change served as a peaceful defense for what was most important to them as a people: the survival of their loved ones, the maintenance of communities where nobody was left behind no matter how much everyone suffered, and the retention of at least some of the land where their ancestors were buried, their ghosts haunted, and their culture's heroes once walked. Indians had little choice than to take up some English ways, but they could influence the pace and extent of change by making bold reforms in one area while hesitating in another, and by using skills and institutions borrowed from the colonists to advance Indian priorities. Such an approach meant that their sense of peoplehood rested on an increasingly slim foundation of land, communalism, and historical sensibility, but it proved to be solid.

Like Epenow, who discovered that appealing to greed was the best way to manipulate his profit-minded abductors, island Wampanoags learned to mediate their relations with New England's religious-minded colonists through Christianity. Although historians now emphasize that Puritanism contained (and often failed to contain) a wide range of Protestant reformist beliefs, still, those beliefs, the debates they provoked, and the institutions they created, were the foundation for the region's peculiar English culture and society.[28] And if Christianity was the key to colonial New England in general, it was all the more so on Martha's Vineyard, since for most of the seventeenth century the island was either an independent or semiautonomous colony ruled almost entirely by Thomas Mayhew Sr., whose family also happened to head the Indian mission and the English congregation. Wampanoags embraced Christianity, in part, to broker an alliance with Mayhew. However, whereas Epenow led the English on a fool's errand, his descendants' approach involved more than political calculation. Attracted to the faith by numerous considerations, soon many of them became knowledgeable believers, and then, with a level of determination and enthusiasm rarely seen in anyone but new recruits, they transformed Christianity into a bulwark for Wampanoag communities and an expression of their own culture.

---

[28] Even a summary listing of the historical literature on New England's Christian culture and society would be too extensive for this space. For superb overviews, see Francis J. Bremer, *The Puritan Experiment* (New York: St. Martin's Press, 1976); and Richard Archer, *Fissures in the Rock: New England in the Seventeenth Century* (Hanover, N.H.: University Press of New England, 2001).

Gorges was quick to believe that Epenow had become a gold-digging ally, but English colonists and their descendants were far more skeptical about Indian Christians, thereby writing the first chapter in the long history of a racial double bind that has restrained American Indians across space and time. On the one hand, the Vineyard Wampanoags, like most Indians in sustained contact with Euro-Americans, felt outside pressure to take up Christianity and adopt alien practices and values such as male plow agriculture, private property holding, monogamous lifelong marriage, formal education, Judeo-Christian law, a six-day sunrise to sundown work schedule, clothes that cover nearly all of the body, and more. On the other hand, whenever the Wampanoags yielded to the most stringent demands, they learned there was yet another standard they had failed to meet, which enabled colonists to justify consigning them to third-class status. This was particularly the case after King Philip's War when the Mayhews' authority weakened, a pattern reflective of other colonial regions in which central power that espoused assimilating the Indians or at the very least treating them with justice, gave way to a white settler democracy intent on dispossessing and even destroying them.[29] Gradually, and almost imperceptibly over time, this rising bar of civilization shifted the focus of difference between Indians and Europeans from culture, which could change, to race, which in many people's minds could not.[30]

---

[29] The classic statement on this point is Edmund S. Morgan, *American Slavery, American Freedom: The Ordeal of Colonial Virginia* (New York: W. W. Norton, 1975). Among more recent works, see Merrell, *Into the American Woods: Negotiators on the Pennsylvania Frontier* (New York: W. W. Norton and Co., 1999); Michael Leroy Oberg, *Dominion and Civility: English Imperialism and Native America, 1585–1685* (Ithaca, N.Y.: Cornell University Press, 1999).

[30] Among many relevant studies of white attitudes toward Indians, see Roy Harvey Pearce, *Savagism and Civilization: A Study of the Indian and the Idea of Civilization*, rev. ed. (Berkeley: University of California Press, 1988); Robert F. Berkhofer Jr., *The White Man's Indian* (New York: Vintage, 1979); Axtell, *The Invasion Within*; Neal Emerson Salisbury, "Conquest of the 'Savage': Puritans, Puritan Missionaries, and Indians, 1620–1660" (Ph.D. diss., University of California at Los Angeles, 1972); Brian W. Dippie, *The Vanishing American: White Attitudes and U.S. Indian Policy* (Lawrence: University of Kansas Press, 1982); Richard Drinon, *Facing West: The Metaphysics of Indian Hating and Empire Building* (Minneapolis: University of Minnesota Press, 1980); Bernard Sheehan, *Savagism and Civility: Indians and Englishmen in Colonial Virginia* (Cambridge: Cambridge University Press, 1980); Sheehan, *Seeds of Extinction: Jeffersonian Philanthropy and the American Indian* (Chapel Hill: University of North Carolina Press for the Institute of Early American History and Culture, 1973); Reginald Horsman, *Race and Manifest Destiny: The Origins of American Racial Anglo-Saxonism* (Cambridge, Mass.: Harvard University Press, 1981); Ronald Takaki, "The Tempest in the Wilderness: The Racialization of Savagery," *JAH* 79 (1992), 892–912; Jennings, *Invasion of America*; Kathleen Brown, "Native Americans and Early Modern Concepts of Race," in Martin Daunton and Rick Halpern, eds., *Empire and Others: British Encounters with Indigenous Peoples* (London: UCL Press, 1999), 79–100; Joyce Chaplin, *Subject Matter: Technology, the Body, and Science on the Anglo-American Frontier* (Cambridge, Mass.: Harvard University Press, 2001); Jill Lepore, *The Name of War: King Philip's War and the Origins of American Identity* (New York: Alfred K. Knopf, 1998); and John Wood Sweet,

The Wampanoags' adaptability, especially to Christianity, provided them with sanctuary and even some leverage when they seemed hopelessly over-powered by the English, and it promoted an uneasy peace, but it could not overcome the pernicious influence of race. As Epenow might have warned his people, the best they could hope to achieve was an imperfect coexistence with their white neighbors and assurance of their own identity.

Bodies Politic, Negotiating Race in the American North, 1730–1830 (Baltimore: The Johns Hopkins University Press, 2003).

"Here Comes the Englishman"

Wuttununohkomkooh knew of God long before the English settled on Noepe. For years, she and her husband, Pammehannit, had unsuccessfully tried to build a family, thrice conceiving and pouring their hopes into the promise of a forthcoming child, only to lose each infant within days of delivery. The would-be mother turned to Indian shamans and doctors for help, but their medicine was of no use; two more births ended just like the ones before. Wuttununohkomkooh's sixth pregnancy in 1638, then, was not a time of joy and anticipation but of overwhelming anxiety.

Filled one day with a sense of impending doom, Wuttununohkomkooh went to a solitary field where she could grieve unrestrained. But as she bewailed her former losses and cringed at the prospect of another, an invisible herald brought her news that his master, the source of all life, was willing to spare her forthcoming babe if she petitioned him for mercy. The expectant mother took this message seriously and carefully followed the instructions. Some time later she bore a son, and within a few weeks it was clear that Wuttununohkomkooh's and Pammehannit's years of suffering were over; this child would live. Overjoyed, Wuttununohkomkooh dedicated the newborn, later known as Japheth Hannit, to serve the deity that had lifted the curse on her family.

Yet the identity of this force was elusive. He went without a name, without form. Four years would pass before an Englishman named Thomas Mayhew Jr. arrived on Noepe to teach Wuttununohkomkooh and her Wampanoag people about the guardian spirit. According to one of Mayhew's descendents, the "Discovery of the true God to her, before she was favoured with the Light of the Gospel, did wonderfully prepare her for a ready Reception of it, when the Providence of God brought it to her." Perhaps, but nothing could have readied her for the epidemics, land losses, and Machiavellianism that would afflict her people after the English began colonizing Martha's Vineyard. Five Indian children dead and just one saved were but a taste of the devastation to come, and Wuttununohkomkooh would be only the first of many Wampanoags to turn to the Christian God at the height of desperation.[1]

I

In 1641, Thomas Mayhew Sr., a merchant from Watertown, Massachusetts, stumbled out of several business failures into the unique opportunity to buy the royal patent to Martha's Vineyard, the adjacent Elizabeth Islands, and Nantucket.[2] These lands were remote and contained a large Indian population with a fearsome reputation, but Mayhew believed them to be worth the £40 asking price. The glistening of Aquinnah's clay cliffs after a rainfall hinted at mineral wealth, just as Epenow had said.[3] At the very least, the islands offered abundant salt grass pasture for livestock and a base from which to fish for cod and mackerel. However, the patent's main attraction for Mayhew might have been the chance to restore his family to the genteel status it had once enjoyed but since lost in England. The title, free from any other colony's jurisdiction, authorized him to act as an independent proprietor with the exclusive right to govern, bargain for Indian territory, and collect quit rents from colonial tenants.[4] Mayhew must have considered himself blessed, and perhaps all the more so when he found a Vineyard sachem, Tawanquatuck, willing to sell him some land on the eastern half of the island. The next year, slightly fewer than one hundred colonists arrived to build a settlement under Mayhew's son and proxy and the community's interim preacher, Thomas Mayhew Jr.

[1] Wuttununohkomkooh's and Japheth Hannit's stories can be found in Cotton Mather, *Magnalia Christi Americana, or, The Ecclesiastical History of New England, From Its First Planting, in the Year 1620, Unto the Year of Our Lord 1698*, 2 vols. (1702; Boston, 1853), 2:440–2, and *Indian Converts*, 44–5, 129, 135–7.

[2] On Watertown during Mayhew's era, see Roger Thompson, *Divided We Stand: Watertown, Massachusetts, 1630–1680* (Amherst: University of Massachusetts Press, 2001).

[3] Emanuel Altham believed the Vineyard contained "a mountain of bole armeniac and divers other metals." See his letter to Sir Edward Altham in Sydney V. James Jr., ed., *Three Visitors to Early Plymouth* (Plymouth, Mass.: Plimouth Plantation, 1963), 27. John Smith thought likewise. See Philip L. Barbour, ed., *The Complete Works of Captain John Smith (1580–1631), in Three Volumes* (Chapel Hill: University of North Carolina Press for the Institute of Early American History and Culture, 1986), 1:341.

[4] Lloyd C. M. Hare, *Thomas Mayhew: Patriarch to the Indians, 1593–1682* (New York, 1932), chaps. 3–5; Charles Edward Banks, *The History of Martha's Vineyard, Dukes County, Massachusetts*, 3 vols. (Boston: George H. Dean, 1911), 1:80–8, 104–26; Margery Ruth Johnson, "The Mayhew Mission to the Indians, 1643–1806" (Ph.D. diss., Clark University, 1966), 21–33; Neal Salisbury, "Prospero in New England: The Puritan Missionary as Colonist," in William Cowan, ed., *Papers of the 6th Algonquian Conference* (Ottawa: Carleton University Press, 1974), 253–73. On the origin of Mayhew's patent, see Isabel Macbeath Calder, "The Earl of Stirling and the Colonization of Long Island," in *Essays in Colonial History, Presented to Charles McLean Andrews by His Students* (New Haven, Conn.: Yale University Press, 1931), 74–95.

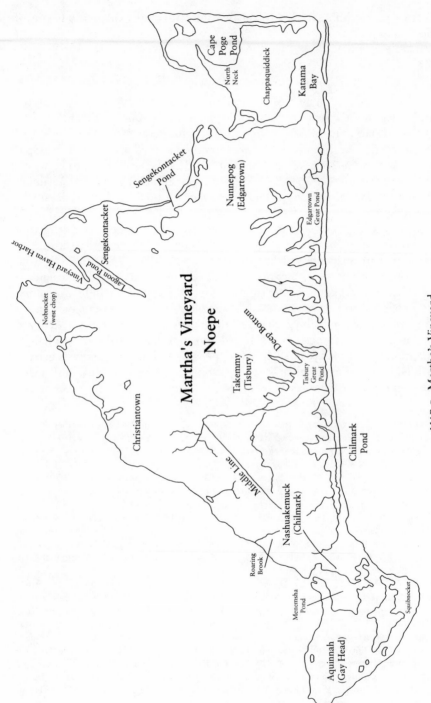

Martha's Vineyard
Noepe

Sengekontacket Pond
Sengekontacket
Nunnepog (Edgartown)

Cape Poge Pond
North Neck
Chappaquiddick
Katama Bay

Edgartown Great Pond

Vineyard Haven Harbor
Lagoon Pond
Nobnocket (west chop)

Christiantown

Takemmy (Tisbury)
Deep Bottom

Tisbury Great Pond
Chilmark Pond

Middle Line

Nashuakemuck (Chilmark)

Roaring Brook

Menemsha Pond

Aquinnah (Gay Head)

Squibnocket

MAP 1. Martha's Vineyard.

18

Despite his weighty responsibilities at the age of just twenty-two, Mayhew Jr. shouldered the added burden of a Christian mission to the Indians in the hope that a shared faith would broker a shared, peaceful future between the island's two peoples. Mayhew, like most Puritans, thought of New England's colonization as a religious undertaking. They believed that God would reward them with blessings on this earth – if not necessarily the next one – if they created a society that upheld proper worship, biblical law, and Christian neighborliness. The Indians' conversion to Christianity was supposed to be a part of this vision, as exemplified by the Massachusetts Bay colony seal that pictured an Indian pleading "come over and help us." Yet as late as 1640 there were still no missionaries in the field. Religious and political infighting, the Pequot War, and the surrounding Indians' near annihilation by epidemic disease provided the English with plenty of distractions and excuses.[5] Mayhew, though, had special incentives to be vigilant. As many as 3,000 Wampanoags resided within the Vineyard's one hundred square miles. A few Indians continued to live and fish inside the borders of the new English town of Great Harbor (later renamed Edgartown), and within a compass of less than five miles they maintained three populous villages: Sengekontacket to the northwest, Nunnepog to the south, and Chappaquiddick to the east. Further off to the west were the sachemships (the basic Wampanoag social unit) of Takemmy and Aquinnah, and between them in the border territory of Nashuakemuck were several small family settlements. Island settlers courted disaster if they neglected missionary work with so many Indians this close at hand. God might unleash punishment for disregarding his order to proselytize. Englishmen might degenerate into "savagery" enticed by Wampanoags nobody had tried to reform. The Natives might suddenly lash out unrestrained by ties of Christian brotherhood, followed by mainland authorities stepping in to quash the Mayhews' proprietorship. By contrast, a dedicated, politically savvy missionary effort had the potential to bring the Wampanoags under English influence and attract God's smile. Such an enterprise was unprecedented to this point in New England history, but so were the circumstances of Indian–English life on the Vineyard.

Less determined men would have resigned this lofty vision to fantasy, since the first task was to learn the "very difficult, irregular, and anomalous" Wampanoag language.[6] The Indians' tongue was full of "Dipthongs

---

[5] On the slow start of the mainland mission, see James Axtell, *The Invasion Within: The Contest of Cultures in Colonial North America* (New York: Oxford University Press, 1985), 220; Richard W. Cogley, *John Eliot's Mission to the Indians Before King Philip's War* (Cambridge, Mass.: Harvard University Press, 1999), 5–22, 43–5; Dane Morison, *A Praying People: Massachusett Acculturation and the Failure of the Puritan Mission, 1600–1690* (New York: Peter Land, 1995), 38–41; Francis Jennings, "Goals and Functions of Puritan Missions to the Indians," *Ethnohistory* 18 (1971), 197–212; Neal Salisbury, "Red Puritans: The 'Praying Indians' of Massachusetts Bay and John Eliot," *WMQ* 31 (1974), 29–31.

[6] *Strength out of Weaknesse*, 181. See also, *Good News*, 591.

or Duble sounds... as ai, au, ei, ee, eau, oi, oo," and threw together multiple consonants in words like "Ahquehuhkg." Nouns varied according to
whether an object was animate or inanimate, past or present, or associated
with a particular direction. There seemed to be an endless array of "com-
pounding words, making one out of several."[7] Worse yet, the English had no
competent interpreters, since the few colonists who knew any Indian phrases
seem to have been taught pidgins, a kind of "baby talk" useful for trade and
diplomacy but not for expounding Christianity.[8] But if Mayhew wanted to
spread God's teachings, he would have to do so in Wampanoag. As one settler observed of the Indians, "they love any man that can utter his mind in
their words."[9] Any man who could not, he might have added, stood little
chance of holding their attention.

Luckily for Mayhew, shortly after arriving on the island he struck up a
friendship with an Indian named Hiacoomes who was willing to assist him.
The Wampanoags spurned Hiacoomes as a "harmlesse man" and "contemptible person" who was "scarce worthy of their notice or Regard," but
when he began loitering around the colonists' settlement Mayhew opened
up his door to him.[10] Through their meetings, by 1644 Hiacoomes commanded basic reading skills while Mayhew boasted some proficiency in

---

[7] Experience Mayhew "Letter of Experience Mayhew, 1722, on the Indian Language," *NE-
HGR* 39 (1885), 12–17. The authoritative study of New England Indian grammar is *Native
Writings*, 2:chap. 3.

[8] Ives Goddard, "Some Early Examples of American Indian Pidgin from New England," *International Journal of American Linguistics* 43 (1977), 37–41; idem., "A Further Note on
Pidgin English," *International Journal of American Linguistics* 44 (1978), 73. More generally, see Axtell, "A Babel of Tongues: Communicating with the Indians," in his *Natives and
Newcomers: The Cultural Origins of North America* (New York: Oxford University Press,
2001), 46–78; James H. Merrell, *Into the American Woods: Negotiators on the Pennsylvania Frontier* (New York: W. W. Norton & Co., 1999), 57–65; Yasuhide Kawashima, "Forest
Diplomats: The Role of Interpreters in Indian–White Relations on the Early American Frontier," *American Indian Quarterly* 13 (1989), 1–14.

[9] William Wood, *New England's Prospect*, ed. Alden T. Vaughan (1634; Amherst: University
of Massachusetts Press, 1977), 110. Wampanoag is a member of the Algonquian language
group spoken by Natives along much of the eastern coast of North America, the Great Lakes,
and the Great Plains. Linguists subdivide Algonquian into a Proto-Algonquian family and a
Proto-Eastern Algonquian family. The Massachusett, Narragansett, and Mohegan–Pequot
dialects fall into the latter grouping and belong, respectively, to the peoples of eastern Massachusetts and northern Rhode Island, western Rhode Island, and southeast Connecticut.
Following the counsel of the Mashpee Wampanoag linguist Jesse Little Doe Fermino, I use
"Wampanoag" to refer to the dialect spoken by people living along Buzzard's Bay and on
Cape Cod, Martha's Vineyard, Nantucket, and the Elizabeth Islands. Personal conversation
with Fermino, October 1999.

[10] *Light Appearing*, 112 ("harmlesse"); *Conquests and Triumphs*, 23 ("contemptible"); *Indian
Converts*, 1–3 ("scarce worthy..."). Hiacoomes might have belonged to the lowest
Wampanoag social order, whose members "were known to be Strangers or Forreigners,"
and "were not Priviledged with Common Right" such as accompanying the sachem on his
annual hunting drives. See *Conquests and Triumphs*, 14–15 (quote), 23; and Roger Williams,

Wampanoag. Three years later Mayhew reportedly spoke Wampanoag with "good understanding" and Hiacoomes and his wife had declared themselves Christians.[11]

For perhaps the first time in his life, Hiacoomes began to attract his neighbors' attention, although probably not the kind he would have preferred. Wampanoags lived in constant fear of witchcraft, which they associated with deviant behavior by socially marginal, and thus, bitterly jealous people yearning for revenge: people just like Hiacoomes.[12] At first Hiacoomes's tribesmen couched their suspicion in laughter, teasing "here comes the Englishman" whenever he passed by.[13] However, they were only half joking and their tone grew more urgent as Hiacoomes began to flaunt a primer Mayhew had given him, for during the early stages of colonization Indians often associated writing's soundless transfer of thought with shamanistic magic.[14] It could not have comforted anyone to learn that Hiacoomes also read the Bible, a book the English revered as the very word of God.[15] In just a few short years, this once-passive fellow had tapped into the colonists' spiritual power – power that had shielded them from the epidemics and perhaps

---

A Key into the Language of America, eds. John J. Teunissen and Evelyn J. Hinz (1643; Detroit: Wayne State University Press, 1973), 96.

[11] *Light Appearing*, 108 (quote); *Glorious Progress*, 78.

[12] Anthony F. C. Wallace, *Death and Rebirth of the Seneca* (New York: Alfred A. Knopf, 1970), 254–5; Bruce G. Trigger, *The Children of Aataentsic: A History of the Huron People to 1660* (Montreal: McGill-Queen's University Press, 1976), 66–7; and David J. Silverman, "Native American Witchcraft," in Richard Golden, ed., *Encyclopedia of Witchcraft: The Western Tradition* (Santa Barbara, Calif.: ABC-Clio, forthcoming).

[13] *Light Appearing*, 110.

[14] *Indian Converts*, 4. Axtell, "The Power of Print in the Eastern Woodlands," in his *After Columbus: Essays in the Ethnohistory of Colonial North America* (New York: Oxford University Press, 1988), 86–99, limits his discussion to New France and discounts the power of writing in New England for three reasons: (1) by the time Eliot launched his mainland mission, the novelty of print had worn off on Indians; (2) unlike their Jesuit counterparts, Puritans were unwilling to put the Indian impression of their writing skills as shamanistic power to missionary ends; and (3) religious works were quickly available in Algonquian and Native children were taught to read or write, hence distributing the skill. All of these points certainly apply to coastal Massachusetts. On the Vineyard, however, Indians did not have steady contact with colonists before 1642. Nor were Mayhew and, more importantly here, Hiacoomes, as inflexible as Eliot. Lastly, Algonquian-language writings were neither available for another ten years nor widely distributed for another twenty years.

Peter Wogan, "Perceptions of European Literacy in Early Contact Situations," *Ethnohistory* 41 (1994), 407–29, challenges Axtell's argument that Indians associated literacy with shamanism, pointing out that the skill failed to meet basic Indian standards for shamanistic success, especially curing. The crux of his argument, though, is that European observations of Native awe at writing stemmed from Westerners' inclination "to see literacy as a central symbol of their identity" (p. 420). This blanket explanation for the content of eyewitness accounts cannot be proved and obviously runs counter to available evidence.

[15] David D. Hall, *Worlds of Wonder, Days of Judgment: Popular Religious Belief in Early New England* (Cambridge, Mass.: Harvard University Press, 1989), 22–3, 63–5.

caused them as well. Hiacoomes's change of fortune suggested that danger was afoot.

Indeed it was. In 1643, a "strange disease" breached the island shore for the first time, carrying off an indeterminable number of victims but spreading an unmistakable pall of terror.[16] Wampanoags began "to run up and down till they could run no longer" and "made their faces black as coale, snatched up any weapon, spake great words, but did no hurt," to frighten off the ghosts of the dead or the spirits behind the killing.[17] The end of this crisis must have renewed their faith in the blackface rite, but only temporarily, for in 1645 they were attacked again, this time by a "universall" "sore Distemper" that was "mortall to many of them."[18] These two outbreaks swept off as many as half of the Vineyard Wampanoags and shook survivors to their core.

The diseases Europeans brought to America were so violent and strange as to unnerve the Indians' stoutest men. Smallpox, the most lethal new contagion of all, turned its victims into pustulated, oozing monsters, gasping for air, clinging desperately to life.[19] Worse yet, virtually all Indians were immunologically vulnerable to such ailments because of their lack of previous exposure, meaning that during an outbreak almost everyone became ill, leaving no one to gather food, water, or firewood or to tend to the sicks' other needs. Simple nursing during an epidemic, even without medicine, can reduce fatalities by two-thirds or more, but without it death rates often reach catastrophic levels, as they did in the Indians' case.[20] The sudden loss of elites, shamans, elders, warriors, and caregivers would have been a formidable blow to any society, but it was particularly damaging to one without writing since specialized knowledge died out with its keepers. Then, beyond the practical challenges of replacing the dead and making up for lost

---

[16] *Light Appearing*, 110.

[17] *Light Appearing*, 110. On the blackface mourning ritual, see "Historical Collections," 153; Thomas Morton, *New English Canaan*, ed. Charles F. Adams, *Publications of the Prince Society* 14 (1632; Boston, 1883), 170; Williams, *Key into the Language of America*, 115–16, 247–50; John Josselyn, "The Second Voyage," in Paul J. Lindholdt, ed., *John Josselyn, Colonial Traveler: A Critical Edition of "Two Voyages to New-England"* (1674; Hanover, N.H.: University Press of New England, 1988), 95.

[18] *Light Appearing*, 111 ("universal"); *Indian Converts*, 77 ("sore Distemper", "many of them"); Morrison, *A Praying People*, 6. The identity of this sickness is also unknown. However, in 1646 Indians on the Kennebec River suffered "a malady which caused vomiting of blood" and "destroyed a good part of their nation." That outbreak also opened the door for a Christian mission. See Kenneth M. Morrison, *The Embattled Northeast: The Elusive Ideal of Alliance in Abenaki–Euramerican Relations* (Berkeley: University of California Press, 1984), 83.

[19] Alfred W. Crosby, "Virgin Soil Epidemics as a Factor in the Aboriginal Depopulation in America," *WMQ* 33 (1976), 289–99.

[20] Crosby, "Virgin Soil Epidemics." See also David S. Jones, "Virgin Soils Revisited," *WMQ* 60 (2003), 703–42.

food production, there was the psychological fallout. In a study of modern disasters like toxic poisonings, sociologist Kai Erikson finds that people who have watched an unknown force waste away their relations' bodies from within, tend to become nervous and depressed, plagued by flashbacks and nightmares, and overwhelmed by a feeling of helplessness. Collectively experienced, this ordeal is best understood as social trauma, which "at its worst, can mean not only a loss of confidence in the self but a loss of confidence in the scaffolding of family and community, in the structures of human government, in the larger logics by which humankind lives, and in the ways of nature itself."[21] Or, as one mainland colonist wrote of Indians coping with the devastation of epidemic disease, "their courage is much abated, and their countenance is dejected, and they seem as a people affrighted."[22]

The Wampanoags, no less than their Puritan neighbors, inhabited a world of spirits in which there were no accidents. They searched for order in a deeply uncertain world by scrutinizing even commonplace troubles like failed crops and hunts for signs of godly displeasure or witchcraft. Crises such as repeated devastation by invisible, anonymous killers only prompted them to interrogate their world with greater urgency.[23] Years earlier, some mainland Indians attributed the new epidemics to a comet, and others to a curse uttered by a shipwrecked Frenchman they had enslaved, but the Vineyard Wampanoags had their own ideas.[24] A number of them suspected Hiacoomes because the diseases had spared him, his family, and his English friends despite his rejection of Wampanoag curing rituals. Even Indians he proselytized "did not taste so deeply of it."[25] These were no idle theories. Anyone who held Hiacoomes responsible for the death of a loved one was liable to seek revenge despite the risk of provoking his magic and allies. Rather than wait for vigilante justice to unfold, the Chappaquiddick sachem,

---

[21] Kai Erikson, *A New Species of Trouble: Explorations in Disaster, Trauma, and Community* (New York: W. W. Norton & Co., 1989), 242. See also William McNeil, *Plagues and Peoples* (Garden City, N.Y.: Anchor Press/Doubleday, 1976), esp. 206; and Rodney Stark, *The Rise of Christianity: How the Obscure, Marginal Jesus Movement Became the Dominant Religious Force in the Western World in a Few Centuries* (San Francisco: Harper Collins, 1997), 73–94.

[22] William Cronon, *Changes in the Land: Indians, Colonists, and the Ecology of New England* (New York: Hill and Wang, 1983), 90.

[23] On New England Indian beliefs, see William S. Simmons, "Southern New England Shamanism: An Ethnographic Reconstruction," in William Cowan, ed., *Papers of the Seventh Algonquian Conference* (Ottawa: Carleton University, 1976), 218–53; Simmons, *Spirit of the New England Tribes: Indian History and Folklore, 1620–1984* (Hanover, N.H.: University Press of New England, 1986), 37–66; Kathleen J. Bragdon, *Native People of Southern New England, 1500–1650* (Norman: University of Oklahoma Press, 1996), 184–99, 207–8.

[24] Edward Johnson, *Johnson's Wonder-Working Providence, 1628–1651*, ed. J. Franklin Jameson, (New York: Charles Scribner's Sons, 1910), 39–40; Nathaniel Morton, *New-England's Memorial, or, A Brief Relation of the Most Memorable and Remarkable Passages of the Providence of God* (Boston, 1721), 36.

[25] *Light Appearing*, 110–11 (quote), 116; "Historical Collections," 155.

Pakeponesso summoned Hiacoomes and "reproached him for his fellowship with the English, both in their civil and religious wayes, railing at him for his being obedient to them." Wampanoags would have expected a marginal figure like Hiacoomes to defer to a sachem's order. Instead, he vowed defiantly to stay the course, even after receiving "a great blow on the face."[26] Hiacoomes told a friend that Jehovah would punish Pakeponesso for this treatment, and, to everyone's amazement, shortly a bolt of lightning nearly killed the sachem. Mayhew related that "now Hiacoomes (as himself saith) did remember his former thoughts of God, and then thought God did answer him, and that he was brought more to rejoyce in God, and rest more upon him."[27] Awestruck and scared, his neighbors too entered "upon serious consideration" of Hiacoomes's newfound powers.[28]

Accordingly, the petty sachem of Nunnepog, Myoxeo, invited Hiacoomes to address an assembly about what he had learned during his conferences with Mayhew.[29] This was a remarkable change of fortune for a man the Wampanoags once derided for having "nothing to say in all their meetings." Yet now, filled with confidence by his new guardian spirit and English contacts, Hiacoomes rose to the task, opening with a lengthy speech about "all the things he knew concerning God the Father, Son and Holy Ghost." Then he turned to the real test: fielding the questions of a skeptical but forlorn audience. Myoxeo wondered just how many gods the English worshipped. "Hiacoomes answered ONE, and no more. Whereupon Miohqsoo reckoned up about 37 principal gods which he had; and shall I, said he, throw away all these 37 for the sake of one only?" Hiacoomes's response burrowed to the heart of the audience's interest in Christianity. He declared, "he did fear this great God only," not the ancestral spirits, adding "For my part I have thrown away all these, and many more, some Years ago, and yet I am preserved as you see [to] this Day."[30] He went on to explain, "in a speciall manner," basic Protestant tenets such as the Fall, Original Sin, Jesus's sacrifice for believers, and the need to confess and repent for one's offenses to God, but probably the message that rang through was the need to strive against a long list of "sins" to secure Jehovah's protection.[31]

In lieu of these reforms, Wampanoags began soliciting medical attention from Mayhew, who brilliantly played the role of Christian *powwow* the Indians cast for him. Called to the bedside of a diseased sixty-year-old man named Ieogiscat, Mayhew "by reasoning with him convinced him of the weaknesse and wickednesse of the Pawwaws power; and that if health were

[26] *Light Appearing*, 109–10 (quote); *Conquests and Triumphs of Grace*, 23–4; *Indian Converts*, 3.
[27] *Light Appearing*, 110–11; *Indian Converts*, 4.
[28] *Light Appearing*, 111.
[29] *Light Appearing*, 111; *Conquests and Triumphs*, 5.
[30] *Light Appearing*, 111; *Indian Converts*, 78 (all quotes).
[31] *Light Appearing*, 111–12.

to be found, it must be had from him that gave life, and breath, and all things; I commended this case unto the Lord." Ieogiscat's recovery after the Wampanoags were resigned to his death seemed to confirm Mayhew's words. Still, Saul, the ailing son of Pakeponesso, ignored Mayhew's counsel, including the warning that God would smite him down if he reverted to the *powwows* in full knowledge of Christianity. Just as the missionary predicted, "so it shortly came to passe." [32] Mayhew's luck peaked when he cured the son of the Nunnepog sachem Tawanquatuck. Missionaries universally acknowledged their need for the support of Indian leaders, yet previously Mayhew found "the Sagamores [or sachems] were generally against this new way." [33] The recovery of his son, especially following Hiacoomes's transformation, convinced Tawanquatuck that his people's future lay in the mission. He confided to Mayhew, "a long time ago the Indians had wise Men among them, that did in a grave manner teach the People Knowledge, but they, said he, are dead, and their Wisdom is buried with them." [34] In the hopes of restoring wisdom, confidence, and spiritual power to his followers, Tawanquatuck arranged for Mayhew to lead Christian instruction in Nunnepog every other week. [35] The mission now had a foothold in the Wampanoag community.

That foothold was tenuous at first, but little by little Tawanquatuck's encouragement brought more of his people to Christianity. Mayhew reported that in 1646 "there were about twelve which came to the meeting as it were halting between two opinions," while "others came to hear and see what was done." [36] By 1650 more than twenty men and perhaps even more women had entered the Christian ranks, a figure that might have represented as much as half the community. [37] Their reasons were expressed by an elder of some one hundred years of age. He announced that his people had "fallen into a worse condition than their forefat[hers]" and that Christianity was a better way. To emphasize the point, the old man "rose up, and in a solemn manner tooke the young Sagamore," Tawanquatuck's son, "by the hand, and having made

[32] *Glorious Progress*, 77 (quote), 78.
[33] *Some Account of those English Ministers*, 283 (quote); Axtell, *Invasion Within*, 143; Salisbury, "Red Puritans," 37.
[34] *Light Appearing*, 112; *Indian Converts*, 80 (quote).
[35] *Glorious Progress*, 78; *Light Appearing*, 112.
[36] *Light Appearing*, 113.
[37] In *Light Appearing*, 115, Mayhew reported that at a 1648 meeting twelve young men publicly committed themselves to "God's way" and that by 1649 "twenty two Indians were found to resolve . . . to walk with God." In all likelihood he did not include women in these figures, but observers often noted that females showed greater enthusiasm for Christianity. See Thomas Shepard, *The Clear Sun-shine of the Gospel Breaking forth upon the INDIANS in New-England* (London, 1648), MHSC 3d ser., 4 (1834), 41; *Indian Converts*, 135. In 1698, the earliest date for which population figures are available specifically for Nunnepog, the community's population stood at 84 ("Indian Visitation," 132). This was eight years after a fever that swept off a hundred adults, mostly on the east end of the island. Given the outbreaks in 1643 and 1645, Nunnepog's population in 1650 might have been even lower.

a shorte speech to him, sate down behind him, in the like manner did 14 more."[38] Nothing was certain in the Wampanoags' world, least of all Christianity, but its offer of solidarity, direction, and quickening was precisely what this shell-shocked community craved. Joining the Christian meeting as a group with the sachem offered some guarantee that Nunnepog's social fabric would remain intact no matter how the experiment turned out. Indeed, Tawanquatuck argued that Christianity would bring his followers even closer together by encouraging them to "know one another's minds... that they might have one heart, & keep it, and walk in God's way with heart."[39] It was an attractive, if untested, vision for a people devastated by epidemic disease.

Throughout their history in North America, missions have torn Indian communities into angry pro- and anti-Christian factions that usually merge with other divisions centered on trade, diplomacy, and clan politics.[40] The Vineyard was no different at this early stage. Even before the mission began, Wampanoags recalling their people's violent history with European explorers protested Tawanquatuck's decision to sell Mayhew land, that is, until "he to quiet them, gave several parts of his Sachemship to them, and then sold the English a considerable Part of what he reserved to himself."[41] This time, however, they expressed their dissent forcefully. Shortly after public prayer meetings began, the sachem lay sleeping next to a fishing weir when "an Indian came down, as being ready fitted for the purpose, and being about six or eight paces from him, let flie a broad headed arrow." The missile struck Tawanquatuck in the forehead, but left him alive. Mayhew Jr. reported, "the cause of his being shot, as the Indians said, was for his walking with the English" and especially "his forwardnesse for the meeting."[42] Settlement had been bad enough, but now Tawanquatuck was allowing outsiders to interfere with the sacred. Much was at stake.

II

At risk was the continuity of beliefs and rituals that had evolved with the Wampanoags throughout the ages to help them make sense of their world. Native religion guided the people through the life cycle, everyday activities, seasonal changes, common ills, and when given the chance, even crises such as epidemics. It differentiated common people from exceptional

---

[38] Thomas Mayhew Jr. to John Winthrop, August 15, 1648, Mayhew Papers.
[39] Ibid.
[40] Daniel K. Richter, "Iroquois versus Iroquois: Jesuit Missions and Christianity in Village Politics, 1642–1686," *Ethnohistory* 32 (1985), 1–16; Rebecca Kugel, *To Be the Main Leaders of Our People: A History of Minnesota Ojibwe Politics, 1825–1898* (East Lansing: Michigan State University Press, 1998).
[41] *Indian Converts*, 80
[42] *Light Appearing*, 113 (quote); *Indian Converts*, 81–2.

FIGURE 2. Assassination Attempt against Tawanquatuck. A nineteenth-century artist's rendering of the attack on the Nunnepog sachem Tawanquatuck by an Indian opposed to his support for the Mayhew mission. Indians were known to be sure shots, so when the arrow only grazed the sachem's eye, some Wampanoags took it as a sign in favor of Christianity. Courtesy American Antiquarian Society.

ones. It kept order between humans and spirits. Even after the epidemics, most Wampanoags asserted they "strongly stood for their own meetings, wayes, and customes, being in their account more profitable then [sic.] ours [the colonists'], wherein they meet with nothing but talking and praying."[43] They viewed their survival as testimony to the efficacy of the people's traditional rites. Innovators like Hiacoomes and Tawanquatuck threatened to turn everything upside down.

Indian religious life in the early seventeenth century was largely concerned with the pursuit of spiritual force, or *manit*, a power that coursed through the world and enabled one entity to influence another. Holders and conduits of *manit* included prominent topographical features, striking works of human artifice, certain animals, and especially spirits, all of which Indians called *manitou*. One could locate *manit* in quartz crystal, which Indians believed came from lightning bolts shot from the eyes of thunderbirds. It was strong in great rocks, mountains, and particularly swamps because they connected the layers of the universe – underworld, land, and sky – and housed powerful *manitous*, such as horned serpents, panthers, and birds, that traveled back

[43] *Light Appearing*, 113.

and forth between the zones like the shape shifters of mythic times.[44] *Manit* was in everything fantastic. Roger Williams wrote of the Narragansetts that "there is a generall Custome amongst them, at the apprehension of any Excellency in Men, Women, Birds, Beasts, Fish, &c. to cry out *Manittóo*, that is, it is a God, as thus if they see one man excell others in Wisdome, Valour, strength, Activity, &c. they cry out *Manitóo*; a God: and therefore when they talke amongst themselves of the English ships, and great buildings of the plowing of their Fields, and especially of Bookes and Letters, they will end thus, *Mannittôwock* They are Gods," or more precisely, they are full of spiritual power.[45]

The Wampanoags' earthly success depended on harnessing *manit* or influencing its course by forging reciprocal relationships with spirit beings. Mayhew Jr. found that the Wampanoags "had their Men-gods, Women-gods, and Children-gods, their Companies, and Fellowships of Gods, guiding things amongst men, besides innumerable more feigned gods belonging to many Creatures, to their Corn, and every Colour of it."[46] The Indians' "divine powers" also included "the sun, Moon, Fire, Water, Snow, Earth, the Deer, the Bear, &c."[47] Behind every animal, plant, fish, or meteorological force was a "boss spirit" or giant lookalike that controlled the abundance and distribution of its smaller kind.[48] People allied with these spirits by taking a vision quest. At adolescence, a boy was guided into the woods, where he would remain alone for weeks, perhaps months, with only a few tools and weapons. He spent this time fasting, depriving himself of sleep, and imbibing emetics in order to picture a spirit. The ideal was that one or more *manitous* would finally appear in the form of beaver person, bear person, hawk person, or any one of a variety of other-than-human "persons," to take the boy on a fantastic shape-shifting journey. They might dive together

---

[44] Kathleen J. Bragdon, "The Shamanistic 'Text' in Southern New England," *Kroeber Anthropological Society Papers* 79 (1995), 165–76; Bragdon, *Native People of Southern New England*, 191–2, 207, 220; Kevin McBride, "Prehistoric and Historic Patterns of Wetland Use in Eastern Connecticut," *MNE* 44 (1992), 10–24; George R. Hamell, "Mythical Realities and European Contact in the Northeast During the Sixteenth and Seventeenth Centuries," *MNE* 33 (1987), 69–70.

[45] Williams, *Key into the Language of America*, 191 (quote). For the best discussions on *manit*, see Constance A. Crosby, "From Myth to History, or Why King Philip's Ghost Walks Abroad," in Mark P. Leone and Parker Potter Jr., eds., *The Recovery of Meaning: Historical Archaeology in the Eastern United States* (Washington, D.C.: Smithsonian Institution Press, 1988), 192–8; and Bragdon, *Native Peoples of New England*, 184–90.

[46] *Tears of Repentence*, 201–2.

[47] Roger Williams to John Winthrop, February 28, 1638, in *The Letters of Roger Williams*, ed. John R. Bartlett, vol. 6 of *The Complete Writings of Roger Williams* (New York: Russell and Russell, Inc., 1963), 88. See also Williams, *Key into the Language of America*, 189–91; Gookin, "Historical Collections," 154.

[48] Calvin Martin, *Keepers of the Game: Indian–Animal Relationships and the Fur Trade* (Berkeley: University of California Press, 1978), 71.

under the waters and converse with Turtle or Serpent and then surface to commune with Wind or Deer. They might visit Bear's den or Beaver's lodge. Each experience was unique in detail, but the lesson was the same: humans would find power by collapsing the boundaries of their fleshy selves and entering a spirit world where human, plant, animal, and element were kin, just as it was during the mythic age of origins before the world took its present hardened form. At the end of the trip, the encountered spirits pledged to serve as lifetime guardians to the boy and gave him songs and fetishes with which to petition them for *manit* in times of need like war or hunting. The boy, in turn, promised to show the *manitous* respect: to address these powers with humility, treat their flesh-and-blood manifestations as representatives of the spirits behind them, and to cherish the gift offered during the vision. With this relationship sealed, the boy returned home for the community to recognize him as a man – as a person with special access to *manit* – and to bestow a new name upon him.[49] For girls, an equivalent rite of passage was their seclusion at first and subsequent menses, a custom resting on the belief that menstruating women exuded intense and possibly dangerous power. Unfortunately, accounts written by European men unfamiliar, unconcerned, or simply uncomfortable with female rites, do not include detailed descriptions of girls' rites of passage into womanhood.[50]

Soul wandering during dreams exposed Wampanoags to a blurrier version of the spirit world. New England Indians believed that every individual had two souls. The first, called *Míchachunck* in Narragansett, resided in the human heart and served as the body's animating force. It remained in the sleeping person during the dream state to keep him or her alive. The other soul, the ghost soul or *Cowwéwonck* (in Narragansett), traversed the evening in the form of a light to interact with other spirits.[51] These ghost

[49] "Isaack de Rasiers to Samuel Blommaert (1628)," in James, ed., *Three Visitors*, 79; Bragdon, *Native Peoples of Southeastern New England*, 170; Patricia E. Rubertone, *Grave Undertakings: An Archaeology of Roger Williams and the Narragansett Indians* (Washington, D.C.: Smithsonian Institution Press, 2002), 148. The works of Calvin Martin speak most eloquently about the guardian relationship and vision experience. See his *Keepers of the Game*, 33–9, 69–93; *The American Indian and the Problem of History* (New York: Oxford University Press, 1987), 207–20; *In the Spirit of the Earth: Rethinking History and Time* (Baltimore: Johns Hopkins University Press, 1992); and, especially, *The Way of the Human Being*. See also Åke Hultkrantz, *The Religions of the American Indians*, trans. Monica Setterwall (Berkeley: University of California Press, 1979), 66–83.

[50] Theda Perdue, "Writing the Ethnohistory of Native Women," in Donald L. Fixico, ed., *Rethinking American Indian History* (Albuquerque: University of New Mexico Press, 1997), 79; Bruce M. White, "The Woman Who Married a Beaver: Trade Patterns and Gender Roles in the Ojibwa Fur Trade," *Ethnohistory* 46 (1999), 127, 134–5; Carol Devens, *Countering Colonization: Native American Women and Great Lakes Missions, 1630–1900* (Berkeley: University of California Press, 1992), 78–9.

[51] Williams, *Key into the Language of America*, 193–4; Josselyn, "The Second Voyage," 95–6; Bragdon, *Native People of Southern New England*, 191.

souls gained access to the truth during their wanderings: they discovered the location of lost or stolen objects and the identity of witches; they peered into the future and scanned across the landscape; animal spirits told them where to hunt; *manitous* taught and demanded new rituals.[52] *Cowwéwonck*, in short, brought sleeping humans into contact with the shadowy but ever-present world of *manit*.

The most powerful spirit who appeared in visions and dreams was "the god of the Dead," known as Hobbomock, Abbomocho, or, on the Vineyard, Cheepi. Although this figure's center of strength was the underworld, Indians encountered his presence far and wide. He captured the souls of "Murtherers, thieves, and Lyers," and maybe drowning victims (since water was a pathway to his lair), and condemned them to haunt the living.[53] He could be felt in the color black, the cold northeast wind, serpents, probably the moon, and an illuminative blur that hovered around the dying. Jealousy, which Indians considered to be the most tragic character flaw and the driving force of witchcraft, dominated Cheepi's personality, leading him to torment humans "with incurable Diseases... Apparitions and panick Terrours."[54] Colonists accused the Indians of devil worship when they petitioned Cheepi for relief, but the Natives countered, "the Evil Power hurts us, does all the Mischief, and who should we seek to prevent or remove Mischief but to him that does it."[55]

Wampanoags depended on their *pniesok* and *powwows* to channel Cheepi's awesome power to productive ends. *Pniesok* (the plural of *pniese*) were carefully selected males who underwent elaborate preparations for the vision quest, including imbibing emetics "till they cast, which they must disgorge into the platter, and drink again, and again, till, at length, through extraordinary oppressing of nature, it will seem to be all blood."[56] Exposure,

[52] Williams, *Key into the Language of America*, 107. This discussion of dreams is also informed by Jesuit accounts of Great Lakes peoples like the Hurons. See Reuben Gold Thwaites, ed., *Jesuit Relations and Allied Tracts*, 73 vols. (Cleveland, 1896–1901), 10:169–73, 183; 12:13; 19:133; 30:171; 54:141.

[53] Williams, *Key into the Language of America*, 194 (quote); *Tears of Repentance*, 202; Wood, *New England's Prospect*, 111–12. See also the discussion of the Narragansett word for northeast wind, *chepewéssing*, in James Hammond Trumbull, *Natick Dictionary*, Bureau of American Ethnology Bulletin No. 25 (Washington, D.C.: Govt. Printing Office, 1903), 250, under the heading "east." On the souls of drowning victims, see M. Mayhew, *Conquests and Triumphs of Grace*, 21; Cotton Journal, 88.

[54] Josselyn, "The Second Voyage," 95 (quote); *Tears of Repentance*, 202.

[55] Franklin Bowditch Dexter, ed., *The Literary Diary of Ezra Stiles, D.D., LL.D.*, 3 vols. (New York: Charles Scribner's Sons, 1901), 1:385–6 (quote). See also John Eliot, *The Day Breaking, If Not The Sun-Rising of the GOSPEL With the INDIANS in New-England* (1647), MHSC 3d ser., 4 (1834), 17.

[56] *Good News*, 586. On Native emetics, see "Samuel Sewall to Nehemiah Grew, ca. 1690," *Publications of the Colonial Society of Massachusetts, Transactions* 14 (1911–1913), 149, 151.

vicious beatings, and other trials followed until finally Cheepi appeared to vow to protect the seeker in war. This gift filled the recipient with "courage and boldness" and launched him into the Indian elite, with a seat on the sachem's council and the responsibilities of collecting the sachem's tribute and protecting him in battle. "One of [the *pniese*] will chase almost a hundred men," wrote Edward Winslow, "for [the Indians] account it death for whomsoever stand in their way."[57]

Some Indians who envisioned Cheepi became *powwows*, or shamans, respected by neighbors for their varying abilities to heal, divine the future, find lost objects, and conjure the weather, but often suspected for witchcraft. As one *powwow* explained to Thomas Mayhew Jr.,

he came to be a Pawwaw by Diabolical Dreams, wherein he saw the Devill [Cheepi] in the likenesse of four living Creatures; one was like a man which he saw in the Ayre, and this told him that he did know all things upon the Island, and what was to be done; and this he said had residence over his own body. Another was like a Crow and did look out sharply to discover mischiefs coming towards him and had residence in his head. The third was like to a Pidgeon and had its place in his breast and was very cunning about any businesse. The fourth was like a Serpent, very subtile to doe mischiefe, and also to doe great cures, and these he said were meer Devills, and such as he had trusted for safety, and did labour to raise up for the accomplishment of any thing.[58]

Generally, when a family or community hired a *powwow's* services, the people would drum and chant in a circle while the *powwow* worked himself into a state of ecstasy, which released his *cowwéwonck* to consult with Cheepi or lesser spirit familiars.[59] But the spectacle did not end there, for then he broadcast the *cowwéwonck's* interactions with the *manitous*, "sometimes roaring like a bear, other times groaning like a dying horse, foaming at the mouth like a chased boar, smiting on his naked breast and thighs with such violence as if he were mad. Thus he will continue half a day."[60] The *powwow* might return to consciousness with directions for a ceremony to appease an angry spirit, or knowledge that a witch had implanted the sick person with an enchanted substance, which he then removed by magically sucking it out through unbroken skin. But if an ailment was caused by the dream-soul spirit of another *powwow*, the solution was to capture it in a fly or mosquito and crush it dead.[61] Such talents made the *powwow* much admired; however, like Cheepi, the slightest offense could turn his cure into a curse.[62]

---

[57] *Good News*, 569, 571, 585–6 (quote).
[58] *Strength Out of Weaknesse*, 186–7. See also Eliot, *Day Breaking*, 19–20.
[59] Those rituals are described in Williams, *Key into the Language of America*, 145, 192.
[60] Wood, *New England's Prospect*, 101 (quote); Eliot, *Day Breaking*, 20.
[61] *Conquests and Triumphs*, 20; C. Mather, *Magnalia Christi Americana*, 2:445.
[62] For general accounts of powwowing, see *Good News*, 583–4; *Tears of Repentence*, 202–4; *Strength Out of Weaknesse*, 186–7; Edward Johnson, *Wonder-Working Providence*,

Whereas Cheepi was the god of the dead, the spirit Kiehtan (also known as Tisquantum and Cautantowit) was the god of life for Wampanoags past and present. He had created the original people during ancient times and sent a giant crow to bring them their first seeds of corn and beans, the very staff of their existence.[63] Wampanoag souls spent the afterlife in his "house" toward the Southwest, where he treated them to a steady round of pleasant weather, robust harvests, and plentiful game.[64] The living enjoyed his patronage of their farming too, that is, when he was able to thwart Cheepi's obstructions, and in exchange they dedicated their harvest celebrations to him.[65] But in recent years the Wampanoags had become "more and more cold in their worship to Kiehtan," with tragic results.[66] The epidemic of 1616–1618 had raged southward from Maine's Saco River until it stopped suddenly at the doorway of the Narragansetts' country, apparently because that tribe alone held a ritual destruction of property for Kiehtan.[67] It was a lesson that bore constant reemphasis in Indian life: even the kindliest personalities could turn belligerent without proper courtesies.

The Wampanoags' giant culture hero, Moshup, fell into a more passive role than Kiehtan or Cheepi following his seminal influence during the time of origins. Legend held that Moshup discovered Noepe in the process of chasing down a thunderbird that had snatched up his child from the mainland. Liking what he saw, he settled down there with his wife, Squant, and their children in the Aquinnah cliffs at a spot later known as Devil's Den. The landscape then became a transcript of their adventures: Aquinnah lacked large trees because Moshup used them for firewood to roast whales;

J. Franklin Jameson, ed., *Original Narratives of Early American History* (1654; New York, 1910), 263; *Conquests and Triumphs*, 17–21; Eliot, *Day Breaking*, 19–20; "Historical Collections," 154. The best secondary treatments of New England *powwows* are Simmons, "New England Shamanism," and Bragdon, *Native People of Southern New England*, 203–14. See also Micea Eliade, *Shamanism: Archaic Techniques of Ecstasy* (Princeton, N.J.: Princeton University Press, 1964); Hultkrantz, *Religions of the American Indians*, 84–102.

   Alfred A. Cave, "Indian Shamans and English Witches in Seventeenth-Century New England," *Essex Institute Historical Collections* 128 (1992), 239–54, tries to challenge accounts that *powwows* sometimes used their magic to harm others, but the weight of historical and ethnographic evidence to the contrary is overwhelming.

[63] Williams, *Key into the Language of America*, 163–4.

[64] Wood, *New England's Prospect*, 111; Roger Williams to Thomas Thorowgood, December 20, 1635, *The Correspondence of Roger Williams*, ed. Glenn LaFantasie, 2 vols. (Hanover, N.H.: Brown University Press/University Press of New England, 1988), 1:30. More generally on Indian beliefs about Cheepi, Cautantowwit, and the afterworld, see Simmons, *Cautantowwit's House: An Indian Burial Ground on the Island of Conanicut in Narragansett Bay* (Providence, R.I.: Brown University Press, 1970), chap. 4.

[65] Morton, *New English Canaan*, 168; Wood, *New England's Prospect*, 100; *Good News*, 582–3; Simmons, *Cautontowwit's House*, 52.

[66] *Good News*, 585.

[67] Ibid.

the giant dragged his toe through the sand to sever Noman's Land island from the Vineyard proper; his tobacco smoke produced the thick island fog; Nantucket island was the deposit of his ashes; he produced the multicolored clay in Aquinnah's cliffs by smashing whales against them; the shoals known as Devil's Bridge were boulders he had tossed into the sea as fishing spots. Finally, when Moshup had enough, he turned his children into whales, tossed his wife across the water where she turned into a rock formation at Sakonnet Point along Narragansett Bay, and then retired into the island mist. The Wampanoags proffered differing accounts of Moshup's disappearance, but in time many of them would point to his disgust at the arrival of Englishmen.[68]

Gathering together to hear the legend of Moshup, participate in a curing ritual, dance at a harvest feast, or celebrate an adolescent's rite of passage into adulthood, enabled the Wampanoags to create order in their spiritual and social worlds. Telling stories and directing ceremonies won elders and *powwows* respect. Families assembled into a larger community as a reflection of their shared concerns and destinies. Rituals and stories about the mythic times reaffirmed seminal lessons like the need to treat *manitous* with the same consideration as one's human relatives. Furthermore, since these traditions were supposed to have been a part of Wampanoag life since time immemorial, they linked the living to the dead. Just as these activities had enabled the ancestors to thrive by structuring their interactions with the spirits and channeling the flow of *manit* through the community, they would protect current and future generations.

III

Transforming the Wampanoags' interest in Christianity into a commitment required Mayhew and Hiacoomes to filter Christian teachings through Wampanoag religious ideas, terminology, and practices – an approach one might call religious translation. Mayhew could fantasize about the Wampanoags "converting" in the sense of their making a blanket rejection of ancestral identity, beliefs, and practices in favor of Christian substitutes, but they would not, and probably could not, do that in the real world.[69] The

---

[68] Several versions of the Moshup story are conveniently gathered in Simmons, *Spirit of the New England Tribes*, 172–234. My thanks to Aquinnah Wampanoag tribal member Tobias Vanderhoop for sharing his own account with me.

[69] For some insightful attempts to define conversion, see David A. Snow and Richard Machalek, "The Sociology of Conversion," *Annual Review of Sociology* 10 (1984), 167–90; Robert W. Hefner, ed., *Conversion to Christianity: Historical and Anthropological Perspectives on a Great Transformation* (Berkeley: University of California Press, 1993). Nicholas Griffiths and Fernando Cervantes, eds., *Spiritual Encounters: Interactions between Christianity and Native American Religions in Colonial America* (Lincoln: University of Nebraska Press, 1999),

Wampanoags had far too much to learn to adopt Christianity wholesale all of a sudden and, in any case, they simply would have stopped coming to the meetings if it did not address their culture's concerns. This was not Spanish Florida or New Mexico where Franciscans were backed by military force, or New France where Jesuits could entice followers with trade and diplomatic advantages. Here on Martha's Vineyard, where Wampanoags were the dominant power, missionaries first had to persuade Indians with ideas. The best way to accomplish that task was to invest Christianity with traditional Indian meanings and concede to Natives doing the same.

Yet religious translation was more than a temporary expedient in the hope of future purification, for Christian and Native beliefs were indeed analogous at several critical points. For instance, to encourage the Natives' acceptance of monotheism, Mayhew, no doubt in consultation with Hiacoomes, proposed that they had "an obscure Notion of a greater god than all, which they call *Manit*, but they knew not what he was and therefore had no way to worship him."[70] Now they did, since Mayhew argued that God was the wellspring of all the *manit* in the world. Similarly, Mayhew identified Cheepi as Satan, who, after all, also dwelt in the underworld, terrorized the living with his minions, and had a penchant for shape-shifting into snakes and other chilling forms. The epidemics, as Mayhew interpreted them, resulted from the Indians' futile attempts "to pacifie the Devil by their sacrifice, and get deliverance from their evil."[71] Any favors granted by the Evil One were designs to lure gullible souls deeper into his clutches. Moreover, appeals to him now after Indians had learned "the truth" would only provoke God's jealous wrath as never before. A *powwow* followed up, "had his Imps [guardian spirits] gone from him, what he should have instead of them to preserve him?" Mayhew alluded to the Wampanoags' belief that spirit familiars lay "treasured up in their bodies" by answering "that if he did beleeve in Christ Jesus, he should have the Spirit of Christ dwelling in him, which is a good and strong Spirit, and will keep him so safe, that all the Devils in Hell, and Pawwaws on Earth, should not be able to do him any hurt."[72] In fact, Mayhew asserted, God was so strong that he could make Cheepi and the other Wampanoag spirits "all flee away like Muskeetoes," a subtle reference to the *powwows'* ability to imprison dream souls in insects.[73] Mayhew's overall point was that Christianity obviated

and Salisbury, "Embracing Ambiguity: Native Peoples and Christianity in Seventeenth-Century North America," *Ethnohistory* (2003), 247–59, provide strong arguments against use of the term. See also the trenchant discussion of missionary encounters in John Webster Grant, *Moon of Wintertime: Missionaries and the Indians of Canada in Encounter since 1534* (Toronto: University of Toronto Press, 1984), 239–63.

[70] *Tears of Repentance*, 202.
[71] Ibid.
[72] Ibid., 205.
[73] Ibid.

Wampanoag spirits by providing its followers access to the supreme source of *manit* and, as such, all the power they needed to protect themselves from danger.

Yet Wampanoags did not embrace Christianity in large numbers until Hiacoomes convinced them that Mayhew's words were truthful. God's power was unmistakable, but so was the *powwows'*, a fear Mayhew judged to be "the strongest cord that binds [the Indians] to their own way."[74] Shamans intimidated even Christian Indians. During one prayer meeting in 1649, they "fell to a great discourse about the Pawwawes power to kill men, and there were many stories told of the great hurt they had done by their witchcraft many wayes," which led them to conclude, "there is not any man who is not afraid of the Pawwawes." Then and there Hiacoomes proved otherwise by announcing that his faith in God made him impervious to the *powwows*. It was a critical moment, for although Hiacoomes's declaration shocked and frightened some of the meeting Indians, it inspired a courageous few to make similar claims. But the *powwows* did not give up so easily. Shortly after this insurgence, an "enraged" shaman barged into a Christian gathering and thundered, "the Pawwawes could kill all the meeting Indians if they set about it." Hiacoomes took up the challenge, daring "that he would be in the midst of all the Pawwawes on the Iland that they could procure, and they should do their utmost they could against them, and when they did their worst by their witchcrafts to kill him, he would without fear set himself against them." For good measure he added, "that he did put all the Pawwawes under his heel." In other words, with his new spirit protector, *he* could destroy *the shamans'* dream souls.

Neither Hiacoomes nor any other meeting Indians fell to *powwow* sorcery after this confrontation, which convinced several now-impotent shamans, including the "very notorious" Tequanomin, to enter the Christian meeting, a painful transition by any measure.[75] One *powwow* said of his craft, "I throw it from me with hatred of it, being sorry that ever I meddled with it. And now I have heard of Jehovah, by his help I put it under my feet, and hope to trample it down in the dust with the Devill and Pawwawnomas (or Imps) I throw it into the fire and burn it."[76] Yet the past emerged phoenixlike from the ashes over and over again. One *powwow* was haunted by his *manitous* for months so "that he could never be at rest."[77] Another's family refused to condone his decision, which "hereby hath made those of his owne house to be his Enemies."[78] Nevertheless, the benefits of praying

[74] *Light Appearing*, 113. All the following quotes are from pp. 115–16.
[75] *Tears of Repentance*, 203–5; *Strength Out of Weaknesse*, 186–7 (quote); *Conquests and Triumphs*, 49–50.
[76] *Strength Out of Weaknesse*, 186.
[77] *Tears of Repentance*, 205; *Strength Out of Weaknesse*, 186–7; *Indian Converts*, 7.
[78] *Strength Out of Weaknesse*, 187.

to Jehovah were so clear and convincing to these *powwows* that they stayed the course.

Large numbers of Wampanoags followed them, making the *powwows'* defeat a watershed for the mission. After the first *powwows* joined the meeting, "there came pressing in at the same time about fifty Indians, desiring to joyne with the Worshippers of God in his service," mostly in family groups, including children.[79] All of them pledged to abide by the Ten Commandments, show fealty to God, and recognize the meeting's moral authority over members. By 1651, there were 199 meeting Indians, enough to permit the establishment of two assemblies, one on Chappaquiddick run by Hiacoomes, another at Nunnepog under Momonaquem, the son of a high-ranking Aquinnah man and an east-side mother.[80] By 1653, 283 adults, including eight shamans, had been persuaded "to renounce their false gods, Devils, and Pawwaws, and publicly in set meetings before many witnesses . . . to embrace the Word and Way of God."[81] The number of meeting Indians continued to grow as members won over friends and relatives, some of whom simply wanted domestic peace, and others who wanted to pacify the god who plagued their families with disease.[82] As anthropologist William Simmons writes, Mayhew and Hiacoomes had neutered the *powwows* with a foolproof argument: "to continue to believe in shamans denied one the greater healing power of the English God, and made one vulnerable to the injuries believed to be caused by shamans to which Christians were immune. Furthermore, [Mayhew] interpreted all suffering among nonbelievers as punishment from God for their sins, which included foremost the refusal to accept God's way. Mayhew thereby usurped the shamans' final power, the ability to cure sorcery victims, by interpreting sorcery as an expression of God's displeasure with those who continued to believe in shamans."[83]

---

[79] *Strength Out of Weaknesse*, 187 (quote), 188. As Sergei Kan notes, when men dominate a mission's ranks, it is probably a signal that politics is Christianity's main draw. But when women and children participate, it suggests something more complicated. See his *Memory Eternal: Tlingit Culture and Russian Orthodox Christianity through Two Centuries* (Seattle: University of Washington Press, 1999), 125.

[80] *Strength Out of Weaknesse*, 188; *Some Account of Those English Ministers*, 289.

[81] *Tears of Repentance*, 202–3 (quote); *Some Account of those English Ministers*, 290.

[82] Wives were particularly effective in drawing their husbands into the fold. See *Indian Converts*, 147, 156, 163, 179, 180, 197, 202, 213.

[83] Simmons, "Conversion from Indian to Puritan," *NEQ* 52 (1979), 209; Morrison, *A Praying People*, 10–17; Cogley, *John Eliot's Mission to the Indians*, 172–6. For comparative purposes, see James Axtell's discussion of Jesuits targeting shamans in New France, in his *Invasion Within*, 93–104. Cogley, "Two Approaches to Indian Conversion in Puritan New England: The Missions of Thomas Mayhew Jr. and John Eliot," *Historical Journal of Massachusetts* 23 (1995), 44–60, argues that whereas Mayhew focused his attention on the *powwows*, Eliot "never made a sustained effort to discredit the *powwows'* powers of healing and sorcery" (p. 57). Cogley overstates the difference between the two missionaries. To be sure, compared to Mayhew's writings Eliot's tracts devote less space to his confrontations with shamans.

Certainly *powwows* continued to terrify some Vineyard Wampanoags well into the seventeenth century and perhaps beyond, but their hold over the general Indian populace was broken.[84]

The Christian population continued to grow with evidence of the meeting Indians' superior health.[85] Although there is little hard evidence to explain this pattern, from a modern secular perspective one can hypothesize that Mayhew and perhaps other colonists provided Christian Indians with food, water, blankets, and fuel when most Natives were debilitated and unable to procure such needs. Doubtless some Christian Indians benefited from the psychological strength of claiming Jehovah's protection against witchcraft, and the abandonment of counterproductive treatments prescribed by *powwows* like fasting, dancing in crowded, smoke-filled *wetus*, and following up sauna baths with dips in frigid waters.[86] But the Natives interpreted their luck differently. In a desperate attempt to reverse their fortunes, they had shown respect for an obviously potent Jehovah by forgoing certain customary rituals and spirits and petitioning him alone for assistance; since gods could not hope to retain their followers without providing them earthly rewards, it was only fitting that Jehovah had eased their suffering, just as he protected the English.

With this critical mass in place, the "praying Indians," as they were called, took the essential next step toward forming a bona fide congregation of saints: agreeing to a Puritan church covenant, in which believers pledged themselves to one another and God to uphold Christian worship and community life. In early 1652, the meeting Indians asked Mayhew to help them gather a covenanted church and to "have some men Chosen amongst them with my Father and my self, to see that the Indians did walk orderly and that such might be incouraged, but that those that did not, might be dealt with according to the word of the Lord."[87] Six months earlier, John Eliot's mainland charges had taken a similar step, and certainly the Vineyarders wanted to keep pace.[88] Furthermore, a covenant would bind Wampanoag subscribers closer to God and, not incidentally, to the colonists. Mayhew

---

Nevertheless, Eliot repeatedly told his charges that all good was to be had through God, not Cheepi. By 1648, Eliot and others submitted that this argument was eroding shaman status among mainland praying Indians. See Eliot, *Day Breaking*, 19; Shepard, *Clear Sun-Shine*, 50–1, 56–7; *Glorious Progresse*, 82, 96; *Light Appearing*, 134, 142.

[84] Cotton Journal, 82, 87. Note that the June 12, 1667 entry is marked by Hiacoomes asking John Cotton Jr. whether a *powwow* can kill a believer. I am assuming that this was a rhetorical question designed to instruct the assembly.

[85] *Light Appearing*, 116.

[86] *Strength Out of Weaknesse*, 187; Sewall to Grew, ca. 1690, 151; William A. Starna, "The Biological Encounter: Disease and the Ideological Domain," *American Indian Quarterly* 16 (1992), 512–19; Jones, "Virgin Soils Revisited," 739.

[87] *Tears of Repentance*, 206.

[88] *Strength Out of Weaknesse*, 172.

38   *Faith and Boundaries*

advised the Indians to consider the implications of their proposal for a time, but eventually he encouraged the process to go forward.

The Wampanoags' solemnity at the covenant ceremony indicates that they viewed this moment as a turning point in their people's history rather than just a pro forma way to please the English. They began with two nonconsecutive days of fasting and prayer "to repent of our sins." Then a number of especially knowledgeable and eager Christians made public confessions of faith and led the group in prayer, "not with any set Form like Children, but like Men I[mb]ued with a good measure of the knowledg[e] of God." Finally, the meeting Indians had a document read in Wampanoag that acknowledged their people's historic ignorance of God, prompting the Lord to "justly vex us for our sins." They renounced those sins, declared their sorrow for them, and then subjected "Wee, our Wives, and Children, to serve JEHOVAH ... and to trust in Him alone for Salvation ... through his mercy in Christ Jesus our Savior, and Redeemer, and by the might of his Holy Spirit."[89] With this the meeting Indians had committed themselves to punish sin and backsliding among their members, and the appointment of Tawanquatuck as magistrate provided them an established leader to see this transition through.[90] God's law was supposed to be the Indians' law, and any failure to uphold it invited divine punishments unlike any the Natives had ever seen.

IV

Up to this point, Christianity's appeal to the Wampanoags' was primarily ideological in character. Indians joined the meeting in anticipation of worldly results, particularly good health, but that hope was ultimately grounded in their conviction that a spirit of unrivaled power favored Christians for their adherence to him. Hiacoomes might have been an exception to this trend, at least initially. As an outcast he had much to gain by attaching himself to the English and very little to lose. The same cannot be said for political leaders such as Tawanquatuck and Myoxeo or *powwows* like Tequanomin. It would not have made sense for them to suffer the disdain of unbelieving kith and kin if their Christianity had been a cynical pursuit of material or political advantage, since the Wampanoags' true measure of wealth was those very people's love and respect. By the same token, it would have been suicidal for them to risk attack by *powwows* if they did not trust in the Christian God's protection. In a world wracked by epidemic disease, their choice rested on

[89] *Tears of Repentance*, 206–7 (all quotes); *Indian Converts*, 82. On the importance of the covenant to New England colonial culture, see Kenneth A. Lockridge, *A New England Town: The First Hundred Years* (New York: W. W. Norton, 1970), 24–30.
[90] *Indian Converts*, 82.

the belief that Christianity was the best way to regain some control over their lives.

The Mayhews' involvement in the praying Indians' choice of officers ushered in a new stage in which the prospect of allying with that ascendant family dramatically enhanced the mission's appeal. Since 1645, Thomas Mayhew Sr. had shared power on the Vineyard with a group of popularly elected assistants, but sometime in the mid-1650s he withdrew this concession to establish himself as an independent magistrate, thereby fulfilling the range of powers entitled to him by his patent. Mayhew also wielded considerable authority over the young English colony on Nantucket. In 1659, he sold his Nantucket rights to a group from Salisbury, Massachusetts, but reserved himself extensive tracts of land and oversight of Wampanoag affairs, including missionary work. Mayhew's prerogatives, unrivaled in early New England except perhaps by John Pynchon in the middle Connecticut River Valley, led his English neighbors to call him "Governor."[91]

The Wampanoags had their own name for him. Sometime around 1650, Mayhew received a visit from "an Indian Prince, who ruled a large part of the Main-land" accompanied by an entourage of eighty armed men. Given the size of this guard, the "Prince" must have been Massasoit, the paramount Wampanoag sachem from the mainland village of Pokanoket, who occasionally toured his dependencies to collect tribute and parcel out justice. Mayhew demonstrated his gamesmanship and fluency in Wampanoag protocol by ignoring the sachem's presence, "it being with them in point of Honour incumbent on the Inferiour to salute the Superiour." Only after a silence of "considerable time," Massasoit ended the power play and saluted Mayhew with the honorific "sachem."[92]

The Governor deserved this title because he protected his followers, something island Wampanoags appreciated in the 1650s under the rising threat of Narragansett attack. The Narragansetts had begun to raid other coastal

---

[91] Banks, *History of Martha's Vineyard*, 1:131–8; Hare, *Thomas Mayhew*, 72–9; Johnson, "The Mayhew Mission to the Indians," 103–5; Alexander Starbuck, *The History of Nantucket, County, Island and Town, Including Genealogies of the First Settlers* (Boston, 1924), 17–22; Obed Macy, *The History of Nantucket* (Mansfield, Mass., 1880), 17–22, 31; Edward Byers, *The Nation of Nantucket: Society and Politics in an Early American Commercial Center, 1660–1820* (Boston: Northeastern University Press, 1987), 28–35. On Pynchon, see Stephen Innes, *Labor in a New Land: Economy and Society in Seventeenth-Century Springfield* (Princeton, N.J.: Princeton University Press, 1983).

[92] *Conquests and Triumphs*, 16. In a letter dated September 7, 1650, Mayhew Jr. mentioned some Vineyard Indians "having a discourse with Ussamequin [Massasoit] a great Sachem or Governour on the Maine Land (coming amongst them) about the wayes of God." See *Light Appearing*, 117. The only other mainland sachem documented as visiting the island during this period was Tispaquin (Wuttuspaquin), the "Black Sachem" of Assawompset (Middleboro). He is unlikely to have commanded such a large entourage. See, *Cotton Journal*, 68.

tribes for wampum (beads made from whelk or quahog shells) in order to
pay a massive tribute they owed to the mainland New England colonies
as part of the Pequot War's settlement.[93] There is no documentary or archaeological evidence of Vineyard Wampanoags manufacturing wampum
despite being surrounded by suitable materials, perhaps because they had
a lingering distaste for English merchants extending back to Epenow's era
and a desire to avoid the mainland's contentious Indian trade rivalries.[94]
Nevertheless, in April 1654, John Mason of Connecticut wrote, "I am reli-
ably enformed that the Narragansetts are gone six dayes since in a hostile
way against Martins vineyard."[95] It is entirely possible that this statement
was just one in a series of rumors spread by the Mohegan sachem, Uncas, through Mason to alienate the Narragansetts from the English, but the
Wampanoags' fear of the Narragansetts was quite real and thus a factor in
their political choices.[96] Luckily for them, just two months earlier Mayhew's

[93] Alden T. Vaughan, *New England Frontier: Puritans and Indians, 1620–1675*, 3rd ed.
(Norman: University of Oklahoma, 1995), 150–1, 169–73; Francis Jennings, *The Invasion
of America: Indians, Colonialism, and the Cant of Conquest* (New York: W. W. Norton
for the Institute of Early American History and Culture, 1975), 273–9; Eric S. Johnson,
"'Some by Flatteries and Others by Threatenings': Political Strategies among Native Americans of Seventeenth-Century New England" (Ph.D. diss., University of Massachusetts at
Amherst, 1993), 127–9, 156; Paul A. Robinson, "The Struggle Within: The Indian Debate
in Seventeenth-Century Narragansett Country" (Ph.D. diss., State University of New York
at Binghamton, 1990), 148–70; John Strong, *The Algonquian Peoples of Long Island from
Earliest Times to 1700* (Interlaken, N.Y.: Empire State Books, 1997), 206–10, 218, 239;
John A. Sainsbury, "Miantonomo's Death and New England Politics, 1630–1645," *Rhode
Island History* 30 (1971), 111–23; Salisbury, "Social Relationships on a Moving Frontier:
Natives and Settlers in Southern New England, 1638–1675," *MNE* 33 (1987), 89–98; Leices-
ter Bradner, "Ninigret's Naval Campaigns against the Montauks," *Rhode Island Historical
Society Collections* 18 (1925), 14–19.
[94] A series of archaeological excavations at shell-rich sites on the island has uncovered no
signs of colonial-era wampum production, such as stone or metal drills, half-worked shell
columnae, or partially finished beads. See Elizabeth S. Chilton and Dianna L. Doucette, "Archaeological Investigations at the Lucy Vincent Beach Site (19-DK-148): Preliminary Results
and Interpretations," manuscript in the possession of the author; personal correspondence
with University of Massachusetts archaeologist Elizabeth Chilton and Holly Herbster of
Public Archaeology Laboratories, Pawtucket, Rhode Island. Moreover, as late as 1671, long
after the trade had become a standard feature of cross-cultural relations on the mainland,
colonial authorities still had to ask Mayhew to pressure island Wampanoags "to worke
the Sewan [wampum] making," though apparently to no avail. See New York Colonial
manuscript, 3:68–71, cited in Charles E. Banks, ed., *History of Martha's Vineyard, Dukes
County, Massachusetts*, 3 vols. (Boston, 1911), 1:150.
[95] Mass. Archives, 30:30.
[96] On the Uncas–Mason relationship, see Wendy B. St. Jean, "Inventing Guardianship: The
Mohegan Indians and Their 'Protectors,'" *NEQ* 72 (1999), 362–87; Michael Leroy Oberg,
Uncas: First of the Mohegans (Ithaca: Cornell University Press, 2003), 139–70. On the ways
Indians used raids as political "statements," see Eric Johnson, "Released from Thraldom by
the Stroke of War: Coercion and Warfare in Native Politics of Seventeenth-Century Southern
New England," *Northeast Anthropology* 55 (1998), 9.

government had ruled to allow "meeting Indians" to borrow two guns "to Fowl or hunt."[97] Over the next few years, while the Narragansetts' campaign of intimidation was at its height, Mayhew further liberalized the praying Indians' access to firearms. Mainland authorities were startled to hear of Mayhew's "training of the Indians and furnishing them with guns powder and shott."[98]

The Narragansetts' looming shadow encouraged sachem holdouts to reconsider their opposition to Christianity. Hiacoomes's old nemesis Pakeponesso, whose territory included the shellfish-rich Cape Poge Bay, began falling over himself to prove his friendship to the English, selling them Chappaquiddick land, grazing rights, and access to beached whales (one of the Indians' most valued resources) upon exceedingly generous terms, and, not least of all, joining the Christian meeting.[99] Sengekontacket's sachem, Ohkohtonat (or Autumsquin), and his son Wompamog (sometimes Wobamuck, Nabamuck, or Mr. Sam), followed suit in 1660 by deeding the colonists an extra square mile of territory.[100] These transactions meant more to the Wampanoags than just profit. Exchange between peoples signaled peace and mutual support consistent with the metaphorical kin terms like "brother" and "cousin" Indians addressed to their trade partners. Coupled with the ties of Christian brotherhood, land sales gave Indians reason to believe that Englishmen would come to their aid in the spirit of family.[101]

Mittark, the sachem of Aquinnah (or Gay Head), had fewer options than Pakeponesso and Ohkohtonat. His location at the southwest end of the island exposed him to the Narragansetts but also to the oversight of Massasoit, "a great Enemy to our Reformation on the Island."[102] Massasoit had probably objected to the mission in his earlier meeting with Mayhew, but instead of forcing a confrontation he shifted the pressure onto his followers, including the Aquinnahs, who became "obstinately resolved not to admit the Glad-Tydings of the Gospel among them."[103] Mittark's deference to

[97] Edgartown Records, 1:137.
[98] *Plymouth Records*, 10:210.
[99] *Indian Converts*, 4 (becomes Christian); Edgartown Records, 1:149 (land); FNPR, 1:18 (land); Testimony of Sarah Natick, Suffolk Files #14047 (grazing rights); DCD, 1:388 (beached whales and grazing rights).
[100] DCD, 2:253; *Indian Converts*, 73–4.
[101] Johnson, "Some by Flatteries," chap. 7; Salisbury, *Manitou and Providence*, 48; Cronon, *Changes in the Land*, 92–3; Robert A. Williams, *Linking Arms Together: American Indian Treaty Visions of Law and Peace, 1600–1800* (New York: Oxford University Press, 1997), 71–82; Richard White, *The Middle Ground: Indians, Empires, and Republics in the Great Lakes Region, 1650–1815* (New York: Cambridge University Press, 1991), 50–93.
[102] *Tears of Repentance*, 209 ("Enemy"); William Hubbard, *A Narrative of the Troubles with the Indians in New England, From the first Planting thereof to the present time* (1677; Boston, 1775), 47–8; *Glorious Progress*, 81.
[103] *Conquests and Triumphs*, 29.

Massasoit left him isolated and vulnerable to challenges by Christian rivals. Most threatening of all were developments in Nashuakemuck, a loosely organized territory right on Aquinnah's doorstep. There, a local elite named Momonaquem and a minor sachem named Pammehannit filled the vacuum by forming two Christian meetings and assuming their offices.[104] Momonaquem not only claimed descent from a principal Aquinnah man, but became a Christian minister and teacher. He traveled to the mainland with Thomas Mayhew Jr. to visit the praying Indians of Natick. His son, John Momonaquem, preached on the east end, later served as a counselor at Gay Head, and eventually married into a large Takemmy family.[105] Traditionally, Indian leaders used polygamous marriages to broaden their kin ties and thus their base of support, but Momonaquem was showing that monogamous Christians could use the church to fashion networks across the island that boosted their reputations at home.[106]

Pammehannit made a similar climb up the Wampanoag ranks. As one of the earliest Christians and a founding member of the Nunnepog congregation, he had strong ties to the most influential colonists and Wampanoags on the east end. His younger brother, Janawanit, served as Nashuakemuck's minister and teacher. Later, Pammehannit's son, Japheth Hannit, added further luster to the family name despite the pressure of the Wampanoags' belief that God had blessed him in the womb. As an adult, Hannit ministered at the east end and Nashuakemuck, and he married Sarah, who was the daughter of Ketsumin, first deacon of the Nunnepog congregation, and the niece of Nahnehshehchat, a prominent church member of Chappaquiddick.[107] Mittark could not help but worry that minor elites like Momonaquem and Pammehannit might draw off his supporters or contest his authority by combining their inherited status with the long reach of Christianity's institutional linkages.[108]

Mittark felt most at risk when an unlikely combination of Englishmen, praying Indians, and the paramount Wampanoag sachem began encroaching on his jurisdiction. In 1653, Nashuakemuck sachems Wassulon

---

[104] *Indian Converts*, 13, 20, 46–7, 129; personal conversation with Tobias Vanderhoop, June 2000.

[105] *Strength Out of Weaknesse*, 176–7 (Natick; note that Momonaquem is spelled "Hamanequinn" in this tract); *Plymouth Records*, 10:261–3 (teacher; where he is referred to as "Memeekeen"); *Indian Converts*, 140 (son).

[106] Ann Marie Plane, *Colonial Intimacies: Indian Marriage in Early New England* (Ithaca: Cornell University Press, 2000), 22–3.

[107] *Indian Converts*, 20 (Janawanit), 44–5 (Japheth), 87 (Ketsumin), 129 (Pammehannit), 166 (Sarah); DCD, 1:83.

[108] For shared concerns among mainland sachems, see Harold W. Van Lunkhuyzen, "A Reappraisal of the Praying Indians: Acculturation, Conversion, and Identity at Natick, Massachusetts, 1646–1730," *NEQ* 63 (1990), 402, 404; Daniel Mandell, "'Standing by His Father': Thomas Waban of Natick, circa 1630–1722," in Robert S. Grumet, ed., *Northeastern Indian Lives, 1632–1816* (Amherst: University of Massachusetts Press, 1996), 167–70.

and Inittuane granted Thomas Mayhew Jr. a huge tract between Chilmark Pond and the southern half of Menemsha. Christians Myoxeo and Annawanit witnessed the deed, but a more ominous name appeared beside theirs: "Ussamequin," otherwise known as Massasoit.[109] Eight years later, Massasoit's successor, Wamsutta or Alexander, went even further, selling William Brinton of Newport, Rhode Island, part of Nashaquitsa within Aquinnah's eastern bounds.[110] This transaction was part of a larger pattern of Wamsutta alienating his tributaries' lands to compensate for the plummeting value of wampum.[111] Wamsutta's fire sales, paired with the spread of Christianity and English influence in Nashuakemuck, warned Mittark that he could no longer resist the mission and defend his authority and territory. It no longer made sense to follow mainland directives against Christianity with Wamsutta acting more like a pariah than a protector. If he could claim suzerainty over Aquinnah by virtue of its tributary status and then have that claim recognized by land-hungry settlers, he wielded the power to sell the ground from under Mittark's feet. And since Mittark had no moral standing in the Vineyard's Christian community, he could not hope to restrain the English from purchasing land in or near Aquinnah or praying Indians from selling it. The safest course under these circumstances was for Mittark to throw in Aquinnah's lot with Mayhew and the Christians.

However, sachems worried that praying Indians would reduce or halt their tribute payments to them, since Indian churches and English authorities could fulfill the sachem's roles of mediating disputes, caring for the needy, and offering protection. Indeed, during the 1660s, Christian Indians frequently asked about portions of scripture that challenged the rights of their traditional leaders: Galatians 3:25, "But after that faith is come, we are no longer under a schoolmaster"; Matthew 23:10, "Neither be ye called masters: for one is your Master, *even* Christ"; and Matthew 4:10, "It is written, Thou shalt worship the Lord thy God, and him only shalt thou serve."[112] Nevertheless, Governor Mayhew insisted that Christians were obligated to follow their traditional rulers in civil matters.[113] The Massachusetts Bay missionary, John Eliot, made the same sorts of arguments, but with a wink.[114] The difference on the Vineyard was that, for the moment, Mayhew remained true to his words.

---

[109] New York Deeds, 3:66, cited in Charles Banks Papers, vol:Chilmark, p. 4, MHS.

[110] DCD, 3:12, 13.

[111] *Plymouth Records*, 4:16; Laurie Lee Weinstein, "Indian vs. Colonist: Competition for Land in Seventeenth-Century Plymouth Colony" (Ph.D. diss., Southern Methodist University, 1983), 175–9.

[112] Cotton Journal, 80.

[113] *Conquests and Triumphs*, 39; *Some Account of those English Ministers*, 293–4.

[114] *Strength Out of Weaknesse*, 176–7; Vaughan, *New England Frontier*, 263–4; Axtell, *Invasion Within*, 146–8; Van Lunkhuyzen, "A Reappraisal of the Praying Indians," 402–3; Cogley, *John Eliot's Mission to the Indians*, 55–6, 199.

Mayhew's integrity convinced Mittark once and for all that Aquinnah's future rested in the mission. However, his plan backfired temporarily when his people sent him into exile rather than consent to his will. Certain of his course, Mittark spent the next three years on the east side of the island educating himself in Christianity until he was ready to become one of the praying Indians' "magistrates," or enforcers of the moral law.[115] He also launched a campaign to work himself back into his community's good graces, but on his own terms.

By 1666, Aquinnah had experienced a change of heart due to Mittark's own missionary work and the rapid spread of Indian Christianity. Mittark had convinced two Aquinnah elites, his brother Abel Wauwompuhque and a *powwow* named Lazarus, to give Christianity a hearing, and through them he must have reached several others.[116] Meanwhile, one Wampanoag community after another entered the mission. Fourteen years of evangelical work on Cape Cod by William Leverich and Richard Bourne bore fruit in 1665 when two sachems designated a swath of land thereafter known as Mashpee to be a "praying town" permanently reserved to Christian Indians.[117] Four years later, Bourne reported that the Wampanoags of Mashpee "and other places neere adjoyning they are Generally Praying Indians," while on the eastern reaches of Cape Cod "there is some praying Indians & App[e]areth great inclination to receive the knowledge of God & forsake their former wayes."[118] The mission's expansion in Wampanoag country coincided with the formation of six praying towns among the Massachusett Indians near Boston. The historic relationship between coastal Wampanoags and the Massachusetts that had once centered around opposition to the Narragansetts, seemed about to revive through a shared Christianity.[119]

These developments prodded Aquinnah towards Christianity, but the crowning factor was a raid on Gay Head by two or three French warships

---

[115] *Conquests and Triumphs*, 47–8; *Indian Converts*, 21–2. Mittark's position as "magistrate" is mentioned in NCD, 2:39.

[116] *Indian Converts*, 98, 130.

[117] Mass. Archives, 33:149–50; *Strength Out of Weaknesse*, 177, 180–4; Gideon Hawley, "Biographical and Topographical Anecdotes," *MHSC* 1st ser., 3 (1794), 189–90; Mary Farwell Ayer, "Richard Bourne: Missionary to the Mashpee Indians," *NEHGR* 62 (1908), 139–43; Francis G. Hutchins, *Mashpee: The Story of Cape Cod's Indian Town* (West Franklin, N.H.: Amarta Press, 1979), chap. 2; Jack Campisi, *The Mashpee Indians: Tribe on Trial* (Syracuse, N.Y.: Syracuse University Press, 1991), 78.

[118] "Richard Bourne to the Commissioners of the New England Company, 1 Sept. 1669," NE Co. MSS, 7957, p. 1.

[119] Praying towns founded among the Massachusetts, Penacooks, Nipmucs, and Pawtuckets before Aquinnah's shift to Christianity were Natick (1650), Punkapoag (1653–7), Wamesit (1653), Hassamessit (1654), Okommakamesit (1654), and Nashobah (1654). See Cogley, *John Eliot's Mission*, 140–71. On historic ties between the Massachusetts Indians and Wampanoags, see *Glorious Progress*, 81; *Indian Converts*, 67, 72; Suffolk Files #12248; DCD 3:129, 133, 134, 154; Sidney Perley, ed., *The Indian Land Titles of Essex County, Massachusetts* (Salem, Mass., Essex Book and Print Club, 1912), 86–7.

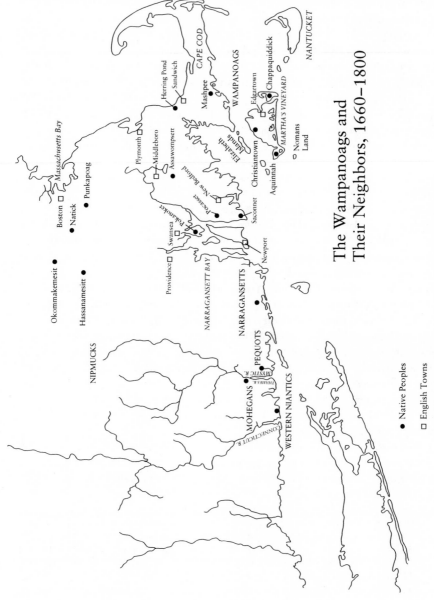

MAP 2. The Wampanoags and Their Neighbors, 1660–1800

45

on July 24, 1666. According to Metacom, or Philip, Wamsutta's successor as the paramount Wampanoag sachem, the foreign sailors "killed and carryed eighteen persons, both men and women, of his from Martins Vineyard."[120] Weary and confused from their struggles against disease, surrounded by an alliance of Christian Indian and English communities, forced to cope without their banished leader, and now subject to renewed assaults from foreign sailors after a generation of calm, the people of Aquinnah finally welcomed back Mittark and his Christian engagement policy. By the spring of 1667, Mayhew was preparing "to settle the Ind[ians] [in] some orderly way of defense in case the Dutch or French should come," and preaching the gospel above Aquinnah's clay cliffs.[121]

Although some sachems, like Tawanquatuck and Mittark, led their communities to Christianity while others, like Pakeponesso, followed them into it, other leaders unintentionally pushed their subjects toward the new faith. One of them was Keteanummin or Josias, sachem of Takemmy, whose territory west of Nunnepog lay directly in the path of English expansion. With so many other sachemships shrinking in size, the people of Takemmy questioned whether Keteanummin and his Massachusett-born son-in-law, Wannamanhut, with whom he sometimes shared decision making, could resist the pressure to sell. The people brooded silently when Thomas Mayhew Sr. acquired Chickemoo (near northern Takemmy) in the late 1650s, but they could not hold their tongues with the threat of renewed sales in 1664.[122] Thirty-three Takemmy men gathered together to announce that "there shall bee noo land sold within the bounds of takemmie with out the consent of the two sachems . . . wannamanhut[,] kotoanum and the rest of the Sachems or gontillmon and common indians of takommie" – meaning just about everyone. They placed the onus on Mayhew "to keep [or restrict] the sale of land" in the future, which was well within his proprietary powers. As for the transaction that had sparked this protest, "wee all agree as one man to with stand & reject that bargain."[123]

Regardless of these pronouncements, Keteanummin began treating the sachemship like a personal estate. In 1668, he sold a huge tract of land to four colonists authorized by Thomas Mayhew Sr. to create a new township,

[120] *Plymouth Records*, 4:151 (quote), 165–6; Mass. Archives, 60:277–9; E. B. O'Callaghan, *Documents Relative to the Colonial History of the State of New York*, 3 vols. (Albany, 1856–1883), 2:585; John Pynchon to John Winthrop, Jr., July 30, 1666, in Carl Bridenbaugh, ed., *The Pynchon Papers: Letters of John Pynchon, 1654–1700* (Boston: Colonial Society of Massachusetts, 1982), 63–4.

[121] Cotton Journal, 81.

[122] DCD, 1:182.

[123] DCD, 1:58. Reprinted as Appendix A to *Report of the Commissioners to Determine the Title of Certain Lands Claimed by Indians, at Deep Bottom, in the Town of Tisbury, on the Island of Martha's Vineyard, Under the Resolve of May 17, 1855*, Massachusetts House Document No. 47 (Boston, 1856).

later known as Tisbury.[124] Wampanoags who lived and worked on this land had few options before them. Customarily, Indians moved to another jurisdiction when they were unhappy with their own sachem. But with land sales plaguing almost every other sachemship there was nowhere else to go. So instead they decided to stay and fight. According to colonist Joseph Merry, the Indians' opposition to Ketanummin's sales became "so much that Mr. Mayhew had hard work to quiet the matter."[125] Ultimately the two sides reached a compromise. In exchange for the Takemmies' approval of their sachem's previous deals they would receive a square mile of land between Great James Pond and Cedar Tree Neck to live on without fear of English encroachment. This land was already in the possession of four praying Indians, Tequannum, Poxim, Nohnosso, and Ketanummin's uncle, Papamick, who probably advocated making the life of the grant contingent upon the Natives' maintenance of Christianity. The agreement specified "th[a]t if the inhabitants [stray] from god his wayes other praying indians of takemmy shal have their land if there be any: if not then the other praying men of this island." Ketanummin promised to enlarge this tract once twenty families had moved to the spot, subsequently known in Wampanoag as *Manitouwatooan* (God's Town), and in English as "Christiantown" and "the Indian Town."[126] The contract also stipulated that no future land sales would take place in greater Takemmy without the consent of four prominent men, Papamick, Tickipit, Joseph, and Taunosan, as well as Ketanummin and Thomas Mayhew Sr. All of this met "with the consent and approbation of most of the inhabitants at meeting."[127] The danger of Ketanummin and the English trampling on the common peoples' rights seemed to be over.

The praying Indians of Takemmy, and indeed, of southeastern New England generally, came to Christianity because it offered them protection not only from the English God but from other threats to the social order.[128] In lieu of war, only Christianity brought the rights of common Indians to the attention of high-ranking colonists, who were as capable of forcing a sachem to respect his followers' rights as they were of encouraging him to

---

[124] DCD, 1:239.

[125] Testimony of Joseph Merry, March 3, 1688/89, Misc. Bound MSS, MHS (mistakenly grouped with documents from 1699–1705). Note that Merry misdates this event by some 10 years. See also Deposition of James Skiff, March 6, 1700, in Suffolk Files #4714.

[126] DCD, 1:357, 378, 402, 2:142; Thomas Mayhew, Declaration of the transfer of title of land to himself and his posterity . . . January 9, 1670, Ayer MS 589, Newberry Library, Chicago, Ill.

[127] DCD, 1:402.

[128] Elise M. Brenner, "To Pray or to Be Prey: That Is the Question: Strategies for Cultural Autonomy of Massachusetts Praying Town Indians," *Ethnohistory* 27 (1980), 135–52, which should be read with Axtell, "Were Indian Conversions Bona Fide?" in his *After Columbus*, 100–21. See also Cogley, *John Eliot's Mission to the Indians*, 55–7, 75, 138, 162–3.

gut the land base.[129] With respect to the land crisis, Christianity did not pose a simple choice between tradition and change, but between some land and no land; between having a strong voice or a weak voice in centers of English power; and between a sachem who, for all his traditional authority, was grasping for new powers, and a church that, for all its novelty, functioned like a traditional counsel that brought the people together, culled their opinions, and mandated leaders to act. Embracing Christianity was not cultural suicide. Similar to the process of religious translation begun by Mayhew and Hiacoomes, the praying Indians appropriated Christianity to secure their collective future as Takemmies, as Aquinnahs, and as Wampanoags.

V

Like Wuttununohkomkooh, who abandoned herself to Jehovah in a moment of dire need, one by one, the Wampanoags of Martha's Vineyard turned to Christianity for answers to the difficulties that plagued them in the colonial world. This new religion promised freedom from illness, upward mobility, links to the English and other praying Indians, and protection from the sachems' prodigality. Overall, the faith provided hope in a very uncertain era. And because Thomas Mayhew Jr. had worked so closely with Hiacoomes in crafting the mission's pitch, the new religion resonated with several traditional Wampanoag beliefs. Thus, the phrase "Here Comes the Englishman" evolved over the years from an alarm during Epenow's lifetime, to an insult during Hiacoomes's courtship with the newcomers, and, finally, to a slogan encouraging reform during the decades of the Mayhew mission. The extent to which the Christian God lived up to his billing would determine the saying's next incarnation.

---

[129] For other examples of the importance of personal cross-cultural alliances to Indians in colonial America, see James H. Merrell, *The Indians' New World: Catawbas and Their Neighbors from European Contact through the Era of Removal* (New York: W. W. Norton for the Institute of Early American History and Culture, 1989), 198–200; Jane T. Merritt, *At the Crossroads: Indians and Empires on a Mid-Atlantic Frontier, 1700–1763* (Chapel Hill: University of North Carolina Press for the Omohundro Institute of Early American History and Culture, 2003).

2

To Become All Things to All Men

John Cotton Jr.'s maiden voyage to Martha's Vineyard in 1665 must have been a time of soul searching and low expectations. Two years earlier, this Harvard-educated son of a Puritan divine was run out of the Wethersfield, Connecticut, pastorate for sexual indiscretion and a sharp tongue. To rehabilitate his name, Cotton had to perform good Christian service while behaving himself; so some time later, when the opportunity arose to proselytize the Vineyard Wampanoags, reluctantly he accepted the position. One imagines Cotton sailing toward his destination, eyes fixed on the shrinking mainland shoreline, reflecting on his fall from an elite family, college, and pulpit, to become a poorly compensated missionary on a remote island responsible for filling "poor ignorant savages" with a sense of God.[1]

Cotton spent the next year preparing for his work by studying the notoriously complex Wampanoag tongue, but this was hardly enough training, as he discovered when he finally met with an Indian audience at Chappaquiddick on March 6, 1666. He plodded through his inaugural Native-language sermon, and then perhaps breathed a sigh of relief assuming the hard work was done, only to have the Wampanoags shower him with a volley of questions sharpened by two decades of Christian education: "How conscience came to be asleepe or silent in a man at any time?" "Whether Judas was saved or damned?" And perhaps most surprisingly: "Whether John Baptist onely sprinkled christs face with water or plunged him under water?" The following week at Nunnepog, John Tackanash said he believed it was "Gods revealed will" to answer prayers only if he deemed them good, even though Thomas Mayhew Sr. preached otherwise. Before the month was out, Sengekontacket's Panunnut (or William Lay) asked for Cotton's exegesis of several passages from Revelation, a book missionaries tended to

---

[1] Cotton's career is traced in Mark A. Peterson, "The Plymouth Church and the Evolution of Puritan Religious Culture," *NEQ* 66 (1993), 582–91.

avoid, as if to advertise his independent access to the Bible.[2] Cotton had gone head-to-head with New England's greatest minds during his college days, but handling sensitive challenges like these from lay congregants, never mind Indians, was startlingly unfamiliar. Contrary to two competing English opinions about the Natives' capacity for Christianity, neither were the Indians so hopelessly "savage" that they could not comprehend the Word, nor were they passive schoolchildren waiting for a paternal teacher to fill their minds with *the* truth. Only some twenty years after Hiacoomes became the first Wampanoag to adopt the faith, a broad cross section of his people was critically yet knowledgably engaged with it too.

The Wampanoags' questions also contained hints that their Christianity was informed by and even consistent with their people's traditional faith. Seantan (or Sissetome) wanted to know "how God may be said to be a rock & fort to his people," like Wampanoag guardian spirits. Hearkening to the Wampanoag belief that *manitous* resided in their wards' bodies, William Lay asked, "How is a sinners heart satans house? How doth sat[an] [kno]w the heart is empty of grace," while Tackanash observed, "God had waited long knocking at the doore of their hearts before they would let him in." Hiacoomes's wife questioned "whether those that are buried in the sea shall rise againe at the last day, as well as those that are buried on land?" She might have puzzled Cotton, but Wampanoags would have nodded in approval, since their ancestors taught that water was the opening to the underground lair of Cheepi, whom they had learned recently to identify with Satan.[3] The Wampanoags were well on their way to becoming Christians by any reasonable standard, but it was a distinctly Indian kind.

John Cotton Jr. entered a mission that was by now premised on shaping the faith to Wampanoag culture and Wampanoag culture to the faith without sacrificing the integrity of either one. Certainly, Wampanoags who joined the meeting experienced the life-altering drama of allying with an unprecedentedly powerful god and his English followers and of reshaping their public identities to include Christianity. Nevertheless, their attraction to Christian precepts derived from Mayhew, Hiacoomes, and their growing number of Native assistants relating these ideas to what the Indians already knew and having their teachings reinforced by social conditions such as disease, politics, and colonial encroachment. Knowing this, missionaries were reluctant to diverge from the proven formula of religious translation, even in the midst of introducing the Wampanoags to complicated doctrines and pressing them to undertake more substantial social reforms. Often the progress was excruciatingly slow and as subject to mistranslation as epiphany. Yet as Cotton could attest, by the 1660s island Wampanoags were receiving a sound Christian education through a variety of institutions, many boasted a sophisticated knowledge of Christian principles, and colonial religious leaders judged a

[2] Cotton Journal, 59–60.
[3] Cotton Journal, 77, 80, 86, 88.

handful of them to be "visible saints," showing evidence of God's grace. All this and the Wampanoags had not become "Englishmen," as Hiacoomes's enemies once teased and as colonial spokesmen hoped. They had found room within the faith for the traditions that mattered most to them.

I

One of Mayhew's first tasks as a missionary was to create institutions in which to educate his charges and make Christian ritual a regular part of their lives, beginning with the Sunday meeting. Praying Indians gathered each Sabbath day to hear Mayhew or a Native preacher like Hiacoomes, Momonaquem, or John Tackanash direct communal prayer, lecture on theological principles, lead a catechism and psalm, and then answer questions, all in the Wampanoag tongue.[4] By at least the 1660s, the mission's expanding staff permitted a midweek lecture as well, which, combined with the Sabbath, led John Cotton Jr. alone to make 119 visits to six different Wampanoag villages in the span of just twenty months.[5] Wampanoags throughout the island were receiving steady instruction and so were their children, for in the winter of 1652, Mayhew established a day school that quickly enrolled thirty students. With financial support from the New England Company, a London-based charity that raised donations for evangelical work and distributed them through a board of Massachusetts elites, he expanded this program, adding colonist Peter Folger as a full-time teacher plus eight Wampanoag schoolmasters.[6] Their straightforward curriculum focused on the catechism, reading, and writing, mostly in Wampanoag and to a much lesser extent in English. Yet the implications of this learning were profound.

---

[4] *Light Appearing*, 118; *Strength Out of Weaknesse*, 188.

[5] The number of visits per village was as follows: Chappaquiddick (forty-two); Nashamoiess/Nunnepog (thirty-five); Sengekontacket (twenty-one); Takemmy (seventeen); Tawanquatuck's Neck (two); Nashuakemuck (two). Native teachers were responsible for the outlying areas of Aquinnah, Nashuakemuck, and Menemsha. Data culled from Cotton Journal.

[6] *Tears of Repentence*, 208; *Conquests and Triumphs*, 28; *Plymouth Records*, 9:203; 10:120, 124, 167, 217, 294, 317–18. *Some Account of those English Ministers*, 289; William Kellaway, *The New England Company, 1649–1776: Missionary Society to the American Indians* (Westport: Greenwood Press, 1961), chaps. 1–2. "The New England Company" was a shorthand for "The New England Company for the Promoting and Propagating of the Gospels of Jesus Christ in New England." After the Restoration of Charles II, the organization was renamed the "Society or Company for the Propagation of the Gospel in New England and the parts adjacent."

More generally on Indian education in early New England, see James Axtell, *The Invasion Within: The Contest of Cultures in Colonial North America* (New York: Oxford University Press, 1985), chap. 8; Margaret Connell Szasz, *Indian Education in the American Colonies, 1607–1783* (Albuquerque: University of New Mexico Press, 1985), chap. 4. On curricula in New England schools, see Axtell, *The School upon a Hill: Education and Society in Colonial New England* (New Haven: Yale University Press, 1974), chaps. 7–8

Literacy opened up a world of reading to Wampanoag scholars even though the majority studied only their natal language. In the 1650s, the mainland missionary John Eliot began to publish a series of religious works in Massachusett, an Algonquian dialect closely related to the island tongue. The first volume of this "Indian Library" was a primer or catechism, followed in 1655 by the books of Genesis and Matthew, then in 1661 by 1,500 copies of the New Testament, and in 1663 by another 1,500 complete Bibles, or about 1 for every Christian Indian family in New England.[7] New editions followed, plus inspirational and instructional tracts such as Richard Baxter's *Call to the Unconverted*, Bishop Lewis Bayly's *Practice of Piety, The Logic Primer, The Day which the Lord hath made*, and a variety of sermons. Handwritten manuscripts, including a Wampanoag catechism authored by Thomas Mayhew Sr. then copied by Native preachers, supplemented this printed material. Taken as a whole, this literature showed praying Indians that God's written word was indeed meant for them and was no less sacred when printed in their language than in English.[8]

Formally educated Wampanoags generously shared their knowledge so the entire community could benefit from the Indian Library. During Cotton's short tenure on the Vineyard, dozens of Wampanoags asked him questions about more than 200 passages of scripture. The unlikelihood that most of these Indians were literate or that they had heard all these verses in English sermons suggests that Mayhew's students held Bible readings at which their neighbors, trained in the context of an oral culture to have sharp ears and deep recall, memorized the selections verbatim.[9] The content of this exercise was new, but its form and function were not. Since time out of mind, Indians had gathered together to have their learned ones transmit sacred knowledge for collective application and safekeeping. The Puritans' emphasis on

---

[7] Jill Lepore, *The Name of War: King Philip's War and the Origins of American Identity* (New York: Alfred A. Knopf, 1998), 34–5. Lepore suggests one native language Bible was printed for every 2.5 praying Indians but her figure does not take into account Christians among the coastal Wampanoags.

[8] On the "Indian Library," see Frederick L. Weis, "The New England Company of 1649 and its Missionary Enterprises," *Publications of the Colonial Society of Massachusetts, Transactions* 38 (1947–1951), 216–18; Kellaway, *New England Company*, chap. 6; Kathleen J. Bragdon, "'Another Tongue Brought In': An Ethnohistorical Study of Native Writings in Massachusett" (Ph.D. diss., Brown University, 1981), chap. 2; Lepore, *Name of War*, 30–41; Richard W. Cogley, *John Eliot's Mission to the Indians before King Philip's War* (Cambridge, Mass.: Harvard University Press. 1999), 119–24; Edward Gray, *New World Babel: Languages and Nations in Early America* (Princeton: Princeton University Press, 1999), chap. 3. On Thomas Mayhew Sr.'s catechism, see "Letter of Experience Mayhew, 1722, on the Indian Language," *NEHGR* 39 (1885), 13.

[9] Walter J. Ong, *Orality and Literacy: The Technologizing of the Word* (New York: Methuen & Co., 1982); Ruth Finnegan, *Literacy and Orality: Studies in the Technology of Communication* (New York: Basil Blackwell, 1988).

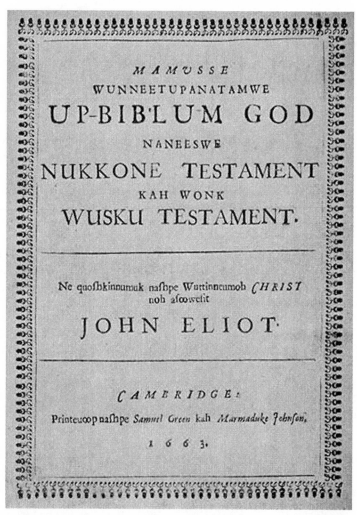

FIGURE 3. Native-Language Bible, 1663. This Bible was the crown jewel in a series of religious works printed in the mid–seventeenth century by John Eliot in the Massachusett language, a close relative of Wampanoag. Such works contributed immeasurably to the Vineyard Wampanoags' religious education and high rates of literacy.

small communities of worship and moral support leant itself easily to the Wampanoags' customs.[10]

[10] A list of works on the Puritans' communal ethic is too lengthy to cite in its entirety. The classic statement is Kenneth A. Lockridge, *A New England Town: The First Hundred Years* (New York: W. W. Norton and Co., 1970).

Mission schools taught Christian fundamentals and literacy, but if the Indians wanted pastors from their own ranks fully trained to interpret scripture, they needed to enroll some of their boys in Harvard College. To that end, in 1659 the New England Company paid for five Wampanoag scholars to join Thomas Mayhew Jr.'s son, Matthew, at the Cambridge Grammar School for preparatory courses. Of them, just two, Joel Hiacoomes, the son of Hiacoomes, and Caleb Cheeschamuck, the son of the Nobnocket (or West Chop) sachem Cheeschamuck, managed to survive the virulent disease environment of the busy colonial town to complete their qualifying studies and enter the college. Tragically, Caleb Cheeschamuck died of consumption shortly after finishing his degree, and before commencement Joel Hiacoomes was murdered (and presumably robbed) by Nantucket Indians when a shipwreck stranded him on their shores. Vineyard Wampanoags were left to imagine the contributions these gifted young men could have made to their peoples' lives.[11]

Whether praying Indians read the Bible themselves or heard it delivered at meetings, whether they attended local schools, Harvard, or just Sunday services, they all had access to a solid Christian education. However, after 1657 their instruction no longer came from Thomas Mayhew Jr., who disappeared at sea on his way to England to promote the mission and attend to his family's homeland estate.[12] It took Thomas Mayhew Sr. years to accept that his son was dead, not just missing, yet he needed to replace him to sustain the mission's expansion to the west side of the island. The question was who to choose. The Wampanoags' leading Christians, Hiacoomes, John Tackanash, Momonaquem, and John Nanoso, might have been capable, but appointing an Indian would have delegitimized the mission (and Mayhew's authority) in the eyes of mainland officials. Qualified Englishmen

[11] Commissioners of the United Colonies to Robert Boyle, September 13, 1665, in *Some Correspondence*, 13–14; John Eliot, *A further Accompt of the Progresse of the GOSPEL amongst the INDIANS in NEW-ENGLAND* (London, 1659), 36 (postscript); "Historical Collections," 173; *Indian Converts*, 148, 164; *Plymouth Records*, 10:277, 296; Walter T. Meserve, "English Works of Seventeenth Century Indians," *American Quarterly* 8 (1956), 264–76; Margery Ruth Johnson, "The Mayhew Mission to the Indians, 1643–1806" (Ph.D. diss., Clark University, 1966), 126–30; Axtell, *Invasion Within*, 182–3, 239; Szasz, *Indian Education in the American Colonies*, 124–6. A letter written in Latin by Caleb Cheeschamuck is translated and discussed in Wolfgang Hochbruck and Beatrix Dudensing-Reichel, "'Honoratissimi Benefactores': Native American Students and Two Seventeenth Century Texts in the University Tradition," in Helen Jaskoski, ed., *Early Native American Writing: New Critical Essays* (New York: Cambridge University Press, 1996), 1–13; and Bernd C. Peyer, *The Tutor'd Mind: Indian Missionary-Writers in Antebellum America* (Amherst: University of Massachusetts Press, 1997), 48–51.

[12] "Historical Collections," 202–3; *Conquests and Triumphs*, 28 (note that a misprint in this source puts the date at 1647); *Some Account of those English Ministers*, 291–2; Charles Edward Banks, *The History of Martha's Vineyard, Dukes County, Massachusetts*, 3 vols. (Boston: George H. Dean, 1911), 1:228–9.

with any alternatives were not about to take a job proselytizing "savages" in a backwater with a resident potentate.[13] Possessing few options himself, the Governor picked up his son's mantle, even though he was sixty-four years old and weighed down with other political responsibilities.[14] Over the next few years he made a few concessions to age and the enormity of his task by leaning on his Wampanoag-speaking son-in-law, Thomas Daggett, and the local schoolteacher, Peter Folger, and then hiring John Cotton Jr., but he was determined not to let the mission slip out of his control.

Unfortunately, Folger and Cotton had not been vetted for the special forbearance needed to be a colleague of Thomas Mayhew Sr. Once Mayhew caught wind of Folger's Anabaptist sympathies, he disparaged him to the Indians as "quite [fall]en from the good way," and "a very bad man & his way very naught." Evidently Folger responded in kind, for his staunchest Indian followers criticized Mayhew for failing to prove his sermons with scripture, and one of them, Washaman of Chappaquiddick, stopped attending Congregationalist services altogether. Turning the other cheek could have turned this dispute into a lesson about Christian ethics, but both men were unable to practice what they preached. Discouraged, Folger left the island in 1662 for Rhode Island before ultimately settling at Nantucket, where he continued to serve as an interpreter and missionary to the Indians.[15] Cotton sailed in on Folger's wake and almost immediately fell out with the Governor too by siding against him in a seemingly innocuous debate with John Tackanash about God's fulfillment of prayer. Just two weeks after Cotton's first sermon at Chappaquiddick he learned that "Mr. Mayhew was very much ag[ain]st my preaching," spreading rumors that "laste year, I said the Indians stunk," and reprimanding Natives who went to Cotton for advice instead of him.[16] Cotton fired back, and shortly the "mutuall contesions and Invictuns against another" grew so intolerable that in 1667 Cotton moved to Plymouth to become the town's minister and missionary to the surrounding mainland Wampanoags.[17] This left Mayhew as the sole English missionary on the island, happily it would appear, since he kept it that way for the next decade until his grandsons, Matthew and John, grew old enough to take his orders.

[13] *Some Correspondence*, 4; Allan B. Forbes, ed., *Winthrop Papers* (Boston: Massachusetts Historical Society, 1929–1947), 7:36–7.

[14] Thomas Mayhew Sr. to John Winthrop Jr., August 29, 1659, *MHSC* 4th ser., 7 (1865), 37; "Historical Collections," 202–3.

[15] Cotton Journal, 60–61 (quotes); Edward Byers, *The Nation of Nantucket: Society and Politics in an Early American Commercial Center, 1660–1820* (Boston: Northeastern University Press, 1987), 38, 57; Carl Bridenbaugh, *Fat Mutton and Liberty of Conscience: Society in Rhode Island, 1636–1690* (Providence: Brown University Press, 1974), 35–6; Nathaniel Philbrick, *Abram's Eyes: The Native American Legacy of Nantucket Island* (Nantucket, Mass.: Mill Hill Press, 1998), 108.

[16] Cotton Journal, 60–1.

[17] Cotton Journal, 89–101; *Plymouth Records*, 10:329 (quote); *Some Correspondence*, 47; *Conquests and Triumphs*, 30–1; *Some Account of those English Ministers*, 299.

II

Mayhew's penchant for alienating coworkers might have killed a weaker mission, but the hard work of his son, devoted Wampanoags, and, not least of all, Folger and Cotton, to establish Native-run churches and schools, and teach Christian doctrine accurately while engaging Wampanoag traditions, had prepared the Indians to tend to their own Christianity. The Wampanoags, no less than their English counterparts, included some who were uninspired Christians, and others, no doubt, who went to church begrudgingly and silently mocked what they heard. They had their pious and profane, orthodox and heterodox. But the latter were in full retreat by the 1660s, outnumbered by those committed to knowledgeable participation in a faith they now counted as an expression of their people's past, present, and future.

Some Wampanoags had to test Christianity's limits and familiarize themselves with its innumerable peculiarities before they could concentrate on basic principles. They reasoned that if Christianity was the key to the great mysteries of the world, their missionaries must know the answers to questions such as "How did God make the fat in candlewood" and "Why doe old men loose their [te]eth and grow blind."[18] The Wampanoags could slow the most targeted agenda to a crawl by fixating on details colonists took for granted, or by interpreting metaphorical passages literally. Cotton found himself answering: Did God want believers to meet indoors or out doors?[19] What fruit did Eve eat (apples were foreign to North America)?[20] What were the *wheels* referred to in Ezekiel 1:19, the *oven* in Matthew 6:2, and "The *Keyes* of the *Kingdome*" in Matthew 16:19? – Indians possessed none of these things.[21] Was it truly God's law that "if thy right eye offend thee, pluck it out, and cast it from thee?"[22] "What it is to Kisse the son of God," one confused Wampanoag asked.[23] Frustrating as it must have been, missionaries had no choice but to address this minutia before moving on.

They also had to participate in the Natives' efforts to place Christian ideas within a Wampanoag framework or else their meetings would have gone nowhere. Women, who otherwise rarely spoke at Cotton's meetings, were conspicuous in putting their customs in dialogue with the new faith.

---

[18] Cotton Journal, 74, 84. For an astute analysis of questions asked by Indians in John Eliot's mainland mission, see Robert James Naeher, "Dialogue in the Wilderness: John Eliot and the Indian Exploration of Puritanism as a Source of Meaning, Comfort, and Ethnic Survival," *NEQ* 62 (1989), 351–5
[19] Cotton Journal, 65.
[20] Ibid., 64.
[21] Ibid., 62, 83. Emphasis mine.
[22] Ibid., 65.
[23] Ibid., 63.

John Amanhut's wife was interested in Revelation 12:1–2, which tells of "a woman... being with child cried, travailing in birth, and pained to be delivered." She must have used this passage to consider the Indians' stigma against expressing the physical strain of childbirth.[24] Hiacoomes's wife asked if drowning victims would rise on the last day like those buried on land, probably because of her people's belief that water led to Cheepi's underworld or, by Christian logic, Hell.[25] Matthew of Chappaquiddick thought along similar lines, but Native women could not have been pleased to hear him question their household authority by citing 1 Corinthians 11:3, which states "that the head of every man is Christ, and the head of a woman is the man; and the head of Christ is God"?[26] Joshua was unsure what to make of Luke 14:12, which reads, "When thou makest a dinner or a supper, call not thy friends, nor thy bretheren, neither thy kinsmen, nor thy rich neighbors; lest they also bid thee again, and recompense be made thee?"[27] Was this a condemnation of the Wampanoags' communal ethic? Fear of entering heaven without the ancestors led Nunnanennumuck to ask, "whether our fathers that died before they heard of God or knew him are saved or not."[28] Another wanted to know what happened to the souls of dead infants, presumably out of concern for their lack of baptism or Christian education, but perhaps in reference to a belief held by other northeast Indians that a baby's spirit might implant itself in a pregnant woman to be reborn.[29] The terror of the Wampanoags' recent devastation by epidemic disease was unmistakable when Joseph of Chappaquiddick pleaded "whether faith will... heal the sick," and one of Hiacoomes's sons mentioned the unspeakable: "what is meant by Gods visiting the Iniquity of the fathers upon the children to the 3rd & 4th generation?"[30] Whatever Cotton's answers (he did not record them), the very act of joining together to address these distinctly Indian concerns was a means of investing Christianity with Wampanoag meanings.

Despite the mission's uneven progress, the growing sophistication of the praying Indians was unmistakable. Wampanoags refused to overlook Christianity's inconsistencies and ambiguities, demanding: "Why some good men died young & wicked men lived till they were old?"[31] "Why Judas betraying

---

[24] Ibid., 68; Ann Marie Plane, "Childbirth Practices of Native American Women of New England and Canada, 1600–1800," in Peter Benes, ed., *Medicine and Healing: Annual Proceedings of the Dublin Seminar for New England Folklife* (Boston: Boston University Press, 1992), 1–12.

[25] Cotton Journal, 88.

[26] Ibid., 69.

[27] Ibid., 74.

[28] Ibid., 68.

[29] Ibid., 71; Reuben Gold Thwaites, ed., *Jesuit Relations and Allied Tracts*, 73 vols. (Cleveland, 1896–1901), 10:273.

[30] Cotton Journal, 66, 79.

[31] Ibid., 60–1.

c[hris]t was a sin seeing God had appointed it?"[32] "Seeing God rewards a
sinner with [de]ath for his evill actions, why doth he not reward him with a
good [re]ward for any good actions he doth?"[33] "Seeing God made all the
world, who then can glorify him?"[34] And "how can wee know that God
hath chosen some & not others?"[35] Such questions spoke directly to the
Puritans' hottest debates over the tension between God's omnipotence and
humankind's free will, between faith and works, and the transparency of
grace.[36] Some Wampanoags brought sectarian perspectives to these issues,
having been exposed to Anabaptists and Quakers before Mayhew could
drum them off the island, and to unorthodox churches located throughout
the colonies of New Plymouth and Rhode Island.[37] One can see Cotton's
teeth clench as the Indians asked, "why all believers are not Baptized," "why
children are baptised," "if that wash [them] from sin, why doe they sin any
of them when growne up," and "what is the Reason that now the sabbath
day is changed" (from the Hebrew Saturday to Sunday, reflecting the doctrine of Seventh Day Baptists).[38] The praying Indians were not blank pages
waiting to be filled by their missionaries with absolute Christian truths. They
guided the evangelical pen and even authored their own passages by pursuing
dissenting opinions and exposing the faith's contradictions.

Cotton saw no need to record his answers to these questions, and neither
Thomas Mayhew Jr. nor Senior left a sizable record of the terms they used to
translate Christian concepts, but given the pattern of collaboration between
New England missionaries, probably their words corresponded to those in
Eliot's Indian Library and Native language writings by other contemporaries.
Although Eliot preferred to leave "God" and "Jesus Christ" untranslated for

---

[32] Ibid., 64–5
[33] Ibid., 72.
[34] Ibid., 84.
[35] Ibid.
[36] See for instance, Michael P. Winship, *Making Heretics: Militant Protestantism and Free Grace
in Massachusetts, 1636–1641* (Princeton: Princeton University Press, 2002); Stephen Foster,
*The Long Argument: English Puritanism and the Shaping of New England Culture, 1570–
1700* (Chapel Hill: University of North Carolina Press for the Institute of Early American
History and Culture, 1991).
[37] George Bishop, *New England Judged* (London, 1661), 123; "Historical Collections," 123,
203; *Indian Converts*, 49. William G. McLoughlin, *Soul Liberty: The Baptists' Struggle in
New England* (Hanover, N.H.: University Press of New England, 1991), 5, 21–2; George
D. Langdon, *Pilgrim Colony: A History of New Plymouth, 1620–1691* (New Haven: Yale
University Press, 1966), 70. Generally on dissenters in New England, see Philip F. Gura,
A Glimpse of Sion's Glory: Puritan Radicalism in New England, 1620–1660 (Middletown,
Conn.: Wesleyan University press, 1984), chap. 4; Foster, *The Long Argument*, chaps. 4–
5; Carla Gardina Prestana, *Quakers and Baptists in Colonial Massachusetts* (New York:
Cambridge University Press, 1991).
[38] Cotton Journal, 65 ("why children"; "why doe they sin"), 66 (children again), 68 (why not
all believers), 79 ("sabbath day"); Eliot, "Account of the Indian Churches in New England
(1673)," *MHSC* 1st ser., 10 (1809), 127.

fear of corrupting the meaning, occasionally he, like Mayhew Jr., consented to using *Manitoo* for "God," as did Abraham Pierson in a catechism for the Montauks of Long Island.[39] *Matcheanitto* stood for "the Devil" in Eliot's writings, combining the Native word for "bad," *matchit*, with *manitou*, but he followed Mayhew's conflation of Satan and Cheepi in his translation of "Hell" as *Chepiohkomuk*. Other missionaries, including John Cotton Jr.'s son, Josiah, used the word *Awakompanaonganit* for Hell, which meant something like "lost people."[40] Indians might have understood this term as a reference to the souls of malicious evildoers sentenced to haunt under Cheepi's rule before being admitted to Kiehtan's House. Pierson called those souls *Mittachonkq*, the force in the Natives' dual-soul scheme that sustained the body while the other explored the dreamworld.[41] In the early eighteenth century, Cotton Mather, who probably drew on Eliot's writings for Indian terminology or consulted with Josiah Cotton or the Vineyard's Experience Mayhew, used *negonne kuh-quttum* for "predestination," which literally translated meant, "previously appointed." His choice for "resurrection" was *pomatamooganit*, combining the words *pomantam* (he lives) and *moocheke* (much, many more).[42] Christianity was filled with novel concepts, but applying Wampanoag names to them and then qualifying the definitions over and over again through face-to-face meetings had the potential to bring

---

[39] Abraham Pierson, *Some Helps for the Indians, Showing Them how to improve their natural Reason*, 25, app. to John Eliot, *A further Accompt of the Progresse of the Gospel among the Indians in New-England* (London, 1659), 25. To analyze Native language terms in Eliot's writings, I use James Hammond Trumbull, *Natick Dictionary*, Bureau of American Ethnology Bulletin No. 25 (Washington, D.C.: Government Printing Office, 1903). For other texts, I depend upon *Native Writings*, vol. 2. This paragraph compresses a fifty-year span of Native language texts while recognizing the need for a study of the evolution of Massachusett and Wampanoag religious terminology.

For Eliot's approach to translation, see Gray, *New World Babel*, 56–85; Stephen Andrew Guice, "The Linguistic Work of John Eliot" (Ph.D. diss., Michigan State University, 1990), 101–85. For a contemporary's thoughts on using loanwords in translation, see Increase Mather, *A Letter Concerning the Success of the Gospel, amongst the Indians in New England* [1687], in C. Mather, *Triumphs of the Reformed Religion* (Boston, 1691), 92. Some Catholic missionaries working in the Spanish Empire also preferred to leave certain Christian terms untranslated. See Vicente Rafael, *Contracting Colonialism: Translation and Christian Conversion in Tagalog Society under Early Spanish Rule* (Ithaca: Cornell University Press, 1988), 29; and David J. Weber, *The Spanish Frontier in North America* (New Haven: Yale University Press, 1992), 110.

[40] *Auwa, auwog, auwate* = them, people, anyone; *ompenumanut* = to lose them; *ompenum* = he looseth it. The term is found in Josiah Cotton, "Vocabulary of the Massachusetts (or Natick) Indian Language," *MHSC* 3d ser., 2 (1830), 155.

[41] Pierson, *Some Helps for the Indians*, 29.

[42] C. Mather, *An Epistle to the Christian Indians, Giving them a Short Account, of what the English Desire them to Know and to Do, In order to their Happiness* [*Wussukwhonk En Christianeue asuh peantamwae Indianog, Wahteauwaheonaount Teanteaquassinish, Nish Englishmansog Koktantamwog Indianog Wahteaunate kah Ussenate, En michemohtae Wunniyeauonganit*] (Boston, 1706), 4.

the Indians' Christian knowledge into close – if not always exact – alignment with that of their English counterparts, all the while emphasizing that the faith belonged to them.

The most active disseminators of these ideas were Wampanoags themselves, beginning with Hiacoomes then expanding to include schoolteachers such as Momonaquem and John Tackanash, sachem/preachers like Mittark and Wompamog, and shortly a variety of ordained church officers and male and female lay leaders.[43] Although no contemporary accounts of the Indians' pedagogy survive, a transcript of a chance conversation in 1708 between Governor Lovelace of New York and an unnamed Wampanoag from the mainland village of Dartmouth offers suggestive hints.[44] Lovelace quizzed the Indian on his Christian knowledge, which he answered (recorded in the vernacular) by using his hand as a mnemonic device, a common Indian method. The Wampanoag responded to Lovelace's question about the Trinity as follows: "He is one God (pointing to the Palm of his Hand.) and yett he Dree (pointing to his Three extended Fingers on that Hand.) – what you callum, my Lord – methink, you calum, Dree Person." As to whether all people were condemned to hellfire, the Wampanoag man exclaimed:

Maybe no! ... You see my-Lord! (Extending Three Fingers & pointing to his middle Finger,) He speakum Him (pointing then to his For-finger,) You so big Angry with Man. Me Luvum Man. What me do you no Angry[?] Then He (pointing to his Forefinger,) speakum Him (so pointing to his middle Finger,) You go down; You be man; you do all Good Things for man who can do nune. You Dy, that man no Dy. Then you rise again. Then you come up here. Then you show man how to com here; You Lead Man here.

Lovelace was astounded to learn that the Wampanoag's instruction had come only from other Indians, certainly his Vineyard tribesmen, who began proselytizing at Dartmouth in the late 1670s. This might very well have been an exercise used to pass on Christian knowledge during the heyday of the island mission.[45]

The most foreign yet essential Christian concept of all, Original Sin, was not so easily communicated, even in the hands of the most determined and linguistically skilled missionaries. Traditionally Wampanoags believed that spirits might punish individuals and perhaps even groups for their offenses, but they shared nothing of the Puritan idea of corruption inherited by all generations since the time of origins, tainting their best deeds and condemning everyone to eternal torture who did not open his or her heart to a selectively granted divine dispensation. Literal translation had no answer for this

---

[43] *Indian Converts*, 18, 20, 23, 27, 29, 31, 32, 36, 38–9, 49, 58, 64, 92, 99, 107, 144.

[44] A Conference with an Indian of New England, December 1708, NE Co. MSS, 7957, p. 3.

[45] For an extensive discussion of the use of gesture and metaphor in New England missions, see Laura J. Murray, "Joining Signs with Words: Missionaries, Metaphors, and the Massachusett Language," *NEQ* 74 (2001), 62–93.

conceptual rift, which led David Brainerd, an eighteenth-century missionary to the Wampanoags' linguistic relatives, the Delawares of New Jersey,
to conclude, "tis next to impossible to bring them to a rational Conviction that they are Sinners by Nature, and that their Hearts are corrupt and
sinful... they seem as if they thought 'twas only the Actions that were sinful,
and not their Hearts."[46] Like Brainerd, New England missionaries could
barely find the words to begin. They used *Matchit*, the Native word for
"bad," as the root for "ungodly" (*Matchtukeg*), "sin" (*Matchuk*), and "sinners" (*Matchessecheg*).[47] These terms failed to distinguish between, on the
one hand, permanent "badness" stemming from humankind's base evil and,
on the other, "badness" related to an isolated act or an individual tendency
toward bad acts – which from a Puritan's perspective would have missed the
point. Not surprisingly, then, Wampanoags tended to struggle with the notion of limited human means, a pattern historians have also noticed among
mainland praying Indians.[48] John Kossunnut appears to have been confused
by the jousting ideas of predestination and the believer's responsibility to
prepare for grace when he asked Cotton "whether man had power to convert himself."[49] Another unnamed Indian questioned "what comes betweene
[a] state of sin and a state of grace," and Wompamog could not fathom,
"Why god commands sinners to turne from their evil wayes, seeing they
have noe strength of their owne to turne?"[50] Answers would have come
automatically to most *English* Congregationalists, although they had their
doubters too.

Gradually, after sitting through one meeting after another at which
the missionaries addressed these questions, Wampanoags began to cross
this widest of cultural gaps. In the early 1650s, Thomas Mayhew Jr. and

[46] Brainerd, *Mirabilia Di inter Indios, or the Rise and Progress of a Remarkable Work of Grace
    Amongst a Number of the Indians in the Provinces of New-Jersey and Pennsylvania, Just
    Represented in a Journal Kept by the Order of the Honourable Society (in Scotland) for
    Propagating Christian Knowledge. With Some General Remarks* (Philadelphia, 1742), 230.
[47] Trumbull, *Natick Dictionary*; Pierson, *Some Helps for the Indians*, 27; Indian Grammar,
    Experience Mayhew Papers, MHS.
      David Murray, "Spreading the Word: Missionaries, Conversation and Circulation in the
    Northeast," in Nicholas Griffiths and Fernando Cervantes, eds., *Spiritual Encounters: Inter-
    actions between Christianity and Native American Religions in Colonial America* (Lincoln:
    University of Nebraska Press, 1999), 47; and Harold W. Van Lunkhuyzen, "A Reappraisal
    of the Praying Indians: Acculturation, Conversion, and Identity at Natick, Massachusetts,
    1646–1730," *NEQ* 63 (1990), 417, suggest that acceptance of the idea of sin is the key
    moment in Native American acceptance of Christianity.
[48] Charles Cohen, "Conversion Among Puritans and Amerindians: A Theological and Cul-
    tural Perspective," in Francis J. Bremer, ed., *Puritanism: Transatlantic Perspectives on
    a Seventeenth-Century Anglo-American Faith* (Boston: Massachusetts Historical Society,
    1993), 233–56; Daniel K. Richter, *Facing East from Indian Country: A Native History of
    Early America* (Cambridge, Mass.: Harvard University Press, 2001), 111–29.
[49] Cotton Journal, 62.
[50] Ibid., 63–4, 68.

Momonaquem traveled to the mainland to preach and take the Lord's Supper with the praying Indians of Natick, and during a pause the Wampanoag took some time to discuss his spiritual beliefs with several colonists, including William French. According to French, Momonaquem defined sin as "a continuall sickness in my heart" as well as "a breach of all God[']s Commandments," that could be overcome only "by the satisfaction of Christ," a realization that came to him after God "stripped me bare as my skinne."[51] Momonaquem was not alone in his orthodoxy. In 1659, a handful of Vineyard Wampanoags rose before a mixed audience of Indians and Englishmen to narrate the evolution of their faith that Christ died for them – the essential act for becoming a full member of many Puritan churches. Convinced of the Indians' sound doctrine and grace, the baptized colonists recognized them as "visible saints" and proclaimed their meeting a "gathered church" possessing equal standing to English congregations.[52] Eleven years later, Eliot and Cotton traveled to the Vineyard to ordain Hiacoomes as a pastor and John Tackanash as a teacher – the first North American Indians to ever hold such positions – and to install John Nahnoso and Joshua Momatchegin as ruling elders.[53] The missionaries' confidence in them speaks volumes.

The Wampanoags' leading lights proved that they belonged in the Congregationalist fold, but because they carried their entire communities with them rather than formed segregated Christian reserves, their churches contained room for the tepid, unorthodox, and even profane. Some Wampanoags avoided complex theological issues such as the nature of the Trinity, claiming these mysteries were "too deep for us to understand."[54] Others refused to send their children to school, neglected family prayer, or persisted in immorality, and yet called upon God when in trouble.[55] The devotion of some Natives to Jehovah ebbed and flowed with his blessings.[56] One *powwow* tried to hedge his bets by encouraging his wife to adopt Christianity while he kept his old *manitous*, explaining that although "she served a God that was

---

[51] *Strength Out of Weaknesse*, 176–7, 192–3 (quotes).

[52] "Historical Collections," 204, 205. Cf. Neal Salisbury, "Red Puritans: The 'Praying Indians' of Massachusetts Bay and John Eliot," *WMQ* 31 (1974), 29–31; and Jean M. O'Brien, *Dispossession by Degrees: Indian Land and Identity in the Natick, Massachusetts, 1650–1790* (New York: Cambridge University Press, 1997), 54–5, 57, who doubt the extent to which praying Indians understood and accepted the Congregationalist message.

[53] John Eliot, *A Brief Narrative of the Progress of the Gospel Among the Indians of New England*, W. T. R. Marvin, ed. (1670; Boston, 1868), 20–1; idem., "Account of the Indian Churches (1673)," 124, 126; "Historical Collections," 205; Increase Mather, *A Letter Concerning the Success of the Gospel amongst the INDIANS in New-England*, app. to *Conquests and Triumphs*, 66; *Indian Converts*, 10, 14, 34; *Some Account of those English Ministers*, 300. C. Mather, *Magnalia Christi Americana*, 1:567, 569, incorrectly dates the ordination as 1666.

[54] *Indian Converts*, 265.

[55] *Indian Converts*, 113.

[56] *Indian Converts*, 113, 244–5.

above his; but that as to himself, his gods kindness, obliged him not to forsake his Service."[57] Perhaps some stalwart traditionalists took their ancestral religious rituals underground, even though secrecy robbed these events of their social significance.[58] Massachusetts superintendent of Indian affairs, Daniel Gookin, thought so, asserting that although most praying Indians "do fear God and are true believers," others were "hypocrites, that profess religion, and yet are not sound hearted."[59] Governor Mayhew belied his own suspicions when he wrote to John Winthrop Jr., "I doe speake to them sometimes about an howre. I ask them sometimes where they understand; they say yes; and I know they doe, for in generall I really know they understand me, but sometimes I doubt my sellfe, & then I ask."[60] There were and always would be people like the mother of Job Soomanan "who was by some thought to be a Heathen, yet she owned the true God and did sometimes call upon him," but this did not make them much different from English "horse-shed Christians" who professed Christianity but privately dabbled in the occult.[61] Recognizing that there was a range of devotion in any Christian population, and that faith was a deeply personal and invisible quality, Mayhew admitted that the sincerity of praying Indians was simply impossible to determine absolutely.[62]

III

Despite their emphasis on faith over works, Puritans knew that only individuals could know their own hearts, thus making the Indians' behavior the best, if imperfect, measure of their Christianity. "Things that are secret belong to God," explained Gookin, "and things that are revealed, unto us and our children."[63] Accordingly, the Christian Indians' behavior was a mix of new and old, much like their beliefs. Sometimes the Wampanoags' "piety" was adherence to custom.

Missionaries faced the tall task of convincing Indians to conform not only to biblical precept but English definitions of "civilized manners," including modesty in hairstyle, ornament, and clothing.[64] Wampanoags wore "long

---

[57] *Conquests and Triumphs*, 18–19.
[58] See the discussion in Iris Gareis, "Repression and Cultural Change: The 'Extirpation of Idolatry' in Colonial Peru," in Griffiths and Cervantes, ed., *Spiritual Encounters*, 241.
[59] "Historical Collections," 183.
[60] Thomas Mayhew to John Winthrop Jr., August 29, 1659, *MHSC* 4th ser., 7 (1865), 37.
[61] *Indian Converts*, 110. On horse-shed Christians, see David D. Hall, *Worlds of Wonder, Days of Judgment: Popular Religious Belief in Early New England* (Cambridge, Mass.: Harvard University Press, 1989), 243.
[62] "Historical Collections," 205.
[63] "Historical Collections," 183.
[64] The following paragraph draws on Axtell, *Invasion Within*, 171–7. For more on Puritan dress ways, see David Hackett Fischer, *Albion's Seed: Four British Folkways in America* (New York: Oxford University Press, 1989), 139–46.

hair to their shoulders, only cut before, some trussed up before with a feather, broad-wise, like a fan, another a fox tail hanging out."[65] They tattooed their bodies with geometric patterns and the totems of *manitous*, painted their faces red, black, white, and yellow, and bedecked themselves in jewelry of wampum, copper, and bone. But above all, missionaries found Indian clothing, or the lack thereof, inappropriate. The problem was that Indians were equally unimpressed with colonial garb, at least at first. Manufactured clothing was expensive, slow to dry, and restrictive and coarse. Even Indians who willingly put on trousers before entering English towns, "pull of[f] all, as soone as they come againe into their owne Houses, and Company."[66] Eventually most Indians adopted English shirts and hats and turned trade blankets into mantles and breechclouts, but they still resisted pants and did little to tone down their ostentation.[67]

Such limited adjustments would not do for Christians, at least as far as missionaries were concerned. Although the Mayhews were less insistent than Eliot about the outward trappings of "civility," they still encouraged reform of "the great Sins of which the Indians were guilty."[68] In 1649, when Hiacoomes was asked to identify these sins, "he presently found 45 or 50." With the hot breath of God at their backs, twenty-two Natives "were found to resolve against those evils," which certainly included "wild" appearance alongside polygamy, fornication, and adultery.[69]

The praying Indians' desire to symbolize their Christianity provided an equally strong impetus to follow "the English mode."[70] They cut their hair "in a modest manner as the New English generally doe," which encouraged

---

[65] Dwight B. Heath, ed., *Mourt's Relation: A Journal of the Pilgrims at Plymouth* (1622; Bedford, Mass.: Applewood Books, 1963), 53. See also Roger Williams, *A Key into the Language of America*, eds. John J Teunissen and Evelyn J. Hinz, (1643; Detroit: Wayne State University Press, 1973), 185–8; William Wood, *New England's Prospect* (London, 1634), ed. Alden T. Vaughan, (Amherst: University of Massachusetts Press, 1977), 85; John Josselyn, "The Second Voyage," in Paul J. Lindholdt, ed., *John Josselyn, Colonial Traveler: A Critical Edition of "Two Voyages to New-England"* (1674; Hanover, N.H.: University Press of New England, 1988), 92–93; Martin Martin Pring, "A Voyage set out from the Citie of Bristoll... in the yeere 1603," in David B. Quinn and Alison M. Quinn, eds., *The English New England Voyages, 1602–1608* (London: The Hakluyt Society, 1983), 222; Lawrence C. Wroth, ed., *The Voyages of Giovanni da Verrazzano, 1524–1528* (New Haven, Conn.: Yale University Press, 1970), 138; Charles Herbert Levermore, ed., *Forerunners and Competitors of the Pilgrims and Puritans* (Brooklyn, N.Y.: The New England Society of Brooklyn, 1912), 127; *Good News*, 589.

[66] Williams, *Key into the Language of America*, 187 (quote); Wood, *New England's Prospect*, 84.

[67] Josselyn, "The Second Voyage," 293 (quote); "Historical Collections," 152.

[68] *Indian Converts*, 12 (quote); Dane Morrison, *A Praying People: Massachusett Acculturation and the Failure of the Puritan Mission, 1600–1690* (New York: Peter Land, 1995), 67–74.

[69] *Light Appearing*, 115.

[70] "Historical Collections," 152.

unchurched neighbors to "revile them and call them Rogues."⁷¹ By 1660, some Englishmen considered Vineyard Wampanoags "more civilized than anywhere else wh'ch is a step to Christiantiy," and in subsequent decades, various writers described them as "well clothed, and mostly in decent English apparell," "generally Cloathed as the English are," and "well attired with a surprising Gravity and Decency beyond what I have met with in other [Indian] plantations."⁷² Some Wampanoags became so enchanted with English fashion that they traveled to the Boston area for seasonal work in exchange for "necessary clothing which is scarce and dear upon those Islands."⁷³

Missionaries hoped that Wampanoag dancing would become scarce and dear as well because of its close association with the Indians' ancestral religion. Puritans felt the presence of the devil when they saw Natives dancing in fire-lit settings accompanied by drumming and chanting.⁷⁴ It did nothing to dispel their fears to learn that some of these dances were prayers for rain, cures, military victories, or other favors, and that sometimes the *manitous* joined in themselves. Praying Indians were supposed to spurn these *manitous* as demons, or offenders of Jehovah, and the Puritans' insistence that Christians no longer received direct revelation closed off the possibility of claiming that the dancing spirits were God or his angels. Indian feasts and festivals continued on the Vineyard, but by at least the early eighteenth century, the dancing sites had fallen out of use and went by names like "the *old* pow[wow] field."⁷⁵

Missionaries also targeted mourning rites in their campaign to purge Indian activities of their traditional religious meanings. Before the Wampanoags adopted Christianity, mourners were expected to blacken their faces, shriek, contort themselves, tear their hair and clothing, and collapse into sobs. Rhode Island's Roger Williams observed that "bewailing is very

⁷¹ John Eliot, *The Day Breaking, If Not the Sun-Rising of the GOSPELL With the INDIANS in New England, MHSC* 3d ser., 4 (1834), 22.
⁷² Samuel Maverick, *A Briefe Description of New England* (1660), Massachusetts Historical Society, *Proceedings*, 2d ser., 21 (1885), 243 ("more civilized"); "Indian Visitation," 132 ("well cloathed"); E. Mayhew, *A Brief Account of the State of the Indians on Martha's Vineyard, & the Small Island adjacent in Dukes County, from the Year 1694 to 1720*, app. to his *A Discourse Shewing that GOD Dealth with MEN As with Reasonable Creatures* (Boston, 1720), 11 ("generally ....)"; Samuel Sewall to William Ashhurst, May 8, 1714, NE Co. MSS, 7955/1, pp. 56–7 ("Gravity.... "). See also *Indian Converts*, 51, 167.
⁷³ Daniel Gookin, "An Historical Account of the Doings and Sufferings of the Christian Indians in New England, in the Years 1675, 1676, 1677," *Archaeologia Americana: Transactions and Collections of the American Antiquarian Society*, vol. 2 (1836), 434.
⁷⁴ "Historical Collections," 153; Levermore, ed., *Forerunners and Competitors of the Pilgrims*, 145; William Simmons, "Cultural Bias in the New England Puritans' Perception of Indians," *WMQ* 38 (1981), 56–72.
⁷⁵ DCP, 1:30 (my emphasis). Such places were also known as "Dancing Fields." See DCD, 6:436. On feasts and other social occasions, see *Indian Converts*, 90, 93, 141, 175, 222.

solemne amongst them morning and evening and sometimes in the night they bewaile their lost husbands, wives, children, brethren or sisters &c. Sometimes a quarter, halfe, yea, a whole yeere, and longer, if it be for a great Prince."[76] Puritans thought death should be marked by ceremonial and emotional restraint because it represented God's will. It was not a time to question his decisions, but a sober occasion to contemplate one's own eternal fate.[77] Wampanoags appear to have been convinced by this argument, for when Hiacoomes's five-day-old son expired around 1650, they showed "no black faces for it as the manner of Indians is," and made no "hellish howlings over the dead." "One of the Indians," Thomas Mayhew Jr. added, "told me he was much refreshed in being freed from their old customes."[78] Mainland praying Indians made similar reforms, and by the 1670s Gookin could write with confidence that they had abandoned black-face mourning.[79]

The dead had their own role in expressing the Wampanoags' Christianity. Praying Indians made their funerals more like English ones by incorporating shrouds, coffins, headstones, and footstones, laying the dead in an extended position rather than a fetal crouch, and abandoning sprinkling the corpse in red ochre as a symbol of rebirth. They also discarded the palisades, mounds, and posts decorated with luxury goods that once marked the graves of prominent leaders.[80] When eighteenth-century Wampanoags asked to be buried "in a Christian manner," their relatives fully understood what they meant.[81]

John Eliot had on a straight face with both eyes trained on the Indians' men when he told them that "we labour and work in building, planting, and clothing ourselves, &c. And they doe not."[82] Indeed, praying Indians learned that their subsistence patterns were yet another affront to the English and their God. From the colonists' perspective, Indian men violated proper

---

[76] Williams, *Key into the Language of America*, 125. See also Wroth, ed., *Voyages of Giovanni da Verrazzano*, 140; *Good News*, 588.

[77] Fischer, *Albion's Seed*, 111–16; David E. Stannard, *The Puritan Way of Death: A Study in Religion, Culture, and Social Change* (New York: Oxford University Press, 1977), chap. 5.

[78] *Light Appearing*, 116.

[79] "Historical Collections," 153. See also Shepard, *Clear Sun-Shine*, 65.

[80] Susan Gibson, ed., *Burr's Hill: A 17th Century Wampanoag Burial Ground in Warren, Rhode Island* (Providence: Haffenreffer Museum of Anthroplogy, Brown University, 1980), 13; William B. Taylor, "The Taylor Farm Site," *Bulletin of the Massachusetts Archaeological Society* 43 (1982), 40–6; Preliminary Site Reports of Cedar Tree Neck, Chilmark, and Gay Head sponsored by the Massachusetts Historical Commission, Courtesy of Jill Bouck, Martha's Vineyard Historical Society (hereafter MV Site Reports); Elizabeth A. Little, "The Nantucket Indian Sickness," in William Cowan, ed., *Papers of the 21st Algonquian Conference* (Ottawa: Carleton University Press, 1990), 181; James Axtell, "Last Rites: The Acculturation of Native Funerals in Colonial North America," in his *The European and the Indian: Essays in the Ethnohistory of Colonial North America* (New York: Oxford University Press, 1981), 119, 123–7.

[81] DCD, 6:380 (quote); DCP, 1:30.

[82] Shepard, *Clear Sun-Shine*, 50.

gender conventions and God's dictate "to be fruitful and multiply" by leaving their women to tend the cornfields while they followed the "slothful" activities of hunting, fishing, trading, and warring.[83] Puritans expected men, not women, to raise society's staple crops, and to do so with plows dragged by horses or oxen, not with the Indians' simple hoes. They wanted fields to be replenished with fertilizer and fenced in as permanent property, not to be worked to exhaustion and then abandoned. Adopting these reforms would please God while also making the Indians more sedentary, predictable, and controllable, which were among the colonists' main priorities.

Having Indians exchange their spiritually charged interactions with wild animals for pastoral animal husbandry was essential to this vision. Indian men talked, danced, and even copulated with the "boss spirits" of game animals while in the dream or ecstatic state. This contact was nothing short of sacrilege to Puritans, who believed Satan shape-shifted into animal form to recruit witches and then often sealed the hellish compact with sex.[84] Understandably, then, missionaries instructed praying Indians to ask God, not costumed demons, for success on the trail. Better yet, the Indians would abandon hunting for animal husbandry. Husbandmen lorded over livestock rather than communed with them, and followed their calling in the safe confines of the pasture rather than in the dark howling wilderness.

Christian Indians nearest to Boston were under the greatest pressure to take up animal husbandry, and by the mid–seventeenth century enough of them raised and trafficked in small herds of pigs, horses, and cows that Englishmen began to complain about Natives underselling them on the meat and livestock markets.[85] Yet the praying Indians' animal husbandry was less a major new economic activity than a supplement to a dwindling deer population and a way to establish a visible claim to land otherwise at risk of being appropriated by colonists. For it was only *in addition* to their traditional mix of horticulture, hunting, fishing, and gathering that they began to graze domestic animals.[86] Similar to religious translation, experimenting in English economic activities did not involve exchanging of one way of life for another, but adjusting familiar forms. Although animal husbandry

---

[83] Edward Johnson, *Wonder-Working Providence* (1654), J. Franklin Jameson, ed., *Original Narratives of Early American History* (New York, 1910), 262; Cotton Mather, *Magnalia Christi Americana, or, The Ecclesiastical History of New England, From Its First Planting, in the Year 1620, Unto the Year of Our Lord 1698,* 2 vols. (1702; Boston, 1853), 1:559 (quote); Axtell, *Invasion Within,* chap. 7; David Smits, "The 'Squaw Drudge': A Prime Index of Savagism," *Ethnohistory* 29 (1982), 281–306.

[84] Elizabeth Reis, "The Devil, the Body, and Feminine Soul in Puritan New England," *JAH* 82 (1995–96), 15–36.

[85] "Historical Collections," 184, 185, 189; Josselyn, "The Second Voyage," 105; Virginia DeJohn Anderson, "King Philip's Herds: Indians, Colonists, and the Problem of Livestock in Early New England" *WMQ* 51 (1994), 601–24.

[86] "Historical Collections," 184, 185, 189; David J. Silverman, "'We chuse to be bounded': Native American Animal Husbandry in Colonial New England," *WMQ* 60 (2003), 511–48.

distinguished the praying Indians from most unbelievers, their weak devotion to the new activity meant that they also remained apart from their would-be English brethren.

There is no evidence to suggest that more than a few island Wampanoags took up animal husbandry, plow agriculture, or male fieldwork before the late seventeenth century. They simply had little economic reason and no political rationale to do so. Unlike their Boston-area counterparts, who competed with thousands of colonists and even larger numbers of livestock for resources, Vineyard Natives confronted a minuscule English population that had not even reached one hundred by 1660.[87] Certainly the newcomers brought livestock with them, but not enough to overrun Indian cornfields or spoil clam banks to any substantial degree, at least not initially. Fish and shellfish were plentiful along the Vineyard's shores and in its streams and brackish ponds, while deer lived in its forests. Christian Indians were urged to conform to English economic patterns, but that pressure was purely moral and, judging from the lack of response, mildly felt.

Wampanoags also rejected missionary arguments to "break the will" of their young people. Well into the eighteenth century, Englishmen like Cotton Mather bemoaned that Native children were "the most humored, cockered, indulged things in the world."[88] Indians breastfed children well into their toddler years. They allowed them to explore and speak at will. They gave no punishment besides glares, "gentle words," and an occasional splash of water.[89] The Mayhews praised Jannohquisso (or Ianoxsoo) of the nearby Elizabeth Islands for using corporal punishment to discipline his children. His wife, on the other hand, was like the rest of the Indians. She "too much countenanced her Sons in their ungodliness, contending with her Husband for Punishing their Offences, insomuch that he would sometimes say to her, that she acted as tho she desired to cast her Children into everlasting Burnings."[90] Of course she did not. She, like many Indians, knew that some of their own customs were no less Christian than the practices missionaries would have had them adopt.

Certain continuities between the Wampanoags' pre- and post-Christian behavior were less visible to the untrained eye, but equally critical to the

---

[87] Banks, *History of Martha's Vineyard*, 2:Annals of Edgartown:15–16.

[88] Cotton Mather to Dr. John Woodward and Dr. James Jurin, October 1, 1724, in Kenneth Silverman, ed., *Selected Letters of Cotton Mather* (Baton Rogue, La.: Louisiana State Press, 1971), 398. See also Williams, *Key into the Language of America*, 115–16; "Historical Collections," 149.

[89] Axtell, ed., *The Indian Peoples of America: A Documentary History of the Sexes* (New York: Oxford University Press, 1981), 31–43. Along similar lines, see Russell Smandych and Anne McGillivray, "Images of Aboriginal Childhood: Contested Governance in the Canadian West to 1850," in Mary Daunton and Rick Halpern, eds., *Empire and Others: British Encounters with Indigenous Peoples, 1600–1850* (London: UCL Press, 1999), 238–59.

[90] *Indian Converts*, 124 (quote), 176, 247.

Indians' sense of tradition and cultural independence.[91] Even though the Natives made some changes to their mourning and burial rituals, they continued to inter the dead with grave goods such as kaolin pipes, metal pots, glass bottles, and shell beads, for use in the hereafter. Well into the twentieth century, stories circulated around Aquinnah that specters haunted those who selfishly withheld grave goods from their relatives.[92] Praying Indians sent ghosts on their way by pointing their graves westward toward Kiehtan's House, a practice steeped in the idea that the soul exited the body through the skull and should begin its journey to the afterlife heading in the right direction.[93] The Wampanoags no longer colored their corpses red, but during the nineteenth century one observer noted that Gay Head Indians buried their dead in coffins stained with red clay; in this sense, Wampanoag tradition had indeed gone underground.[94] Even if Christians publicly referred to their spirits by new names, they still received death's notice from an illuminated blur resembling Cheepi and souls continued to leave their bodies in flashes of light.[95] Wampanoag-speaking "angels" and ancestral ghosts appeared in dreams to reassure the living of their salvation or to

---

[91] The following paragraph draws on James P. Ronda, "Generations of Faith: The Christian Indians of Martha's Vineyard," *WMQ* 38 (1981), 369–94; Axtell, "Some Thoughts on the Ethnohistory of Missions," and "Were Indian Conversions Bona Fide?" in his *After Columbus: Essays in the Ethnohistory of Colonial North America* (New York: Oxford University Press, 1988), 47–57; and Van Lunkhuyzen, "A Reappraisal of the Praying Indians," 397–98, all of whom caution against seeing Christianity as antithetical to Indian tradition. Instead they emphasize that Christianity offered many opportunities for Indians to change with their times while maintaining important ties to their past. See also Erik R. Seeman, "Reading Indians' Deathbed Scenes: Ethnohistorical and Representational Approaches," *JAH* 88 (2001), 17–47.

[92] Simmons, *Spirit of the New England Tribes: Indian History and Folklore, 1620–1984* (Hanover, N.H.: University Press of New England, 1986), 127.

[93] MV Site Reports; Little, "Nantucket Indian Sickness," 181; Gibson, ed., *Burr's Hill*, 13; Brenda J. Baker, "Pilgrim's Progress and Praying Indians: The Biocultural Consequences of Contact in Southern New England," in Clark Spencer Larsen and Geroge R. Milner, eds., *In the Wake of Contact: Biological Consequences of Conquest* (New York: Wiley-Liss, 1994), 39; Axtell, "Last Rites," 122; Taylor, "Taylor Farm Site"; Constance A. Crosby, "From Myth to History, or Why King Philip's Ghost Walks Abroad," in Mark P. Leone and Parker Potter Jr., eds., *The Recovery of Meaning: Historical Archaeology in the Eastern United States* (Washington, D.C.: Smithsonian Institution Press, 1988), 186–8; Elise Melanie Brenner, "Strategies for Autonomy: An Analysis of Ethnic Mobilization in Seventeenth Century Southern New England" (Ph.D. diss., University of Massachusetts at Amherst, 1984), 174. For a thorough discussion of Narragansett burial practices in the late seventeenth century, see Patricia E. Rubertone, *Grave Undertakings: An Archaeology of Roger Williams and the Narragansett Indians* (Washington, D.C.: Smithsonian Instutition Press, 2002), 132–64, 191–8.

[94] Edward S. Burgess, "The Old South Road of Gay Head," *Dukes County Intelligencer*, v. 12, no. 1 (1970), 24.

[95] *Indian Converts*, 33, 150, 160, 201, 221–2, 262; Simmons, *Spirit of the New England Tribes*, 116, 120–1, 134, 137.

portend the future.[96] "Devils" in the employ of an "apostate" Indian attacked Aquinnah preacher Elisha Paaonut.[97] Indians still did all they could
to avoid mentioning the names of the deceased, using circumlocutions like
"nickanoose his father" (Nickanoose's father), in order to leave their souls
undisturbed.[98] Through such subtle means, even those who adopted the
colonists' religion and many of their ways could retain a sense of cultural
distinctiveness.

In important ways, Christianity *promoted* continuity with and even ex-
aggerated traditional belief and practice.[99] Although Wampanoags possessed the Bible, the spoken word remained their way to the sacred. Many
Wampanoag preachers either could not or would not read scripture to the
Sunday meeting but rather memorized it, thus establishing themselves as
keepers of the community's hallowed words. Preacher Joseph Popmechohoo
of the east end was renowned "for the excellent Memory wherewith God
favoured him...He could remember a great number of excellent Texts of
Scripture, and had a Heart to improve them for the Edification of his Neighbors." Elisha Paaonut "used no notes in preaching, nor did he seem to
need any...yet he used to illustrate the Observations which he raised from
his Text, by other Places of Scripture pertinently alledged."[100] The broader
Indian populace, explained John Eliot, "doe not know the Book, chapter,
and Verse, but distinguish my Lectures by the first material word in it."[101]
The singing of Paaonut's congregation was marked by the same kind of simple rhythmic organization and lack of musical accompaniment that distinguished traditional Indian music. Indeed, Native congregations were praised
in colonial circles for having excellent voices.[102] Normal feminine roles such
as housekeeping, washing clothes, instructing children, nursing, and family
government, now indicated pious Christian living.[103] Work colonists once associated with Indian women's "helplesse condition" and "drudgery" became
a measure of the praying Indians' "industriousness."[104] Sickness caused by a

[96] *Indian Converts*, 147–8, 232, 262.
[97] *Indian Converts*, 58–9, 241.
[98] Elizabeth A. Little, "Three Kinds of Indian Land Deeds at Nantucket, Massachusetts," in
   William Cowan, ed., *Papers of the 11th Algonquian Conference* (Ottawa: Carleton University, 1980), 65.
[99] The following paragraph draws from Kathleen J. Bragdon, "Native Christianity in
   Eighteenth Century Massachusetts: Ritual as Cultural Affirmation," in Barry Gough and
   Christie Laird, eds., *New Dimensions in Ethnohistory: Papers of the 2nd Laurier Conference on Ethnohistory and Ethnography* (Hull, Quebec: Canadian Museum of Civilization,
   1991), 119–26.
[100] *Indian Converts*, 57–8, 83. See also, *Strength Out of Weaknesse*, 170.
[101] *Strength Out of Weaknesse*, 174.
[102] Axtell, *Invasion Within*, 235–6.
[103] Ronda, "Generations of Faith," 385–6; *Indian Converts*, 137, 139, 141, 149, 153, 157, 159,
   163, 171, 198, 202, 229.
[104] *Indian Converts*, 16, 17, 18, 20, 25, 29, 31, 36, 39, 48, 60–1, 68, 82, 85, 88, 112.

powwow's magic became "witchcraft."[105] Indian leaders who mediated disputes became Christian harbingers of peace, and their eloquent, metaphorical speechmaking was seen by missionaries as evidence of Christian calling rather than as traditional Wampanoag oratory. In some areas of life, then, Indians could demonstrate their piety and devotion while barely breaking stride.

Christian prayer also drew on Wampanoag custom. Praying Indians called themselves "pitiful" and "corrupt" in their petitions to God, not unlike the cautious though perhaps less deprecating addresses of pre-Christian rituals. As in the days of powwowing, Christian Indians believed certain people were closer to the spirits than others. Someone lying on the deathbed might be asked to deliver a message to heaven, or a sick person might call for a pastor to intercede with God.[106] William Lay was deathly ill in 1690 when he summoned Japheth Hannit to come and pray for him. Hannit began by singing the first eleven verses of the eighty-eighth psalm, but as Lay faded Hannit shifted to prayer. Suddenly Lay revived, exclaiming that God had heard and acted upon the holy man's words.[107] Congregationalism was a priesthood of all believers, but the Wampanoags considered Hannit to be first among equals.

Such parallels between Christianity and traditional Wampanoag religion buttressed a long-standing Wampanoag argument that Christianity was less a new faith brought by the English than a colonist-spurred revival of ancient Indian practices. One Cape Cod Wampanoag explained to his stunned English audience, "That these very things which Mr. [John] Eliot had taught them as the Commandments of God, and concerning God, and the making of the world by one God, that they had heard some old men who were now dead, to say the same things." Since then, however, the Indians had fallen into a "great sleep" and forgotten these truths.[108] The mission, by this train of thought, was a return to tradition, not an abandonment of it. For others, the spread of Christianity was a fulfillment of precolonial prophecy. One Indian recalled that during the epidemic of 1616–1618,

Hee fell into a dream, in which he did think he saw a great many men come to those parts in cloths, just as the english now are apparelled, and among them there arose up a man all in black, with a thing in his hand which hee now sees was all one English mans book; this black man he said stood upon a higher place than all the rest, and on the one side of him were the English, on the other a great number of Indians: this

---

[105] *Indian Converts*, 214.

[106] *Indian Converts*, 19, 31, 149.

[107] C. Mather, *Magnalia Christi Americana*, 2:442–3. See also *Indian Converts*, 85, 105, 108, 152; E. Mayhew, "A Brief Account," appendix to his, *God Dealeth with Men*, 8–9. Cf. Bragdon, "Native Christianity," 120, who argues that Native ministers "seem to have been accorded authority because of their knowledge and rhetorical skill, rather than as a result of their direct communication with God, as the traditional shaman would have been."

[108] Shepard, *Clear Sun-shine of the Gospel*, 43–4.

man told all the Indians that God was *moosquantum* or angry with them, and that he would kill them for their sinnes, whereupon he said himself stood up, and desired to know of the black man what God would do with him and his Squaw and Papooses, but the black man would not answer him a first time, nor yet a second time, untill he desired the third time, and then he smil'd upon him, and told him that he and his Papooses should be safe, and that God would give unto them *Mitcheu*, (i.e) victualls and other good things, and so hee awakened.[109]

God's blessing of Wuttununohkomkooh while she was pregnant with Japheth Hannit was cut from the same cloth. Nobody would have denied that becoming Christian entailed many changes. Yet the big picture, according to these perspectives, was that it was a return to the purity of old ways and a rediscovery of spiritual power.[110]

III

Over the course of just a few decades the hard work and flexibility of the Vineyard's missionaries and their charges made Wampanoag Christianity the preeminent Native religion. This religion adapted some old practices to new circumstances, gave fresh meaning to familiar words, replaced ineffective beliefs and behaviors with more satisfying ones, and sealed political alliances across the island and the region, thereby addressing a wide range of Wampanoag needs. Subsequently, Thomas Mayhew could report in 1674 that all but one of some 300 Indian families on the Vineyard and about half of the fifteen Indian families on the Elizabeth Islands considered themselves Christian, though he had admitted three years earlier that "many practice litl yet."[111] They were led by fifty Indian visible saints, divided into six meetings, and served by ten Indian preachers. Colonial authorities judged their faith genuine enough that on special occasions, like the ordination of Wampanoag church officers, Native and English islanders gathered together for bilingual services. Some of the "godly English People" even took the administration of the Lord's Supper from Native ministers occasionally, since no ordained colonists served the Vineyard between 1667 and 1684.[112]

---

[109] Ibid., 44.
[110] *Glorious Progress*, 73, 95; *Indian Converts*, 45, 56; C. Mather, *Magnalia Christi Americana*, 2:440–2; Simmons, "Of Large Things Remembered: Southern New England Indian Legends of Colonial Encounters," in Anne Elizabeth Yentsch and Mary C. Beaudry, eds., *The Art and Mystery of Historical Archaeology: Essays in Honor of James Deetz* (Boca Raton, Fla.: CRC Press, 1992), 322–3. For a similar argument about Tlingit views of Russian Orthodoxy, see Sergei Kan, *Memory Eternal: Tlingit Culture and Russian Orthodox Christianity through Two Centuries* (Seattle: University of Washington Press, 1999), 404–53, esp. 409.
[111] "Historical Collections," 205; *Some Correspondence*, 40 (quote).
[112] Eliot, *Brief Narrative of the Progress of the Gospel*, 20–1; idem., "Account of the Indian Churches," 126; *Indian Converts*, 15–16.

The future looked bright for the mission as well. Gradually, the Indians were moving toward congregational independence, in which they ordained their own officers, admitted their own church members, ran their own services, and educated their own children. Thomas Mayhew Sr. continued his evangelical labors while Matthew and John Mayhew honed their skills to succeed him.[113] Most impressive of all was the Wampanoags' own missionary work, particularly on Nantucket, where by 1673 they could claim the bulk of responsibility for 90 of 300 Indian families gathering into a recognized church.[114] The network of praying Indian communities now stretched from central Massachusetts, east to Massachusetts Bay, and then south along the coast to the Cape and islands.

Yet nowhere were missions so successful as on Martha's Vineyard, where the rough figure of 1,500 Wampanoag Christians exceeded the number of praying Indians on the more populous mainland. To explain this pattern, scholars have correctly highlighted the proximity of the Indians and Englishmen on the island, Thomas Mayhew Jr.'s targeting of the *powwows*, and the timing of the epidemics just after the beginning of the mission. Additionally, they have noted the Mayhews' respect, relative to Eliot, for the Natives' political and property rights, tolerance for Natives' syncretization of traditional and Christian ways, and formidable knowledge of Wampanoag language and culture.[115] However, other factors were at play. For one, after the first wave

---

[113] "Historical Collections," 202.

[114] *Plymouth Records*, 10:383–4; "Historical Collections," 206; Rev. John Eliot to the Commissioners of the United Colonies, Aug. 25, 1664, *NEHGR*, 9 (1855), 131; Eliot, *Brief Narrative of the Progress of the Gospel*, 21; idem., "Account of the Indian Churches," 124–9; *Conquests and Triumphs*, 37.

[115] Ronda, "Generations of Faith," 371; Simmons, "Conversion from Indian to Puritan," *NEQ* 52 (1979), 215–17; David C. Stinebeck, "The Status of Puritan–Indian Scholarship," *NEQ* 51 (1978), 85; Francis Jennings, "Goals and Functions of Puritan Missions to the Indians," *Ethnohistory* 18 (1971), 200; Neal Salisbury, "Missionary as Colonist," in William Cowan, ed., *Papers of the 6th Algonquian Conference* (Ottawa: Carleton University, 1974), 264; Richard W. Cogley, "Two Approaches to Indian Conversion in Puritan New England: The Missions of Thomas Mayhew Jr. and John Eliot," *Historical Journal of Massachusetts* 23 (1995), 44–60; Cogley, *John Eliot's Mission to the Indians*, 172–6.

Jennings and Ronda contrast John Eliot, who they see as having used Christianity for "political" ends, with the Mayhews, whose missionary activities supposedly were not marked by "either coercion or material reward . . . On the Vineyard, Indian rights in property were fully respected" ("Goals and Functions," 200). Similarly, Simmons contrasts Eliot's demand that the Indians adopt civilized behavior before conversion, with Mayhew's strategy of beginning "with the implanting of English religious symbols, after which the converts voluntarily restructured their families and political institutions in the direction of English modes." These authors depend exclusively on Mayhew missionary tracts, thereby missing the story contained in the Dukes County Deeds that the protected Christiantown reserve required its residents to be praying Indians. Only Salisbury correctly notes that Governor Mayhew, no less than Eliot, had a long-term goal of bringing the Indians under Christian government. Vaughan and Cogley suggest that the island setting left the Indians with nowhere to retreat in the face of English expansion, thereby promoting their conversion.

of Indians joined the meeting following the epidemics of 1643 and 1645, the island did not experience another serious outbreak of disease until the 1690s, which verified Christianity's power. If the Wampanoags had suffered another epidemic, probably they would have abandoned the faith or at least backslid into complacency. Second, although island Wampanoags lost about half of their people during the 1640s, they still outnumbered the English by as many as 15 to 1. The Wampanoags' vast majority encouraged the Mayhews' acceptance of (or rather, resignation toward) Indians determining the pace of reform. Island Wampanoags never experienced the same pressure as Indians near Boston to abandon far-flung territories in favor of English-style towns with parallel streets, measured house lots, and square-framed meeting houses. The Mayhews neither followed Eliot's plan to overhaul his charges' economy, nor were they so bold as to issue "Town Orders" like Eliot's, which fined Natives for picking lice, wearing traditional hair styles, greasing their bodies, and adhering to "the old Ceremony of the Maide walking alone and living apart so many dayes."[116] Wampanoag strength forced "civility" to become a handmaiden, not a prophet, of Indian Christianity. The irony was that Mayhews' concession to emphasize Christianity's religious content rather than English customs produced larger numbers of Indian Christians and a higher degree of Indian acculturation than could be found anywhere else in English America.

Thomas Mayhew Jr.'s close relationship with Hiacoomes and other Indian leaders, such as Tawanquatuck and Momonaquem, was equally critical to the mission's success. Learning one another's language enabled Mayhew and Hiacoomes mutually enhance their influence over Wampanoag society. Hiacoomes tutored Mayhew about the Indians' tongue, religious beliefs, social structure, and respect for metaphorical speech, thus allowing the missionary to construct persuasive arguments for Christianity and to target the most important members of the Native community. In exchange, Mayhew educated Hiacoomes until he was well versed in Christian doctrine, skilled at reading and writing, and prepared to deliver polished defenses of monotheism and biblical authority. It took both parties' working in tandem to win over the first group of meeting Indians and then attract even greater numbers of the unchurched.

Martha's Vineyard's mission did not take place in a political vacuum. John Winthrop Jr. encouraged Thomas Mayhew Jr. to leave the island for Connecticut with its larger Indian population and more lucrative opportunities.[117] Yet Mayhew turned down the invitation in acknowledgment of his

---

The Indians had limited choices, to be sure, but less because of their island location than because their mainland allies confronted similar difficulties.

[116] Shepard, *Clear Sun-shine*, 39–40.

[117] John Winthrop to John Winthrop Jr., July 3, 1648, Forbes, ed., *Winthrop Papers*, 5:236.

work's importance to Indian–English relations within his father's grant. The mission was more than a program to save Indian souls. It opened up political dialogue between island peoples and provided a shared set of values and rituals to control tensions when diplomacy failed. An active mission also meant that Thomas Mayhew Sr.'s proprietary rights carried moral and legal weight in English circles. Undoubtedly he knew that the risk of interference by mainland colonies decreased proportionately as Wampanoags entered the Christian fold. His family's task, then, was to move cautiously but deliberately to convince the Natives that Christianity was the only real choice without antagonizing them to loud protest or violence. The Mayhews also had to keep praying Indians from disowning their sachems, which might provoke a Pakeponesso, Mittark, Massasoit, Wamsutta, or Philip to bring down the club of Wampanoag strength on the island's tiny English population. Missionaries and their Indian charges trod a fine line between cross-cultural peace and war.

Wampanoag ties with mainland peoples, and the lack thereof, was an additional influence on the mission. Assuredly, the Nunnepogs and Chappaquiddicks weighed the progress of Eliot's mission among their long-standing Massachusett Indian allies when deciding to join the meeting. The people of Nashuakemuck entered the mission just as William Leverich and Richard Bourne began to proselytize Wampanoags on Cape Cod. The Takemmies' movement to form the Christiantown reserve was informed by the mainland praying towns Natick, Punkapoag, and Hassanamessit. And Mittark's acceptance of Christianity was partially shaped by the threat of land sales by the paramount Wampanoag sachems. Greater security seemed to lie in an alliance with the English and a burgeoning, closely knit population of Christian Indians extending along the coast.

The Vineyard Wampanoags had extensive contacts with mainland Indians, but not with multiple European powers. Thus, quite unlike Natives who lived along the northern borderlands of New France, New Netherland, and New England, or in the Southeast between Louisiana, Florida, and South Carolina, the Wampanoags did not associate the Christian meeting with one alliance over another. Furthermore, for reasons that are somewhat unclear, island Indians did not produce wampum to exchange with the English, so foreign trade was not a major issue. The Wampanoags' option was to engage the English to one degree or another or withdraw at the risk of appearing hostile, an unappealing option in light of the Pequot War and the Narragansett threat. The Wampanoags' lack of foreign policy choices ultimately muted religious civil strife despite some early signs that it was emerging.

All of these factors culminated in the main reason for the Mayhew mission's success: at each stage there were more and more people, English and Indian, who believed in Christianity, however they understood it, and therefore dedicated time, energy, and resources to spreading its tenets and institutions. Colonial missionaries were compensated for their efforts on an island that otherwise lacked reliable sources of income, but they were not paid handsomely.[118] Profit seekers had more lucrative paths to follow. Certainly Indians received some trade advantages through Christianity and created special niches for themselves as cross-cultural diplomats. Yet the earliest praying Indians absorbed the wrath of spouses, siblings, friends, and other relatives who remained committed to old ways. In a face-to-face society that valued material items as gifts that consolidated relationships, what profit was there in antagonizing one's home and village? No factor greater than faith adequately explains why an Englishman would stand in a *wetu* full of potentially hostile Indians whom he saw as devil worshippers in order to proselytize them. Nothing else justifies a *powwow* enduring torture by his *manitous* week after week and alienating himself from his loved ones, just to attend the meeting. Why else would Natives, who knew people who had been killed by a shaman's magic, publicly renounce the *powwows*, or why would a sachem like Mittark voluntarily abandon his political office rather than end his pursuit of Christian knowledge? Be they English or Indian, the people of seventeenth-century New England lived in a world of spirits. On Martha's Vineyard, Christianity was the way they both decided to come to terms with that world.

By the late 1660s, Christianity had moved to the center of Vineyard Wampanoag life: some Indians had been attracted by its intellectual content and spiritual power, others by its organizational strength, and still more by the hope of English alliance or just household peace. One by one these various paths merged until the entire community began to gather for Sunday meetings, midweek lectures, Bible readings, and ordinations. And whether they came to these events primarily to worship God, socialize, or discuss politics, the Indians could not help but learn more about the religion in which they had staked their collective future. No one questioned that adopting Christianity was painful; adhering to this religion required the abandonment of certain time-tested, cherished ways. It strained relations with Indians outside of the meeting, and sometimes brought unwelcome interference by Englishmen in Native life. Yet the missionaries' use of Wampanoag religious traditions to explain Christianity, and the Indians' integration of Christianity into their community life, made the adjustments seem less awkward and at times even natural. As such, increasingly the Wampanoags told their individual and collective histories as a struggle to abate God's wrath by opening their hearts

---

[118] *Plymouth Records,* 10:120, 124, 167, 217, 294, 317–18; *Light Appearing,* 108; Langdon, *Pilgrim Colony,* 122. On this theme, see Cogley, "Idealism vs. Materialism in the Study of Puritan Missions to the Indians," *Method and Theory in the Study of Religion* 3 (1991), 165–82.

to grace and overcoming sin.[119] Pangs of doubt must have followed every step the praying Indians took through Christianity's stages of education and spiritual growth. But at a time when an entire generation or more could be swept off by a single disease, disrupting nearly every conceivable aspect of life, walking with Jesus was the greatest certainty in their lives.

---

[119] On using autobiographical narrative plots as a measure of "conversion," see David A. Snow and Richard Machalek, "The Sociology of Conversion," *Annual Review of Sociology* 10 (1984), 167–90; and Robert W. Hefner, ed., *Conversion to Christianity: Historical and Anthropological Perspectives on a Great Transformation* (Berkeley: University of California Press, 1993), esp. 17–18.

3

The Lord Tests the Righteous

An islander's life is ever attuned to the weather, and that was particularly true in colonial New England. Throughout any given day, salt-crusted fishermen and sun-bleached farmers scanned the horizon for signs of the next nor'easter, a torrent of wind and water that devoured boats and flattened crops during the warm months, and dumped ungodly amounts of snow in just a few hours in winter. One can be certain that Vineyarders were watching the sky during the last week of June 1675, and, if it was clear, Indians atop Menemsha's hills or Aquinnah's shoreline cliffs might have seen smoke billowing from the smoldering mainland towns of Swansea, Rehoboth, and Taunton. After nearly annual rumors of an Indian conspiracy and, more recently, heightened tensions between mainland Wampanoags and Plymouth, one question would have immediately flashed through their minds: "Had Philip's men finally struck against the English?" To find out, messengers would have raced to alert all the Vineyard sachems and the Mayhews in Edgartown, followed by a scramble for reliable news. While awaiting confirmation, Indians and Englishmen who commonly worked and traded together would begin to eye one another suspiciously. The future was very uncertain in the summer of 1675.

Still, there was reason to believe that this was just another in a string of false alarms, that the smoke rose from a mere house fire or forest blaze that had spread out of control. For in recent years missionaries had brought Natives all along New England's southeastern coast into the Christian fold with the promise that the Gospel of Peace extended to worldly as well as heavenly affairs. In 1675, this formidable Christian network encompassed over 1,300 Penacooks, Pawtuckets, Massachusetts, and Nipmucs in east and central Massachusetts, and 3,500 Wampanoags on Martha's Vineyard, Nantucket, Cape Cod, and the nearby mainland, totaling nearly one-third of the region's Indians. Even Philip, paramount sachem of the Wampanoags, had accepted the counsel of a praying Indian named

John Sassamon and briefly considered hosting a missionary at the tribal seat.[1]

There was also hope to be found in recent measures by mainland Indians, Christian and otherwise, to adjust peacefully to colonial expansion. As profits from the fur and wampum trades plummeted in the 1660s, a number of Indians shifted to wage labor to obtain manufactured goods like cloth clothing, brass kettles, and iron-edge tools that had become basic to their lives. When Massachusetts Bay tried to encroach on the Narragansetts' jurisdiction, the Indians craftily placed themselves under the protection of their adversaries' own king, thereby staying the threat. Indians living in and around colonial settlements were increasingly subject to English courts run by alien judges, juries, and procedures, which naturally heightened tensions, but a handful of cases demonstrated that Indians who studied the system or forged alliances with legal-minded colonists could win favorable verdicts in New England courtrooms. Combined with reluctance of either party to end nearly forty years of peace, these adaptations suggested there might be light behind the dark horizon across the water.[2]

By the time the horrible truth reached the islands, the north shore of Buzzard's Bay was already pockmarked with charred homes and awash in blood. Apparently the peace was not as durable as it once seemed, but merely served to postpone a showdown between two incompatible ways of life, two peoples whose cultural inertia left them unable to live together peaceably. Indeed, it seemed only a matter of time before the Vineyard itself entered the fray. Offshore Wampanoags shared many of the same grievances that drove their mainland tribesmen to the warpath, and to add insult to injury their Christianity had done little to convince Englishmen that they were equals. For their part, island colonists had ample reason to suspect their

---

[1] John Eliot to the Commissioners of the United Colonies, August 25, 1664, *NEHGR* 9 (1855), 131–2.

[2] Alden T. Vaughan, *New England Frontier: Puritans and Indians, 1620–1675*, 3d ed. (1965; Norman: University of Oklahoma Press, 1995), chaps. 6–11; Vaughan, "Tests of Puritan Justice," in his *Roots of American Racism: Essays on the Colonial Experience* (New York: Oxford University Press, 1995), 200–325; Peter A. Thomas, "In the Maelstrom of Change: The Indian Trade and Cultural Process in the Middle Connecticut River Valley, 1635–1665" (Ph.D. diss., University of Massachusetts at Amherst, 1979), chaps. 4–6; Francis Jennings, *The Invasion of America: Indians, Colonialism, and the Cant of Conquest* (New York: W. W. Norton for the Institute of Early American History and Culture, 1975), 254–81; Yasuhide Kawashima, *Puritan Justice and the Indian: White Man's Law in Massachusetts, 1630–1763* (Middletown, Conn.: Wesleyan University Press, 1986), chaps. 5–7; Neal Salisbury, "Social Relationships on a Moving Frontier: Natives and Settlers in Southern New England, 1638–1675," *MNE* 33 (1987), 89–99; Joshua Micah Marshall, "'A Melancholy People': Anglo–Indian Relations in Early Warwick, Rhode Island, 1642–1675," *NEQ* 68 (1995), 402–28; Jean M. O'Brien, *Dispossession by Degrees: Indian Land and Identity in the Natick, Massachusetts, 1650–1790* (New York: Cambridge University Press, 1997), chap. 2.

TABLE 1. *Praying Indian Population in 1674*

Community	Families and Warriors[a]	Population
Massachusett, Penacook/Pawtucket, and Nipmuc		
Natick	29	145
Punkapoag	12	60
Hassanamessit	12	60
Okommakamesit	10	50
Wamesit	15	75
Nashobah	10	50
Magunkaquog	11	55
Manchage	12	60
Chabanankongkomun	9	45
Maanexit	20	100
Quantisset	20	100
Wabquissit	30	150
Pakachoog	20	100
Waeuntung	10	50
Weshakim	?	?
Quabaug[b]	?	?
Subtotal	220	1320
Wampanoag		
Noepe (Martha's Vineyard)	300	1500
Nantucket	300	1500
Meeshawn and Punonakanit	14	72
Nauset	9	44
Manamoy	14	71
Sawkattuckett, Nobsquassit, Mattakees, and Weequakut	24	122
Satuit, Pawpoesit, Coatuit, Mashpee, and Wakoquet	19	95
Codtanmut, Ashimuit, and Weesquobe	4	22
Pispogutt, Wawayontat, and Sokones	7	36
Titicut and Assawompset	7	35
Subtotal	918	3497
Total	1138	4817

[a] The number of warriors given here is approximate, based on the conservative ratio of one male of fighting age per family.

Source: "Historical Collections," 180–201, 205.

Indian neighbors, since they were all too aware that some of Eliot's praying Indians had spilled English blood and that the Wampanoags' leading sachem headed the Native war effort. The Vineyard was a tinderbox of cross-cultural anxieties always threatening to combust.

Yet for all its fragility, the island's peace held fast supported by cross-cultural institutions, leadership, and visions of the nightmare a first blow would unleash. Through each stage of the war crisis, Thomas Mayhew Sr. exercised his formal power and cultivated influence, refusing to sacrifice his goal of Indian–English coexistence to the prejudiced demands of the colonial mob. His farsighted governance, combined with the skillful diplomacy of Indian sachems and churchmen, enabled Vineyarders to control the fires of King Philip's War. However, in the process of defending the peace, one lingering fear of the Indians was confirmed: they could share a land and faith with the English, but the two peoples were not Christian brethren and would remain separate, with the colonists in firm control.

I

For nearly thirty years after arriving on Martha's Vineyard, Thomas Mayhew had used his proprietary rights and missionary influence to advance peaceful Wampanoag–English relations, but imperial initiatives following the Restoration of the English crown in 1660 placed his authority in peril. In March of 1664, King Charles II granted his brother James Stuart, Duke of York, title to the entire area between the Delaware and Connecticut Rivers, plus Long Island, part of Maine, Nantucket, the Elizabeth Islands, and Martha's Vineyard. This patent quite deliberately hemmed in New England, partially to revenge the Puritans' beheading of Charles I in 1649, partially to halt the spread of religiously intolerant Puritan governments in America, since the Stuarts advocated freedom of conscience for Christian dissenters. James wasted little time making good on this opportunity. By late August, his agent, Colonel Richard Nicolls, had conquered the Dutch colony of New Netherland and announced the creation of New York in its place, and was preparing to rein in the other ducal territories. Mayhew delayed acknowledging James's authority as long as he could, but by July of 1671 he had exhausted his tactics. With the proverbial writing on the wall, grudgingly Mayhew sailed for New York. He came armed with his old proprietary rights and a stellar record of managing Indian affairs, but had every reason to expect a dressing down and an ignominious end to his family's ascendancy.[3]

[3] Noel A. Sainsbury et. al., *Calendar of State Papers, Colonial Series, America and the West Indies...Preserved in the Public Record Office, 1661–1668* (London, 1880), 534–5; Peter R. Christoph and Florence A. Christoph, eds., *New York Historical Manuscripts: English [:] Books of General Entries of the Colony of New York*, 2 vols. (Baltimore: Genealogical

To Mayhew's relief, York was no lover of participatory government, but instead envisioned for America what was politically impossible back home: a near autocracy that could force peoples of different faiths and ethnicities to live alongside one another quietly and that used generous manorial grants to win the support of elites.[4] Thus, after several days of negotiations, Nicolls' successor as governor, Francis Lovelace, appointed Mayhew "Governor and Chief Magistrate" of Martha's Vineyard for life (he was already 78 years old) and assigned Indian affairs "wholly" to his "prudent Management." Mayhew would preside, first, over a council on the Vineyard with executive, legislative, and minor judicial powers, and, second, over a General Court that would manage the joint concerns of the Vineyard and Nantucket, try major lawsuits, and hear appeals from lower courts. At each level, Mayhew was supposed to consult with a small number of elected assistants, but his double vote ensured that his voice would be loudest. Next, Lovelace appointed Mayhew's grandson, Matthew, the Vineyard's collector and receiver of customs and, with his grandfather, gave him the exclusive right to negotiate for all unsold Indian land. If all this were not enough, Lovelace created the "Manor of Tisbury" out of a huge swath of Nashuakemuck, part of Takemmy, and the Elizabeth Islands, and then dubbed Thomas and Matthew Mayhew lords, with the power to collect quitrents and, technically, to preside over special courts. Within several years, similar grants would line the Hudson River Valley, but this was the only feudal establishment of its kind in colonial New England. In exchange for these honors, the family was to deliver two barrels of codfish to Manhattan annually. They also agreed to rename Great Harbor "Edgartown" in honor of James's infant son. It was a small gesture of gratitude for such lavish privileges.[5]

Publishing Co., Inc., 1982), 1:1–4, 17, 343–4, 345–6; John M. Murrin, "The New York Charter of Liberties, 1683 and 1693," in Stephen L. Schechter, ed., *Roots of the Republic: American Founding Documents Interpreted* (Madison, Wisc.: Madison House, 1990), 47–65; Michael Kammen, *Colonial New York: A History* (New York: Oxford University Press, 1975), 71–87; Robert C. Ritchie, *The Duke's Province: A Study of New York Politics and Society, 1664–1691* (Chapel Hill: University of North Carolina Press, 1977), 9–46.
[4] John M. Murrin, "The Menacing Shadow of Louis XIV and the Rage of Jacob Leisler: The Constitutional Ordeal of Seventeenth-Century New York," in Stephen L. Schechter and Richard B. Bernstein, eds., *New York and the Union: Contributions to the American Constitutional Experience* (Albany: New York State Commission on the Bicentennial of the United States Constitution, 1990), 29–71; Murrin, "English Rights as Ethnic Aggression: The English Conquest, the Charter of Liberties of 1683, and Leisler's Rebellion in New York," in William Pencak and Conrad Edick Wright, eds., *Authority and Resistance in Early New York* (New York: New York Historical Society, 1988), 56–94; Sung Bok Kim, *Landlord and Tenant in Colonial New York: Manorial Society, 1664–1775* (Chapel Hill: University of North Carolina Press for the Institute of Early American History and Culture, 1978), 8–43.
[5] Franklin B. Hough, ed., *Papers Relating to the Island of Nantucket, with Documents Relating to the Original Settlement of That Island, Martha's Vineyard, and Other Islands Adjacent, Known as Dukes County, While under the Colony of New York* (Albany, 1856), 27–30, 33–51; Charles Edward Banks, *The History of Martha's Vineyard, Dukes County,*

New York strengthened Thomas Mayhew's already formidable clout. Before 1671, Mayhew's legitimacy rested upon purchased proprietary rights, an uneasy basis for denying English islanders elective government, but now his power was justified by grants from a royal agent. At least on paper, Mayhew's authority over the English was more secure than ever. Moreover, officially New York reinforced his proven oversight of the colonists' Wampanoag affairs. However, the Wampanoags' allegiance still needed to be earned, and thus when cross-cultural disputes arose he threw his support to them. For example, in the early 1670s Simon Athearn charged that Mayhew had an Indian steal Jacob Perkins' livestock after Perkins complained about the island's impartial justice. The Indian then attacked Perkins for calling him a "lying Rogue," and Mayhew's only response was to tell Perkins to complain to New York if he liked.[6] Doubtless there was another side to this story, since Athearn was a perennial thorn in Mayhew's side, but Mayhew himself admitted to Thomas Prence of Plymouth, "my favour to the Indians hath been thought to be overmuch."[7] The royal seal buttressed Mayhew's standing among the English, but years of experience taught him that he could persuade the Wampanoags only with mutual respect and affection.

Mayhew already had a favorable reputation among the Wampanoags by virtue of his missionary work; now, with his enhanced power and defense of Indian interests, they were ready to consider him as one of their own. In 1670, the Wampanoags invited him to become their pastor, yet surprisingly he declined the offer.[8] He was already tired and overextended, and, more to the point, he no longer needed to man the pulpit himself to sustain his influence. He continued to preach informally to Wampanoag communities across the island, and his grandson, John, was about to become Tisbury's pastor and missionary to the west side of the island.[9] After years of worry and toil, Mayhew was securely in power.

The Indians' confidence in Mayhew and Mayhew's faith in them brought calm to moments of cross-cultural suspicion. In 1671 rumors buzzed through the region that Philip was plotting to strike against the English, possibly in

Massachusetts, 3 vols. (Boston: George H. Dean, 1911), 1:chaps. 11–12, 2:Chilmark, 17–22; Lloyd C. M. Hare, *Thomas Mayhew: Patriarch to the Indians, 1593–1682* (New York: D. Appleton, 1932), chap. 13.

[6] Peter R. Christoph and Florence A. Christoph, eds., *Files of the Provincial Secretary of New York During the Administration of Governor Sir Edmund Andros*, 3 vols. (Syracuse, N.Y.: Syracuse University Press, 1989), 1:217–21.

[7] Thomas Mayhew Sr. to Governor Thomas Prence, June 19, 1671, *MHSC* 1st ser., 6 (1799), 196–7.

[8] John Eliot, *A Brief Narrative of the Progress of the Gospel among the Indians of New England, 1670* (Boston, 1868), 22.

[9] Christoph and Christoph, eds., *Files of the Provincial Secretary*, 1:123–6; *Some Account of those English Ministers*, 303–5.

league with the Narragansetts. Mainland officials responded by forcing the sachem to "agree" to turn over his people's firearms, pay a substantial fine, admit to conspiracy, and publicly submit to the colony and the crown. Then Plymouth threatened to march against the Wampanoag sunksquaw (female sachem), Awashunks of Saconnet, until she too signed a statement of fealty and pledged to relinquish all her people's guns.[10] These injuries to mainland Wampanoag pride festered for years.

Thomas Mayhew brought a lighter touch to his investigation. Just before sailing to New York for his fateful meeting with Lovelace, he visited all the Vineyard Wampanoag villages to ask about the supposed plot. The Natives pleaded ignorance of it and as evidence of their fidelity pledged allegiance to King Charles and promised, "to fight against his enemies and the enemies of his subjects if called thereunto." The Wampanoags served up an even greater display of friendship when Mayhew returned to the island with his royal commission. "I sent for all the sachems and chief men," wrote the Governor, "acquainting them with what was done [in New York]. All the sachems, with many others, as well non-praying as praying men, did, with much thankfulness, submit unto his honour's act in setting me over them; and every person present by holding up his hand, did promise to advance the worship of God. The like was never of them heretofore attained."[11] Christian Wampanoags on Cape Cod responded similarly to the panic by publicly disowning Philip and expressing their hope that Indians and Englishmen as fellow believers "would no more be strangers and forraigners."[12] Future generations might read these statements as empty rhetoric or hopeless utopianism, but in the context of a rapidly expanding mission and the coastal Wampanoags' dramatic reforms, they were enough to defuse a severe crisis and sustain the region's experiment in coexistence.

II

Indian declarations of fidelity pulled the Cape and islands back from the cusp of war, but teetering on the edge sent a double warning that God was not yet satisfied with the Wampanoags' Christian reforms and many colonists still doubted their loyalties. Both threatened future disaster. If the praying Indians had been less certain of their course, they might have foreseen that their best

[10] *Plymouth Records*, 5:63–5, 73–5, 77, 79; Jennings, *Invasion of America*, 293–4; George D. Langdon Jr., *Pilgrim Colony: A History of New Plymouth* (New Haven, Conn.: Yale University Press, 1966), 159–61; Douglas Edward Leach, *Flintlock and Tomahawk: New England in King Philip's War* (New York: W. W. Norton & Co., 1958), 26–9; James D. Drake, *King Philip's War: Civil War in New England, 1675–1676* (Amherst: University of Massachusetts Press, 1999), 66–8.
[11] *Some Correspondence*, 39–40. On the symbolic importance of Indian submission to Englishmen, see Drake, *King Philip's War*, 36–8.
[12] *Plymouth Records*, 5:70–1.

efforts would never be good enough, but recent history suggested otherwise. For three decades the Wampanoags had hosted the Mayhew mission, and during that time epidemic diseases had vanished and cross-cultural calm had persevered. Even the recent alarm could be read as something of a victory given that war had been averted without resort to the mainland's gunpoint diplomacy. The key to future peace, then, seemed to lie in the Christian Wampanoags' strengthening their relationships with God and the English, namely by intensifying their campaign against sin, the very root of evil and war.

To this point, Wampanoags had depended solely upon peer pressure to direct sinners to the godly path. At Sunday meeting, drunkards, fornicators, thieves, and slanderers, all fell under the discipline of ruling elders, called *"Aiuskomuaeninuog*, i.e. Reprovers, or Men of Reproofs, because [the Wampanoags] judge that their Office mainly consists in reprooving of Sinners and censuring Offenders."[13] The elder called sinners before the congregation and then "searched out Matters very diligently, and examined strictly into the Nature and Degrees of the Faults and Offences whereof they were guilty, and would sharply reprove them for their Sins, endeavouring with all his Might to convince them of the Evil of what they appeared to be just charged with, and would most affectionately press them to a thorow and hearty Repentance of their Miscarriages."[14] Obstinate sinners were banned from the Lord's Supper and thereby symbolically cast out from the religious community, not unlike the Wampanoag custom of expelling heinous criminals from the sachemship.[15]

Including civil authorities in the church campaign against sin was the Wampanoags' answer to their need for a stronger symbol of their peaceful intent and commitment to Christianity after the war scare of 1671. Four years earlier, during one of John Cotton Jr.'s visits to Nashuakemuck, "the Indians, as they had Many times formerly, soe now they complained greatly for want of rulers according to the manner of xians [Christians], much disliking Mr. M[ayhew]'s Compelling them still to owne the present sachem."[16] Mayhew could see the diplomatic and moral value of having Indians enforce Christian law, but his priority in those days was to reassure the sachems that Christianity and government were separate spheres. However, by 1671 Mayhew's hand was strengthened by New York and the mission no longer

[13] *Indian Converts*, 17.

[14] *Indian Converts*, 61. See also pp. 16–18, 41, 57.

[15] E. Mayhew, *A Brief Account of the State of the Indians on Martha's Vineyard...1694 to 1720*, appended to E. Mayhew, *A Discourse Shewing that God Dealeth with Men as Reasonable Creatures* (Boston, 1720), 5–6; Bragdon, "Native Christianity in 18th Century Massachusetts: Ritual as Cultural Reaffirmation," in Barry Gough and Christie Laird, eds., *New Dimensions in Ethnohistory: Papers of the 2nd Laurier Conference on Ethnohistory and Ethnography* (Hull, Quebec: Canadian Museum of Civilization, 1991), 119.

[16] Cotton Journal, 81. See also, *Some Account of those English Ministers*, 292–3.

had to tiptoe around the sachems since virtually all of them were churchgoers. Sensing the opportunity, he and the praying Indians arranged to have each Wampanoag village elect three Christian magistrates to hold formal courts. The local sachem would preside and exercise a veto over all court decisions, but if he declined to serve, a fourth person would be chosen. Indian rulers and constables would assist these courts, with the former responsible for policing and filing indictments, and the latter for apprehending the accused. It was a judicial system for Wampanoags by Wampanoags, but for the meantime they agreed to consult with Mayhew on their choice of magisterial candidates.[17]

These reforms sent a clear message that the Wampanoags intended to co-exist with the English and honor their shared God. Indian magistrates, no less than their English peers, "handled cases in the way they imagined God would judge them were He to appear visibly in the court," by awakening sinners to their corruption and the ways their offenses hurt the entire community.[18] Typically, Native courts opened with the magistrate's prayers to God "for his Help and Direction," followed by attempts "to convince [evil-doers'] Consciences of the Sins of which they were guilty, and bring them to a humble sense and Confession of their Faults." Sinners confronted by magistrate William Lay (or Panunnut) were wise to confess, for if they did, "he dealt all the more tenderly and gently with the Persons offending... but if they appeared stubborn and obstinate, he would very severely chastise them for their Offences, making them know what Stripes for the Backs of Fools do intend." Lay defended his harsh methods by claiming his fellow Wampanoags "have no shame in them."[19] Herein was the primary difference between the old and new order. Previously, Wampanoag churches only shamed sinners. Lay's court was prepared to beat them into repentance.

The Wampanoag courts harkened to the Puritan notion of a "federal covenant" in which Christian communities experienced God's favor or wrath according to their enforcement of his law and support for his church. Puritans argued that one reason Indians suffered epidemic disease and social decay while the English grew healthy and strong was that they rigorously suppressed sin while the Indians did not. Although Puritans believed that only select individuals received God's grace and the accompanying power to live righteously, nevertheless they punished a wide range of transgressions and forced lawbreakers to declare their sinfulness on the principle of revering God's law and edifying the public about humankind's corruption. Fulfillment

---

[17] *Some Account of those English Ministers*, 293–4; Bragdon, "Crime and Punishment among the Indians of Massachusetts, 1675–1750," *Ethnohistory* 28 (1981), 24.
[18] Murrin, "Magistrates, Sinners, and a Precarious Liberty: Trial by Jury in Seventeenth Century New England," in David D. Hall, Murrin, and Thad Tate, eds., *Saints and Revolutionaries: Essays on Early American History* (New York: W. W. Norton, 1984), 173.
[19] *Indian Converts*, 25–6 (quote), 26–7, 48, 89, 93–4, 99.

of these obligations brought the peace and prosperity of God's blessing, whereas neglecting them unleashed divine retribution.

This was a new way for Christian Wampanoags to think about their mutual responsibilities and fate. Traditionally, Wampanoags did not consider the people as a whole responsible for an individual's relations with the spirits since, for the most part, violations of taboo put the offender alone at risk. On occasion, an unpredictable *manitou* might afflict the entire community with disease, poor weather, or wartime defeat for neglecting its favorite rites or ignoring its directives for new ones, but the Indians could only handle these crises singularly. As such, the Wampanoags had no tradition of prosecuting nonviolent religious offenses like Sabbath breaking or blasphemy. Sachems and their counselors punished crimes such as rape, murder, witchcraft, and treason because these crimes threatened to launch a cycle of revenge killings and undermine the established authority. Antisocial but otherwise benign behavior was not their concern. On the surface, the new magisterial system could not have been more different. If William Lay is representative, Wampanoag civil officers used public humiliation and corporal punishment against a long list of sins that previous generations had not defined as crimes. In earlier times, sachems who dared to mete out such discipline would have lost their supporters if not their lives. But by 1671, Christianity and the English had become such indelible parts of the Indians' world that it was difficult to imagine a peaceful future without placating God and easing the colonists' suspicions. Adopting colonial-style courts and magistrates to suppress sin appeared to be a means toward those ends.

These reforms were unprecedented but their radicalism should not be overstated since the Wampanoags' church and court officers came disproportionately from historically elite families. At least six of nine known magistrates from the late seventeenth century held the status of sachem, a sachem's relative, or a sachem's counselor. Two were of unknown backgrounds, and the other was Samuel Coomes, the son of Hiacoomes. Of thirty church officials (ministers, preachers, deacons, and teachers), a minimum of sixteen were from leading families.[20] At the same time, Wampanoag

[20] The magistrates were Mittark (Aquinnah sachem), Japheth Hannit (son of "petty sachem" Pammehannit), Tawanquatuck (Nunnepog sachem), Abel Wauwompuhque Sr. (brother of Mittark), Ekoochuck (son-in-law of Mittark), and William Lay (son of "a noted Indian called Panunnut"). The church officials were Momonaquem (preacher; son of Aquinnah sachem Annawantoohque), John Nahoso (ruling elder; son-in-law of "petty sachem" Cheeschamuck), Wunnanuahkomun (preacher; son-in-law of Cheeschamuck), Janawanit (minister; brother of Pammehannit), Jonathan Amos (deacon and preacher; son-in-law of sachem Myoxeo), Elisha Paaonut (preacher; nephew of Mittark), Joah Panu (pastor; grandson of Mittark), Abel Wauwompuhque Jr. (deacon; nephew of Mittark), John Amanhut (preacher; grandson of a mainland sachem), Wompamog (preacher; Sengekontacket sachem), and Panuppaqua (preacher; brother of William Lay and son of the "noted" Panunnut). All of the above information is contained within *Indian Converts'* entries for these individuals. However, the high status of several church officials only becomes clear by cross-checking

church figures doubled as political rulers. The sachems Mittark, Wompamog, and Tawanquatuck all held Christian offices, and in 1675 nine of Mittark's ten counselors served as preachers, deacons, or magistrates.[21] The appropriation of new titles by old leaders had made the Wampanoags' political, court, and church leadership all but indistinguishable, reflecting the Indians' well-established practice of hanging a Christian edifice on customary scaffolding.[22]

With rare exceptions, Indian justices continued to focus on the same matters that traditionally concerned them as sachems and counselors. The only glimpse into a Wampanoag courtroom during this period, a brief record of appeals sent by the Nantucket Indians' own court to English authorities in the late 1670s and early 1680s, lists only crimes against actual people, such as theft, spousal abandonment, physical abuse, and property disputes, not victimless moral offenses like Sabbath breaking or swearing.[23] Of course, there is no way to know what rulings the Indians did not appeal, yet several other signs point to continuity in the duties of Wampanoag leaders. For instance, magistrates doubled as Indian headmen by treating the people with hospitality and funding community business. Sachem descendant, magistrate, and

---

Indian Converts against other records. Kequish, who was paid as a teacher and schoolmaster in 1662, and Sam Mackakunit, who preached at Nunnepog, were both related to Towtoowe, sachem of the Kophiggon area of Nashuakemuck. Nanosco, brother of Momonaquem and grandson of principal Aquinnah man, Annowantooque, was paid by the New England Company as a teacher in 1662. Christiantown preacher Joel Sims was the son of Pockqsimme, or Poxim, one of seven Indians who approved Wamsutta's 1661 sale of Nashaquitsa land, and a Christiantown proprietor. And Christiantown pastor Hosea Manhut was son of Wannamanhut, the Massachusett-born Takemmy sachem. On Kequish and Sam Mackakunit, see *Plymouth Records*, 10:277; DCD, 1:93–4; FNPR, 1:320, 322; and Banks, *History of Martha's Vineyard*, 2:Chilmark:14–15. On Nanosco, see *Plymouth Records*, 10:277; DCD, 1:257. On Joel Sims, see *Indian Converts*, 73; DCD, 1:357, 3:12. On Hosea Manhut, see *Indian Converts*, 207; *Native Writings*, 1:159–61; Suffolk Files #12248.

[21] DCD, 6:369–73; *Native Writings*, 1:82–9. The counselors, their offices, and pertinent relatives were as follows: Yonohummuh – no supporting data; Samuel Coomes – magistrate and son of Hiacoomes (*Indian Converts*, 91–3); Abel Wauwompuhque – magistrate and brother of Mittark (*Indian Converts*, 67, 98); Wompamog, alias Mr. Sam – Sengekontacket sachem and preacher (*Indian Converts*, 73–4); Akoochuck – magistrate and Mittark's son-in-law (*Indian Converts*, 101–2); John Momonaquem – east-end preacher and son of Nashuakemuck minister Momonaquem (*Indian Converts*, 12, 140); Wuttinomanomin – magistrate and Nashuakemuck deacon (*Indian Converts*, 31–3); Nashcompait – no office but one of Aquinnah's first Christians (*Indian Converts*, 100–1); Elisha – on New England Company dole in 1710–11 for unspecified service (New England Company Ledger, p. 25, MHS); Wuttahhonnompisin – early Aquinnah Christian (*Indian Converts*, 131–2).

[22] James P. Ronda, "Generations of Faith: The Christian Indians of Martha's Vineyard," *WMQ* 38 (1981), 375; Susan MacCulloch, "A Tripartite Political System among the Christian Indians of Early Massachusetts," *Kroeber Anthropological Society Papers* 34 (1966), 63–73.

[23] All the following data appears on the reverse side of the indicated page: Land disputes: NCD, 2:3, 7, 8, 29, 30. Theft: NCD, 2:3, 15. Broken marriage: NCD, 2:3, 11. Physical abuse: NCD, 2:3, 28. Destruction of property: NCD, 2:7.

minister Japheth Hannit was "frequently visited, both by Neighbours and Strangers, they were always kindly and generously entertained in his House with the best he had, or could readily procure."[24] "None would contribute more liberally" than magistrate Samuel Coomes toward meeting-house repairs, and "when there was a Day of publick Thanksgiving, and Provision to be made for it, which among our Indians is brought into common Stock, (which the Poor as well as the Rich may come to and be filled) this our Samuel was one of the principal Providers for that Feast."[25] Any Native leader who neglected conspicuous acts of generosity could expect to find his tongue, if not his whip, lose its sting. The Wampanoags hinted at these points of compatibility by calling their Christian civil rulers *negonshaenin*, which derived from a word meaning "the man who goes in front" – the long-standing function of high-ranking Natives.[26]

The mainland Wampanoag sachem, Philip, probably failed to appreciate these parallels since the Indians' new court system linked them more firmly to the colonists and weakened their ties to him. Since at least the earliest days of English colonization, Cape and island Wampanoags had paid tribute to the sachem of Pokanoket (of which Philip was the most recent) in exchange for his arbitration of high-level disputes, leadership in foreign affairs, and military protection; with justification, Philip referred to Vineyarders as "his" people. However, it appears that Vineyard Wampanoags, and perhaps the Christian Wampanoags of Cape Cod and Nantucket as well, rejected Philip after they declared allegiance to Charles in 1671 and established their new magistracy. In 1672, the Vineyard General Court ruled that "any Indian shall have Liberty in any Case to appeal from such courts as they shall hold amongst themselves to the Quarter Court and from the Quarter Court to the General Court according to Law."[27] This decision signaled the colonial magistrates' preemption of Philip's role as the Wampanoags' supreme arbiter, which helps to explain Philip's heightened opposition to the missions and other English infringements on the eve of the war. The Vineyard Wampanoags were committed to living as Christians alongside the English. They could not continue along this path by following an unchurched sachem who was constantly implicated in war scares.

The praying Indians had taken several steps toward peacefully resolving their differences with colonists by campaigning against sin, pledging their friendship to the king, and joining the English court system. As Christians, both peoples shared a basic understanding about the definition of common

---

[24] *Indian Converts*, 49.
[25] Ibid., 93.
[26] Kathleen J. Bragdon, "'Another Tongue Brought In': An Ethnohistorical Study of Native Writings in Massachusett" (Ph.D. diss., Brown University, 1981), 134.
[27] DCD, 1:211; New York Deeds 1:78, cited in Charles Banks Papers, vol:1600–99, pp. 80–5, MHS. See also, *Some Account of those English Ministers*, 293–4.

crimes, who should judge those crimes, and, to a lesser degree, how they should be punished. Furthermore, the Indians had the Mayhews as allies to introduce them to English jurisprudence and defend them from colonists who might exploit them during their orientation.

Yet the Wampanoags' compromises exacted substantial costs. Englishmen ruling on appeals from Indian courts were by definition evaluating the performance of Native magistrates, thereby influencing their future decisions. This was not an idle threat to Wampanoag self-determination. According to the Nantucket appeals records, colonial judges repeatedly overturned Wampanoag rulings.[28] Whereas earlier, a sachem issued punishments only after consulting with his leading supporters, now magistrates cracked the whip by weighing English demands as well.[29] Perhaps that is why Nantucket Indian Obadiah refused to obey Native justices, charging that "the[y] doe not Love him and the like," in stark contrast to the flatteries that Indians customarily heaped upon their leaders.[30]

The colonists' creeping jurisdiction also threatened to intervene in Wampanoag family life. Most Wampanoags understood, and seem to have accepted, that God would not tolerate polygamy (which in any case was mostly limited to elites) or spousal abuse, but they were less convinced than English authorities that divorce was wrong. As early as 1667, Thomas Mayhew Sr. had reconstituted a broken Indian marriage even though "the body of the Indians did manifest their dislike of it," and Hiacoomes himself cited Deuteronomy 24:1–4, a passage that calls a man taking back an adulterous woman an "abomination."[31] Englishmen were even more likely to impinge on Wampanoag marriage customs once the Natives were subordinate within the colonial court system. In August of 1677, Nantucket's Court of Sessions ordered an Indian and his wife to live together again after a recent separation. Three years later, Manshoquen successfully appealed a divorce granted to her husband Johaboy (or Johnboy), and the following year, Wessoah's wife complained "against her husband for leaving of her," for which "the Court finds him gilty of having to doe with another woman in an Evil way: the court orders [the husband] Wessoah and the woman to be severely whipt." Then in 1683 Nantucket ruled that Nanepopo could

---

[28] NCR, 2:10 (verso), 11 (verso), 23 (verso), 24 (verso), 28 (verso). See also Ann Marie Plane, *Colonial Intimacies: Indian Marriage in Early New England* (Ithaca, N.Y.: Cornell University Press, 2000), 88–93.

[29] Eric Johnson, "Released from Thraldom by the Stroke of War: Coercion and Warfare in Native Politics of Seventeenth-Century Southern New England," *Northeast Anthropology* 55 (1998), 6. See also, *Plymouth Records*, 10:405.

[30] NCR, 2:11 (verso).

[31] Cotton Journal, 79. See also pp. 71, 87. Colonial leaders also struggled to undermine their own people's toleration of "serial monogamy." See Richard Godbeer, *Sexual Revolution in Early America* (Baltimore: Johns Hopkins University Press, 2002).

renounce his wife only if she refused to return to him within six weeks, even though she "hath forsaken him about one year and followed other men."[32] As these litigants discovered, the colonists' high standard for divorce, premised on the idea that society rested on the sanctity of the family, put the Indians' principle of household peace over marriage at risk.[33]

The responsibility of Indian magistrates to have "Records kept of all Actions, and Acts passed in their several Courts, by such who having learned to write fairly," also challenged the Native custom of having collective memory serve as the people's archive.[34] Under the new system, charges, testimony, and verdicts became official only after they were put down in ink. English appellate judges were likely to favor the printed word if any discrepancies arose between that record and the Native community's recollections of lower-court proceedings. Young Natives who could read and write thereby emerged as potential rivals of Native elders, the keepers of the oral record.

To this point in time, the threat of written records was more theoretical than real. Nothing in the earliest court dockets suggests that any appeal hinged on a disparity between oral and written record keeping. Rather, some evidence indicates that Wampanoags used their own cursory writings as mnemonic devices to recall more extensive proceedings.[35] Yet Englishmen did not use court records in such a manner, and since a few literate Natives and English clerks controlled the official court record, rather than an entire courtroom audience, it did not take much foresight to see the potential for corruption and conflict. Already Indians on the mainland complained that Englishmen manipulated land deeds to claim more acreage than the Natives had agreed to sell. Even Indians got in on the act. Recently a literate praying Indian named John Sassamon had recorded a will dictated by the illiterate sachem Philip, inserted a secret clause granting himself a tract of Philip's land, and then cunningly read a version of the document back without mentioning

---

[32] NCR, 2:3 (verso), 10 (verso), 11 (verso; 1677 case), 23 (verso), 24 (verso; Manshoquen), 29 (verso; Wessoah), 34 (verso), 35 (verso; Nanepopo). See also, *Indian Converts*, 191; Plane, *Colonial Intimacies*, 88–93.

[33] On English standards, see Edmund Morgan, *The Puritan Family*, rev. ed. (New York: Harper and Row, 1966); John Demos, *A Little Commonwealth: Family Life in Plymouth Colony* (New York: Oxford University Press, 1970), chap. 5; Cornelia Hughes Dayton, *Women before the Bar: Gender, Law, and Society in Connecticut, 1639–1789* (Chapel Hill: University of North Carolina Press for the Omohundro Institute of Early American History and Culture, 1995), chap. 3; Plane, *Colonial Intimacies*. On the Indian emphasis on household peace, see Irving A. Hallowell, "Some Psychological Characteristics of the Northeastern Indians," in his *Culture and Experience* (Philadelphia: University of Pennsylvania Press, 1955), 125–50.

[34] *Conquests and Triumphs*, 40.

[35] Elizabeth A. Little, "Three Kinds of Land Deeds at Nantucket, Massachusetts," in William Cowan, ed., *Papers of the Eleventh Algonquian Conference* (Ottawa: Carleton University Press, 1980), 61–70; Bragdon, "Vernacular Literacy and Massachusett Worldview," in Peter Benes, ed., *Algonkians of the Northeast: Past and Present* (Boston: Boston University, 1993), 32–3; *Native Writings*, 1:16, 19.

this section.[36] The danger of such figures gaining control of the court record was immediate.

The Vineyard Wampanoags could temper any resentment they felt about the island courts' violation of their customs by witnessing the patterned bias against Natives in Plymouth and Massachusetts.[37] Although Indians in these colonies received equal sentences for offences such as murder, manslaughter, and rape in which the victim was English, they had higher conviction rates than settlers for theft and drunkenness and were more likely to receive corporal punishment. Furthermore, when the victim was Indian and the perpetrator was English, the courts were much more lenient. This was not the case on Martha's Vineyard and Nantucket or, for that matter, Connecticut and Rhode Island, where Indians still posed a military threat and therefore could not be casually abused without repercussions. As the handful of offshore Indians who fell into trouble while on the mainland could attest, the sharp lash of Puritan justice was scarcely felt at home.[38]

Indeed, despite the obvious inequities of the Vineyard's judicial system, it did give the Wampanoags redress against colonists for trespass, property damage, and illegal liquor sales without having to resort to violence.[39] All islanders were fortunate, though, that their courts never had to endure a trial for rape or murder. The only violent act to be tried took place in 1665, before the creation of the Indian courts. That year, a group of Nantucket Wampanoags murdered Joel Hiacoomes and a few of his English companions whom they found cast by a shipwreck onto the shore. Officials from New York and Plymouth demanded Nantucket authorities to bring the killers to justice. Island colonists, in turn, pressed the sachem Nickanoose to hand over the men, prompting Nickanoose to seek Philip of Pokanoket's intervention. True to his family's historic responsibility to resolve the islands' "interescine quarells," Philip traveled to Nantucket, witnessed the local sachems pledge their "subjection" to the English, and then allowed the offenders to be hanged.[40] The process was tense, improvised, and fragile, yet it managed

---

[36] James P. Ronda and Jeanne Ronda, "The Death of John Sassamon: An Exploration in Writing New England Indian History," *American Indian Quarterly* 1 (1974), 99.

[37] The following paragraph is based on Lyle Koehler, "Red–White Power Relations and Justice in the Courts of Seventeenth-Century New England," *AICRJ* 3 (1979), 1–31; and James P. Ronda, "Red and White at the Bench: Indians and the Law in Plymouth Colony, 1620–1691," *Essex Institute Historical Collections*, 110 (1974), 200–15, esp. 210 and 214, note 46. See also Vaughan, "Tests of Puritan Justice," 208–9.

[38] *Plymouth Records*, 4:22. As Drake, *King Philip's War*, 77, notes, "the decision to join or fight against Philip's forces hinged largely upon the extent to which an individual or group – Indian or English – felt marginalized by the colonial political structure."

[39] DCD, 1:2; Alexander Starbuck, *The History of Nantucket, County, Island, and Town, Including Genealogies of the First Settlers* (Boston, 1924), 130.

[40] NCR, 2:70; Commissioners of the United Colonies to Robert Boyle, Sept. 13, 1665, NE Co. MSS, 8010, p. 6; Nathaniel Philbrick, *Abram's Eyes: The Native American Legacy of*

to uphold the appearance of joint Wampanoag and English sovereignty. No one knew if the Vineyard's new integrated court system could also manage an execution for a heinous cross-cultural crime, and it is telling that no one on the island, Wampanoag or English, decided to test it.

The new courts were a microcosm of the tensions in praying Indian life between community autonomy and custom, on the one hand, and Christianity and English relations, on the other. Colonists hearing appeals from Native courts had the power to overrule Wampanoag leaders and affect Wampanoag life on the basis of distinctly English values. Combined with the upper courts' favoring of written records over collective memory, these changes weakened the Indians' consensus mode of government in which sachems responded to the needs of commoners, commoners deferred to the rulings of sachems and counselors, and the community as a whole honored the wisdom of elders. Yet the Vineyard Wampanoags concluded that these drawbacks were worth having a structure to resolve cross-cultural grievances and symbolize their commitment to Christianity, particularly when it was largely under Indian control. The looming question was whether the courts would bring the parties closer together or, by providing a new forum for the colonists to express their prejudices, push them farther apart.

III

Offshore Wampanoags had adopted the colonists' religion and legal forms, but the two peoples remained deeply divided and even distrustful of one another. Like colonists throughout New England, many and perhaps most Englishmen on the Vineyard considered Christian Indian imposters. "Tis hard to find amongst the English a moderate Interpretation of the word and actions of Indians," Thomas Mayhew complained to the New England Company in 1671.[41] Not that they could generally understand one another's words. In 1674, the number of island Indians able to read and write English was "very few...none, to any great purpose; not above three or four; and those do it brokenly."[42] By the same token, only four Vineyard colonists had a firm command of the Wampanoag language on the eve of King Philip's War: Mayhew, two of his grandsons, and his son-in-law Thomas Daggett.[43]

Nantucket Island (Nantucket, Mass.: Mill Hill Press, 1998), 111–14. For similar improvisations in another North American setting, see Richard White, *The Middle Ground: Indians, Empires, and Republics in the Great Lakes Region, 1650–1815* (New York: Cambridge University Press, 1991).

[41] NE Co. MSS, 7936, p. 17.
[42] "Historical Collections," 205 (quote); *Conquests and Triumphs*, 33–4.
[43] Thomas Mayhew to John Winthrop Jr., Aug. 29, 1659, Banks Papers, vol:1600–99, p. 45, MHS; "Historical Collections," 205.

The language barrier was nearly as high on the island as it was throughout the mainland.[44]

Perhaps Daggett's younger brother, Joseph, also boasted Wampanoag language skills, since it appears that sometime around 1667 he married the sister (whose name is unknown) of the petty sachem Puttuspaquin of Sengekontacket; yet Joseph Daggett's example was an isolated one.[45] No other recognized marriages took place between Vineyard colonists and Wampanoags during this period. Given the continent-wide Indian custom of using exogamous marriage to broker foreign relations, it is obvious that the English rejected such unions. Thus, the Vineyard, no less than the New England mainland, lacked a substantial *métis* population (or at least a legitimate one) to bridge cultural misunderstandings and signal that the English really pursued the universal Christian brotherhood proclaimed by their missionaries.[46]

Liquor sales were another blow to the spirit of fellowship. Profiteering Englishmen regularly peddled alcohol to Indians, knowing full well that "a very

---

[44] Kawashima, "Forest Diplomats: The Role of Interpreters in Indian–White Relations on the Early American Frontier," *American Indian Quarterly* 13 (1989), 2–3; Edward G. Gray, *New World Babel: Languages and Nations in Early America* (Princeton, N.J.: Princeton University Press, 1999), 44–49

[45] The evidence of this union rests on a 1685 deed (DCD 1:251) in which Puttuspaquin referred to Hester and Ellis Daggett, Joseph's daughters, as his "cousins" and "near kindred," and a 1698 deed in which Puttuspaquin is identified as the girls' "uncle." Correspondence with Vineyard genealogist Andrew Pierce, May 14, 2002. Pierce notes that Banks, *History of Martha's Vineyard*, 2:West Tisbury, 44–6, 118, misidentified Daggett's spouse as Alice Sissetom, the daughter of Wompamog, through a series of imaginative leaps. See also, Samuel Bradlee Doggett, *A History of the Doggett–Daggett Family* (Boston: Rockwell and Churchill, 1894), 84–5.

[46] David D. Smits, "'We Are Not to Grow Wild': Seventeenth-Century New England's Repudiation of Anglo–Indian Intermarriage," *AICRJ* 11 (1987), 1–32. On the roles played by *métis* and mixed marriages elsewhere, see James H. Merrell, *Into the American Woods: Negotiations on the Pennsylvania Frontier* (New York: W. W. Norton, 1999), 77, 87; Jacqueline Peterson, "Prelude to Red River: A Social Portrait of the Great Lakes Métis," *Ethnohistory* 25 (1978), 41–67; Peterson, "Ethnogenesis: The Settlement and Growth of a 'New People' in the Great Lakes Region, 1702–1815," *AICRJ* 6 (1982), 23–64; Jennifer S. H. Brown, *Strangers in Blood: Fur Trade Company Families in Indian Country* (Vancouver: University of British Columbia Press, 1980); Sylvia Van Kirk, *"Many Tender Ties": Women in Fur-Trade Society, 1670–1870* (Winnipeg: Watson and Dwyer, 1980); Peterson and Brown, *The New Peoples: Being and Becoming Métis in North America* (Lincoln, Neb.: University of Nebraska Press, 1985); Alexandria Harmon, "Lines in the Sand: Shifting Boundaries between Indians and Non-Indians in the Puget Sound Region," *Western Historical Quarterly* 26 (1995), 429–53; Dannis F. K. Madill, "Riel, Red River, and Beyond: New Developments in Métis History," in Colin G. Calloway, ed., *New Directions in American Indian History* (Norman: University of Oklahoma Press, 1988), 49–78; Susan Sleeper-Smith, *Indian Women and French Men: Rethinking Cultural Encounter in the Western Great Lakes* (Amherst: University of Massachusetts Press, 2001); and James F. Brooks, *Captives and Cousins: Slavery, Community, and Kinship in the Southwest Borderlands* (Chapel Hill: University of North Carolina Press for the Omohundro Institute of Early American History and Culture, 2002).

little matter will intoxicate their brains," and "being drunk, are many times outrageous and mad, fighting with and killing one another, yea sometimes their own relations."[47] In 1660, the Vineyard's court ordered fines against anyone caught selling strong drink to the Wampanoags, but it was impossible for authorities to monitor commerce along the island's lengthy coastline.[48] Clearly there was little popular support for the law since the Vineyard's General Court had to reissue the ban repeatedly "uppon applycation to that End made by the Indian sachimes."[49]

Wampanoags were equally sore about the pace and process by which colonists engrossed their land. In 1660, the freemen of Great Harbor voted that "the Indians upon the town Bounds that is within the Purchased Lands are to be Removed within this ten days Except Two families which are Not to be put off in Respect to the Sachims two Commonages... and if they Refuse to Remove them by force."[50] The Christiantown affair pitting the Takemmy Indians against their sachem and his English customers followed four years later, and praying Indians began to wonder aloud "whether it be a Righteous thing for Mr M[ayhew]: to buy away soe much of the Indians['] lands?"[51] On Nantucket, in 1662 and 1668, colonists threatened to fine any Wampanoag remaining on "English" land five shillings per week, even though four Natives protested that the sachem's land sales included places "they formerly lived on."[52] To avoid a confrontation, the English court assigned each displaced Indian a twenty-acre plot well inside the Wampanoags' bounds "without paying any tribute to said sachims." It also ordered "that all other Indians who formerly inhabited the west end of the island, the said sachims shall Entertain them, to live on the land unsold, as the Indians, and common people do within their presincts."[53]

Troubles of this sort were common on the Vineyard despite its small English population. Natives refused to budge from deeded territory, arguing that the sachem either had no right to sell or that he had merely sold the English the right to use the land alongside Indians, not to take sole possession of it. Frustrated colonists like Simon Athearn consistently raised the stakes. In the early 1670s, Athearn purchased land at Tississa in southern

[47] Gookin, "An Historical Account of the Doings and Sufferings of the Christian Indians in New England, in the Years 1675, 1676, 1677," *Archaeologia Americana*, Transactions and Collections of the American Antiquarian Society 2 (1836), 515 (quote); "Historical Collections," 151. Generally, see Peter C. Mancall, *Deadly Medicine: Indians and Alcohol in Early America* (Ithaca, N.Y.: Cornell University Press, 1995).

[48] Edgartown Records, 1:130; *Plymouth Records*, 10:404–5.

[49] New York Deeds, 1:178, cited in Banks Papers, vol:1600–99; DCCR, 1:12 (quote); DCD, 1:1.

[50] Edgartown Records, 1:148.

[51] Cotton Journal, 71.

[52] NCR, 1:3 (verso), 9 (verso).

[53] DCD, 1:6, 12. See also Philbrick, *Abram's Eyes*, 103–7.

Takemmy from a Native grantor without legitimate right to the tract and refused to acknowledge the Indians' rejection of the sale. Ultimately, the Vineyard's General Court had to fine Athearn £5 5s. for forcibly entering the territory and frightening the inhabitants, and another £1 12d. for allowing his livestock to trample the Wampanoags' corn.[54]

Other colonists were only slightly more diplomatic than Athearn. In the late 1650s or early 1660s, the sachem Towtowe of Nashuakemuck sold Thomas Mayhew Sr. the southern half of his sachemship, encompassing most of the land between the east side of Stonewall Pond and the west side of Tisbury Great Pond. Mayhew permitted Indians already living on the tract to stay with "the free use and benefit of such portions and parcells of Lands as he did sett out to each one." However, Mayhew equivocated that "if at any time they did remove and Leave the same," which was part of their seasonal round, he would enact his exclusive use rights.[55] Lest there remain any question about Mayhew's ownership, regardless of the Natives' tenancy, Mayhew and the Indians ran a border several miles long from Waskosim's Rock near the head of Mill Brook and the Nashuakemuck–Takemmy boundary, southwest to Menemsha Pond. Land to the south of what was thereafter called "the middle line" belonged to Mayhew, whereas land to the north was the Indians'. Before long, Mayhew was in full possession of his side and more.[56] His initial consent to have Indians on the land was a temporary concession to quiet Indian protest, not an acknowledgement of the common Indians' rights. The Chappaquiddick sachem, Pakeponesso, was so troubled by these sorts of events that he bypassed his eldest son, Pecosh, as heir in favor of a younger son, Seeknout, out of fear that Pecosh "would sell land to the English."[57] John Eliot's observation that praying Indians generally revered and esteemed the English, "but the business about land giveth them no small matter of stumbling," applied equally to the islands.[58]

English livestock was as much a threat to Wampanoag land as the colonists themselves.[59] On the Vineyard, the English allowed their stock to wander

---

[54] DCD, 1:2; DCCR, 1:9, 12. See also William S. Swift and Jennie W. Cleveland, eds., *Records of the Town of Tisbury, Mass., Beginning June 29, 1669, and Ending May 16, 1864* (Boston, 1903), 10–11.

[55] Mass. Archives, 31:19.

[56] DCD, 1:327–8; 3:202; 9:400; Titles and Deeds, etc., Relating to Martha's Vineyard, NE Co. MSS, 8003.

[57] Suffolk Files #12965, p. 104.

[58] John Eliot, "An Account of the Indian Churches" (1673), *MHSC* 1st ser., 10 (1809), 128.

[59] Edgartown Records, 1:121, 124; FNPR, 1:268; NCR, 1:21 (verso), 2:4 (verso), 7(verso); "Deed: Cheichatesset of Manomet to John Alden, 17 May 1661," Pilgrim Hall, Plymouth, Mass., available online. The following paragraph also draws on William Cronon, *Changes in the Land: Indians, Colonists, and the Ecology of New England* (New York: Hill and Wang, 1983), chap. 7; Robert E. Gradie, "New England Indians and Colonizing Pigs," in William Cowan, ed., *Papers of the Fifteenth Algonquian Conference* (Ottawa: Carleton University Press, 1984), 147–69; Peter A. Thomas, "Contrastive Subsistence Strategies and Land Use

free on the uninhabited dry plain in the middle of the island until it was time for shearing or slaughter. They also put animals on Chappaquiddick to graze at large during the late fall and winter months, and as of 1655 this herd contained fifty head of "Great Cattle" or its equivalent of 200 calves or 500 goats.[60] Time and time again, Indians found these animals feasting on their corn or digging up their clam banks, but it was of little use to drive them away into the woods because then they encroached on the feed of wild game and thus undermined the hunt. One answer would have been for the Indians to fence in their cornfields, but the Natives were reluctant. Fencing was time-consuming, expensive, and a waste of valuable firewood. Moreover, fences gave Englishmen a basis to argue that Natives owned just their bounded lands, which the Wampanoags flatly rejected. Yet there were few other solutions given the colonists' unwillingness to control their herds. Nantucket Wampanoags erected pounds to hold trespassing animals until their owners paid damages, but the violations continued unabated.[61] Fifteen years later, Keteanummin saw no other better option than to have the English pay him to have their livestock run loose in Takemmy.[62] And so it remained. In 1677 the Vineyard court acknowledged the Wampanoags' "continuall complaint... of trespass don[e] in their corn fields by cattle... continually abroad in the woods," but it offered no redress.[63] As late as 1708, Samuel Sewall observed that "a Great part of the Island is barren and unfit for tillage, and being free from wolves; the Flocks of Sheep & Goats go at large without a Keeper, rambling over the Island. And if any sheep be stolen and killed; the English owner is ready to be jealous the Indians did it."[64] Offshore Wampanoags must have echoed mainland Indians in calling English livestock "filthy cut-throats."[65]

The spread of English jurisdiction enabled colonists to impose their own answers on the livestock question. After finding cattle swinging upside down in Wampanoag spring-nooses or with heads crushed from free-falls of bundled stones, they banned Indian traps in purchased territory despite deed clauses that guaranteed the Natives' right to hunt anywhere.[66] They also

as Factors for Understanding Indian–White Relations in New England," *Ethnohistory* 23 (1976), 1–18; Virginia DeJohn Anderson, "King Philip's Herds: Indians, Colonists, and the Problem of Livestock in Early New England," *WMQ* 51 (1994), 601–24.

[60] Edgartown Records, 1:124; Suffolk Files, #1047, Testimony of Thomas Mayhew and Sarah Natick.

[61] NCR, 2:1 (verso).

[62] FNPR, 1:268.

[63] DCCR, 1:15.

[64] Sewall to John Bellamy, 9 March 1708, NE Co. MSS, 7955/1, p. 12.

[65] Roger Williams, *A Key into the Language of America*, eds. John J Teunissen and Evelyn J. Hinz, (1643; Detroit: Wayne State University Press, 1973), 182.

[66] Edgartown Records, 1:114; William Wood, *New England's Prospect*, ed. Alden T. Vaughan, (Amherst: University of Massachusetts Press, 1977), 106–7; Williams, *Key into the Language of America*, 224.

outlawed forest fires Indians used to drive wild game into ambushes and clear the dense underbrush that hindered travel in the woods and promoted the growth of deer feed.[67] One of those fires set around the year 1659 by Keteanummin's uncle, Pamick, "Broake out and run so that it killed many of the English their Goats."[68] Clearly these measures made livestock safer, but at the expense of Indian hunting.

Some Wampanoags responded by stalking the colonists' animals, only to be charged with destroying someone else's "property."[69] They found this to be an odd double standard since colonists often killed Indian dogs for attacking sheep and hunted the Indians' deer without paying compensation.[70] A few Natives decided to adjust to the colonists' example by taking up animal husbandry themselves, but this experiment met English opposition too, particularly in Nantucket.[71] By a 1660 deed, the English could graze livestock in Wampanoag cornfields between October and May, when planting grounds lay fallow but contained barren corn stalks valued as cattle feed.[72] The English premised this agreement on the assumption that Indians would never graze animals themselves. Yet shortly after signing, the Indians began to purchase livestock from island settlers and pasture them alongside the colonists' beasts.[73] Citing the "over breeding" of Indian horses and cattle, in 1669 Nantucket authorities outlawed these sales and impounded the Indians' stray animals.[74] It smacked of hypocrisy for settlers to tell Indians to respect property and become civilized, then to turn around and obstruct the Natives' animal husbandry and permit their own herds to destroy Indian resources.

In the years leading up to King Philip's War, Vineyard colonists antagonized their Wampanoag neighbors with alcohol sales, xenophobia, and

---

[67] Starbuck, *History of Nantucket*, 125; Cronon, *Changes in the Land*, 49–51; Gordon Day, "The Indian as an Ecological Factor in the Northeastern Forest," in Michael K. Foster and William Cowan, eds., *In Search of New England's Native Past: Selected Essays by Gordon M. Day* (Amherst: University of Massachusetts Press, 1998), 36–43.

[68] Suffolk Files #72789.

[69] DCCR, 1:59; NCR, 1:10 (verso).

[70] Edgartown Records, 1:22; Starbuck, *History of Nantucket*, 12.

[71] Nathaniel Shurtleff, ed., *Records of the Colony of the Massachusetts Bay*, 5 vols. (Boston, 1853), 3:398, 4:255–6; Mass. Archives, 30:65; *Plymouth Records*, 11:221–2, 229; John R. Bartlett, ed., *Records of the Colony of Rhode Island and Providence Plantations in New England*, 10 vols. (Providence, 1856–65), 2:172–3; NCR, 1:11 (verso); David J. Silverman, "'We chuse to be bounded': Indian Animal Husbandry in Colonial New England," *WMQ* 60 (2003), 511–48.

[72] Starbuck, *History of Nantucket*, 125, 133, 140. On corn stalks as cattle feed, see John Winthrop Jr. "On Indian Corn (1662)," *NEQ* (March 1937), 125–33, esp. 129.

[73] Daniel Vickers, "The First Whalemen of Nantucket," *WMQ* 60 (1983), 571.

[74] Starbuck, *History of Nantucket*, 128 (quote); Elizabeth A. Little, "Sachem Nickanoose of Nantucket and the Grass Contest," *Historic Nantucket*–(1976), 23:15–22, 24:21–30; Idem., "Indian Horse Commons at Nantucket Island, 1660–1760," Paper presented at the 1986 meeting of the American Society of Ethnohistory, Charleston, S.C.

encroachment on Native land and jurisdiction, which were among the grievances that incited the mainland tribes to battle. The Indians' willingness to address their complaints through colonial institutions, combined with leadership by Mayhew, the sachems, and Christian Indian officers had kept these issues from becoming violent. Yet they continued to arise again and again, and so no one could feel confident that tensions between the communities would ease in the near future. When news arrived that mainland Wampanoags had taken to the warpath, island Indians had to wrestle with the question of whether joining Philip and possibly eliminating the settlers was worth the risk of blood.

IV

Just before the war erupted, Philip made an unequivocal statement to Rhode Island's Lieutenant Governor John Easton about his grounds for rising against the English.[75] Philip railed that colonists plied Indians with alcohol and used falsified writings to claim more land than Indians had intended to sell them. But even then the English were not satisfied with the rewards of their graft. Their cattle strayed from as far as thirty miles away into Indian cornfields, and the colonists' response to Indian complaints was not to fence the animals in, but to tell the Indians to fence them out. Englishmen demanded restitution when intoxicated Indians killed these animals even though it was colonists who had provided them with the liquor. On all of these points, Wampanoags from the mainland and the islands could agree that living alongside the English was an ongoing struggle.

Yet Philip's other complaints appealed only to his core supporters at Pokanoket and the nearby Wampanoag communities of Saconnet, Pocasset, and Assawompsett. The mission's progress was among their foremost concerns. Unlike minor sachems such as Sengekontacket's Wompamog or

---

[75] This conversation is recorded in John Easton, "A Relacion of the Indyan Warre, by Mr. Easton of Roade Isld, 1675," in Charles H. Lincoln, ed., *Narratives of the Indian Wars, 1675–1699*, Original Narratives of Early American History (New York, 1913), 10–11. The following section draws from Leach, *Flintlock and Tomahawk*, chaps. 2–3; Ronda and Ronda, "The Death of John Sassamon," 91–102; Jennings, *Invasion of America*, chap. 16; Philip Ranlet, "Another Look at the Causes of King Philip's War," *NEQ* 61 (1988), 79–100; Russell Bourne, *The Red King's Rebellion: Racial Politics in New England, 1675–1678* (New York: Oxford University Press, 1990), chap. 3; James Drake, "Symbol of a Failed Strategy: The Sassamon Trial, Political Culture, and King Philip's War," *AICRJ* 19 (1995), 111–41; Vaughan, *New England Frontier*, xxix–xxxv; Jill Lepore, *The Name of War: King Philip's War and the Origins of American Identity* (New York: Alfred A. Knopf, 1998), chap. 1; Richard W. Cogley, *John Eliot's Mission to the Indians before King Philip's War* (Cambridge, Mass.: Harvard University Press, 1999), 196–206; and Yasuhide Kawashima, *Igniting King Philip's War: The John Sassamon Murder Trial* (Lawrence: University Press of Kansas, 2001).

Aquinnah's Mittark, who used church offices to reinforce their local power, a regional sachem like Philip was weakened by the spread of Christianity. Increasingly, praying Indians looked to churches and courts rather than Philip to mediate their quarrels and to the English to protect them from outside threats. Thus, Philip had become superfluous to Wampanoags on the Vineyard, Nantucket, and Cape Cod, which probably led them to halt their tribute payments to him shortly after their submission to King Charles in 1671.[76] This would mean that Philip had lost as many as half his followers to the mission during the early 1670s. It was no coincidence that Philip told Easton of his "great fear to have ani of ther indians should be Caled or forsed to be Christian indians," because "the English made them not subject to ther kings." Worse yet, the mission had crept perilously close to Pokanoket through the preaching of John Sassamon at Nemasket, and of John Cotton Jr. at Acushnet and Saconnet.[77] If this trend continued, Philip might find himself with only a village-sized area to lead. The sachems of the nearby Narragansetts and Mohegans must have sympathized with his plight, but Christianity was not an immediate threat to them because they had consistently repelled English missionaries. Seven praying towns had recently formed among the Nipmucs of central Massachusetts, but that tribe did not organize under a single paramount leader. In his pique against the mission, Philip basically stood alone.

A number of Philip's grievances stemmed from specific disputes with New Plymouth that were not shared by Indians living outside of that colony's jurisdiction. Philip's charge that the English would "make a nother king that wold give or sell them land" when he refused to bargain with them referred to two isolated but inflammatory incidents. The first, in 1671, involved colonist Josiah Winslow filing suit in Plymouth court against William, the son of Tispaquin, the sachem of Assawompset and Philip's relative and subordinate. Winslow claimed William owed him £10 8s to pay for a horse, and although horses normally cost between £2 and £4, the jury awarded him £20. Tispaquin could pay off his son's fine only by selling land Plymouth had craved for a long time, as the court knew all too well.[78] Three years later, Plymouth encouraged a Saconnet Wampanoag named Mammanuah to sue the sunksquaw Awashunks, Philip's kinswoman, for denying him permission to sell territory. A colonial jury awarded Mammanuah £5 in damages, the costs of the suit, and his "chiefe right" to alienate the disputed tract.[79] Such artifice left Philip with "no hopes left to kepe ani land."

[76] *Some Account of Those English Ministers*, 292–5.
[77] Cotton Journal, 93, 94; "Historical Collections," 196–207.
[78] Deed: Tispaquin and William to Edward Gray and Josiah Winslow, 30 June 1672, Pilgrim Hall, Plymouth, Mass., available online. The territory sold is mapped in Thomas Weston, *History of the Town of Middleboro, Massachusetts* (Boston, 1906), 582.
[79] Ann Marie Plane, "Putting a Face on Colonization: Factionalism and Gender Politics in the Life History of Awashunkes, the 'Squaw Sachem' of Saconet," in Robert S. Grumet, ed.,

The death of Philip's brother, Wamsutta or Alexander, was a final bone of contention for mainland Wampanoags. The death of Massasoit in 1660 and the ascension of Alexander represented a new era in Wampanoag–English relations after forty years of uninterrupted peace. Within two short years rumors had Alexander plotting to cut off the English, and when Plymouth summoned him to explain, he ignored the order. Then, in a belligerent violation of Wampanoag sovereignty, Plymouth retrieved Alexander at gunpoint, only to release him when he fell ill during the forced march east. He died a few days later and his people suspected the worst. Philip found it cruelly ironic that "when the English first Came their [the Wampanoags'] king['s] father was as a great man and the English as a litell Child, he [Massasoit] Con-straened other indians from [w]ronging the English and gave them Coren and shewed them how to plant and was free to do them ani good and let them have a 100 times more land, then now the king [Philip] had for his own peopell, but the[i]r king['s] brother [Alexander] when he was king Came miserably to dy by being forsed to Court as thay judged poysoned." This event not only incensed the people of Pokanoket, but three other main-land Wampanoag strongholds: Pocasset, where Alexander's wife and Philip's sister-in-law, Weetamoo, ruled as sunksquaw; Saconnet, under the direction of Alexander's cousin, the sunksquaw Awashunks; and Assawompset, led by Tispaquin, Alexander's brother-in-law.[80] Wampanoag communities led by sachems unrelated to Alexander, like those on the Vineyard, Nantucket, and Cape Cod, found the event less incendiary, if troubling.

For Philip, these issues revealed the colonists' contempt for his office, his people's sovereignty, and, with Plymouth having forced him in 1671 to submit to the crown, even the Wampanoags' supposed rank as fellow subjects of the crown. Philip had inherited Massasoit's legacy of peaceful relations with the English, but in just a few years he had accumulated a laundry list of humiliating episodes that individually would have been just causes for war. Nevertheless, instead of lashing out, he set the grinding machinery of Native politics in motion to build a coalition of neighboring tribes. Philip wanted to fight the English, but not alone, not yet. Ultimately, it took the death of John Sassamon in 1675 and Plymouth's outrageous response to sum up years of indignity and finally prove to Philip's Wampanoags that their only hope for a tolerable future lay in battle, with or without the coalition in place.

Sassamon had been raised among the English of Massachusetts Bay after his parents (one of whom was Wampanoag) died in the epidemic of 1633.

Northeastern Indian Lives, 1632–1816 (Amherst: University of Massachusetts Press, 1996), 144–5.

[80] Robert Steven Grumet, "Sunksquaws, Shamans, and Tradeswomen: Middle Atlantic Coastal Algonkian Women during the Seventeenth and Eighteenth Centuries," in Mora Etienne and Eleanor Leacock, eds., *Women and Colonization: Anthropological Perspectives* (New York: Prager Press, 1980), 51.

He fought on the side of colonial troops during the ferocious Pequot War, assisted John Eliot in translating the Bible, taught school at Natick, and even attended Harvard College for at least a semester in 1653. Despite his impressive credentials, Sassamon eventually fell out with Eliot and therefore left Natick to serve as the interpreter and scribe to Alexander and eventually to Philip.

Sassamon's credibility with Philip deteriorated in lockstep with the sachem's English affairs. The war scare of 1671 began when Sassamon leaked to Plymouth that Awashunks was entertaining high-ranking Narragansetts. In fall of that same year, Sassamon arranged for Massachusetts and Connecticut to arbitrate Philip's refusal to turn over his people's firearms to Plymouth in accordance with an earlier promise. The arbiters came down heavily in Plymouth's favor, issuing Philip a steep £100 fine to be paid within three years, which could only be met by selling more Wampanoag land.[81] Perhaps in the course of those sales, Philip discovered that Sassamon had forged his will. Sassamon would have been wise to leave Wampanoag country altogether, but he resurfaced in Assawompset, where he became preacher to the small Nemasket congregation and married the daughter of the petty sachem Tispaquin.

For unknown reasons, Sassamon would not stay out of Philip's path. In January of 1675, he snuck to Plymouth to tell the governor, Josiah Winslow, that Philip was recruiting allies to strike against the English. Winslow doubted this news "because it had an Indian original" and dismissed Sassamon, but not before the informant uttered one fateful last prediction: Philip would surely seek his life for his treachery. True enough, in February Sassamon's body was found beneath the ice of Assawompset Pond. Philip was an obvious suspect, but an investigation uncovered no sign of wrongdoing, and so Sassamon received a proper burial, the matter of his death apparently fated to remain unsolved. However, shortly a praying Indian named Patuckson came forward to testify that he had witnessed three of Philip's chief men – Tobias, his son Wampapaquan, and Mattshunannamo – murder Sassamon and bury him under the ice to make it appear that he had drowned. William Nahauton, minister of the praying town, Punkapoag, provided hearsay to the same effect. In response, colonial authorities disinterred the corpse, performed a coroner's inquest, and determined that Sassamon had indeed been killed before he entered the water. On June 1, Plymouth hauled in the accused men to be tried by Englishmen with the slaying of a Wampanoag within Wampanoag territory. A jury of twelve Englishmen advised by a nonvoting group of "the most indifferentest, gravest, and sage Indians" (certainly Christians) found the three defendants guilty, and a week later the court marched Philip's men to the gallows for hanging.

[81] Cogley, *John Eliot's Mission*, 200–6.

To mainland Wampanoags, the trial crystallized everything that was wrong in their relationship with the English. For one, Sassamon's death took place in Wampanoag country and, if it was indeed murder and not simply drowning, involved only Wampanoags. Philip raged that "what was only between ther indians and not in towneshipes that we had purchased, thay wo[u]ld not have us prosecute." Then there was the testimony of Nahuaton and the role of the Indian advisors to the jury. Christianity, Philip was convinced, encouraged Natives "by ther lying to rong their kings." English officials and English procedures ran the trial, and English standards of evidence determined how the case would be judged. The entire matter seemed designed to provide the colonists with an excuse to "kill [Philip] to have his land." Plymouth showed nothing but scorn for Wampanoag jurisdiction, custom, and even lives in this trial, without any sense of equity in judging the word of a Christian Indian against that of a non-Christian. Worst of all, there was no relief in sight. In the future, more Wampanoags were sure to enter the Christian fold, Englishmen would acquire more land by means fair and foul, and if Philip survived, he would find himself a third-rate official at the bottom of the colonial hierarchy with nothing to bequeath to his progeny. English justice had proved to be a sham many times over, so there was little hope for redress. Philip's cause was now desperate.

Philip had to strike against the colonists to maintain the respect of his enraged followers even though he did not yet have committed allies. Beginning on June 11, three days after Plymouth executed Tobias and Mattashunannamo, Englishmen reported the Pokanoket Wampanoags were preparing for war. By the 20th, Philip's warriors had begun looting and burning homes near the English village of Swansea that had been wisely abandoned by their inhabitants. Then, on the 24th, the Wampanoags finally attacked the English directly. After nearly forty years of uneasy peace, New England was at war again.[82]

V

For all of their shared grievances with Philip, Christian Wampanoags were not about to join him on the warpath. None of their sachems had ever been seized at gunpoint by colonial authorities. None of their people had been sentenced to death by English courts. They paid the English no tribute and suffered no confiscation of their arms. A shared faith produced a certain degree of trust and open channels of communication between Wampanoag and English leaders, while common mechanisms of social control, such as church discipline and the courts, lent hope that stubborn problems could be addressed nonviolently. Mayhew's official power insulated him from popular

---

[82] Leach, *Flintlock and Tomahawk*, chap. 3, is the quintessential account of the war's opening events.

pressure to dispossess or disadvantage the Indians, which allowed him to continue his policy of easing the Indians into the structures of colonial society. The two groups were far from being a single people, but they had managed to coexist peacefully.

Yet never did that coexistence appear as tenuous as during King Philip's War. When news of the war reached Boston, Vineyard Indians working as field hands on nearby farms were forced to return home because "the English were so jealous and filled with animosity against all Indians without exception."[83] They left at just the right time, for a few weeks later Plymouth seized 160 mainland Wampanoags who had surrendered themselves as a show of loyalty and transported them out of the colony, probably to slavery in the West Indies. A short time later, fifty-seven more Wampanoags entered Sandwich "in a submissive way," yet English authorities judged them to be "in the same condition of rebellion as those formerly condemned to servitude" and thus sentenced them to the same fate.[84] "Innocent Indians" everywhere were now exposed to "the rash cruelty of our English," as colonist Thomas Walley put it.[85] William Hubbard judged the Natives to be "in a kind of maze, not knowing well what to do, sometimes ready to stand with the English, as formerly they had been wont to do; sometimes inclining to strike in with Philip."[86]

The disintegration of cross-cultural relations in the interior did nothing to clarify matters. Although some Nipmucs supported Philip, most of them preferred neutrality, as did Indians along the Connecticut River (the Woronocos, Agawams, Norwottucks, Pocumtucks, and Squakheags). These people had traded amicably with the region's settlers for years and won the title "friend Indians," which some of them made good upon by volunteering to guard exposed English towns.[87] But the English did not trust even long-standing Indian allies. They accused friend Indians with shooting over the heads of

[83] Gookin, "Historical Account," 434.

[84] *Plymouth Records*, 5:173, 174 (quote); Almon Wheeler Lauber, "Indian Slavery in Colonial Times within the Present Limits of the United States" (Ph.D. diss., Columbia University, 1913), 146. On mainland Indian reactions to such treachery, see Drake, *King Philip's War*, 117, 121.

[85] Thomas Walley to John Cotton Jr., Nov. 18, 1675, Curwen Family Papers, Box 1, File 3, AAS.

[86] William Hubbard, *A Narrative of the Indian Wars in New England, From the first Planting thereof in the year 1607 to the Year 1677* (1677; Boston, 1775), 56. This and the following paragraphs draw on Leach, *Flintlock and Tomahawk*, chaps. 4–5 and 8; Richard Melvoin, *New England Outpost: War and Society in Colonial Deerfield* (New York: W. W. Norton, 1989), 41–7, 97–107; and Jenny Hale Pulsipher, "Massacre at Hurleberry Hill: Christian Indians and English Authority in Metacom's War," *WMQ* 53 (1996), 459–86.

[87] On the history of Indian–colonial relations in this region, see Thomas, "Bridging the Cultural Gap: Indian/White Relations," in John W. Ifkovic and Martin Kaufman, eds., *Early Settlement in the Connecticut Valley* (Deerfield, Mass.: Historic Deerfield, Inc., and Westfield State College 1984), 5–21; Melvoin, *New England Outpost*, chaps. 1 and 3.

the enemy and conspiring to ambush English soldiers from behind, with celebrating Philip's victories and hosting his ambassadors.[88] Rumor fed upon rumor until colonists could no longer distinguish between friend and foe.

In a critical miscue, Englishmen in the Connecticut Valley demanded local Indians to turn over their arms, only to receive a blunt refusal. The Indians were not about to expose themselves either to the Mohawks, who had launched several raids against them in recent years, or to the colonists' palpable rage. They were equally unwilling to allow the English to force the issue. Just days later, River Indians launched devastating attacks against the unsuspecting towns of Hadley and Springfield. This, Hubbard argued, "did more than any other discover the said actors to be the children of the devil."[89] In what was becoming a self-fulfilling prophesy, panicked colonial authorities announced "the plott is generall (if not universall) among the Indians, and strikes at the interest of all the English in New England," all the while failing to acknowledge that their own people's brashness had forced erstwhile Indian allies into Philip's camp.[90] When Philip captured three Nipmuc praying towns and enlisted, perhaps forcibly, the men of those villages, the colonists' Indian-hating became even more intense. Initially, Massachusetts confined all of its praying Indians to the limits of five Christian reserves, but then English mobs threatened these places, whereupon the legislature interned the Natives on Deer Island, a desolate, windswept finger of land in Boston Harbor. The lesson for offshore Wampanoags could not have been clearer: in this war, an Indian community's Christian status and support for the colonial militia was not enough to earn the colonists' trust. Settlers viewed Christian Indians as Philip's and Satan's minions, not friends. The praying Indians were a people trapped in between and hated by all.

Island politics had been especially strained in the years leading up to 1675 and under the pressure of war it threatened to burst into anarchy and bloodletting. The Vineyard Wampanoags' primary concern was a sudden challenge to the rule of Mittark by his brother Ompohhunnut, who took advantage

---

[88] In addition to the sources cited above, see Richard R. Johnson, "The Search for a Usable Indian: An Aspect of the Defense of Colonial New England," *JAH* 64 (1977), 626–7.

[89] Hubbard, *Narrative of the Indian Wars*, 92.

[90] Commissioners of the United Colonies to Anonymous, Nov. 12, 1675, *Further Letters on King Philip's War* (Providence: Society of Colonial Wars, 1923), 18–19. See also, Gookin, "Historical Account," 450, 454; William Harris, *A Rhode Islander Reports on King Philip's War: The Second William Harris Letter of August, 1676*, Douglas Leach, ed. (Providence: Rhode Island Historical Society, 1963), 66; Increase Mather, *A Brief History of the Warr with the Indians in New-England* [Boston, 1676], in Richard Slotkin and James K. Folsom, eds., *So Dreadfull a Judgment: Puritan Responses to King Philip's War, 1676–1677* (Middletown, Conn.: Weselyan University Press, 1978), 94–5; Drake, *King Philip's War*, 84–90, 103; Drake, "Severing the Ties That Bind Them: A Reconceptualization of King Philip's War (Ph.D. diss., University of California, Los Angeles, 1996), 195–6; and Pulsipher, "'The Overture of this New-Albion World': King Philip's War and the Transformation of New England (Ph.D. diss., Brandeis University, 1999), 161–4.

of the wartime uncertainty to declare, "I am older than you, and I should be sachem, for I was first of our father Nohtouassuet [or Notooksact]." Not one to overreact, Mittark gathered together "my chief men, and also the (common) people of Gay Head, accordingly we appointed a great court and we called the sachems of this island as far as the mainland." This body, in turn, appointed a smaller council of Wampanoag church and civic leaders and gave them "complete power[:] whatever they did, we would do it." By traditional rules of inheritance, Ompohhunnut, as the eldest son, stood on firm ground. Yet Mittark had already proven himself to Indians and Englishmen alike by guiding his people out of Philip's alliance into the missionary fold, and Aquinnah needed his battle-tested leadership now more than ever. Ultimately, the council reached a sage decision that balanced each parties' legitimate demands: the elder brother would receive one quarter of Aquinnah's land and nothing else.[91]

The colonists settled their own troubles less amicably, most of which stemmed from the brief Dutch reconquest of New York in the summer of

---

[91] DCD, 6:369–73 (Wampanoag version); translation in *Native Writings*, 1:82–9. The eleven-man jury consisted of the following men: (1) Samuel Coshomon – future Sengekontacket minister and husband of Johannah, daughter of Sengekontacket sachem Wompamog; (2) Hosea Manhut – future Christiantown pastor; (3) Mashquattuhkooit – Nunnepog deacon; (4) Joshua Momatchegin – east-end ruling elder; (5) Stephen Tackanash – Takemmy preacher; (6) Japheth Hannit – Nashuakemuck preacher; (7) Isaac Ompany – Christiantown magistrate; (8) Samuel James – son of well-respected east-end Christian; (9) Pattompan – brother of Christiantown ruling elder John Shohkow, Takemmy magistrate Stephen Shohkow, and Christiantown preacher Micah Shohkow; (10) Matthew Nahnehshehchat – Chappaquiddick church member and relative of several Natives of pious reputation; (11) Joseph Popmechoo – island magistrate and sometime preacher. Witnesses to the deed conveying the land were Abel Wauwompuhque – Mittark's and Ompohunnut's brother; Wompamog (alias Mr. Sam) – Sengekontacket sachem and preacher; Akoochuck – magistrate and Mittark's son-in-law; John Momonaquem – east-end minister; Wuttino-manomin (probably David Wuttinomanomin) – Nashuakemuck deacon, sometime magistrate, and Aquinnah counselor; James Nashcompait – early Aquinnah convert; Elisha – on New England Company payroll in 1710–11; and Wuttahhonnompisin – early Aquinnah Christian. This data has been culled from a cross-section of sources too lengthy to list here. Citations are available upon request from the author.

All data relating to Ompohunnut's challenge are contained in deeds that were not registered until 1740, and then only to facilitate an underhanded attempt by Israel Amos, Ompohunnut's grandson, to engross Aquinnah land (as detailed in Chapter 5). This sequence raises the possibility that Ompohunnut's challenge was a fiction invented by Amos (suggested to me by Vineyard genealogist Andrew Pierce). However, the deeds' internal evidence – from the subdivision of a sachemship to avoid internecine squabbles, to the participation of almost every known Indian elite from that period – is consistent with seventeenth-century Wampanoag custom. Moreover, there is no record of any Indian challenging the legitimacy of these documents, which they were not reluctant to do in other cases of fraud. The deeds, I believe, were drawn up or copied in 1740, but recounted an actual event – not unlike many Wampanoag deeds of the late seventeenth and early eighteenth centuries.

1673.[92] As soon as the islands learned of the Dutch victory, disaffected colonists began renouncing local authority. On the Vineyard, the rebels' issues were Mayhew's lifetime appointment as "Governor," his liberal approach to Indian affairs, his family's stranglehold on secondary political offices, and the island courts' arbitrary procedures. Twenty Vineyard men (about half of the English heads of household) demanded Mayhew to open his seat for election. Predictably he refused, whereupon the dissenters formed a rump government and disowned his rule. Mayhew could not proceed against his opponents until the English retook New York in October of 1674 and the new governor, Major Edmund Andros, reaffirmed his power, but the long wait did not sap his vigor. Mayhew punished one dissenter after another by fine, sequester of estate, and revocation of franchise. Proceedings bled into the early months of 1675. Tensions lasted much longer.

The "half-share men" who sparked Nantucket's "Dutch Rebellion" were angry that as latecomers to the island, their farm plots and shares in future divisions of English common lands were only half the size of those enjoyed by the original proprietors, "the full-share men." Furthermore, they were forbidden from purchasing Indian territory, which otherwise could have compensated for these disadvantages.[93] Thus, when New York fell to the Dutch, the half-share men took control of Nantucket's government, reapportioned English lands, and threw out restrictions on bargaining with the Natives. The conflict was still in full bloom when Philip's warriors took up arms.

King Philip's War exacerbated these tensions on both islands. Colonists suddenly became "unreasonably exasperated against all Indians" for fear they conspired with Philip.[94] The leader of the Vineyard's "Dutch Rebels," Simon Athearn, worried that Mayhew would use the crisis as an excuse to unleash the Indians against his enemies, "we being about 38 English men on the Iland able to bare arms: and the Indians a multitud [of] Mr. Mayhews tennant[s]."[95] The numerical superiority of island Wampanoags,

---

[92] The following two paragraphs are based on DCD, 1:5, 7; Christoph and Christoph, eds., *Files of the Provincial Secretary*, 1:22–3, 24–30, 123–6, 128, 137–8, 141–3, 217–19, 219–21, 2:34–8, 47–51, 68–9, 266–7, 273–5; Hough, ed., *Papers Relating to the Island of Nantucket*, 51–128; Banks Papers, vol:1600–99, pp. 89–107, MHS; Banks, *History of Martha's Vineyard*, 1:155–69; Hare, *Thomas Mayhew*, chaps. 14–15; Edward Byers, *The Nation of Nantucket: Society and Politics in an Early American Commercial Center, 1660–1820* (Boston: Northeastern University Press, 1987), chap. 3.

[93] On the business of town proprietors, see John Frederick Martin, *Profits in the Wilderness: Entrepreneurship and the Founding of New England Towns in the Seventeenth Century* (Chapel Hill: University of North Carolina Press for the Institute of Early American History and Culture, 1991).

[94] *Conquests and Triumphs*, 40.

[95] Christoph and Christoph, eds., *Files of the Provincial Secretary*, 1:219.

which Matthew Mayhew put at "Twenty to one, having arms," would be daunting if hostilities broke out.[96] Isolation and preparedness seemed the best course, so the islands' joint General Court outlawed all nonofficial commercial contact with the mainland, excessive drinking, all sales of powder and shot to Indians, and required every house to keep firearms repaired and accessible.[97]

Local Wampanoags had every cause for alarm, but they adopted more conciliatory measures. Like their Cape Cod tribesmen, who immediately distanced themselves from Philip's raids by reaffirming their allegiance to the English and pledging to defend them, eight Nantucket Wampanoags presented themselves to the English on August 5 to "freely submit themselves to King Charles, the Second." They also "brought in som armes and left with this as a testimony to their fidelity to the English."[98] The latter act was more symbolic than substantive, the weapons amounting to just three muskets and a bow, but the Indians believed they had made their intentions clear.

They had not. Plymouth showed its lack of confidence in the Cape Wampanoags by ruling, "though divers of those Christian Indians manifested themselves ready and willing to engage with the English against their enemies," they were "to come noe further toward Plymouth than Sandwich...on paine of death or imprisonment."[99] Attacks by the Connecticut Valley friend Indians led Englishmen on the islands and elsewhere to conclude that any Indian refusal to disarm revealed deep-seeded hostility, not that seizing the Indians' guns risked driving them to war.[100] Mayhew pleaded for moderation, but he could not quell Vineyard colonists from "rising to assay the disarming of the Indians." Unwilling to goad the Dutch Rebels any further, the reluctant Governor appointed militia captain Richard Sarson, who had wed Thomas Mayhew Jr.'s widow, to lead a small party "to Treat the Indians on the West end of Martha's Vineyard [Aquinnah] who were mostly to be doubted."[101]

---

[96] *Conquests and Triumphs*, 40. Nantucket settlers submitted that the number of English fighting men on Nantucket and the Vineyard were thirty and forty, respectively. Indian fighting men numbered 500 to 600 on Nantucket, "not so many" on the Vineyard. See Hough, *Papers Relating to the Island of Nantucket*, 88–9.

[97] DCD, 1:404; DCCR, 1:11; NCD, 1:7 (verso), 36 (printed number) and 35 (handwritten number).

[98] NCR, 2:4 (verso). On Plymouth, see Cotton Journal, 97; and *Plymouth Records*, 5:177–8.

[99] Gookin, "An Historical Account of the Doings and Sufferings of the Christian Indians in New England in the Years 1675, 1676, 1677," *Transactions and Collections of the American Antiquarian Society* 2 (1836), 434; *Plymouth Records*, 5:183.

[100] Kenneth M. Morrison, *The Embattled Northeast: The Elusive Ideal of Alliance in Abenaki–Euramerican Relations* (Berkeley: University of California Press, 1984), 89, 108–9; John A. Strong, *The Algonquian Peoples of Long Island from Earliest Times to 1700* (Interlaken, N.Y.: Empire State Books, 1997), 252–3.

[101] *Conquests and Triumphs*, 40–1.

This envoy put Mittark and his council in a precarious spot. The order to disarm came from Mayhew's rivals, who seldom employed a light touch in Indian affairs. What if Mayhew were unseated or died (he was, after all, 83 years old) after the Indians turned over their weapons? If Mittark submitted, his brother might use the issue to revive his claims to the sachemship and lead the people into Philip's camp. What if mainland colonies extended their combative Indian policies to the islands? There was another issue as well. The Aquinnahs told Sarson "that the delivering their Arms would expose them to the will of the Indians ingaged in the present War, who were not less theirs than the Enemies of the English." Asserting "that they had never given occasion of the distrust intimated," the Indians rejected the colonists' demands.

However, they also proposed a way out of the stalemate to avoid a reenactment of the Connecticut Valley debacle. First, they drew up a document in the Wampanoag language "that as they had Submitted to the Crown of England, so they resolved to Assist the English on these Island against their Enemies, which they esteemed in the same respect equally their own, as Subjects to the same King." They promised that if Philip's men crossed over from the main, they would turn them over to the English. If Philip's forces attacked, they would resist them. The way to protect the island, Aquinnah contended, was not to disarm the Wampanoags but to outfit them as a guard.[102]

Now the difficult choice lay with the colonists. To force the weapons issue might very well bring war to the island, but to accept the Natives' plan was to surrender everything to trust despite abundant proof that "friendly Indians" were all too willing to take colonial lives. Furthermore, Massachusetts had established a precedent by disarming and confining its praying Indians. However, unlike Massachusetts, where the colonists' population majority and the rule of comparatively democratic governments made it more difficult for officials to control Indian-hating mobs, on the Vineyard the power and leadership of Thomas Mayhew was able to carry the day. Somehow he raised enough support to pass an audacious ruling to *furnish* the Wampanoags "with suitable Ammunition" and coordinate their maneuvers with the island militia.[103]

Leadership by Indian church officials such as Japheth Hannit was critical to seeing the peace plan through. Hannit was an ideal cultural broker during these tense times, for he mixed elite ancestry with personal accomplishments and ties to the English community.[104] He was already famous among the

---

[102] *Conquests and Triumphs*, 40–1; *Some Account of those English Ministers*, 296.
[103] *Conquests and Triumphs*, 41.
[104] On these types of figures, see Margaret Connell Szasz, ed., *Between Indian and White Worlds: The Cultural Broker* (Norman: University of Oklahoma Press, 1994); Daniel K. Richter, "Cultural Brokers and Intercultural Politics: New York–Iroquois Relations, 1664–1701," *JAH* 75 (June, 1988), 40–67; Merrell, *Into the American Woods*; Frances E. Karttunen, *Between Worlds: Interpreters, Guides, and Survivors* (New Brunswick, N.J.:

Wampanoags for having been blessed by the Holy Spirit in the womb of his mother, Wuttununohkomkooh. Then, after being raised in the family of the Nashuakemmuck sachem, Pammehannit, Japheth distinguished himself in virtually all of the Indians' new Christian institutions. He learned to read and write English at the Mayhew school, delivered a conversion narrative to become a full member of the Indian church, and later won election as "Chief Indian Magistrate." As a leading church member and civil authority he boasted an island-wide reputation for sobriety, piety, and empathetic judgment. These factors led to Japheth's appointment as "captain" over the newly formed Wampanoag militia, with the added responsibility "to observe and report how things went among the Indians." To "his Faithfulness in the Discharge of this Trust," wrote Experience Mayhew, "the Preservation of the Peace of our Island was very much owing, when the People on the Main were all in War and Blood."[105]

Yet the blood constantly threatened to spill over. Mayhew's political opponents insisted "that no person or persons be suffered to lett any indian or indians have any powder in these perilous times."[106] Nantucket settlers agreed, submitting "an ill consequence may arrive upon the Indyans Trayning in Armes on Martins Vineyard."[107] Mainlanders who fled to Nantucket during the war joined the half-share men to protest against "helping the Indians as the Law directs; and thus they press with vyolence in words."[108] The full-share proprietors' response was to jail the half-share man and missionary, Peter Folger, but this only aggravated the Wampanoags. As Folger cautioned, "I have bin Interpreter here from the Beginning of the Plantation when no Englishman but myself could speak scarce a Word of Indian,

---

Rutgers University Press, 1994); William B. Hart, "Black 'Go-Betweens' and the Mutability of 'Race,' Status, and Identity on New York's Pre-Revolutionary Frontier," in Andrew R. L. Cayton and Fredrika J. Teute, eds., *Contact Points: American Frontiers from the Mohawk Valley to the Mississippi, 1750–1830* (Chapel Hill: University of North Carolina Press for the Omohundro Institute of Early American History and Culture, 1998), 88–113; Alan Taylor, "Captain Hendrick Aupaumut: The Dilemmas of an Intercultural Broker," *Ethnohistory* 43 (1996), 431–57.

[105] *Indian Converts*, 46. Contrast Hannit's diplomacy with Jill Lepore's assessment of Indian literacy during this era. Lepore uses the death of John Sassamon to assert that "Indians who could read and write placed themselves in a particularly perilous, if at the same time a powerful position, caught between two worlds but fully accepted by neither." Sassamon was murdered, she believes, less for his machinations, than because he "negotiated with both peoples." Her argument that "in a sense, literacy killed John Sassamon" misses the bigger point that literate Indians were especially capable of helping their communities to work within, rather than against, the colonial state. Not coincidentally, the most literate Indian towns outlived King Philip's War by many years. See *In the Name of War*, chap. 1, quotes from pp. 25 and 27.

[106] Christoph and Christoph, eds., *Files of the Provincial Secretary*, 1:219.

[107] Hough, ed., *Papers Relating to the Island of Nantucket*, 88–9.

[108] Hough, ed., *Papers Relating to the Island of Nantucket*, 105–8.

at which Time I am sure some of these Men that deal thus with me now, had felt Arrows in their sides from the Indians for the reall Wrong that they did them, had I not stept in between them and made Peace." He could not do so at this critical time while rotting in jail. The Indians were nonplussed by Folger's arrest and by the refugees' claims to power. The Indians "say there is now young men in Place," related Folger, "they do not understand that way. They cannot believe that young Men, especially such Men, can understand things like old Men, and are always in doubt Justice or no." Pleading with New York authorities to intervene, Folger reminded them, "we have had Peace hitherto when our Neighbours just over the Water, have lost so many of their dear Relations in bloody wars." Folger was not being alarmist. One Nantucket sachem warned John Gardner that if things continued as they were, the Indians "could not forbear but must fight."[109]

Threats of this sort blew through the islands like the winter's gusts and gales, chilling English and Wampanoag firebrands until they could reach temperate solutions to their problems. After the confrontation at Aquinnah, Vineyard colonists never again attempted to seize the Indians' arms. For their part, Vineyard Wampanoags followed through on their pledge to defend the shoreline. In the spring of 1676, starved and battered mainland Wampanoags began crossing to the island in search of refuge, which put colonists, "in continuall fear that the other Indians by their Instigation may Joyne with them to doe as they have done."[110] The refugees' hopes and English fears proved to be unfounded. Matthew Mayhew wrote that the praying Indians were "so faithful" that they seized "even some nearly related" and "in observance of general instructions given them . . . immediately brought [them] before the Governour, to attend his pleasure."[111] There was no pleasure for the refugees: Mayhew turned his "many Captives" over to Plymouth, thereby dooming the adults either to turncoat military service against Philip or a life of slavery in the West Indies, and the children to years of indentured servitude.[112] Unlike the Narragansetts, who the English brutally attacked after they reneged on a promise to turn over Wampanoag refugees, offshore Indians made the

[109] Hough, ed., *Papers Relating to Nantucket*, 107–8; Christoph and Christoph, eds., *Files of the Provincial Secretary*, 2:45.

[110] Mass. Archives 30:227.

[111] Mayhew, *Conquests and Triumphs*, 42.

[112] Mass. Archives, 30:234; DCD, 1:3; Kawashima, "Indian Servitude in the Northeast," *Handbook of North American Indians*, vol. 4, *History of Indian–White Relations*, Wilcomb E. Washburn, vol. ed., William C. Sturtevant, gen. ed. (Washington, D.C.: Smithsonian Institution, 1988), 404; Lauber, "Indian Slavery in Colonial Times," 128; Paul R. Campbell and Glenn W. LaFantasie, "Scattered to the Winds of Heaven: Narragansett Indians, 1676–1880," *Rhode Island History* 37 (1979), 69–70; Leach, *Flintlock and Tomahawk*, 225–8; Lepore, *The Name of War*, chap. 6; Drake, *King Philip's War*, 160.

heart-wrenching decision to betray their own blood rather than court destruction.[113] The deep blow to their honor was the price for their lives.

VI

It took several years for King Philip's War to flicker out in Maine and the upper Connecticut River Valley, but the death of Philip aptly symbolizes its end in southeastern New England. The conflict had taken an immense toll on the Indian population.[114] With the exception of a few hundred mainland Wampanoags who had received quarter from the English for switching sides late in the war, and some Narragansetts who had been sheltered by the neutral Eastern Niantics, nearly all of the Indians who had formerly lived along Buzzard's Bay and Narragansett Bay, the upper Connecticut and lower Merrimack River Valleys, and the lakes of central Massachusetts were gone. The survivors fled northward toward the French and Wabenakis, or westward to settle among the Mahicans of the Hudson and Housatonic River watersheds. Over seventy percent of the warring tribes' members were dead or displaced, reducing the region's overall Indian population by forty to fifty percent. These were irreparable losses.

The English were less devastated but certainly reeling. Contemporaries disagreed on the figures, but the loss of colonial life ranged somewhere between a low of 800 to an unlikely high of 3,000 out of a total population of slightly more than 50,000. Philip's men had attacked fifty-two of ninety-two colonial towns, severely damaged twenty-five, and entirely destroyed sixteen. The colonial economy was in shambles and every government was deep in debt, while thousands of refugees called for assistance. Besides the Cape and islands, the only place in southeastern New England to escape disaster was Connecticut, where authorities "acquitted themselves like men

---

[113] On the colonists' strike against the Narragansetts, see Mather, *Brief History*, 107–8; Benjamin Church, *Entertaining Passages Relating to Philip's War* [Boston, 1716], in Slotkin and Folsom, eds., *So Dreadful a Judgment*, 412; Eaton, "Relacion," 14; Leach, *Flintlock and Tomahawk*, chap. 7; Jennings, *Invasion of America*, 302–12; Malone, *The Skulking Way of War*, 98–102; Drake, *King Philip's War*, 119–20.

[114] The following paragraphs draws on Leach, *Flintlock and Tomahawk*, chap. 8; Shelburne F. Cook, "Interracial Warfare and Population Decline among the New England Indians," *Ethnohistory* 20 (1973), 1–24; Patrick Frazier, *The Mohicans of Stockbridge* (Lincoln: University of Nebraska Press, 1992), 15–16, 32, 109; Bourne, *The Red King's Rebellion*, 12, 36, 242–3; Michael J. Pulgisi, *Puritans Besieged: The Legacies of King Philip's War in the Massachusetts Bay Colony* (Landham, Md.: University Press of America, 1991), chap. 4; Drake, "Severing the Ties," 297–8; Colin G. Calloway, *The Western Abenakis of Vermont, 1600–1800: War, Migration, and the Survival of an Indian People* (Norman: University of Oklahoma Press, 1990), 79–89; Evan Haefeli and Kevin Sweeney, "Wattanummon's World: Personal and Tribal Identity in the Algonquian Diaspora, c. 1660–1712," in William Cowan, ed., *Proceedings of the 25th Algonquian Conference* (Ottawa: Carleton University Press, 1993), 212–24.

and like Christians" by recruiting the Mohegans and Pequots to fight along-side the colonial militia.[115] It was a lesson lost on most of Connecticut's English neighbors.

Praying Indians were left to cope with the colonists' residual Indian-hating. When English writers reflected on King Philip's War, they were almost uniformly unable to concede that their opponents had pursued legitimate goals, and instead pointed to the supposedly inherent treachery and savagery of all Indians, not just the fighters.[116] Thus, more than ever, praying Indians became acceptable targets for New Englanders' vitriol. Rhode Island's Mary Pray captured the mood when she charged, "there is no trust in Indians they are subtil to deceiv," in response to a rumor in 1677 that Indian prisoners-of-war condemned to servitude in English homes were going to run away "and Ralley in there forces together and destroy us."[117] This was no mere chatter, for although New England Indians were hobbled, in certain places they retained enough strength to pose a significant threat. In September of 1688, an Indian named Joseph was arrested in Rochester, Massachusetts, for carrying weapons, to which he responded "in an Insulting and taunting manner" that "there was five Hundred [Indians] at Martins Vineyard[,] Seauven Hundred at Nantucket & four hundred at Chappaqquetsett all very well armed & in a better manner than him."[118] After a nightmarish war, Englishmen on the coast were more likely to interpret these words as a threat than an excuse.

Colonists had ample reason to fear their Indian neighbors because they abused them as never before. It did not take long for island Wampanoags to discover that their wartime service did nothing to soften the lash of mainland courts. Instead, penalties became harsher, with heavier fines, more brutal corporal punishment, and a newfound willingness to bind indebted Indians out as indentured servants. Boston authorities seared a "B" into the forehead of a Vineyard Wampanoag named Sam on the charge of burglarizing a house during the Sabbath. They issued a similar penalty to the island Wampanoag, Tom, for assaulting a colonist. Jonas and Abraham returned to the island

---

[115] Mather, *Brief History*, in Slotkin and Folsom, eds., *So Dreadful a Judgement*, 141. On Connecticut's experience in King Philip's War, see Christopher William Hannan, "'After This Time of Trouble and Warr': Crisis and Continuity in the New England Anglo–Indian Community, 1660–1725" (Ph.D. diss., Boston College, 1999), chaps. 6–7.

[116] The literature on Puritan responses to King Philip's War is extensive. For the most enlight-ening recent studies, see Pulgisi, *Puritans Besieged*, chaps. 1–2, 7; Lepore, *The Name of War*, chaps. 4 and 7; and Louise A. Breen, "Praying With the Enemy: Daniel Gookin, King Philip's War, and the Dangers of Intercultural Mediatorship," in Martin Daunton and Rick Halpern, eds., *Empire and Others: British Encounters with Indigenous Peoples, 1600–1850* (London: UCL Press, 1999), 101–21.

[117] Pray to Capt. James Oliver, Jan. 1676/77, *Further Letters of King Philip's War*, 22–4.

[118] Mass. Archives, 35:129a (quote); John Palmer, *The Revolution in New England Justified and the People There Vindicated* (Boston, 1691), in William H. Whitmore, ed., *The Andros Tracts: Being a Collection of Pamphlets and Official Papers*, 3 vols. (Boston: The Prince Society, 1868–1874), 1:101–3.

with their own testimony to English justice: thirty stripes each for pilfering a hog and some cider.[119]

The spread of English Indian-hating and the death of Thomas Mayhew in March of 1681/82 emboldened island colonists to step up their own confrontational behavior. By 1677, Nantucket's half-share men had thrown open the Indian land market without heed to its protocols. A Wampanoag named Obadiah appealed to New York that his "Land is wrun[g]fuly sold from him by Other Indian sachems that had nothing to do with it: and he t[u]rned out: and his Land now Enjoyed by the English without aney satesfaction either to himself or his Ansisters."[120] The Wampanoags hardly dared to protest because Nantucket courts suddenly became as aggressive as those on the mainland, even going so far as to employ branding.[121] On the Vineyard, Indian complaints streamed into the island's General Court about trespasses by English cattle.[122] A Chappaquiddick Wampanoag named Joel added that the Englishman John Wright had confiscated his gun, behavior of a sort rarely seen before the war.[123]

If coastal settlers believed that their Wampanoag neighbors lacked the will to defend themselves, events in 1688 provided them with a timely awakening. That year William and Mary unseated James from the English throne, which inspired mobs in New England and New York to overthrow their unpopular crown-appointed leaders, and people in remote places like the Vineyard to test the bounds of local authority.[124] Matthew Mayhew recalled that "many in hopes there was no King in Israel, expected to have done what they saw good in their eyes," by seizing sheep from the Chappaquiddick Wampanoags on the pretense that they were stolen. An unnamed sachem (probably Seeknout) would not have it, warning Mayhew, "if they persist in that Resolution, it may Occasion Blood-shed." Wise with years, this sachem was uniquely qualified to assess four decades of Indian–English peace on the island and recent developments that put it at risk. He gave Mayhew a lecture he never forgot:

You know that while your Grand-father and my Father lived, there never happened any difference in such things, nor hope will be Occasion given by me. I desire the

[119] *Abstract and Index of the Records of the Inferior Court of Pleas (Suffolk Court) Held at Boston, 1680–1698* (Boston: Historical Records Survey, 1940), 126, 128, 129.
[120] Christoph and Christoph, *Files of the Provincial Secretary*, 2:51. See also pp. 68–69; NCR, 1:2–3.
[121] Compare NCR 2:7 (verso), 8 (verso), and 53 with 1:11 (verso), 12 (verso), 20 (verso), 23 (verso), 24, and 24 (verso).
[122] DCCR, 1:15.
[123] DCCR, 1:19.
[124] David S. Lovejoy, *The Glorious Revolution in America* (New York: Harper Torchbooks, 1972); Johnson, *Adjustment to Empire: The New England Colonies, 1675–1715* (New Brunswick, N.J.: Rutgers University Press, 1981); Murrin, "The Menacing Shadow of Louis XIV and the Rage of Jacob Leisler."

same Amity may be continued, nor can the English say that we have not manifested our Allegiance to the King by a continued subjection. And although it is time, we have desired that your Order should come to us, rather then your Officer, which hath generally been observed; yet we are willing in Case the English pretend any thing ours have injured them in; let an Officer by writ from Authority doe his duty, then we shall known how in an orderly way, to be relieved; yet shall the least Boy bringing your Order, as in your Grandfathers time, Command any thing: and if you see cause on any Complaint about our Sheep, you may Command all of them.

From the sachem's perspective, peaceful coexistence had relied on the Wampanoags subjecting themselves to the English king and accepting the legitimacy of colonial courts; on colonists respecting Wampanoag jurisdictions and issuing complaints through recognized authorities rather than the crowd; and especially on Indian leaders and Thomas Mayhew Sr. conducting serious business in a spirit of "Amity." All Seeknout wanted was a continuation of this remarkable social experiment, that "as hitherto we may have equal Justice, being the King Subjects; and Violence and Riot committed on our People by the English may be esteemed of the same nature and quality as ours against them."[125]

No sooner had the sachem spoken these words than the Vineyard faced one of its gravest tests. In 1689, colonist Thomas West accused a Wampanoag named Pomatook with killing Sarah, a Native woman of Takemmy, only to have Pomatook confess to an unsolved twenty-year-old murder of an Indian woman who had been pregnant with his child. With this, Pomatook sealed his own fate, and on September 17, an English jury sentenced him to hang, the first ruling of its kind on the island. With confrontations between Indians and colonists on the rise, the Chappaquiddick sachem intimating war, and now this trial for the murder of a Wampanoag by a Wampanoag, there were eerie similarities to the summer of 1675. The Vineyard's General Court was guarded but determined to see English justice done, and so on September 20th, it met in emergency session and ordered that any Indian found in Edgartown half an hour after sunset was to be brought before a Justice of the Peace, questioned, and thoroughly whipped if he could not explain his presence. Six days later, the fateful hour came. Pomatook walked from jail to the gallows and then climbed the steps before a throng of bystanders. To the relief of English authorities, he fell into the role of a Puritan gone astray who was now repentant at the brink of death. Pomatook confessed his crime again as well as the rest of his sins, declared his conscience to be clean, and then asked for prayers of mercy from the audience. Those were his last words.[126]

---

[125] Mayhew, *Conquests and Triumphs*, 42–3.
[126] DCCR, 1:61–2; Cotton Mather, *Magnalia Christi Americana; or, the Ecclesiastical History of New England*, 2 vols., ed. Thomas Robinson (1702; Hartford, 1855), 2:444–5. On the importance of these kinds of confessions in Puritan culture, see Murrin, "Magistrates,

Once again the peace held on Martha's Vineyard. Unlike Philip's men fourteen years earlier, the Vineyard Wampanoags accepted the judicial procedure and principles of Pomatook's sentence. Years of Christian education had taught them that so long as their community, as a covenanted community, met its responsibility to punish sins like murder, God's wrath would fall upon the individual sinner, not the sinner's people. Experience with the colonial state taught the Indians a system in which government, not families, held a monopoly on justice and violence. But as the hangman's rope snapped Pomatook's neck, perhaps the greatest force of restraint was the most basic lesson of King Philip's War: that the consequence of a war in a locality with a large Indian population, but in a region with an English majority, would be the near destruction of both sides. Fear was as powerful as "amity" in shaping the peace.

VII

Late in the war, several hundred mainland Wampanoags had been given quarter by Plymouth in exchange for taking up arms against Philip, and now, with the conflict over, they looked to the Vineyard Indians as a model for adapting to the colonists' church and state. They saw that offshore Wampanoags upheld Christian living through their own churches and courts that the English respected. There were seven meetings every Sabbath day, and two organized congregations with forty full members (those who had given conversion narratives), run by twelve preachers and eleven teachers. A full 140 Indians had pledged total abstinence from alcohol. Even the sparsely populated Elizabeth Islands, just off the Vineyard's northwest coast, boasted forty Christian families and a preacher.[127] A who's who of colonial elites accepted them as fellow Christians.[128] Clearly there was something to be learned from the Vineyard Wampanoags. Fortunately for the refugees, the islanders were willing to teach. In a campaign that made Philip turn over in his grave, praying Indians began crossing Vineyard Sound into the sachem's heartland to help his people transition into peacetime.

Sinners, and a Precarious Liberty," 164, 172–82; Jane Kamensky, *Governing the Tongue: The Politics of Speech in Early New England* (New York: Oxford University Press, 1997), chap. 5.; Daniel E. Williams, ed., *Pillars of Salt: An Anthology of Early American Criminal Narratives* (Madison, Wisc.: Madison House, 1993).

[127] *Plymouth Records*, 10:404–5.

[128] "Historical Collections," 183; John Eliot, Letter of November 4, 1680, and Thomas Hinckley, Letter of April 2, 1685, New England Company Collection, File 5, AAS; Samuel Sewall, *Phaenomena Quaedam Apocalyptica, or, Some Few Lines Toward a Description of the New Heaven as it Makes to Those who Stand Upon the New Earth* (Boston, 1697), 34; I. Mather, *Masukkenukeeg Matcheseauwog* [*Greatest Sinners Exhorted*] (Boston, 1698), 163–4; C. Mather, *Triumphs of the Reformed Religion*, 116–17, 123, 127–9; C. Mather, *Bonifacius*, 195, 198; C. Mather, *Letter about the present state of Christianity*, 5, 7–8, 11.

John Hiacoomes, the son of Hiacoomes, was among the first to go, leaving Nunnepog in 1687 to preach to the eighty-person village of Assawompsett.[129] Over the next twenty years, several leading Vineyarders joined him: John Momonaquem, who was the son of the Nashuakemuck minister Momonaquem, a preacher in his own right, and one of Mittark's counsellors; Hannah Ahhunnut, John's wife, a Nunnepog church member and a reputable midwife; Annampanu, the nephew and son-in-law of Mittark; and Jonathan and Rachel Amos, Jonathan having served as deacon of the Nashuakemuck church, and Rachel boasting status as daughter of the Nunnepog elite, Myoxeo.[130] Combined with forays into the surrounding country by Japheth Hannit, Sengekontacket's Thomas Sissetom, and the former Vineyard missionary, John Cotton Jr., Christianity quickly took hold among the mainlanders.[131] As early as 1689, Increase Mather described Saconnet as "a great Congregation."[132] Nine years later, continental Wampanoags had organized four meetings with at least 240 attendees and an array of Native officers ordained by their Vineyard counterparts. Cotton Mather rejoiced that these Indians were "so far Christianized, as they Believe there is a God, and but one God, and that Jesus Christ is the Saviour of the World," providing "just Foundation to hope, That they are Travelling the right way [to] Heaven."[133] Literacy was on the rise too, with ten of forty praying Indians at Saconnet, and most of the men at Cohassit, able to read the Bible.[134]

These Natives used the church to reintegrate themselves into a Wampanoag and Massachusett network comprising twenty to thirty mainland meetings of "some thousands of souls," plus ten meetings on the

[129] "Indian Visitation, 134.

[130] New England Company Ledger, MHS, p. 60; *Indian Converts*, 38, 110, 140; "Indian Visitation," 130.

[131] *Conquests and Triumphs*, 37; John Cotton Jr. to Increase Mather, March 23, 1693, Mugar Library Special Collections (transcription courtesy of Sheila McIntyre and Len Travers), and typescript at the New York Historical Society, New York City; Cotton Journal, 89–101; C. Mather, *Letter about the present state of Christianity among the Christianized Indians of New England* (Boston, 1705), 13; C. Mather, *A Brief Account of the Evangelical Work among the Christianized Indians of New England*, appended to his *Just Commemorations. The Death of Good Men, Considered* (Boston, 1715), 53; C. Mather, *Concerning the Essays that are made, for the Propagation of Religion among the Indians*, appendix to his *Bonifacius: An Essay Upon the Good, that is to be Devised and Designed, by those who Desire to Answer the Great End of Life* (Boston, 1710), 199; *Indian Converts*, 161; *Some Correspondence*, 110; NE Co. MSS, 7953, p. 12.

[132] I. Mather, *A Brief Relation of the State of New England* (London, 1689), in Whitmore ed., *Andros Tracts*, 2:165–6, 168 (quote); idem., *A Letter Concerning the Success of the Gospel, amongst the Indians in New England* [1687], reprinted in C. Mather, *Triumphs of the Reformed Religion in America: The Life of the Renowned John Eliot* (Boston, 1691), 90.

[133] C. Mather, *Letter about the present state of Christianity*, 5, 11.

[134] *Conquests and Triumphs*, 37; J. Cotton to I. Mather, March 23, 1693; "Indian Visitation," 129–30.

Vineyard and Elizabeth Islands, and three on Nantucket.[135] For the first time in decades, the refugees had a ritual basis to gather with offshore communities, this time for marriages, church openings, the Lord's Supper, ordination, school, and Bible readings. Their devotion to Christianity convinced colonial officials that they deserved a place in postwar New England, thus leading to the formation of protected reservations, albeit on tracts much smaller than they had formally enjoyed.[136] How ironic it must have seemed that the Vineyard Indians, after decades of withdrawal from mainland trade, politics, religion, and ultimately war, were now emerging as the Wampanoags' leaders.

VIII

Martha's Vineyard's peaceable history was not lost on English contemporaries. "This Island may even brook the name of Rebekah," wrote New England Company official Samuel Sewall in 1708, "from these two Nations thus struggling together and cro[w]ding one another in it."[137] By "Rebekah," Sewall referred to Genesis 24:60, in which Rebekah leaves her family to marry Isaac, the son of Abraham, thereby joining the people of Israel, God's chosen ones. So too had the Vineyard Wampanoags seemingly detached themselves from their pagan roots to worship in the way of Puritans, the self-proclaimed successors of Israel. Moreover, Rebekah's story expressed hope for the future. Her family said goodbye to her with a blessing, "Thou art our sister; be thou the mother of thousands of millions, and let thy seed possess the gate of those which hate them."

The Wampanoags and English of the Cape and islands had resisted tremendous pressures to shed one another's blood, but Sewall was willfully naive in his inference that the two parties might someday form a single people. So too was John Eliot, who attributed the colonists' "continual disgust and jealousy of all the Indians" to ongoing raids by northern Indians allied

---

[135] C. Mather, *Brief Account of the Evangelical Work*, 49–50 (quote); C. Mather, *Concerning the Essays*, 195–9; *Conquests and Triumphs*, 34–6, 52–68; "Indian Visitation"; *Some Correspondence*, 84; Experience Mayhew, *A Brief Account of the State of the Indians on Martha's Vineyard*, appendix to his *Discourse Shewing That God Dealeth with Men as with Reasonable Creatures* (Boston, 1720), 2–3, 5; Experience Mayhew to Roland Cotton, July [], 1699, Misc. Bound MSS, MHS; NE Co. MSS, 7956, p. 103, 7955/2, pp. 100, 109–10; CPGNE, Box 1, February 25, 1731.

[136] Weston, *History of the Town of Middleboro*, 13, 18, 582 (map), 583; Hugo A. Dubuque, *Fall River Indian Reservation* (Fall River, 1907), 3–4, 10, 61; Frank G. Speck, *Territorial Subdivisions of the Wampanoag, Massachusett, and Nauset Indians*, Indian Notes and Monographs No. 44 (New York: Heye Foundation, 1928), 180; Laurie Weinstein, "We're Still Living on Our Traditional Homeland': The Wampanoag Legacy in New England," in Frank W. Porter III, ed., *Strategies for Survival: American Indians in the Eastern United States*, Contributions in Ethnic Studies 15 (Westport, Conn.: Bergin and Garvey, 1986), 94–5; *Native Writings*, 13.

[137] Sewall to John Bellamy, March 9, 1708, NE Co. MSS, 7955/1.

with New France.[138] Contrary to these men's optimism, their people's Indian-hating fed on a shared Indian–English society that survived among the ruins of King Philip's War. Colonists had successfully convinced large numbers of Indians to take up Christianity and adopt certain "civilized" institutions and behaviors, only to find that the Natives necessarily brought their own culture to these reforms. The Indians worshipped the same God as the English and practiced the same piety, but they did so in distinctly Indian ways through innumerable subtle innovations. This "indigenization" of Christianity, as one might call it, forced the English to confront that "conversion" was not a leap across a broad gulf separating civility and savagery, but a series of sprints, half-steps, and hesitations through a gray area where cultures overlapped, a process that enabled Indians to retain their kin, land, and communal values even as they adopted Christian worship and living and distanced themselves from the Philips of the world.[139] Englishmen had to account for this ambiguity and their own equally unanticipated insistence on treating praying Indians – fellow Christians after all – as third-class members of colonial society or resident aliens. For if Christian Indians remained a people apart after all their reforms, clearly what made them distinct was something else besides the outward manifestations of culture such as religion, government, or dress, as earlier theorists had proposed. Increasingly, settlers explained this conundrum away and their own role in perpetuating it by appealing to race.

New England colonists moved toward the idea of an essential inferior Indian racial identity by staining all praying Indians, regardless of their wartime loyalties, with the savagery and duplicity they attributed to Philip's supporters. This was the case even on Martha's Vineyard. In the 1690s, Matthew Mayhew lamented that many of his English neighbors "have indeavoured to Scandalize so great a work" as the mission because those "who are in no measure qualified for Church Fellowship, think it no small disparagement that Indians should be accounted worthy of what themselves cannot be admitted to." These settlers, he continued, "have not Scrupled to Stigmatize the Indians with greatest opprobry [opprobrium], in particular cases of their complaint, the Indians have been found wholly innocent, and themselves sordidly Villanous." Mayhew consoled himself that "the Sober Religious People here, have done, and doe esteem [the Natives] as Christians indeed" but most of the time sober religious people were outnumbered.[140] Just a few years later, in 1705 Massachusetts considered a bill "against fornication, or marriage of White men with Negros or Indians," for

---

[138] Letter of John Eliot, October 23, 1677, New England Company Collection, File 5, AAS.

[139] On this term, see Antonio R. Gualtieri, "Indigenization of Christianity and Syncretism among the Indians and Inuit of the Western Artic," *Canadian Ethnic Studies* 12 (1980), 47–57; Marshall Sahlins, "The Economics of Develop-Man in the Pacific," *Res* 21 (1992), 12–25.

[140] *Conquests and Triumphs*, 32–3. See also, C. Mather, *Letter about the Present State of Christianity*, 11.

"the Better Preventing of a Spurious and Mixt Issue." Only Samuel Sewall's pleading convinced legislators to leave the Indians out, and the margin was slim.[141] This was the extent of the colonists' acceptance of Christian Indians in postwar New England.

Martha's Vineyard's peace rested on an unstable foundation. It depended upon the unique power of Thomas Mayhew; Wampanoag reforms in government and religion that bound them more closely to colonists and less so to mainland Natives; the war-time refusal of each party to overreact to pernicious rumors despite harboring many doubts about the other's intentions; and the Indians' performance in the English militia. But it was fear that held the weak foundation together, fear that either side could annihilate the other. After the war, this legacy, combined with the colonists' rising Indian-hating and willingness to exploit their power, left little promise of Indians and Englishmen marrying, producing children, and creating a single society. In a region saturated with bloody memories of a war that brought out the worst in humanity, this was too much to expect. For the Vineyard Wampanoags, making do within a crassly unequal society would have to be enough.

---

[141] M. Halsey Thomas, *The Diary of Samuel Sewall, 1674–1729*, 2 vols. (New York: Ferrar, Straus and Giroux, 1973), 532.

4

Deposing the Sachem to Defend the Sachemship

Vineyard colonists engrossed Wampanoag land with particular zeal after King Philip's War, spurred on by the new balance of power, the
death of Thomas Mayhew Sr., and a rise in Indian-hating, but the Takemmy
Indians were supposed to be immune to such pressure. In 1669, Mayhew
and the sachem Keteanummin had guaranteed them a mile-square reserve
called Christiantown in perpetuity and veto power over future land sales
elsewhere in the sachemship. However, the latter clause was rarely honored and with every passing season the Wampanoags lost hunting grounds,
fishing stations, and places for gathering wild plants to English expansion.
Fears leftover from the war had persuaded the Indians to tolerate this encroachment, but by 1695 they had reached their limits. Recently a settler
had constructed an "English-style house" within Christiantown on a tract
known as "the Red Ground." If the praying Indians allowed this breach to
stand, their village border was sure to erode and wash away. It was time for
action.

In June, four Wampanoag men went to expel the intruder, but they found
only a young boy who sensibly refused to unlatch the door. No matter; Isaac
Ompany climbed onto the roof, leapt "down the oven[']s mouth," and then,
with the boy looking on crying, emptied the dwelling of all its contents.
Afterwards, Ompany claimed the house as his own while the other Indians
pulled down crops and a fence in the nearby field. The Takemmies were
sending a clear message that if Englishmen expected to profit from their
work, it was best for them to settle elsewhere.[1]

---

[1] Suffolk Files, #4714 and 4974. The exact location of the land in dispute is undeterminable and
can easily lead to confusion since several documents identify it as lying near "Wampashe," the
same name applied to a neck of land off Tisbury Great Pond. However, testimony by Simon
Athearn in 1700 noted that the "Land in Controversey, was within the bounds of those land
before granted to the Praying Indians." Testimony of Simon Athearn, April 2, 1700, Misc.
Bound MSS, MHS.

On the surface, this brief episode seems part of a familiar history about Indians caught in the path of English expansion. Colonists discard agreements guaranteeing Natives a sliver of their ancestral land, and in response a group of hot-headed Indian men take violent action, achieving what is certain to be a short-lived victory before English power drives them into the woods. But things were rarely so simple on colonial Martha's Vineyard. In this case, Wampanoags and colonists were allies against their own kind as well as opponents of one another, and the supposed cultural gap between peoples was arched by bridges of church, law, and leadership. It was not young warriors who came to the defense of Christiantown. Instead, they were an august cast respected by Indians and Englishmen alike: minister and magistrate Isaac Ompany, the schoolmaster Job Soomanan, justice Obadiah Paul, and a fluent English speaker named Tiesse. The Takemmies did not lash out in a fit of blind rage, but executed a strategy plotted by a legal-minded settler with "the joint consent of the indians of said town" to provoke a courtroom hearing.[2] A colonist did indeed own the "English-style house" the Indians took over, but his tenants were none other than Keteanummin and the sachem's young son. These twists and turns are unfamiliar in part because they do not adhere to the overworked theme of Indians futilely struggling to preserve a doomed culture. Certainly the Wampanoags intended to defend their people's land, and with it, their very ability to survive as a people. But as Christian Indians living in a colonial world, church officers, magistrates and lawyers were now Wampanoag devices to be put to Wampanoag ends.

The land crises that plagued New England Indians after King Philip's War involved more than struggles for acreage and divided society along finer lines than an Indian–English fault. Common Indians had determined that their shrinking land base was a problem of supply as well as demand, of sachems selling territory as well as of colonists buying it. Sachems argued that custom sanctioned their transactions, but their followers countered that the leadership's preeminent traditional responsibility was to further the people's interests, including defense of the homeland. Both sides appealed to history in vain since the land sale problem was without precedent. Yet in the process they raised several fundamental questions about their communities that shook them to the core: At its essence, was a sachemship the personal estate of the sachem on which the sachem's followers happened to live, or a territory that belonged to the people as a whole and that the sachem was obligated to manage and protect? To what extent were Native leaders answerable to the needs of common people? What were the acceptable forms of protest for the Wampanoags against the traditional leadership? Could there be a sachemship without a sachem?

The Vineyard Wampanoags reached a broad range of answers to these questions. In the best of scenarios, the Indians concluded that to retain the

---

[2] Suffolk Files #4974, p. 7.

sachemship they had to rid themselves of the sachem and then undertake a series of equally speculative measures: instituting less-centralized local governments, run not by a sachem and his or her elite counselors, but by meetings of Indian "proprietors," or representatives from the families on the land; forging risky alliances with powerful Englishmen who, while capable of navigating the technical shoals of colonial courts, often blurred the distinction between advocate and pariah; adopting new economic practices and methods of record keeping that established English-style usufruct and written claims to territory; and finally, using limited violence to intimidate trespassing colonists and draw the attention of authorities when peaceful means proved ineffective. Other groups continued to defer to traditional leaders even in the midst of runaway land sales. In the end those parties lost everything, for there could be no leader without the land and there could be no land with the leader. With so many weighty considerations, so many variables, no two communities addressed the intertwined problems of dwindling territory and sachem power in the same way. Yet the choices each made helped determine whether Indian lands would become dismantled with alarming speed or emerge from the fray at least partially intact. Those who were most willing to innovate, who possessed the courage to make difficult, even painful, adjustments to this seminal challenge of the colonial era, were able to preserve some of what was most important to their people.

I

Over the course of just a few decades the Vineyard Wampanoags had adopted new religious practices, political alliances, and civic institutions, but they entered the late seventeenth century with their primary social unit, the sachemship, and leading office, the sachem, intact albeit not unaltered.[3] The sachemship was at once a territory about the size of an English town and a network of villages encompassing usually no more than five hundred people. The sachem advised by a council of elders and elites was responsible for managing his territory's economic resources, hosting prominent visitors, maintaining relations with other communities, caring for the destitute, arbitrating disputes, punishing criminals, and organizing defense. Sachems also collected tribute in food, furs, animal skins, wampum, labor, and military service, but not by and large for strictly personal use. Sachems were hardly

---

[3] The best discussions of the sachem are William S. Simmons and George F. Aubin, "Narragansett Kinship," *MNE* 9 (1975), 21–31; Kathleen J. Bragdon, *Native People of Southern New England, 1500–1650* (Norman: University of Oklahoma Press, 1996), 140–55; and Eric Spencer Johnson, "Some by Flatteries and Others by Threatenings: Political Strategies among Native Americans of Seventeenth-Century New England" (Ph.D. diss., University of Massachusetts at Amherst, 1993).

better off than most of their followers, as Europeans frequently observed with some puzzlement. Unlike European elites, who could translate accumulated wealth into political power, sachems generated status by applying wealth to public ends, not by hoarding it. Poor men could be rich men in a society that paid its leaders with deference.

One of the sachem's privileges was to pass on his title within the family line. Customarily it went to his eldest son, but if the heir was unsuitable it might descend to a younger son, daughter, brother, or paternal nephew. Yet birthright did not make the sachem's rule autocratic. A sachem had to cultivate support among leading families with strategic marriages and council appointments, and among the broader public with generosity and high oratory, for there was always the risk of his followers leaving for another jurisdiction or shifting their allegiance to one of his political rivals. What was more, although the people honored the sachem, they believed the community's welfare ultimately took precedence over his will. As linguist Kathleen Bragdon explains, they conceived that "the sachemship was made up of those who 'defended' it . . . Loyalty went beyond that given to the present sachem, and rested with the sachemship as an ongoing social grouping, to whom one's ancestors had belonged and to which one's own posterity would be loyal."[4] On Martha's Vineyard, the major sachemships from east to west were Chappaquiddick, Nunnepog, Takemmy, and Aquinnah (or Gay Head). A few of these larger units contained semiautonomous "subsachemships" like Sengekontacket in Nunnepog, usually headed by one of the major sachem's relatives. In the border zone of Nashuakemuck there were a number of small family settlements headed by minor sachems, but they do not appear to have been a part of any larger group. As the loci of Wampanoag society these places had always been subject to factional politics, power struggles that took on new meaning once colonists began purchasing Indian land.

Until the English arrived, probably it never occurred to any of the Indians whether a sachem could permanently alienate large tracts of land to outsiders. Although there is evidence of occasional land swaps between sachems and of sachems carving out subsachemships for their relatives, these decisions appear to have been uncontroversial. The relationship between sachems and their people over the land was more reciprocal than adversarial. The sachem controlled access to the sachemship's hunting grounds and determined how unused planting fields would be distributed. When a new sachem rose to power the people were supposed to have their rights renewed in his name. Most families seem to have held their privileges for long stretches of time, even generations, without any interference. As such, when commoners paid

[4] Bragdon, *Native People of Southern New England*, 141.

the sachem tribute, they framed it not as rent but a "gift" given out of one another's "love."[5]

That love was sorely tested after the colonists' arrival. Englishmen likened the sachems to kings and believed that common Indians held no legitimate claim to the land, except perhaps to their own planting fields. Thus, when colonists wanted to extinguish Indian claims they bargained with the sachems. The sachems, in turn, proved more than willing to swap land for European manufactures since the trade simultaneously strengthened their relations with the English, while displaying and circulating the goods enabled them to consolidate influence at home. Additionally, *at first* sachems did not intend to sell exclusive rights to the land, but merely permission for colonists to use the land alongside Indians (in all likelihood they probably expected tribute payments as well). Consequently, in the early years of colonization Indians often gave no second thought to hunting, fishing, and gathering plants on land the English considered their own. There was a basic cultural misunderstanding at play, but the English were not amused, and demanded compensation from Indians who "trespassed" on their "property." Worse yet for the Wampanoags, their sachems continued to sell land even after they realized the colonists' determination to have English customs hold sway. Under these conditions, Indians could not help but wonder if their loyalty to the sachems and their obligation to defend the sachemship might be incompatible.[6]

In the 1660s, Wampanoags began to protest that the sachems overstepped their bounds. Some complained directly to the English that sachems forced them off the land despite their status as "naturall Inhabitants, time out of minde."[7] Others, like the founders of Christiantown, simply refused to move. Their showdowns with colonial deed holders gradually produced two compromises widely recognized by Indian leaders and colonial buyers on the Vineyard: when a sachem intended to sell only particular use rights – for instance, the right to gather hay or graze animals – he would specify those things as well as the privileges Indians reserved. But when a sachem transferred exclusive and permanent title to the land – a sale according to the

---

[5] NCD, 3:39, 41. See also Elizabeth A. Little, "Three Kinds of Indian Deeds at Nantucket, Massachusetts," in William Cowan, ed., *Papers of the Eleventh Annual Algonquian Conference* (Ottawa: Carleton University, 1980), 62.

[6] On the colonists' likening sachems to kings, see Karen Ordahl Kupperman, *Indians and English: Facing Off in Early America* (Ithaca: Cornell University Press, 2000), 77–109. On English measures to secure their land purchases, see Edgartown Records, 1:148 ("the Indians upon the town Bounds..."); NCR, 1:3 (verso), 9 (verso; five-shilling fine). The seminal discussion of clashing Indian and English ways of land use and ownership is William Cronon, *Changes in the Land, Indians, Colonists, and the Ecology of New England* (New York: Hill and Wang, 1983).

[7] DCCR, 1:41.

English understanding – he sold "sachem rights." As part of this agreement, sachems accepted the responsibility of relocating supporters from the
"sachem right" grants. As Experience Mayhew understood it, "some Times
when the Sachems have sold Tracts of land to English men[,] they have given
[Indian] planters part of the price to satisfie them and at other times to
passifie them have given them tracts of Land to be at their own dispose."[8]
Outright grants of land by sachems to their followers to convince them to
move off other tracts sold to the English, eventually expanded the meaning
of "sachem right" to include a common Indian's exclusive claim to a parcel
of territory. In a matter of time, most of the island's "sachem rights" were
not held by sachems at all.

A second compromise emerged from some Indians' rebuff of their
sachems' offers of money, goods, or "sachem rights." These commoners
won unlikely victories in the island courts that they had "planting rights"
Englishmen would have to purchase in addition to the sachem's "sachem
rights." Samuel Mantor testified, only somewhat inaccurately because he
failed to acknowledge the fight to establish these claims, "it hath be[e]n all
ways, the practes upon this Island to b[u]y the Sachem out and also to b[u]y
the planters out of thare fields."[9]

Compromises like these contributed to the decades' old peace on Martha's
Vineyard and even kept land sales from running out of control. But after King
Philip's War several factors reopened debate over the legitimate claims of
sachem versus commoner and accelerated the sale of Indian territory. The loss
of Wampanoag life and leadership to a "sore fever" in 1690 was especially
critical.[10] Out of more than one hundred adult victims, three-quarters ranked
among the most pious Indians, leaving an indelible tear in the Wampanoag

---

[8] Deposition of Experience Mayhew [undated], BPL.

[9] Deposition of Samuel Mantor, April 20, 1758, BPL. The original meaning of sachem rights
can be gleaned from DCD, 1:126; 3:12, 13. See also NCR, 2:52. On reserved rights, see DCD,
1:116, 388, 408, 3:444. On the changing meaning of sachem rights, see Bragdon, "'Another
Tongue Brought In': An Ethnohistorical Study of Native Writings in Massachusett" (Ph.D.
diss., Brown University, 1981), 133; NE Co. MSS, 7955/2, pp. 22–3; DCD, 5:265–75. For
court cases upholding Native "planting rights," see DCCR 1:41, 52, 87; Peter R. Christoph
and Florence A. Christoph, eds., Files of the Provincial Secretary of New York during the
Administration of Governor Sir Edmund Andros, 3 vols. (Syracuse, N.Y.: Syracuse University Press, 1989), 1:138. For historical studies in agreement with the above argument
that Indians quickly grasped the English understanding of land sales, see Emerson W. Baker
"'A Scratch with a Bear's Paw': Anglo–Indian Land Deeds in Early Maine," Ethnohistory
36 (1989), 235–56; Peter S. Leavenworth, "'The Best Title That Indians Can Claime': Na-
tive Agency and Consent in the Transferal of Penacook–Pawtucket Land in the Seventeenth
Century," NEQ 72 (1999), 275–300. Cf. Little, "Daniel Spotso: A Sachem at Nantucket
Island, Massachusetts, circa 1691–1741," in Robert S. Grumet, ed., Northeastern Indian
Lives, 1632–1816 (Amherst: University of Massachusetts Press, 1996), 193–207; John Strong,
"Tribal Systems and Land Alienation: A Case Study," in William Cowan, ed., Papers of the
Sixteenth Algonquian Conference (Ottawa: Carleton University Press, 1985), 183–200.

[10] Indian Converts, 68 (quote), 86. See also, Conquests and Triumphs, 34.

social fabric. Christiantown lost ruling elder Assaquanhut (John Shohkow), deacon Micah Shohkow, and "discourser" Noquittompany.[11] So many eminent believers died on Chappaquiddick that this former wellspring of Native Christianity became known as "unchurched."[12] Meanwhile, replacement ministers, deacons, and elders proved to be poor substitutes. Veteran churchgoer Isaac Ompany criticized the new pastorate because "they too much contented themselves with only teaching and exhorting the People, without sharply reproving and rebuking of them for the Sins and Vices where in they lived."[13] Deacons Jonathan Amos and Elisha Paaonut struggled with drink, which undermined their moral influence.[14] When Keteanummin threatened the Takemmy land base during the 1660s, it was Wampanoag church leaders who rose up and forced the creation of the Christiantown reserve. Their successors were still novices when the epidemic of 1690 brought them to power, and early signs indicated they were not up to the task of using the church to rein in the sachems' abuses of power.

Equally questionable was whether the praying Indians had enough spirit left to defend their collective interests. Some fifty years earlier, Thomas Mayhew Jr. had promised Wampanoags ravaged by epidemic disease that Christianity would bring them health and peace, and the people did almost everything he asked of them. Now, when there was no turning back, sickness revived with a fury. The fever left a number of Wampanoags deaf and others in "very much sorrow" listlessly waiting to enter a less troublesome afterlife.[15] Perhaps the Wampanoags could have healed their collective psyche if they had been able to heal their bodies, but the Vineyard's growing involvement in the whaling trade exposed the island to outside diseases as never before, and the Indians suffered the consequences. Bethia Taphaus lost her husband, a twelve-year-old son, and a four-year-old daughter between 1703 and 1705, and then a fifteen-year-old son nine years later; Peter and Dorcas Ohquonhut lost a five-year-old daughter that same year and an eighteen-year-old daughter the next; Jane Ponit lost her husband and two or three children in less than a decade.[16] Overall, the number of

---

[11] *Indian Converts*, 28, 30, 84. The dead from other communities included "godly men" Matthew/Nahnehshehchat, Amos, Thomas Oonquon, Washamon, Jehu, Adam, and Samuel Kahtohkomut of Chappaquiddick, preacher Lazarus of Aquinnah, and magistrate/preacher William Lay of Nashuakemuck. See, *Indian Converts*, 24, 87, 130, 131; Cotton Mather, *Magnalia Christi Americana: or, the Ecclesiastical History of New England*, 2 vols., ed., Thomas Robinson (1702; Hartford, 1855), 2:442–3.

[12] *Indian Converts*, 34–5 (quote), 88.

[13] *Indian Converts*, 60.

[14] *Indian Converts*, 41, 56–7.

[15] *Indian Converts*, 68, 86, 174 (quote), 195–6; Increase Mather, *Ichabod...A Discourse, Shewing What Cause There is to Fear that the Glory of God is Departing from New England* (Boston, 1702), 108–9.

[16] See, *Indian Converts*, 97, 228–32, 242, 244–7, 251–4.

Vineyard Wampanoags dropped from some 1,500 in 1674 to approximately 956 in 1698 to between 500 and 600 around 1740.[17] "The Indians," Experience Mayhew put it coldly, "are every where decreasing of which [if] I should give you an account of the Occasions it would make my Letter to[o] proli[x]."[18]

Watching good Christians suffer miserable ends plunged many Indians into a depressing meditation on their role in this tragedy. From his deathbed in 1712, Japheth Hannit admonished his flock: "You bring Trouble on the People . . . by your Miscarriages. They procure Distempers & all other Chastisement from the Great God . . . God hath repeated his Chastisements upon us especially by Sickness . . . Yet only how full are all our Towns of Sin!"[19] His words did not fall on deaf ears to judge from marginalia in a Native-language Bible circulated among several Wampanoag readers during the early eighteenth century. "Pitiful people [are] we," one person wrote, "it is not good." Another groaned, "I am not able to defend myself from the happenings of the world." And then a lonely confession: "I am a pitiful man . . . we have disease in the whole world because we do not" – symbolic of the magnitude of the problem, the writer's words suddenly cut off.[20] Clearly, some Wampanoags believed they were responsible for their own disasters. In the early years of the Mayhew mission the same realization had galvanized the praying Indians. This time, however, it weakened their collective will because they saw their best had not been good enough. Such despair, coupled with the uninspiring state of Indian churches, left the Wampanoags in too poor a condition to mount an energetic defense of their land.

Yet the need was greater than ever, for the sachems, with their finances stretched to the breaking point, were anxious to sell. Shrinking resources and the dictates of Indian fashion meant that sachems now bought large amounts of clothes and provisions from colonial merchants, mostly on credit.[21] A few sachems accumulated more debt by helping favorites to pay off their

---

[17] "Historical Collections," 205 (assuming five members to each family); "Indian Visitation," 131–3; Increase Mather, *A LETTER, About the Present State of Christianity; among the christianized INDIANS of New England* (Boston, 1705), 5.

[18] Experience Mayhew to Anonymous, July 20, 1741, Mayhew Papers.

[19] NE Co. MSS, 7957, p. 9.

[20] *Native Writings*, 1:423, 431, 437.

[21] Peter A. Thomas, "Contrastive Subsistence Strategies and Land Use as Factors for Understanding Indian–White Relations in New England," *Ethnohistory* 23 (1976), 1–18; Cronon, *Changes in the Land*; Bragdon, "Native Economy on Eighteenth-Century Martha's Vineyard and Nantucket," in William Cowan, ed., *Actes du Dix-Septième Congrès des Algonquinistes* (Ottawa: Carleton University Press, 1986), 27–42; Robert E. Gradie, "New England Indians and Colonizing Pigs," *Papers of the Fifteenth Algonquian Conference*, ed. William Cowan (Ottawa: Carleton University Press, 1984), 147–69; Virginia DeJohn Anderson, "King Philip's Herds: Indians, Colonists, and the Problem of Livestock in Early New England," *WMQ* 51 (1994), 601–24.

FIGURE 4. Ninigret II, ca. 1681, Sachem of Eastern Niantics/Narragansetts of Rhode Island. This portrait hints at the financial pressures on Vineyard sachems to sell land. Almost all of Ninigret's clothing and jewelry in this portrait was English-made: his mantle, breechclout, leggings, and legging ties were of manufactured cloth; the top three medallions of his wampum necklace were metal; even his wampum beads, the sole item of Indian manufacture, were produced using metal drills. Generally Indians purchased such goods from colonists on credit, but were often unable to meet their debts. As Christians, the Vineyard Wampanoags tended to dress in English garb and thus ran up even higher bills with colonial merchants. Courtesy of the Art Museum of the Rhode Island School of Design.

own bills, and by purchasing livestock to lend out for plowing.[22] Already before 1690, sachems had been unable to meet these costs, but the sudden rise in disease made things worse by sweeping away their tribute payers. The only way to sustain the sachem's traditional generosity was to sell recently depopulated lands and more. Even the best-intentioned leaders found the lure impossible to resist.[23]

There are hints that sachems had grown estranged from their followers after King Philip's War, which must have eased their consciences at the bargaining table. Whereas earlier sachems like Tawanquatuck and Mittark were leading Christians, by the 1680s only one, Wompamog of Sengekontacket, was a force in the praying ranks. The reasons for this development are unclear. Perhaps the next generation resented that their fathers had relinquished the sachem's prerogatives. Before the Wampanoags' adoption of Christianity and submission to the crown, sachems had been essential to the governance and identity of their communities. Now the Wampanoags defined themselves in part through their churches and relied upon ministers and magistrates for leadership. Sachems were increasingly marginal to public life and, as their behavior would suggest, less responsive to their people.

A surge in colonial demand was a final impetus to Indian land sales. Vineyard Indians had outnumbered Englishmen by as many as 1,500 to 225 on the eve of King Philip's War, but by 1720 their numbers were equal at approximately 800 each, and by the 1750s there were only some 400 Natives against more than 1,900 colonists (see Appendix A). This growing English population needed woodland and tillage, but their greatest pressure on Indian territory was for livestock pasture because the slave plantations of the West Indies and especially the whaling fleet represented expanding markets for animal products like wool clothing, meat, and beasts of burden.[24] King

[22] Suffolk Files #12289 (Testimony of Benjamin Hawes, Benjamin Norton, and Thomas Pease); Elizabeth Little, "Probate Records of Nantucket Indians," *Nantucket Algonquian Studies* 2 (Nantucket, Mass.: Nantucket Historical Association, 1980), 19–21; Little and Marie Sussek, eds., "Index to Mary Starbuck's Account Book with the Indians," *Nantucket Algonquian Studies* 5 (Nantucket, Mass.: Nantucket Historical Association, 1981), 10–11.

[23] For studies of the Indians' credit crunch, see Thomas, "In the Maelstrom of Change: The Indian Trade and Cultural Process in the Middle Connecticut River Valley, 1635–1665" (Ph.D. diss., University of Massachusetts, Amherst, 1979), chap. 6; Neal Salisbury, "Social Relationships on a Moving Frontier: Natives and Settlers in Southern New England, 1638–1675," *MNE* 33 (1987), 89–98; Daniel Vickers, "The First Whalemen of Nantucket," *WMQ* 40 (1983), 560–83; Bragdon, "Native Economy."

[24] On the colonists' "great want of wood," see DCD, 1:291 (quote), and Cronon, *Changes in the Land*, chap. 6. On the trade, see Bernard Bailyn, *The New England Merchants in the Seventeenth Century* (Cambridge, Mass.: Harvard University Press, 1955), chaps. 3–4; Richard Pares, *Yankees and Creoles: The Trade between North America and the West Indies before the American Revolution* (Cambridge, Mass.: Harvard University Press, 1956); Stephen Innes, *Creating the Commonwealth: The Economic Culture of Puritan New England* (New York: W. W. Norton, 1995), 280–1, 285–7, 295–7; Carl Bridenbaugh, *Fat Mutton and Liberty of Conscience: Society in Rhode Island, 1636–1690* (Providence, R.I.: Brown

Philip's War had shattered Indian military might, so there were few practical reasons for Englishmen not to engross Indian land, especially when the sachems were willing to oblige them.

The Vineyard Wampanoags all used the distinction between "sachem rights" and "planting rights" to debate the issue of land sales, and they all suffered from weakened leadership and morale, indebted sachems, and unyielding English encroachment. Yet a look at the four main Vineyard sachemships, Takemmy, Nunnepog, Aquinnah, and Chappaquiddick, and some of their smaller villages, illustrates that not every community addressed the land-sale crisis in the same way or with the same effectiveness. Some failed miserably, but the relative success of others demonstrates that even in a time of restricted choices Indians could influence the future of their homelands.

II

Takemmy was the first contested sachemship on Martha's Vineyard after King Philip's War despite the 1669 Christiantown agreement. By 1682 Thomas Mayhew Sr. was dead, sachem Keteanummin was in debt, and the English town of Tisbury had lifted an earlier ban on the purchase of Indian land without official consent.[25] That same year Keteanummin began violating his promises with impunity, beginning with a grant off Tisbury Great Pond to the unsavory Simon Athearn, who had a lengthy record of abusing Indians and buying their territory illegally.[26] Then Keteanummin breached the praying town line in a sale to Isaac Chase, sparking what one colonist remembered as "a great contest between Josias [Keteanummin] Indian sachem and the Christian Indians, so called about the title of some land called the lands of the Christian Town."[27]

Since Keteanummin showed no heart for defending the sachemship, his people seized the responsibility themselves, beginning with the "Red Ground" that Keteanummin had sold in the early 1670s to William Rogers and Athearn. In 1688, Athearn's tenant, John Hillman, reported that several praying Indians entered his enclosure and ran "a line through his Corn

---

University Press, 1974), chap. 3. and pp. 120–6; Margaret Ellen Newell, *From Dependency to Independence: Economic Revolution in New England* (Ithaca, N.Y.: Cornell University Press, 1998), chaps. 4–5. On whaling, see Alexander Starbuck, *History of the American Whale Fishery: From its Earliest Inception to the Year 1876*, 2 vols. (1878; New York: Argosy-Antiquarian, 1964); Daniel Vickers, "Maritime Labor in Colonial Massachusetts: A Case Study of the Essex County Cod Fishery and the Whaling Industry of Nantucket, 1630–1775" (Ph.D. diss., Princeton University, 1981).

[25] *Records of the Town of Tisbury, Mass., Beginning June 29, 1669, and Ending May 16, 1864* (Boston, 1903), 15.

[26] DCD, 1:299, 302; Suffolk Files #4714; Charles E. Banks, Dukes County Court Records, Transcriptions, p. 10, NEHGS. On Athearn's troubled past, see DCCR, 1:9, 12, 17, 31, 37; *Records of the Town of Tisbury*, 10–11.

[27] Suffolk Files, #3834.

field...and asserted the lands on the Northerly side of the said line to be
theirs." To Hillman's relief, after the Indians marked their bounds, they said
that because he was "a poor man they would not disturb him during the
time he had hired said farm."[28] Takemmy was equally generous to William
Rogers, permitting "that he and his might live upon the said land, but might
not sell it, but [it] should remain theirs when he or his children should remove off from it."[29] In other words, Rogers was welcome to stay so long as
he agreed that, consistent with Wampanoag custom, his land would revert
to the community once it was no longer planted. Athearn received no such
leniency, not only because of his checkered history, but because he had recently built a house on the Indians' land and invited Keteanummin to live
there in an effort to strengthen his title. He must have congratulated himself
after Takemmy complained to Thomas Mayhew (grandson of the old proprietor) about the house, only to be told that the sachem "might live theare
as well as any other Indian."[30]

Mayhew's response alerted the Indians that it would take a lawsuit, not
informal persuasion, to contest Athearn's purchase, and yet none of them had
courtroom experience. Fortunately, they were able to enlist outside help in
the form of settler John Pease. In accordance with Pease's advice, the Indians
deliberately gathered together several witnesses, publicly warned Athearn
"to be gone off their Land for they claimed it to be theirs," announced
their intention to evict him, and then acted on their threats. Afterwards,
Pease interviewed eyewitnesses and wrote down their accounts. Through
this painstaking work, the praying Indians and their colonial ally ensured
that they would control courtroom evidence.[31]

Pease also counseled the Wampanoags about how to establish an English
usufruct right – the right of use – to the disputed territory, such as by moving
into Athearn's house, building *wetus* in the surrounding fields, and having
Pease plow and plant the territory anew.[32] Pease knew one of the reasons
colonists had been able to justify seizing unplanted Wampanoag land was
that Indians did not use it in ways the English honored. Generally, they did
not keep livestock, apart from the Indian elite's few cows, hogs, and sheep,
and since these minor holdings did not require huge swaths of pasture, the
Natives had not stripped their lands of trees and lined the boundaries with
fences. Nor had they taken up the plow, with perhaps a few minor exceptions.
Most Wampanoags were still committed to feeding themselves through hoe
agriculture, shellfish and plant gathering, hunting, and, increasingly, wage

[28] Suffolk Files, #4714, p. 127.
[29] Suffolk Files, #4714, p. 127.
[30] Suffolk Files, #4974, p. 12.
[31] Suffolk Files, #4714, 4974.
[32] Suffolk Files, #4714; Deposition of Jabez Athearn, Misc. Bound MSS, MHS, copy in Segel,
     Pierce, Montorosso Collection: Wampanoag Genealogy and Related Documents, Box 1,
     MVHS.

work. Incidents like the contest for the Red Ground taught them of the need to establish an English usufruct claim to the land in order to protect it from the sachem and his colonial grantees.

Keteanummin refused to be denied despite his people's efforts. Colonist William Parlow recalled that the Takemmy Wampanoags, anticipating trouble, gave him an official copy of the Christiantown agreement for safekeeping while they prepared for their lawsuit. As if on cue, shortly Keteanummin appeared to demand the paper:

> The said sachem came to me and desired me to burn said deed or writing, saying that if I would do it he would give me some of the land, but I refusing said I would not undo those praying Indians to whom it was granted. The sachem replied saying it may be you think I will give you but a little piece. Then I said how much will you give me if I burn the deed. He then answered I will give you half. Then I told him he had no love for the Christians and I will not do it if you will give me all of it.[33]

In frustration, Keteanummin demolished the *wetus* his people had erected on the Red Ground, prompting yet another stream of litigation that flowed up and down the justice system for years and cost each side handsomely in attorney bills, court fees, and travel expenses.[34] Initially, the praying Indians lost one trial after another, but eventually they secured legal assistance from the reputable Matthew Mayhew and had all cases settled in their favor.[35] However, along the way the Natives accumulated court costs almost beyond their ability to pay, thereby putting the land they were trying to save in further peril. To restore their coffers and the peace of the sachemship, Christiantown met with Keteanummin one final time and pleaded with him to halt his land sales.

The sachem believed he had not "don[e] anything out of the Indian custom." He alienated sachemship land, he explained, only because his people failed to pay him enough tribute. He had agreed in 1669 to seal off Christiantown because the praying Indians pledged "that they should give twenty shillings every year to me their sachem." They had not fulfilled their part of the bargain and now "being grown old and poor not able to work [I] promised to sell the land to the English, for my maintenance." For a time he had protected his followers by helping them to pay off court fines and the like. What was the incentive for a sachem to be so generous if his people did not reciprocate? Moreover, the men behind the original Christiantown agreement were gone: "my uncle pamick died & his sons are dead &

[33] Suffolk Files, # 3834, p. 134.

[34] DCCR, 1:101, 104; Suffolk Files, #4714, 4974.

[35] DCCR, 1:101, 104; RSCJ, pp. 195, 236–7, 238, 296, 298; Mass. Archives, 31:19; Testimony of Thomas Mayhew, Sept. 2, 1698, Apology of Simon Athearn, April 2, 1700, and Abigail Pease, Isaac Ompany, Job Sooamana, and Tiase, appointment of atty., March 12, 1700/1701, Misc. Bound MSS, MHS.

nonoussa & taqnannum & poxsim are all dead."[36] As far as Keteanummin was concerned, so were his obligations to them.

Nevertheless, Keteanummin knew that his actions had emptied the title
"sachem" of most of its legitimacy, and perhaps fearing that this would be his
eldest son, Zachariah Pooskin's, inheritance, reluctantly he made amends.
"Every man have made much trouble about land I have sold to the English,"
he acknowledged, "and some men say that the praying Indians must have
their town I formerly gave them." To that end, the elderly sachem returned
the money he had received from his illegal land sales and declared, once
again, that the mile square should remain inviolable "forever."[37] He even
went so far as to swear that he would never alienate the remaining half of
Takemmy.[38]

By 1701 Keteanummin was dead and his younger son, Alexander, wasted
no time selling his father's title to the unrelenting Simon Athearn even though
he had not been recognized as sachem. As Sam Nahomon remembered it,
Athearn immediately "declared himself Sachem" and then raised "a fence
upon som[e] part of the Sachemship on the north side of the Island." Eventually the Massachusetts legislature negated this purchase, but in the meantime all eyes turned to Zachariah Pooskin to protect the forty-eight praying
Indians. Although the rules of succession were not hard and fast, generally the sachem's mantle passed to his eldest son. The firstborn could be
rejected, though, if the community judged him inadequate. Accordingly,
in January of 1702, nineteen church officials, magistrates, and other leading figures met with Pooskin to have him address their "fear for the security, tranquillity, and peace of that sachemship, and the protecting of
the possessions and matters that pertain to that from now on." No one
recorded Pooskin's answer, but it was convincing enough to persuade the
council to declare him their sachem and acknowledge that he "owns all
Takemmeh."[39]

Luckily for Christiantown, Pooskin transcended his father's impoverished
example. First, he gathered up his followers and drove Athearn off the
Indians' land, telling him "he had not business there." Then the sachem
twice promised that Christiantown's boundaries should remain inviolate and

---

[36] DCD, 1:357.

[37] DCD, 1:357. Little, "Daniel Spotso," 204, suggests that even as late as the eighteenth century,
when New England Indians used "forever" they actually meant "for my lifetime." Her case
can be argued either way, but I find it exceedingly difficult to believe that after several decades
of land deals and related lawsuits with the English, Natives still misunderstood the meaning
of such terminology in the context of colonial jurisprudence.

[38] Suffolk Files, #4974, p. 5; DCD, 1:379.

[39] DCD 1:132; *Native Writings*, 1:134–5 ("we fear for the security"); Suffolk Files #69495
("declared himself Sachem"); Mass. Archives, 31:19; "Indian Visitation," 131 (population
figure); Daniel R. Mandell, *Behind the Frontier: Indians in Eighteenth-Century Eastern
Massachusetts* (Lincoln: University of Nebraska Press, 1996), 63–4.

put his words to paper. But the clearest sign of Pooskin's fidelity came on August 18, 1702. In a move undoubtedly supported by the maligned people of Takemmy, he transferred almost all his sachem rights to the praying Indians' leaders "and their associates in the Christian religion and Successors for ever," retaining only his annual twenty-shilling tribute, a personal forty-acre parcel, and a preemptive claim to all beached whales. From this point forward the common Indians managed the sachemship and its lands by a "Legall Town meeting" of family representatives replete with moderator and clerk. In effect, the office of sachem was defunct in Takemmy.[40]

Yet Keteanummin's ghost lingered in the form of unregistered deeds issued after his promise to halt all land sales.[41] In 1717, colonists began exhibiting the dubious papers and demanding their execution, which breathed new life into the Indians' land sale troubles. The Natives' first response was to choose three "agents" – minister and deacon Zachariah Papamick, preacher Josiah Pattompan, and ruling elder Thomas Paul – to file suit, but after losing a case at the Superior Court and feeling the financial strain, they shifted to a two-pronged strategy aimed at damage control.[42] They acquiesced to the most determined colonial grantees, giving up smaller tracts of land than the English claimed in exchange for nominal sums. Then they used their planting rights to obstruct the titles of less imposing colonists. As Englishman Samuel Mantor explained, his father bought Christiantown land in 1694, but "the Natives [who] lived upon said Land could not be removed of[f]: for about thirty years . . . and I have been obliged to b[u]y the Natives out of said Land at a Dear Rate before I could come at the Improvement of the Land[.] all I had [was] the Sachem Right and further I am knowing to other English men that has ben obliged to b[u]y out the planters as I have Don[e]."[43]

[40] DCD, 1:123 ("associates in the Christian religion"), 4:173, 6:97 ("Legall Town meeting"), 8:196; Suffolk Files, #43637, p. 81, #69495 ("had no business there"); Mass. Archives, 31:19; *Native Writings*, 1:134–5; Bragdon, "'Another Tongue Brought In'," 113.

[41] Land sales that took place after the sachem's declaration can be found in DCD, 1:33, 3:293; FNPR, 1:312; and *Records of the Town of Tisbury*, 41. On the legalities of deed registration, see Mark DeWolfe Howe, "The Recording of Deeds in the Colony of Massachusetts Bay," *Boston University Law Review* 28 (1948), 1–5; David T. Konig, "Community Custom and the Common Law: Social Change and the Development of Land Law in Seventeenth-Century Massachusetts," *American Journal of Legal History*, 18 (1974), 137–48.

[42] On the Takemmy Indians' lawsuits during this period, see, DCCR, 1:240, 247, 248; Suffolk Files #12248, 23637, 24769; DCD, 3:129, 133, 134, 154; 4:317; Thomas Paul et al. v. Ebenezar Rogers, Superior Court of Judicature at Plymouth, April 29, 1718, catalogued as Dukes County Superior Court Records, File 1, NEHGS; DCCF, Box 4, File 5, Oct. 1735; Box 174A, Env. 42: Documents dated April 29, 1735, March 1736, and March 11, 1737, MVHS; E. Rogers v. A. Ianoxso Jr., April 1735, Rogers v. Ianoxso, March 12, 1736, and Rogers v. Ianoxso, March 11, 1738, Force Papers; Bond Receipt for Ebenezar Paul, January 18, 1734, Box 5S, Env. 3, and Proceedings of the Inferiour Court of Common Pleas, Oct. 1743, Box 5S, Env. 8, MVHS; NE Co. MSS, 7953, p. 48 (verso). On later suits, see DCCP, 1730–1755, p. 822.

[43] Testimony of Samuel Mantor, April 20, 1758, BPL.

The Christiantown Wampanoags' defense of their territory had been imperfect, but three factors ensured that they still commanded a village-sized
area. First, the 1669 agreement slowed Keteanummin's sales and established
a legal basis for a permanent Native claim to at least one square mile of
Takemmy. Second, the praying Indians recruited English advocates to help
them compete in the colonial legal system.[44] Third, and most important,
Christiantown eliminated the office of sachem so no leader could shred
the paper barrier the Indians had raised around themselves. Now a town
meeting of proprietors, not just a single individual, took responsibility for
managing land sales. Compared to greater Takemmy, where the people were
left with only a small tract appropriately named "Deep Bottom," Christiantown was a beacon of stability.[45] It would remain the Indian place in
Takemmy for the next century largely because of decisions made during this
period.

III

Across the island, the Wampanoags of Nunnepog also struggled to keep
their leaders from eviscerating the homeland. Since the 1640s, the Nunnepogs' proximity to Edgartown had required them to fend off land-hungry
colonists, but sachem Tawanquatuck's granddaughter and successor, Wunnattuhquanmow, raised the struggle to new heights by selling land at least
eight times between 1670 and 1690 in her core area along the coastal ponds
of the southeast part of the island.[46] In recompense to her displaced followers, she distributed fee-simple "sachem rights," which several Indians
promptly recorded. "He owns it and forever and his posterity firmly own
it," the sunksquaw and her husband Washamon promised in a 1687 grant
to John Momonaquem. "We and our posterity shall not have the power to
alter it. This is firm. And no one shall have the power to alter it. Because I
am a sachem."[47]

---

[44] For similar emphases on Indians using negotiated land titles and colonial advocates to carve
out a space for themselves in areas dominated by colonists, see James H. Merrell, *The Indians'
New World: Catawbas and Their Neighbors from European Contact Through the Era of
Removal* (New York: W. W. Norton for the Institute of Early American History and Culture,
1991), 106, 212; Wendy B. St. Jean, "Inventing Guardianship: The Mohegan Indians and
Their 'Protectors,'" *NEQ* 72 (1999), 362–87.

[45] Takemmy land sales are documented in DCD, 1:30, 33, 117, 129, 170, 182, 214, 257, 271,
273, 280, 299, 302, 304, 305, 307, 316, 328, 343, 355, 375, 467; 2:24, 29, 49, 60, 65, 138,
218, 303; 3:108b, 116, 140, 141, 314, 351; 4:183, 268, 279; 5:53, 323, 384; 6:216–17, 345;
17:489–91; Scrapbook of Deeds, p. 87, and Box 130B, MVHS; *Records of the Town of
Tisbury*, 11, 21, 24, 25, 33. Material relating to Deep Bottom is conveniently gathered in
*Report of the Commissioners to Determine the Title of Certain Land Claimed by Indians,
At Deep Bottom, in the Town of Tisbury, on the Island of Martha's Vineyard, Under the
Resolve of May 17, 1855* (Boston, 1856).

[46] DCD, 1:257, 273, 285, 316, 352; 3:27; 4:127; NCR, 2:52, 58.

[47] *Native Writings*, 1:106–7 (quote), 108–9, 129–31.

Wunnattuhquanmow was true to her word, but Indian Isaac Tocamo was waiting to pounce on the new market in these sachem right grants. Within a few short years, he bought up at least half a dozen plots in Nunnepog plus a handful more elsewhere on the island. Perhaps he was trying to set himself up as a sachem by allowing Indians to remain on these lands in exchange for their loyalty and tribute. However, all of this would have changed with his eccentric 1709 will. Tocamo specified that after the death of his wife, half of his estate should pass to the Seventh Day Baptist churches of Charlestown and Westerly, Rhode Island, where he worshipped. The other half was to go to Rhode Islanders Peter Tabor Jr. and Thomas Hilcox.[48] With the execution of Tocamo's will, a sizable portion of Nunnepog passed into English hands.

Wampanoag deaths from disease postponed any land shortage, but the loss of tribute was a major blow to Wunnattuhquanmow's and Washamon's finances and thus an impetus to more land sales. In 1698, Nunnepog's population stood at a paltry eighty-four, meaning that perhaps only seventeen households paid the sachems tribute, all at a time when years of credit purchases and lawsuits had put the couple in debt to island merchants and courts.[49] Even before the epidemic, Wunnattuhquanmow had been forced to sell land to fend off her creditors. Now she was mired in a truly impossible situation. She had to sustain a sachem's generosity in order to command her people's loyalty, but she no longer received enough tribute to allow her to show such grace. She had to keep the English at bay in order to fulfill her job of defending the sachemship, but selling them land was the only way she could raise money to treat her supporters and provide them with loans. Thus, like her contemporary, Keteanummin, she conceived of no other choice than to market her inheritance. Even her rights to beached whales and other sea treasure, a primary symbol of her sachem status, went up for sale.[50]

Whatever resentment the people of Nunnepog felt about their shrinking territory, they never moved to unseat the sachem in favor of a community-wide council or to establish a protected praying Indian reserve like Christiantown or Mashpee. The 1690 epidemic killed off many of Nunnepog's church leaders and demoralized the rest, men who otherwise might have led a resistance. Then the Nunnepogs' meetinghouse burned down and the pastorate went unfilled for many years, thus giving disaffected Christians yet another reason to miss the Sunday meeting with all of its political functions.[51]

---

[48] DCP, 1:35. For the purchases of Tocamo (also spelled Tecamo, Takemen, Tuhkemme, Tuhkemen, and Tackomysee), see DCCR, 1:31, 81, 113; 2:71, 337; DCD, 2:335, 334; *Native Writings*, 1:143. On Newport's Seventh Day Bapists, see Richard L. Bushman, *From Puritan to Yankee: Character and the Social Order in Connecticut, 1690–1765* (Cambridge, Mass.: Harvard University Press, 1967), 164; Jon Butler, *Awash in a Sea of Faith: Christianizing the American People* (Cambridge, Mass.: Harvard University Press, 1990), 174.

[49] "Indian Visitation," 131–3; DCCR, 1:97.

[50] DCD, 1:108, 208; 3:98, 444; Little and J. Clinton Andrews, "Drift Whales at Nantucket: The Gift of Moshup," *MNE* 23 (1982), 17–38.

[51] *Indian Converts*, 116–17, 119.

The Nunnepogs had been the first Wampanoags to trust that the Christian God would carry them through their trials, but the community's endless suffering after King Philip's War undermined their faith. The people gave up and turned inward, choosing to manage their own family plots instead of forging a corporate strategy to preserve the entire sachemship. Weak as they were together, they were even more vulnerable alone. In a cruel refrain to their sachem's struggles, by the middle of the eighteenth century, most of the Nunnepog Wampanoags had fallen prey to store debts and court fines and abandoned themselves to the vagaries of the land market.[52]

By the end of her life, Wunnattuhquanmow was a sachem only in name. She had not been a defender of the sachemship but a steward to direct its end. Perhaps appropriately, neither her death nor her successor's received any official notice. The only reason that Nunnepog and "sachem" were ever mentioned in the same breath again was that Sarah Gilbert, the daughter of Peter Mortal (Tawanquatuck's one-time choice as heir), decided in 1742 to pass on her "sachem rights" to her sons Joseph and Peter Gilbert. She clearly meant "sachem rights" in the traditional sense of the term, rather than just a commoner's land title, since her claims stretched between Edgartown Pond and Oyster Pond, most of which Indians no longer possessed. The sons, though, realized they had inherited an anachronism. Peter quietly served as pastor to the east end Indians while Joseph last appeared in 1755 on a list of Indians receiving poor relief. Neither of them bothered to identify themselves as sachems at any point in their lives.[53]

Things were hardly better in the Nunnepog subsachemship of Sengekontacket. By the late seventeenth century, this village-sized area fell under the direction of Ohkohtonat and his son, Wompamog (or Mr. Sam), one of the first Christian Indians and eventually a preacher in his own right.[54] Edgartown colonists greedily eyed the rich salt grasses of their territory, which were ideal for grazing livestock, but for years the sachems were able to keep them at arm's length. The only settler to gain a foothold in the sachemship before the 1680s was John Dagget, who obtained a 500-acre tract later known as "the Farm," and who, not coincidentally, was the father of Joseph Dagget, the lone Vineyard colonist to have married a Wampanoag.[55]

---

[52] DCD, 2:52; 3:10, 33; 4:33; 6:216–17, 227, 230, 231.

[53] Deeds, January 25 and 29, 1742, Box 130B, MVHS; Thomas Walcut Papers, 1671–1866, MHS, January 25, 1742. On Joseph Gilbert Sr., see "Disbursements to the Indian Poor," p. 4, Experience Mayhew Papers, MHS. In 1669, Tawanquatuck chose Peter Mortal as his successor and granted him part of his estate, but this was the last time Mortal appeared in the historical record. See Edgartown Records, 1:83.

[54] *Indian Converts*, 73–4.

[55] DCD, 1:289, 2:253; Charles Edward Banks, *The History of Martha's Vineyard, Dukes County, Massachusetts*, 3 vols. (Boston: George H. Dean, 1911), 2:Annals of West Tisbury:44–5.

Yet English encroachment made rapid progress after King Philip's War. In 1683, the two sachems permitted Indian Thomas Sissetom to sell twenty acres of land to Thomas Daggett.[56] Six years later, Wompamog's sister Alice and her husband mortgaged one hundred acres to Thomas Harlock then failed to pay their £8 debt. Harlock foreclosed and immediately sold his claim to Joseph Daggett. Initially Wompamog refused to permit the conveyance, but after much wrangling, he granted Daggett fifteen acres of land and use rights to Sengkontacket's clay.[57] Wompamog contained his losses but at the cost of setting a dangerous precedent.

The tribute Wompamog received from Sengekontacket's twenty-five or so families was not enough to meet his expenses, and therefore sometime in the 1690s he took his sister's lead and mortgaged land to Samuel Sarson.[58] Needing money and quick, Wompamog realized that he could sell his people the same kinds of "sachem rights" other Indian leaders had been distributing for free to quell opposition to their land sales. Colonist John Norton recalled the moment: "Tokhegun an Indian of said Neck Paid Part of the Money . . . Mortgaged by the Sachim . . . and that he hath understood that said teckhigun had a Lott of Land Laid out to him for the money he paid."[59] Wampanoags throughout Sengekontacket joined Tokhegun in buying fee-simple "shares" from their cash-starved leader and shortly they too were at the mercy of creditors and the courts. By 1710 Vineyarders referred to Indian and English "halves" of the neck.[60] But even this boundary broke down as one family after another lost their lands to poverty.[61] As Indians on the mainland were about to discover, once they divided their communities into individually owned tracts, it was only a matter of time before the English took possession.[62]

---

[56] DCD, 1:15.

[57] DCD, 1:176. Alice's husband, Thomas Tyler, was a Massachusett Indian from Agawam (Ipswich) on the mainland. Thus, his Vineyard business is documented in Sidney Perley, ed., *The Indian Land Titles of Essex County, Massachusetts* (Salem, Mass., 1912), 86–7.

[58] "Indian Visitation," 132; DCD, 5:304–5.

[59] DCD, 5:304–5. See also *Native Writings*, 1:204–5.

[60] DCD, 1:104, 177, 187, 294; 2:221, 285, 334; 3:25, 271; 5:413; 7:506; 10:44; Testimonial of Isaac Norton, Eighteenth and Nineteenth-Century Misc. Docs., Box 3S, MVHS. There is some evidence to suggest that this division took place in 1685, since Edgartown Records, 1:88, mentions that the colonists' meeting "voted that the Lands in this Town Ship that the Indians Now Live upon is to be Devided." However, it is entirely unclear whether this was just an assignment of shares to English proprietors, rather than an actual division of land. There are several examples of Vineyard investors agreeing among themselves about how they would distribute certain tracts of Native territory long before they had actually possessed them. See, for instance, DCD, 4:21–2.

[61] For breaches of the division line between 1710 and 1750, see DCD, 3:266, 311, 434; 5:302; 6:22, 114, 492, 517; 7:37, 38, 115–16, 137, 193, 239, 245, 246–7, 293, 404, 407, 503; 8:619; Scrapbook of Deeds, pp. 25, 39, MVHS; Box 130B (document of 1744), MVHS.

[62] Jean M. O'Brien, *Dispossession by Degrees: Indian Land and Identity in Natick, Massachusetts, 1650–1790* (New York: Cambridge University Press, 1997), 101–15, 184.

Some families retained their land, but they did so without the aid of
a sachem, council, or colonial authorities. Although Wompamog was a
preacher and his supporters were once active churchgoers, Sengekontacket
never organized into a formally recognized praying town reserve. Nor, for
that matter, did the people request English authorities to come to their aid,
perhaps because they lacked the figures to head such a campaign. By the
time Wompamog's heir, Betty Josnin, entered the historical record in 1716,
she lived with her husband in Bridgewater on the Massachusetts mainland
and was in the process of selling off her Vineyard claims. Her largest pur-
chaser, Sengekontacket's magistrate John Talman (or Tolman), had the tal-
ent and reputation to wear the sachem's mantle, but he was so plagued
by debt that he resorted to buying land cheap from Indians to sell dear to
colonists.[63] It was a pattern that his heirs and nephews, Peter and James,
Talman Jr., mimicked until they left for Sengekontacket or Aquinnah rather
than live like so many of their kinsmen, landless on the edge of a colonial
town.[64]

IV

The 500 or so Wampanoags in the sachemship of Aquinnah and the bordering territory of Nashuakemuck were less overwhelmed by colonial encroachment than Indians elsewhere on Martha's Vineyard.[65] Tucked into
the southwest corner of the island, they had a buffer of some fifteen miles
between them and the core English settlement of Edgartown, and perhaps
half that distance between them and the second colonial town of Tisbury.
Nevertheless, a series of bargains enacted far from their watchful eyes confronted them with challenges no other Indians would relish. First, on April
25, 1685, New York's royal governor, Thomas Dongan, created the Manor
of Martha's Vineyard out of Thomas Mayhew Sr.'s preexisting Manor of
Tisbury, and appointed Matthew Mayhew lord. Then Mayhew sold his
new manorial rights back to Dongan for £200, thereby allowing Dongan
to circumvent restrictions against granting himself such privileges.[66] The
dance continued as Dongan hired Mayhew to serve as his agent to purchase Wampanoag lands and secure English tenants. Within five years, the
minor sachem John Philip had signed away his claims to Squibnocket and

[63] DCD, 6:465; *Native Writings*, 1:148–9. On Talman's public service, see CPGNE, December
    entries between 1729 and 1740; New England Company, Ledger, p. 34, MHS. On his sales
    and other purchases see DCD, 2:352; 4:304, 405–6; 6:114, 447–8; 7:109–10; *Native Writings*,
    1:64–5. For his debts, see DCP, 1:107, 134–5, 148–9; 3:28–31; DCCP, 1730–55, 791, 797.
[64] On the sales and purchases of James Jr. and Peter, see DCD, 6:307; 7:3–4, 5–6, 38, 41, 47,
    49–50, 51–2, 115–16, 124, 125–6, 246–7, 293, 404, 503; Scrapbook of Deeds, p. 63, MVHS.
[65] "Indian Visitation," pp. 131–3, put the 1698 population of Nashuakemuck at 231, and the
    number of "Christians" at Aquinnah/Gay Head at 260. Samuel Sewall, in NE Co. MSS,
    7955/1, pp. 13–14, put the number of Aquinnah families at "above Fifty."
[66] DCD, 1:241–47; NE Co. MSS, 8003.

Noman's Land island to Matthew and Thomas Mayhew III.[67] Not to be outdone, Aquinnah sachem Joseph Mittark, in a deed apparently signed in New York in May of 1687, granted Dongan all of his territory in exchange for just £30.[68]

These deals were a shocking demonstration of how papers drawn in distant colonial capitals, without any Native witnesses, could directly affect Indian village life. Matthew Mayhew, acting as Dongan's attorney, began assigning manor Indians in Nashuakemuck forty-acre lots and ordering them to acknowledge the governor "as their Lord and Sachim."[69] This new sachem proved to be more like Keteanummin than Wampanoag leaders of old. No sooner had Mayhew assigned the Natives land than he bought out several of them, seized tracts that had been only temporarily vacated, and turned an approvingly blind eye as his colonial tenants drove many of the remaining Indians away.[70] "I have cause to be troubled by the English of nashoakemok," Jonathan Soomanan complained, "because they made me go away from thence in the winter in a very cold time & when the snow was almost up to my knees with my house & familie as if they ware about to kill me, for the Indians don't use to move there houses in the winter its contrary to our custome."[71] It is unlikely that Joseph Mittark transferred his sachemship to Dongan with this in mind. Judging from similar deals struck by mainland sachems, his intent was to enlist New York to *defend* Wampanoag territory from the unpredictable Englishmen of the island.[72] If so, he had seriously miscalculated and his followers were not in a forgiving mood.

Troubles of this sort were new for the Aquinnah Wampanoags, but they had learned from other Vineyard sachemships of the need to frame their response in legal terms the colonists would recognize. As such, they produced a tattered paper recording a speech by Joseph Mittark's deceased father that called the entire legitimacy of Dongan's purchase into question. Dated September 11, 1681, a translation of the document read

I am Muttaak, sachem of Gay Head and Nashaquitsa as far as Wanemessit. Know this all people. I muttaak and my chief men and my children and my people, these are our lands. forever we own them, and our posterity forever shall own them.

[67] DCD, 1:126, 128, 137.

[68] DCD, 4:128; NE Co. MSS, 8004.

[69] DCD, 1:35, 2:344 (quote).

[70] DCD, 1:27, 68, 71, 84, 107, 110, 124, 125, 166, 196, 204, 212, 216, 223–4, 233, 277, 287, 341, 365, 384–5; 2:71; Mass. Archives, 31:19. See O'Brien, *Dispossession by Degrees*, chap. 6, for a sophisticated analysis of the colonial process of "imposing a construction of place as property and fixity upon Indians, and then dispossessing Indians of their property and defining them as rootless."

[71] Suffolk Files, #4974, p. 14. For similar cases, see DCCR, 1:116, 187.

[72] Paul R. Campbell and Glenn W. LaFantasie, "Scattered to the Winds of Heaven: Narragansett Indians, 1676–1880," *Rhode Island History* 37 (1979), 71; St. Jean, "Inventing Guardianship"; Michael Leroy Oberg, *Uncas: First of the Mohegans* (Ithaca, N.Y.: Cornell University Press, 2003), 154–6.

I Muttaak and we the chief men, and with our children and all our common people present, have agreed that no one shall sell land. But if anyone larcenously sells land, you shall take back your land, because it is forever your possession. But if anyone does not keep this agreement, he shall fall and have nothing more of this land at Gay Head and Nashaquitsa at all forever. I Muttaak and we the chief men, and our posterity, say: And it shall be so forever. I Ummuttaak say this, and my chief men: if any of these sons of mine protects my sachemship, he shall forever be a sachem. But if any one of my sons does not protect my sachemship and sells it, he shall fall forever. And we chief men say this, and our sachem: if any of these sons of ours protects our sachemship, he shall forever be a chief man. But if any of our sons does not protect our sachemship and sells it, he shall fall forever. I Umattaag, sachem, say this and my chief men; that is our agreement. We say it before God. It shall be so forever.[73]

The marks of five chief men followed.

The implications of this document were not lost either upon the Wampanoags who brought it to public attention or English officials sent scrambling to investigate it. Despite the colonists' rhetoric that "wandering" Indians had no legitimate land claims apart from their planting fields, they usually followed the pragmatic course of purchasing Native territory.[74] The colonies of Plymouth, Connecticut, and Rhode Island even used Indian titles, not royal charters, as the initial bases of their jurisdictions. For every corrupt Englishman willing to buy land from fraudulent claimants, there were several others who tried to identify the appropriate seller, if only to avoid future trouble. In this, they had no choice but to rely upon the Natives' collective memory. Usually such preliminary business was not written down, but occasionally (particularly after New England land policies fell under crown scrutiny in the 1680s) a deed would include Indian testimony about a historic council in which a sachem assigned the grantor's ancestors the land in question.[75] Mittark's declaration, with its memory-aiding

[73] DCD, 1:349; *Native Writings*, 1:96–7. I use the translation by Ives Goddard and Kathleen Bragdon here, but I eliminate their editorial symbols, and use "sachemship" instead of "chieftainship" in the declaration of the "chief men," which is in accordance with a contemporary translation in Mass. Archives, 31:10.

[74] On English debates over the necessity of purchasing Indian lands, see Robert Cushman, "Reasons and Considerations touching the lawfulness of removing out of England into the Parts of America," in *A Journal of the Pilgrims at Plymouth: Mourt's Relation*, Dwight B. Heath, ed. (New York: Corinth Books, 1963); Nathaniel B. Shurtleff, ed., *Records of the Governor and Company of the Massachusetts Bay in New England*, 5 vols. (Boston, 1853–1854), 3:281–2; Chester E. Eisinger, "The Puritan Justification for Taking the Land," *Essex Institute Historical Collections* 84 (1948), 131–43; Wilcomb E. Washburn, "The Moral and Legal Justification for Dispossessing the Indians," in James Morton Smith, ed., *Seventeenth-Century America: Essays in Colonial History* (New York: W. W. Norton for the Institute of Early American History and Culture, 1959), 22–5.

[75] William Nahaton, alias Quaanan et al., to Daniel Fisher and others, April 14, 1680, and Confirmation of Charles Josias, 1685, in William Hill, ed., *Ancient Deeds from the Indians to the Town of Dedham* (1881), Ayer MS 279, Newberry Library, Chicago, Ill.; Little,

repetition of important points and references to the chief men witnesses, was consistent with such recorded "speech events" and thus apparently authentic.[76] Moreover, the Aquinnah Wampanoags formed a wall of agreement that this document had indeed been written in 1681. Their attempt to register the paper some twenty years after the fact merely followed the colonists' example of entering deeds for Indian land years and even decades after they had purportedly been signed. Given the colonists' standard and their dependence upon Native testimony to authenticate their own titles, how could Mittark's land-sale ban be dismissed?

Then again, how could it be accepted? Taking recognition of the paper to its logical conclusion would entail seizing Dongan's property, displacing dozens of colonial tenants, and establishing a precedent that might upset English property rights throughout the region. As if to prove the point, almost simultaneously Wampanoags from surrounding communities presented yellowed papers challenging English rights at Squibnocket, Noman's Land island, Nantucket, Naushon Island (of the Elizabeth Islands), and Assawompsett (in the mainland town of Middleboro).[77] The Wampanaogs of these places were linked by strong kin and church ties, which hinted that their documents were part of an organized protest of English expansion. However, proof of any collusion was elusive.

Authorities in Massachusetts Bay, to which the Vineyard, Nantucket, and Plymouth Colony had just been annexed in 1691 as part of King Williams' imperial reordering, must have questioned whether London had invited the proverbial fox into their henhouse. But to the relief of colonial landowners, in 1703 a committee appointed by Boston designed a foolproof way to dismiss the Indians' challenge. They contended that most of the Indians' cases rested on wills that had not "been proved in due Form of Law, nor drawn up in Form as is usual among the English." Regarding the Nantucket "will," they found "by the confession of the scribe that wrote it and by other witnesses, that they did not agree to the time nor place where it was writt... which

---

"Three Kinds of Indian Land Deeds at Nantucket, Massachusetts," in William Cowan, ed., *Papers of the 11th Algonquian Conference* (Ottawa: Carleton University Press, 1980), 61–70, esp. 63–5; Theodore Lewis, "Land Speculation and Dudley Council of 1686," WMQ 31 (1974), 255–72; John Frederick Martin, *Profits in the Wilderness: Profits in the Wilderness: Entrepreneurship and the Founding of New England Towns in the Seventeenth Century* (Chapel Hill: University of North Carolina Press for the Institute of Early American History and Culture, 1991), 262–3; O'Brien, *Dispossession by Degrees*, 74–8.

[76] Kathleen J. Bragdon, "'Emphaticall Speech and Great Action': An Analysis of Seventeenth-Century Native Speech Events Described in Early Sources," MNE 33 (1987), 101–11.

[77] Matthew Mayhew to Wait Winthrop, October 24, 1702, Winthrop Papers, MHS; Mandell, *Behind the Frontier*, 72–3; Little, "Indian Horse Commons at Nantucket Island, 1660–1760," Paper presented at the 1986 meeting of the American Society for Ethnohistory at Charleston, S. C.; Little, "Sachem Nickanoose of Nantucket and the Grass Contest, Parts I and II," *Historic Nantucket* 23 (1976), 14–22, and 24 (1976), 21–30; Little, "Daniel Spotso," 201.

gives us cause to believe that they were not true but forged and false."[78]
The committee also declared the Natives' writing for Squibnocket "forged
and not true."[79] Then outside pressure caused a hairline crack in Aquinnah's
solidarity. Upon inquiry, "an Indian called Jonah Hossewit which seemed to
be a sober honest man comes before the Committee and said that he wrote
that writing long since Mattark's death and by the Testimony of sundry other
Indians wee have good reason to thinke that said writing was forged and not
true."[80]

But was it? After all was said and done, Aquinnah's case still came down
to the word of Jonah Hossueit, who in a few years would emerge as a
heterodox Baptist preacher, against that of his neighbors, the vast majority
of whom remained Congregationalist.[81] Possibly his confession was part of
a religious schism and the Wampanoags had been telling the truth all along.
Another scenario is that the Indians drew up the document around 1703,
but faithfully transcribed the proceedings of a 1681 council, like colonists
who used oral accounts of Indian land genealogies to justify their own land
titles. Or, perhaps, the Indians were shrewdly playing the colonists' old game
of manipulating the printed word.[82] Whatever the case, they could not win
with Englishmen setting the rules. Boston's rejection of the Wampanoags'
claims established that it would rely on Indian memory only when it suited
colonial interests, and that it was not about to let control of the written
record slip into Native hands.[83]

The loss shattered Nashuakemuck into several bickering camps. By 1704,
Natives complained there was "much difference" among them over the place-
ment of the Middle Line.[84] Relatives formerly in "Joynt possession" of land

---

[78] Mass. Archives, 31:17; "Thomas Walcut Papers, 1671–1866," File 4, MHS.

[79] Mass. Archives, 31:17.

[80] Ibid. (quote), and 31:501b, 501c, 505, 505a; *Mass. Acts and Resolves*, 8:118. In 1712,
Nashuakemuck Indians would try again to register an ancient will, attributed to the deceased sachem Chipnock, only to have it rejected as "being unintelligible and the witness
thereto being long since deceased." See DCP, 1:39, and the original Wampanoag language
document, "Chipnock's Will – 1691. Disallowed 1712," Dukes County Superior Court, in
a metal file labeled "Petitions: Common Pleas" among a bundle of papers listed as "Titles."

[81] Halsey Thomas, ed., *The Diary of Samuel Sewall, 1674–1729*, 2 vols. (New York: Farrar,
Straus, and Giroux, 1973), 1:465; Isaac Backus, *A History of New England, with Particular
Reference to the Denomination of Christians Called Baptists*, 3 vols. (Boston, 1777), 1:438–
39.

[82] Daniel Mandell argues that there is "little doubt" that these were oral agreements later put
to paper, but does not adequately entertain the possibility of Native machination. See *Behind
the Frontier*, 72–3.

[83] For more on this theme, see Russell L. Barsh, "Behind Land Claims: Rationalizing Dispossession in Anglo-American Law," *Law and Anthropology* 1 (1986), 15–50.

[84] DCD, 3:48, 435 (quote); 6:129; Suffolk Files, #66753. The north party was composed of
Josias Wesoquin, Judah Chipnock, Joan Kesuckquish, and Thomas Tackonot. The south
party was Hester Janittuwannit, Sarah Poonshomp, Eleazar Comok, Harriet, and Stephen
Comoson.

began dividing and selling off their claims, often in an atmosphere of jealousy and mutual recrimination.[85] Even Japheth Hannit's heirs leapt into the market, despite being instructed by his will to keep the family's lands "till their generations be ended[.] then let the Sachimms (that is the Government) wisely consider who will be next to enjoy it and there let it fall."[86]

With its sachem out of favor and no one poised to replace him, Aquinnah could have fallen headlong in the same direction, but once again off-island English elites, this time from Boston and London, had their own plans for the sachemship. News from the Vineyard left the missionary New England Company concerned that the Wampanoags were "Threatned to be Ousted," and "scattered up and down the Continent, and returning to the barbarous Customes of their Ancestors."[87] Fortunately, the Company had a chance to act; Dongan's frustration at the Indians' challenge to his titles prompted him to sell the Manor of Martha's Vineyard to the Company for £550. Company commissioner Samuel Sewall celebrated the deal as a "Triumph in receiving the Oppressed, and in Helping those who have no helper."[88] As far as the New England Company was concerned, now it was Aquinnah's new "Lord and Sachim."

The Company, whose officials included New England elites like Sewall, Increase Mather, Cotton Mather, and Wait Winthrop, was determined to bring English order to Aquinnah by dividing it into family farms and leasing out territory *it* defined as excess to fund Indian schools and poor relief.[89] Lest the Wampanoags fear a Trojan Horse, the Company wrote to them about its intention to "use all the care of [a] Kind Father, to make your condition comfortable" and to "love you like . . . children."[90] But Aquinnah refused to respond; if the Company wanted to get anywhere it had to conduct business Indian style – in person like real kin – rather than through paternalistic letters. Shortly the Company sent a delegation from Boston to the island to address the wary community.

---

[85] *Mass. House Journals* 13:149; DCD, 3:456–9; 6:41, 129; DCCP, 1730–55, 811, 812; DCCP, 1736–42, 710b; Force Papers, [ ]April, 1737.

[86] Scrapbook of Deeds, p. 77, MVHS. See also DCD, 4:236, 237, 240, 241; 5:17, 30. DCD, 3:413, 450, might also refer to Hannit's land.

[87] NE Co. MSS, 7953, p. 17 ("threatened . . . "); *Some Correspondence*, 94 ("scattered . . . ").

[88] DCD, 2:311–16, 327; NE Co. MSS, 7955/1, pp. 29–30 (quote), 56–7; New England Company Letter Book, 1688–1761, pp. 104, 106–12; Alderman Library, University of Virginia, Charlottesville, Va.; Mandell, *Behind the Frontier*, 114–15.

[89] NE Co. MSS, 7953, pp. 39, 49, 108; NE Co. MSS, 7955/1, p. 42; Cotton Mather to Daniel Parker and Zachues Mayhew, ca. August 1714, and, to the Indians of Gay Head, ca. August 1714, in Kenneth Silverman, ed., *Selected Letters of Cotton Mather* (Baton Rouge: Louisiana State University Press, 1971), 151–2; *Diary of Samuel Sewall*, 2:751. Generally on English efforts to promote Indian "civility," see James Axtell, *The Invasion Within: The Contest of Cultures in Colonial North America* (New York: Oxford University Press, 1985), chaps. 7–10.

[90] Undated Letter, II-56, Box 5, File 1, Mather Family Papers, AAS.

Joseph Mittark's own misguided decisions had brought about this unwelcome meeting, but the Aquinnah Wampanoags were not about to negotiate without some respected person out in front. They chose one "Abel" (either the church elder, Abel Hossueit, or Mittark's nephew, Abel Wauwompuhque Jr.) to speak for them while the sachem kept to the shadows – as he would for the rest of his life. Abel told the Company through the translations of Experience Mayhew that his people welcomed a proposal to run "a good Fence across the [Gay Head] neck assigning one Half for Tillage and the other for herbage."[91] This measure would enable them to experiment with livestock without having to fence off individual family plots as if they shared the colonists' private property ways. The Wampanoags also took advice to run a ditch across the peninsula connecting Aquinnah to the rest of the island. Aquinnah embraced these proposals because they furthered the goals of defending the community's resources against outsiders and demarcating its boundaries without sacrificing the people's communal ethic.

The Wampanoags were less taken with the Company's idea to rent out part of their land as an English farm. Company leaders believed, "calamities have so wasted these Indians" that leases were the best means by which they "might have an Everlasting and Unalienable Claim unto some Little Scraps of a Vast Country, once entirely Possessed by their Ancestors."[92] Englishmen were going to put the land to "use" one way or another; they were not going to leave it "idle" in Native hands. Renting out the land would at least reap the Indians some profit and provide them with a model for their own agricultural reforms. However, Aquinnah was skeptical that inviting colonists to work their land was the best way to retain it. Sewall concluded from their polite but firm opposition that he "could not find it convenient as yet, to Lett out any part to English-men."[93]

The Company found it easier to ignore the Indians' wishes back within the safe confines of Boston, where they negotiated a ten-year lease for 600 Aquinnah acres with colonist Ebenezer Allen. As the Wampanoags might have predicted, laying out Allen's bounds met "with some difficulty in the performance which was unseen, respecting several Indians dwelling on the spot." Ultimately, sixteen Wampanoag families had to be displaced in order to possess Allen of the tract. "Many Indians be aggrieved, the Commissioners will consider them," Company notes tersely mentioned.[94] When the lease came up for renewal in 1723, the Indians' ongoing protests gave the

---

[91] NE Co. MSS, 7955/1, pp. 56–7 (quote); *Diary of Samuel Sewall*, 2:750–1. See also "Letter Book of Samuel Sewall," *MHSC* 6th ser. 1 (1886), 232–3.
[92] Cotton Mather, *A brief Account of the Evangelical Work among the Christianized INDIANS OF NEW-ENGLAND*, appendix to his *Just Commemorations. The DEATH of GOOD MEN Considered* (Boston, 1715), 56.
[93] NE Co. MSS, 7955/1, pp. 56–7.
[94] NE Co. MSS, 7953, p. 45.

Company no pause.[95] Commissioners extended it by fourteen years and added another four hundred acres. This would uproot even more Aquinnah families and once again raise the specter of Englishmen gradually crowding out Wampanoags from "the best tract of land on the Iseland and the most Valluablest."[96] What was more, the new lease would stretch "within one rod of the grave of the Indian Minister Joash which is in the burying place on Gay Head Neck."[97]

For Aquinnah, this was a battle worth fighting. In 1725, the Company ordered its Vineyard agents "to make the Indians at the Gayhead easy about Mr. Allen's last Lease and to induce them peaceably to go off from the said land."[98] But the Wampanoags stood fast. Arguing that "the Land was theirs and their Ancestors and that they never sold it," they began to "hinder not only [Allen] taking possession of the 1000 acres in his last Lease but also his keeping possession of the 600 acres in his former Lease."[99] By 1726, a terrified Allen reported Indians killing and impounding his cattle and tearing down his fences, to the value of some £5,000, all the while "alledging that the land is theirs."[100]

The Company and its lessee were not going to win this fight on the Wampanoags' own ground, so they retreated to the courts and filed suit against Aquinnah's leading men. Aquinnah needed only to compare its scant resources with the Company's deep pockets and legal expertise to reenter negotiations – once again, without a sachem.[101] Ten men agreed to the Farm on behalf of the community in exchange for the Company reducing its size from 1,000 to 800 acres, recognizing the Wampanoags' right to collect its marsh grass, and commissioning Pain and Zacheus Mayhew to police all encroachments on Indian territory. Upon signing, the Company dropped all of its lawsuits, but it was still a bleak day for Aquinnah.[102] The people had to stomach a twenty-one-year lease of the Farm and acknowledge that they "shall be always under the direction, government, & Stint of the said Company or their Agent."[103]

This loss taught the Aquinnah Wampanoags to express their grievances more subtly. Around 1729, they finally instituted a "sheep right" system

95 NE Co. MSS, 7953, pp. 43–47.
96 NE Co. MSS, 7955/1, p. 37.
97 CPGNE, Box 3, File 3, October 16, 1724.
98 NE Co. MSS, 7953, p, 67.
99 NE Co. MSS, 7955/2, pp. 40–1 (quote); NE Co. MSS, 7953, pp. 67, 68, 70.
100 NE Co. MSS, 7953, pp. 69, 70, 7955/2, pp. 22–3.
101 DCGSP, 1722–62, p. 872.
102 DCD, 4:199–200, 242–4; NE Co. MSS, 7955/2, 22–3, 26; CPGNE, Recs., Box 3, File 5, May 10, 1727; New England Company Letter Book, 200, 202, 211–12; William Kellaway, *The New England Company, 1649–1776* (New York: Barnes and Noble, 1961), 223–5.
103 NE Co. MSS, 7955/2, p. 27. On the lease dispute, see also Mandell, *Behind the Frontier*, 114–15.

recommended years before by the Company in which every Native received the privilege of grazing ten sheep or their equivalent, with the option of taking in colonial cattle.[104] Without question, this move was at least in part financially driven. Over the next twenty years, several Wampanoags profitably leased out their sheep rights "on the halves" – meaning for half the value or half the number of the pastured livestock's offspring – thereby providing much needed income in lieu of selling land.[105] Given the timing, it appears that another goal was to establish a firmer usufruct claim to Wampanoag territory. Putting the land to "civilized" use guarded against future extension of the Farm and established the groundwork to reassert Native title. Ironically, animal husbandry, which the Indians had long associated with English trespass, also became a means for Aquinnah to restructure its polity after deposing the sachem for facilitating that trespass. To prevent the land from being "over Stockt and Ruin[ed]," Aquinnah formed a meeting of "proprietors" (adults with customary rights to the land), which annually elected a five-man committee to negotiate grazing leases with colonists, collect and distribute rents, and withhold monies from "several of their young men being addicted to stealing sheep."[106] Yet these authorities turned a blind eye to thefts from the Farm. As late as 1731, Allen still complained to the Company that "his Fences at Gayhead are thrown down in the night by which means his sheep get out and are impounded and to his frequent damage."[107]

The sheep-right system addressed Wampanoag needs for income, firmer land claims, and corporate leadership. It was not, however, a campaign to roll back the English. Years before the people of Aquinnah protected themselves against future land sales by deposing Joseph Mittark and discarding the office of sachem, but at the price of strong individual leadership. Without it, aggressive Indian attempts to seize back the land, like the 1703 deed contest and attacks on the Farm, fizzled out as soon as Boston elites became involved. So long as the sachem's functions remained divided among the Company, the Aquinnah proprietors, and Wampanoag church leaders, the Indians had to settle for modest defense of the land they still retained.

[104] A 1763 document suggests that the sheep-right ratio was 8 sheep::1 oxen and 10 sheep::1 horse. See Cornelius Basset to Peter Norton, 1763, Box 4S, Env. A, MVHS.

[105] John Allen Account Book, 1732–1752, pp. 20 (account of John Occouch), 21 (Josiah Pomit), 22 (Zachariah Hossueit), 24 (Jonah Hossueit), 28 (Nicodemos Demos), 35 (Josiah Pomit), 36 (Aron Ohomo), MVHS.

[106] Ebenezar Allen to Anonymous, undated, Andrew-Eliot Collection, MHS ("over Stockt"); Mass. Archives 31:523 (committee chosen), 32:8; John Allen Account Book, p. 47 ("Gayhe[a]d Indians" account), MVHS. This committee was in place by at least 1739. See CPGNE, Recs., Box 2, March 17, 1739. On Indian theft and killing of English sheep, see DCGSP, October 1730–October 1757, pp. 733, 743, 743b, 746, 746b, 749, 749b, 750, 756, 765; Force Papers, March 9, 1730.

[107] CPGNE, Recs., Box 2, March 27, 1731, NEHGS. Disputes arose again in 1745. See DCCF, Box 4, File 5.

V

Given Chappaquiddick's proximity to Edgartown, one would expect that sachemship to have crumbled more swiftly than those on the west side of the island. However, Pakeponesso's successor, Seeknout, continued his father's strategy of balancing Indian and English needs. He allowed colonists to pasture cattle on Chappaquiddick island during the winter, but refused to sell them land. He restricted Wampanoag animal husbandry to "some particular indians," which satisfied the Native elite and colonists who worried about competition for land, but required Indian husbandmen to plow their neighbors' corn fields, thus pleasing the commoners.[108] Such arrangements allowed the 140 or so Wampanoags of Chappaquiddick and more than 200 colonists of Edgartown to coexist even though just a thin sliver of harbor separated them.[109]

Cooperation broke down after the ascension of Seeknout's son, Joshua Seeknout, in or around 1692.[110] Edgartown's Chappaquiddick Proprietors (as Englishmen with pasture rights called themselves) impounded the sachem's livestock and then used their families' control of the courts to deny him justice when he filed charges of trespass.[111] Yet Seeknout's case caught Boston's attention once it passed to off-island appellate courts and led authorities arbitrate a compromise. In 1715, the sachem and Proprietors agreed that the English could keep one hundred head of cattle, or their equivalent, on Chappaquiddick between October 20 and March 25 of each year, paying Seeknout 1s. 6d. for every "fatted beast." The Indians were free to graze one hundred animals.[112] Supposedly Chappaquiddick's problems were over.

Yet the death of Joshua Seeknout in January of 1716 revived colonial designs to appropriate the Wampanoags' territory.[113] The English Proprietors arranged with an Indian named Sassachuamin to claim the sachemship and let in more English cattle than ever before. Decades earlier, Pakeponneso had rejected his eldest son, Sassachuamin's father, Pecosh, as Chappaquiddick sachem for fear he would sell land. The Proprietors and Sassachuamin concocted that bypassing the firstborn was a violation of Wampanoag custom and therefore Sassachuamin was the rightful sachem of Chappaquiddick – the English had a strange way of dismissing legitimate Indian customs while honoring fictional ones that put the Natives at disadvantage. Then in the fall

---

[108] Suffolk Files, #12289.

[109] "Indian Visitation," 138.

[110] In a 1692 deed, Joshua mentioned his "late" father. See DCD, 1:116.

[111] DCCR, 1:207, 209, 212, 214, 222; 2:212; DCCF, Indian Papers, Box 4; RSCJ, 1700–1714, p. 282. Chief Justice John Worth, Clerk of Courts Matthew Mayhew, and most jury members had financial or family interests in the Chappaquiddick dispute. See Edgartown Records, 90, 91.

[112] DCD, 6:463–4; DCCR, 1:252; Mandell, *Behind the Frontier*, 74–5.

[113] *Native Writings*, 1:459.

of 1716, the Proprietors flooded Chappaquiddick with nearly 1,000 head of livestock. Jacob Seeknout, Joshua's successor, predictably impounded the beasts, whereupon Sassachuamin filed suit against him, certainly with English backing. Simultaneously, the Proprietors suspended their rent payments to Seeknout, thereby forcing him to sue them. In just a matter of months, Seeknout was buried in litigation, probably more than any other Indian to date anywhere in New England.[114]

Jacob Seeknout was literate enough to write his signature, but not to mount an independent legal campaign. Indeed, when he brought charges against the Proprietors, they pleaded for abatement on the basis of technicalities that must have seemed entirely beside the point to him. For one, the Proprietors argued, Seeknout's writ claimed that he was Joshua Seeknout's heir, but "by the law of this province all his children are but one heir; and the suit must be in their names." They submitted that the 1715 agreement requiring them to pay the sachem for every "fatted beast" on Chappaquiddick referred only to slaughtered cattle, not to every animal that grazed upon the land. The English outlined three more foibles in Seeknout's writ, won their motion, and then handed a bill for their court costs to the undoubtedly bewildered sachem.[115]

In the late 1680s, Jacob's grandfather, Seeknout, had warned the English that peace required them to engage his people in a spirit of mutual respect; now, years later, colonists ignored his threat because the Wampanoags were too weak to fulfill it. The lesson was bitter, but Jacob Seeknout realized that his own defense of the Chappaquiddick sachemship had to take place according to English rules. So, wisely, he hired a capable lawyer, colonist Benjamin Hawes, to guide his appeals from Edgartown's corrupted courts to more neutral magistrates in Plymouth. It took only a fair hearing for mainland justices to see that Sassachuamin was a "Naked man" set up by a "Restless people" who were dissatisfied with "halfe the profits of the land which the said Sachem called his owne" and aimed "to make themselves sachems or owners of said Island." The Superior Court threw out Vineyard rulings in favor of Sasschuamin and the Proprietors, and instead awarded Seeknout nominal damages.[116]

[114] DCCR, 1:243, 244, 246, 247, 249.
[115] DCCR, 1:246, 253; Suffolk Files, #12289.
[116] Suffolk Files, #12965, pp. 101–2 (all quotes), #14047; RSCJ, 1700–1714, p. 176; DCCR, 1:178; Testimony of Bethia Tuxit, October 1, 1717, Misc. Bound MSS, MHS.
    Ann Marie Plane, "Legitimacies, Indian Identities, and the Law: The Politics of Sex and the Creation of History in Colonial New England," Law and Social Inquiry 23 (1998), 55–77, demonstrates that to defend Seeknout's office and dismiss Sassachuamin's claim, Hawes had to cast Sassachuamin as an "illegitimate" heir because of his descent from a sachem concubine rather than a wife, and to establish Seeknout's "sexual legitimacy" and "sovereignty by detailing the marriage, paternity, and succession of his ancestors." Plane suggests that "Hawes ignored the subtleties

Yet this was a Pyrrhic victory for Jacob Seeknout. The courts upheld his title against Sassachuamin, but the Proprietors still withheld rent payments, confident that the Vineyard sheriff would never enforce off-island rulings. Seeknout had no choice but to file suit again, financed by marketing the very land his litigation was supposed to protect. In June of 1720, he sold Simeon Butler his "sachem right" to a grassy area called Pocha, and then another tract to none other than Benjamin Hawes.[117] But all this was not enough. In September, with the Proprietors' rents still overdue and his legal costs having reached £281, Seeknout transferred all his remaining land to Hawes and declared him to be heir to the Chappaquiddick sachemship.[118]

It is unlikely that Seeknout ever intended this document to see the light of day. Probably he viewed it as a mortgage of sorts, since Hawes did not enter it until July of 1722, and Seeknout's response was to strip the lawyer of all his powers and former grants and to appeal to Boston for aid.[119] The sachem's followers rallied to his cause with their own petition in which they contrasted themselves as a Christian people with Hawes who was "in a League with

of seventeenth-century Indian marriages," and that his "rejection of polygamy out of hand reveals more about what he wished were true than it does about the historical complexities of seventeenth-century Native marriages." "Indeed," she concludes, "the case was never about the real practices of real Natives, but rather about the construction of ideal Indians."

Plane's argument cannot support uncited evidence that polygamous elite Indians of the early seventeenth century distinguished between women with whom they lived and women with whom they did not, as well as among women who were of sachem status and those from the common ranks. In 1624, Edward Winslow noted that a male sachem "will not take any to wife but such a one as is equal to him in birth; otherwise, they say, their seed would, in time, become ignoble. And though they have many other wives: yet are they no other than concubines or servants" (*Good News*, 587). A 1716 inheritance case involving descendants of the Takemmy sachem, Wannamanhut, confirmed this statement, while addressing issues similar to those in Seeknout's trial. Several Indians in the Takemmy case judged the children from two of Wannamanhut's wives as (in English parlance) legitimate, but the son of another one as illegitimate. Wannamanhut, they explained, "married two women of the nobility among the Indians," and by one he had a son named Nananit and several other children. Ester Aquannhut remembered, "Wannamanhit took a third woman Severall years after the first and had a son by her called John," and Wannamanhut neglected him "as being born of a woman not Noble." Ponit added that "wannamanhut took a woman at nashowakommuck which he some times visited but did not take her home nor keep her as a wife" and thus the sachem "took little or no care for the abovesaid John." Moreover, Takemmy's chief men "never Esteemed" John and "divers Children that the said Wannamanhit had afterwards by women in other parts of said Island... to have any Consern" with Wannamanhut's land. Given such testimony, it seems that Hawes' argument did indeed rest on Indian customs about marriage and legitimacy. See DCD, 3:129, 133, 134, 154, and related testimony in Suffolk Files, #12248. For a similar case on Nantucket, see Thomas Wallcut Papers, File 6, Item 2, MHS; Little, "Daniel Spotso," 203.
[117] DCD, 3:477–8, 537.
[118] DCD, 3:512.
[119] DCD, 3:513; *Mass. Acts and Resolves*, 10:212–13; Mandell, *Behind the Frontier*, 116.

the Devil."[120] Hawes slapped the lead author, Judah Coquit, with a slander suit, but the people remained united against him.

Massachusetts appointed Simeon Butler to replace Hawes as Seeknout's attorney, then found him on the take as well. Butler, Wampanoag John Cockquett objected, "Insinuated himselfe into our good oppinion of him by his Flattering Tongue making many fare speeches and solemn promises" only "to his utmost to gain all that he Can (by any means) to himselfe and make only a prey of us who have betrusted him as it were with our lives." The cancer of land sales and corruption, which had infected every other Indian community on the island and beyond, had finally violated the Chappaquiddick sachemship. Cockquett blamed Butler's "Craft and Cunning" for having "prevailed upon our said sachem as to Joyn with him in a Separate private interest," in which Seeknout "hath in a great measure forsaken us his poore feeble people (which wee Impute Rather to his Excessive Drinking)...he seemeth to be regardless of his own as well as our Interest," evidenced in that "above halfe the Island is already sold."[121] Enoch Coffin investigated the Indians' complaints for Boston and removed Butler after uncovering a poorly covered trail of embezzlement and conflict of interest. Yet eleven years later the Wampanoags charged Coffin too of conspiring against them.[122] Try as it might, Boston could not depend upon local people to resist plundering the Indians when there was no one willing to stop them.

Seeknout's people no longer had any faith in him, so like the Nunnepogs and Sengekontackets before them, they demanded "sachem rights," or fee-simple title, to their own plots of land, in exchange for the money their leader craved.[123] In one grant, a Native even won Seeknout's promise "for ever to warant & defend the said upland," a stark reversal of the commoner's traditional pledge to defend the sachemship.[124] Yet Seeknout did not defend the land, nor did his grantees. As elsewhere, sachem-right grants only accelerated the loss of Indian land by placing the titles with vulnerable commoners.[125] Luckily for the Wampanoags, Seeknout had not yet sold or parceled out a peninsula called North Neck. Seeknout's brothers, Matthew, Hezekiah, and Joseph, guarded this last sanctuary by convincing the sachem to grant them, as a trio, North Neck's planting and mowing privileges and an exemption

[120] Dukes County Inferior Court of Common Pleas, March 28, 1727, Misc. Bound MSS, MHS (quote); DCCP, 1722–36, 662; Suffolk Files, #29178.

[121] Mass. Archives, 31:129 (quote); *Mass. Acts and Resolves*, 10:212–13; *Mass. House Journals*, 4:125, 216; DCD, 4:14, 70, 72–3, 73–4, 218; William John Burton, "Hellish Fiends and Brutish Men: Amerindian–Euroamerican Interaction in Southern New England, An Interdisciplinary Analysis, 1600–1750" (Ph.D. diss., Kent State University, 1976), 316–19; Mandell, *Behind the Frontier*, 116.

[122] *Mass. Acts and Resolves*, 12:418; *Mass. House Journals*, 15:190.

[123] DCD, 3:515, 516, 517, 518, 523; 4:55–6, 57–8, 163–4; 5:400–1, 433–4; 6:82; 10:60.

[124] DCD, 3:523 (quote); Bragdon, "'Another Tongue Brought In'," 129.

[125] DCD, 5:196; 6:49, 531; 7:81, 384, 525; 8:69, 158, 210, 308, 351, 361, 449, 453, 484, 486, 489, 532, 536, 555, 559, 572, 610; 9:40, 154; 10:60; 11:158–59; 12:23.

from having to open the area to colonial livestock. In return, they affirmed Jacob's exclusive right to rents throughout the rest of the island, probably meaning that Seeknout no longer had to share his proceeds.[126] By the 1730s, Jacob Seeknout appeared in deeds, not as a sachem, but a fisherman, prone to defensive rants about "my Lands not Lawfully Disposed of And Still Remaining Mine and Belonging to me by Any ways."[127] They were the words of a fallen leader.

Within four years Seeknout was dead and succeeded by his daughter, Hepzibah. She inherited a skeletal office, but with her husband, Samuel Cagenhew, a Baptist preacher and schoolmaster, she managed to keep the people together by hosting religious services and guarding the bounds of North Neck.[128] In 1740, she even revived her father's failed campaign to win justice for Chappaquiddick by filing suit against Edgartown for recovery of rents outstanding since 1715. But when three local referees found for the defendants with costs, it was, in effect, the Chappaquiddick sachemship's last gasp; there would be no more lawsuits or claimants to the title "sachem." The Cagenhews' son, Israel, occasionally identified himself as the "only surviving Grandson of Jacob Seicknouet Sachim of the Island Chabbaquiddick," but he did not pretend the title applied to him; the sachemship as a political structure was dead.[129]

Jacob Seeknout had made every effort to defend his sachemship, but the new balance of power forced him to work from within the colonial bureaucracy, which he could not do alone, either from a technical or a financial standpoint. He relied upon guardians and lawyers to write up his paper work, collect his rents, deliver his courtroom arguments, and not least of all, lend him money. Even when judges awarded him court costs and rents, it was left to Vineyard sheriffs to collect these sums and the money was never forthcoming. For Indians living among the tight-knit communities of rural New England, enlisting outside support meant hoping against hope that colonial neighbors would act against neighbors and even relatives against relatives. Without a wampum trade or fur trade, the only ways Seeknout could fund his legal activities was to sell land or borrow money from Englishmen, which, ultimately, he had to pay back by selling land. Luckily for the common

---

[126] DCD, 3:530–31.

[127] DCD, 5:429–30 (quote), 433, 434.

[128] CPGNE, Recs., Box 1, December entries, and Box 2, July 25, 1764; Memorial of Zacheus Mayhew, October 1, 1759, Misc. Bound MSS, MHS; Backus, *A History of New England*, 1:438–9; DCD, 6:517.

[129] DCD, 10:591, 625. The only document to connect Israel Cagenhew to the title "sachem" was an 1828 account of the partition of Chappaquiddick Indian lands in which three white commissioners mentioned a tract "which Abishai Merchant purchased of Israel Cagnehau deceased, late sachem of the said Indians." However, no eighteenth-century document made such a link. See "Partition of Land Belonging to the Indians and People of Colour on Chappaquiddick and in Christiantown, as Determined by Commissioners John Hancock, Thomas Fish, and Jeremiah Pease, September 28th, 1828," Indian Collection, Box B, MVHS (unpaginated). Also entered in DCD, 23:292–316.

Indians of Chappaquiddick, Jacob Seeknout's brothers had the foresight to cordon off Northern Neck before he hawked the entire sachemship. They saw that even the most determined sachems could not meet their historic roles as providers for the poor, skilled diplomats, and defenders of the land. The institution no longer had any place in eighteenth-century New England.

VI

It had not always been so with Indian leaders. Well within memory, a sachemship's peace and prosperity had rested upon its sachem's leadership, and he symbolized his followers' links to one another and the ancestors. Yet after King Philip's War pressures to sell the land made even the best-intentioned leaders sources of community division. Under such circumstances, the people's survival required them to unseat their figurehead and ground their collective identity ever more firmly in the territory under siege. They had to depose the sachem to defend the sachemship. By the 1740s, the only three Wampanoag communities on Martha's Vineyard with more than a few families – Christiantown, Aquinnah, and Chappaquiddick – were those that had come to terms with this disturbing realization.

The ability of these communities to respond depended on the vitality of their churches. Despite losing prominent religious leaders to disease and age, the people of Christiantown and Aquinnah remained active, if less enthusiastic, churchgoers. Sunday meeting gave them an opportunity to discuss problems and debate solutions when their sachems' land sales grew excessive. The congregation served as a council, where preachers, deacons, and ruling elders gauged the opinions of their neighbors and determined the best course of action. Then these church leaders, the most formally educated and well-connected members of their communities, organized the campaigns to defend the community's rights, whether by recruiting English allies or monitoring and writing the documents that had become so critical to the Indians' collective lives. The sachemships of Nunnepog, Sengekontacket, and Chappaquiddick on the east side of the island did not possess such figures. Devastated by the 1690 epidemic, overwhelmed by English encroachment, and unable to mobilize their populations, yet again, through a church that had failed to protect them, these peoples left their collective interests to sachems whose ability to govern had passed but who retained the clout to impair their people's future. Only after wallowing for years in indecision, and when it was almost too late, Chappaquiddick began to revive its church polity around the Cagenhews. Nunnepog and Sengekontacket never responded at all and paid the price.

Although at times it seemed that the English were united to double cross the Wampanoags, there were colonists who provided essential help. Christiantown would have been overrun were it not for the legal assistance of John Pease and Matthew Mayhew. Aquinnah's experience with the New England Company was mixed, although ultimately beneficial. The Company was an unsolicited patron with a callous disregard for Wampanoag priorities and property rights. Yet it is equally clear that before the Company stepped in, Aquinnah was on the verge of being consumed by its English neighbors. The Company did not halt the feast, but it did slow it down by consolidating the Indians' titles, halting individual sales, and introducing a "sheep right" system that allowed Indians to raise money from the land without selling it. Not to be overlooked, Company salaries to Wampanoag church officials and magistrates helped to sustain the Indians' leaders and provide them with a focal point of resistance. The Aquinnah Wampanoags justly resented the Company, but it played a formative role in their adjustment to the postwar realities of Indian life in New England.

The least successful sachemships either failed to make outside alliances, as in the cases of Nunnepog and Sengekontacket, or else mistrusted corrupt colonial guardians, as in the case of Chappaquiddick. Among those sachemships, only Chappaquiddick put up much of a fight. Jacob Seeknout failed several times in his quest for justice and then fell apart, but his relatives managed to stop the hemorrhage of Indian land at the North Neck boundary without the aid of – and indeed despite of – the guardians assigned to them by Massachusetts. Their last-ditch effort left the Chappaquiddick Wampanoags with a homeland to defend.

The Chappaquiddicks' struggles most closely paralleled those of tribes on the New England mainland. The Narragansetts and Mohegans, under the Ninigret and Uncas families, respectively, suffered long, arduous contests involving the corruption of their English guardians, their sachems' use of land sales to seal alliances and pay off debts, and competing lawsuits by sachem claimants. The sachems were difficult to unseat because English authorities insisted upon their legitimacy to justify land cessions, irregardless of the Indian public's say. Moreover, the Narragansett and Mohegan sachems did not have to confront popular opposition organized around a church. Their people gave missionaries a chilly reception until the evangelical revivals of the 1740s, well after most of the land was gone. One contest after another weakened the Narragansett and Mohegan sachemships until they collapsed, leaving the commoners with what little scraps of land their minor leaders were able to prevail upon the colonies to defend.[130]

---

[130] On the Mohegans, see John W. DeForest, *History of the Indians of Connecticut* (Hartford, 1852), chaps. 8, 12; David W. Conroy, "The Defense of Indian Land Rights: William Bollan and the Mohegan Case in 1743," *Proceedings of the American Antiquarian Society* 103 (1993), 395–424; St. Jean, "Inventing Guardianship." On the Narragansetts, see Campbell and LaFantasie, "Scattered to the Winds of Heaven," 70–4; John Wood Sweet, *Bodies Politic: Negotiating Race in the American North, 1730–1830* (Baltimore: The Johns Hopkins University Press, 2003), chap. 1; William S. Simmons and Cheryl L. Simmons, "Joseph Fish and the Narragansetts," in their *Old Light on Separate Ways: The Narragansett Diary of Joseph Fish, 1765–1776* (Hanover, N.H.: University Press of New England, 1982), xix–xxxvii; William Simmons, "Red Yankees: Narragansett Conversion in the Great Awakening," *American Ethnologist* 10 (1983), 253–71.

Geography was a final and more ambiguous factor in the struggles of the Vineyard sachemships.[131] It was not coincidental that the two peoples who fared worst, the Nunnepogs and Sengekontackets, were located near Edgartown on land without clear boundaries. They experienced more direct pressure from animals, farmers, and the law than other Native communities on the island. By contrast, Aquinnah was located on the most remote portion of Martha's Vineyard, and a harbor separated Chappaquiddick from the island proper. But geography offered only certain advantages and could not determine a sachemship's fate. Compare Christiantown and Nashuakemuck, neither of which had natural boundaries nor were located near the heart of the English settlement. Christiantown survived, in part, because its bounds were put to paper and marked on rocks and trees across the landscape. When colonists breached those lines, the Natives restaked their claim by plowing and building walls. These things happened as a result of human decisions, not luck. Nashuakemuck also had its official border, the Middle Line, dividing the Mayhews' manor from the bulk of the area's Indian settlements. However, the Wampanoags allowed this line to become permeable. Scattered into tiny neighborhoods at Menemsha, Nashaquitsa, and Roaring Brook, each family was left to go its own way, usually quite literally.

All Indians, even if they had deposed the sachem, continued to struggle to reconcile their immediate material needs with their attachments to the homeland. All were tempted to sell land to provide for their families, but they also yearned to preserve it as an act of ethnic solidarity, spiritual devotion to the ancestors, and inheritance for the young. And all recognized that the few remaining Wampanoag communities were the only guarantees that their people would survive in a region where the majority seemed intent on destroying them. These lessons confronted the Indians with two substantial questions after the fall of the sachemships: first, whether they could achieve the sustained leadership and collective will required to monitor boundaries, leases, and guardians, and to organize effective resistance to colonial encroachment; second, and more important, whether, in an age in which the traditional Native economy was giving way to the colonial marketplace, and Indian justice to English courts, common Indians could afford to keep the land. Ironically, sometimes the campaign to defend these distinct Indian places would require adopting even more English practices. At other times, a renewal of Wampanoag traditions and institutions would be called for. But at no point was restoring the office of sachem the answer. The people knew that in this respect, to secure a collective future they had to discard part of their collective past.

---

[131] On Native survival as a partial byproduct of geography, see Jack Campisi, *The Mashpee Indians: Tribe on Trial* (Syracuse, N.Y.: Syracuse University Press, 1991), 77–8; Simmons, *Spirit of the New England Tribes: Indian History and Folklore, 1620–1984* (Hanover, N.H.: University Press of New England, 1986), 258.

5

Leading Values

When minister Zachariah Hossueit Sr. drew his final breath in June of 1772 it was a time for the people of Aquinnah both to mourn and celebrate. For almost half a century Hossueit had been their unrivaled master of the written word, dispensing the gospels to his flock in plain speech and interpreting the Wampanoag language for colonial authorities.[1] He had used every conceivable tool at his disposal to unite his community behind a landed order based on shared resources instead of personal profiteering. More than once he had called Boston's attention to the corruption of the Indians' guardians and won redress. Not the least of all, he was a role model of sober godly living at a time when the Indians needed it most. The people mourned because now this local hero was gone.

Yet there was cause for rejoicing. Hossueit's career spanned an era in which other New England Indians were starved for leaders to defend their homelands. The Narragansett and Mohegan sachems were in league with colonial land sharks, and every campaign to rein them in became bogged down in bitter factionalism and litigation. Prospects were so dismal by the eve of the Revolution that the mainland Indians' brightest stars, Samson Occum and Joseph Johnson, convinced portions of seven tribes to abandon their ancestral territories for a new start among the Oneidas in upper New York.[2] In Wampanoag country, a handful of communities rallied around

---

[1] Examples of Hossueit's English writings are in ZHP, 1744 Mr 8-1813 Ja 25, #33060–3, 1747 Jly, #33060–5, 1763 Mr 24-N28 #33060–8.

[2] Laura J. Murray, ed., *To Do Good to My Indian Brethren: The Writings of Joseph Johnson* (Amherst: University of Massachusetts Press, 1998); W. De Loss Love, *Samson Occom and the Christian Indians of New England* (1899; reprint, with an introduction by Margaret Connell Szasz, Syracuse, N.Y.: Syracuse University Press, 2000); Harold Blodget, *Samson Occum* (Hanover, N.H.: Dartmouth College Publication, 1935); Bernd C. Peyer, *The Tutor'd Mind: Indian Missionary – Writers in Antebellum America* (Amherst: University of Massachusetts Press, 1997), chap. 3; John W. DeForest, *History of the Indians of Connecticut* (Hartford, 1852), chaps. 8, 11–12; David W. Conroy, "The Defense of Indian Land Rights: William

the church to unseat ineffective sachems before they gutted the entire land base. However, the slow, consensus-driven meetings that took over often proved incapable of policing their jurisdictions with any consistency or energy. Charismatic personalities could make a difference, but the most talented candidates for leadership were reluctant to step forward since that would make them targets of the Indians' fearsome colonial adversaries. The ensuing power vacuum engulfed lower Nunnepog and Nashuakemuck, where only a few Indians remained, and made the Wampanoags' hold on Chappaquiddick, Christiantown, and Sengekontacket more perilous than ever. But Aquinnah's boundaries held firm, largely because Hossueit solved the sachems' dilemma by personally holding multiple offices with salaries paid by the New England Company, and then using his income and connections to battle the Indians' opponents. In the process, he helped his people complete their transition from a government based on the sachem and his counsel to the town meeting and church, without sacrificing their communal landholding practices to the colonists' private-property regime. The people of Aquinnah could celebrate because Hossueit's labors meant that he would be buried on undivided ancestral ground.

The Indians could also rejoice that Hossueit had groomed a successor, his son, Zachariah Howwoswee Jr. (who distinguished himself by this spelling of the surname), a man with ministerial experience and all the skills to serve as the people's scribe and interpreter. Moreover, the son had the example of his father's effective leadership. Yet few Anglo-Americans drew favorable comparisons between the two. Gideon Hawley praised Zachariah Sr. as "a man of Abilities; and as far as I can say of good works," while others were struck by his "solemnity and devotion."[3] By contrast, Jabez Athearn called Howwoswee a "designing man & very Drunken ... not a man of good Morals," Elisha Clap judged him to be "a very intemperate man, grossly inattentive to the business of a missionary," and Joseph Thaxter found him "useless" with "all the subtilty of a Fox."[4] Howwoswee was subtle and designing to be sure, intemperate, perhaps, but not useless, at least to judge from his early

Bollan and the Mohegan Case in 1743," *Proceedings of the American Antiquarian Society* 103 (1993), 395–424; Paul R. Campbell and Glenn W. LaFantasie, "'Scattered to the Winds of Heaven': Narragansett Indians, 1676–1880," *Rhode Island History* 47 (1978), 66–83; William S. Simmons, "Red Yankees: Narragansett Conversion in the Great Awakening," *American Ethnologist* 10 (1983), 257–60; John Wood Sweet, *Bodies Politic: Negotiating Race in the American North, 1730–1830* (Baltimore: The Johns Hopkins University Press, 2003), 316–28; Anthony Wonderly, "Brothertown, New York, 1785–1796," *New York History* 81 (2000), 457–92.

[3] Hawley to Rev. Morse, undated, Hawley Journal ("man of Abilities"); "Report of the Committee on the State of the Indians in Mashpee and Parts Adjacent," *MHSC* 2d ser., 3 (1815), 13 ("solemnity and devotion").

[4] Athearn to Rev. Walker, August 10, 1794, NE Co. MSS, 7956/2, pp. 85–6; Clap to Jedidah Morse, July 22, 1808, Misc. Bound MSS, MHS; Report of Joseph Thaxter on the State of the Indians, to Abiel Holmes, May 8, 1817, SPGNA, Box 6, File 4.

accomplishments. Wampanoags knew that Howwoswee's defense of Indian boundaries, indeed his expansion of them, sharpened his critics' edge. Nevertheless, the Indians could be forgiven if they doubted Howwoswee too; after all, their recent past was filled with leaders who put themselves in the people's good graces before degenerating into pariahs. Fortunately, throughout his fifty-year career Zachariah Hossueit Sr. had shown Aquinnah how to protect itself against such men. The community stood ready if his son became one of those.

I

It is fortunate that even hints of Hossueit's experience growing up in Christiantown can be sifted out of the sparse historical record.[5] He was named after his father, Zachariah Osooit, a man from Aquinnah with a poor reputation, at least in the estimation of Experience Mayhew. According to Mayhew, Osooit "was very apt to follow after strong Drink," which left his family in such a "miserable Condition... miserably clothed," that his wife was embarrassed to have their children appear in public.[6] Perhaps Mayhew knew that in 1704 "Zachariah Hossoo" (either Osooit or another man, Zachariah Wunhosso) was fined for public drunkenness and swearing at Robert Cathcart, and then again for beating Betty Hossueit with a stick "whereby she was much bruised and lamed."[7] Fourteen years later, Ossoit was in "desperate debt" to Cathcart, a shameless liquor peddler.[8] Such behavior left family management squarely on the shoulders of Ossoit's spouse, known to the English as Margaret and to the Indians as Meeksishqune, a daughter of the notorious Takemmy sachem, Keteanummin. A pious and formally educated woman, she diligently taught her "many children" the catechism, reading, and writing in Wampanoag, and "excited her Husband to pray to God in his House, and prevailed with him to do so."[9] Englishmen

---

[5] Researchers must carefully differentiate between the activities of three separate Zachariahs, whose surname was alternatively spelled by whites as Osooit, Hossueit, and Howwoswee. Known to nineteenth-century Natives as "Old Zachary," the youngest of the three died in 1821 at age 83, meaning that he was born in 1738 (Frederick Baylies, "The Names & Ages of the Indians on Martha's Vineyard," MSSA/S53/File 1HA, NEHGS). Old Zachary's father, the Zachariah Hossueit who distinguished himself during the eighteenth century, died on June 6, 1772 (CPGNA, Box 2, File 2, Accounts for June 1772–Nov. 1772). Another Zachariah Hossueit (also Ossooit) Sr. and Jr. duo lived on the Vineyard earlier in the century as well. The two men appeared separately for "desperate debt" in the account books of store owner Robert Cathcart in 1718, and then again in 1730 when Sr. was a ruling elder in the Nashuakemuck congregation and Jr. was a justice at Gay Head (DCP, 1:102; CPGNE, Box 1, December entries). The eldest Zachariah died in 1731.

[6] *Indian Converts*, 197–201.

[7] DCCR, 1:143, 145.

[8] DCP, 1:102.

[9] *Indian Converts*, 197.

thought Meeksishqune was too forceful in criticizing her husband's drinking, but she could take heart that her children had no doubts about her high expectations.

Meeksishqune's last pregnancy "several Years past Child-bearing" forced her into her deathbed where she made one more lasting impression on her family.[10] Witnesses told Mayhew that "having first spoken to her Husband giving him the best Counsel she could, and committing the Care of her Children to him, earnestly desiring him to bring them up in the Nurture and Admonition of the Lord; she called in her Children one by one, giving such Advice to them as she thought they respectively most needed." Wampanoag neighbors remembered that as she took her last breaths, "they then heard a melodious singing in the Air, over the House where this Woman lay."[11]

Meeksishqune's death in 1723 appears to have been a transforming event for the Hossueit family. Seven years later, her widower had reformed and become Nashuakemuck's ruling elder.[12] Her son, Zachariah, had moved to Aquinnah to apply his mother's lessons as magistrate. For the younger Zachariah it was the beginning of a long distinguished career seemingly driven by the dying wishes of his upstanding mother, as well as by the chiaroscuro example of his father, who was sinfully neglectful yet inspiring in his life change.

II

Zachariah Hossueit became a justice when that office was at its ebb among the Indians. During the seventeenth century, magistrates were potent enforcers of social order and esteemed community members. They hailed from elite families, mediated between Wampanoag and English courts, received the colonists' encouragement, and pursued an agenda widely supported by the people they served. Some justices, such as Isaac Ompany and Obadiah Paul of Christiantown, added further luster to the post by leading the defense of Native territory against the sachems and their English co-conspirators. However, the bases of magisterial authority had seriously eroded by the early eighteenth century. New rounds of epidemics drained the Indians' vigor to uphold Christian law. A person's descent from a sachem lineage still mattered, but the bankrupt administrations of Keteanummin, Wunnattuhquanmow, and Joseph Mittark made Indians less deferential toward their leaders and increasingly distrustful of them. All the while, English courts hemmed

---

[10] *Indian Converts*, 200.

[11] *Indian Converts*, 201. For accounts of similar wonders at the deaths of other Christian Indians, see, *Indian Converts*, 33, 147–8, 150, 160, 201, 221–2, 232, 262; Simmons, *Spirit of the New England Tribes: Indian History and Folklore, 1620–1984* (Hanover, N.H.: University Press of New England, 1986), 116, 120–1, 134, 137.

[12] CPGNE, Box 1, December 31, 1729, Dec. 7, 1730.

in the authority of Wampanoag magistrates, to which the Indians responded by informally withdrawing from the judicial system. Experience Mayhew complained to Cotton Mather that Wampanoags suffered "the want of due Exercise of civil Government among them . . . there are a multitude of bold transgressors that continually goe unpunished, especially vile prophanation of the Sabbath day." The reason for Indians' laxity, Mayhew believed, was "they are disgusted that they have not the same authority allowed them as formerly they had, and will seldom inform the English authority of such breaches of law as are among them."[13] In 1746 Boston declared Aquinnah, Christiantown, and Chappaquiddick to be official Indian "plantations" and formally transferred their magistrates' powers to colonial guardians, but the act merely ended a charade that had gone on for many years.[14] Even when guardians reappointed Indian justices to act in their stead, these figures lacked the legitimacy of Wampanoag self-rule.

The collapsing magistracy could not contain Hossueit's talents and ambitions, so in 1737 he also became Aquinnah's schoolmaster, which in previous generations had been a powerful office. On a 1698 trip to the Vineyard, ministers Grindal Rawson and Samuel Danforth found well-instructed children in every Native community except Chappaquiddick.[15] Twenty years later, Experience Mayhew wrote that "considerable numbers of the Indians have learned to read and write," though he equivocated, "yet they have mostly done this after the rate that poor Men among the English are wont to do," and "few of them [are] able to read and understand English Books in any measure well."[16] Mayhew forgot that the Wampanoags' modest literacy was an achievement no other Indian people could match, and more to the point, it met their limited goals. A reading knowledge of Wampanoag was sufficient to use the documents that most affected Indian life – the Bible, religious tracts, deeds, and wills. The select few who were literate in English could shoulder the responsibility of guarding their people against the outside world.

Indian schools had served the community well over the years, but they were also in decline by Hossueit's day. Some struggling parents kept their children at home "for Tillage of the land" or because they could not afford proper books and clothes, while others disapproved of school faculty.[17] In 1717, the New England Company hired Jabez Athearn as the Christiantown schoolmaster and paid him £14 more than his Native counterpart, Hosea

---

[13] Experience Mayhew to Cotton Mather, August 28, 1723, Misc. Bound MSS, MHS.

[14] Yasu Kawashima, "Legal Origins of the Indian Reservation in Colonial Massachusetts," *American Journal of Legal History*, 13 (1969), 46–8.

[15] "Indian Visitation," 131–2.

[16] *Indian Converts*, xxiii. See also E. Mayhew, *A Brief Account of the State of the Indians on Martha's Vineyard . . . 1694 to 1720*, appended to E. Mayhew, *Discourse Shewing that God Dealeth with Men as Reasonable Creatures* (Boston, 1720), 4.

[17] E. Mayhew, *A Brief Account of the State of the Indians on Martha's Vineyard*, 4 (quote); *Conquests and Triumphs*, 45.

Manhut, even though his family had a record of abusing Indians with law-suits and land purchases. The following year, the Company had to dismiss Athearn, "forasmuch as the Indians neglect & refuse to send their children to be taught by him."[18] The Natives' greatest discouragement was the Com-pany's new emphasis on having their children taught in English by English schoolmasters and its termination of Wampanoag language publications.[19] The Indians' response was to abandon the schools, just as they had left the courts. Unfortunately, weakened literacy skills put them at greater risk of exploitation.

Zachariah Hossueit had a great deal of work to do, but he continued to take on new responsibilities. In 1740, after five years of serving as an assis-tant to the Baptist minister Jonah Hossueit, he switched denominations to become the Congregationalists' pastor. Hossueit's shift took place during a critical phase in the Indians' church history, a time of moderate but important growth for a Baptist meeting that would figure prominently in the Indians' future and that today boasts the longest continual existence of any Protestant Indian congregation in North America. The Aquinnah Baptist Church first gathered in 1693 under the former Christiantown preacher Stephen Tacka-masun, and although the profile of its membership is uncertain there was a clear connection to Noman's Land, a tiny island just off the Vineyard's south-west coast. In 1702, Jonah Hossueit, a "kinsman" to sachem John Philip of Noman's Land, was the Baptists' preacher, and most of the Indians who fished at the island were members of his church.[20] This was a fringe base if there ever was one, but the Baptists still managed to unnerve orthodox English authorities. Experience Mayhew, the grandson of Thomas Mayhew Jr. and the most active missionary of his day, tried to dismiss the Baptists as petulant Congregationalists who had been "brought under Church-dealing for their vile Immoralities."[21] Yet his explanation rings hollow. Several years earlier, Mayhew criticized the Congregationalists as moral police and he let slip that Caleb Ohhumuh managed to quit drinking only after attending the

---

[18] NE Co. MSS, 7953, p. 49 (verso). For Jabez Athearn's legal confrontations with Indians, see DCCR, 1:126, 163; Box 174A, Env. 42, November 21, 1735, MVHS; DCGSP, 1730–57, p. 746.

[19] William Kellaway, *The New England Company: Missionary Society to the American Indians* (Westport, Conn.: Greenwood Press, 1961), 195, 228–30; Edward G. Gray, *New World Babel: Languages and Nations in Early America* (Princeton, N.J.: Princeton University Press, 1999), 82–3; Kathleen Joan Bragdon, "'Another Tongue Brought In': An Ethnohistorical Study of Native Writings in Massachusett" (Ph.D. diss., Brown University, 1981), 46; NE Co. MSS, 7953, p. 24.

[20] M. Halsey Thomas, ed., *The Diary of Samuel Sewall, 1674–1729*, 2 vols. (New York: Farrar, Straus, and Giroux 1973), 1:465; Isaac Backus, *A History of New England, with Particu-lar Reference to the Denomination of Christians Called Baptists*, 3 vols. (Boston, 1777), 1:438–9; Gay Head Baptist Church Records, Charles Banks Papers, Vol:Gay Head, MHS; *Conquests and Triumphs*, 31.

[21] *Indian Converts*, 42–3.

Baptist meeting.[22] Doctrine, Mayhew revealed in his most forthright moments, was the Baptists' strongest draw. He recommended to the New England Company "that some short Treastise be drawn up and translated into Indian to prevent the spreading of the Anabaptistical Notions," and years later he accused Baptist Wampanoags of being "uncharitable and censorious" on matters of conscience.[23] It is also possible, indeed likely, that the Baptists embodied a political bloc. Historically, Native American peoples under colonial pressure have divided into "accommodationist" and "traditionalist" wings that overlapped with traditional "peace" and "warrior" moieties. Tribes courted by more than one Christian denomination have tended to express these and other political allegiances through the competing churches, thereby adding a third layer to factional identity.[24] Given scant evidence, there is no way to know for sure whether a similar process accounts for the Wampanoags' Baptist schism, but clearly it involved more than the dissenters' aversion to church discipline.

It could not have been a coincidence that the Baptists' popularity spiked soon after the New England Company pressured the Aquinnah and Nashakemuck Congregationalists to replace their deceased pastor, Japheth Hannit, with Experience Mayhew. Wampanoags were angry enough at their loss of control over their land, schools, and courts; now outsiders were trying to interfere with the community's central institution. The Indians would not have it, and "Contrary to the Advi[c]e of the Commissioners" called one of their own, Sowomog, to the pulpit.[25] The Indians were not opposed to Mayhew, per se, for he had been and would continue to be a cherished advocate of theirs as a missionary, political advisor, and interpreter.[26] The issue was that they were "not being willing to have Englishmen" – any

---

[22] *Indian Converts*, 224, 227–8; E. Mayhew, *A Brief Account of the State of the Indians on Marthas̀ Vineyard*, 6–7.

[23] *Diary of Samuel Sewall*, 1:465 ("Treatise"); *Indian Converts*, 43 ("uncharitable").

[24] Among many studies, see Rebecca Kugel, *To Be the Main Leaders of Our People: A History of Minnesota Ojibwe Politics* (East Lansing: Michigan State University Press, 1998); Daniel K. Richter, "Iroquois versus Iroquois: Jesuit Missions and Christianity in Village Politics, 1642–1686," *Ethnohistory* 32 (1985), 1–16; Karim Michel Tiro, "The People of the Standing Stone: The Oneida Indian Nation from Revolution Through Removal, 1765–1840" (Ph.D. diss., University of Pennsylvania, 1999), 147–99.

[25] NE Co. MSS, 7953, pp. 32, 36 (quote), 45.

[26] CPGNE, Recs., Box 2, May 5, 1740, December 15, 1741, August 19, 1742, June 27, 1743, November 15, 1744, June 2, 1747; Disbursements to the Indian Poor, Experience Mayhew Papers, MHS; Suffolk Files, #43637; NE Co. MSS, 7953, pp. 32–3, 40, 42, 48, 69, 72, 78, 82, 94; "Letter from Experience Mayhew," *NEHGR* 18 (1864), 68; Epistle dedicatory by Samuel Rawson in Increase Mather, *Masukkenukeeg Matcheseanvog* [*Greatest Sinners Exhorted and Encouraged*] (Boston, 1698), 163–4; E. Mayhew, *A Brief Account of the State of the Indians on Marthas̀ Vineyard*, 8, 9; Margery Ruth Johnson, "The Mayhew Mission to the Indians, 1643–1806" (Ph.D. diss., Clark University, 1966), chap. 6; Jean Fittz Hankins, "Bringing the Good News: Protestant Missions to the Indians of New England and New York, 1700–1755" (Ph.D. diss., University of Connecticut, 1993), 260–6, 292.

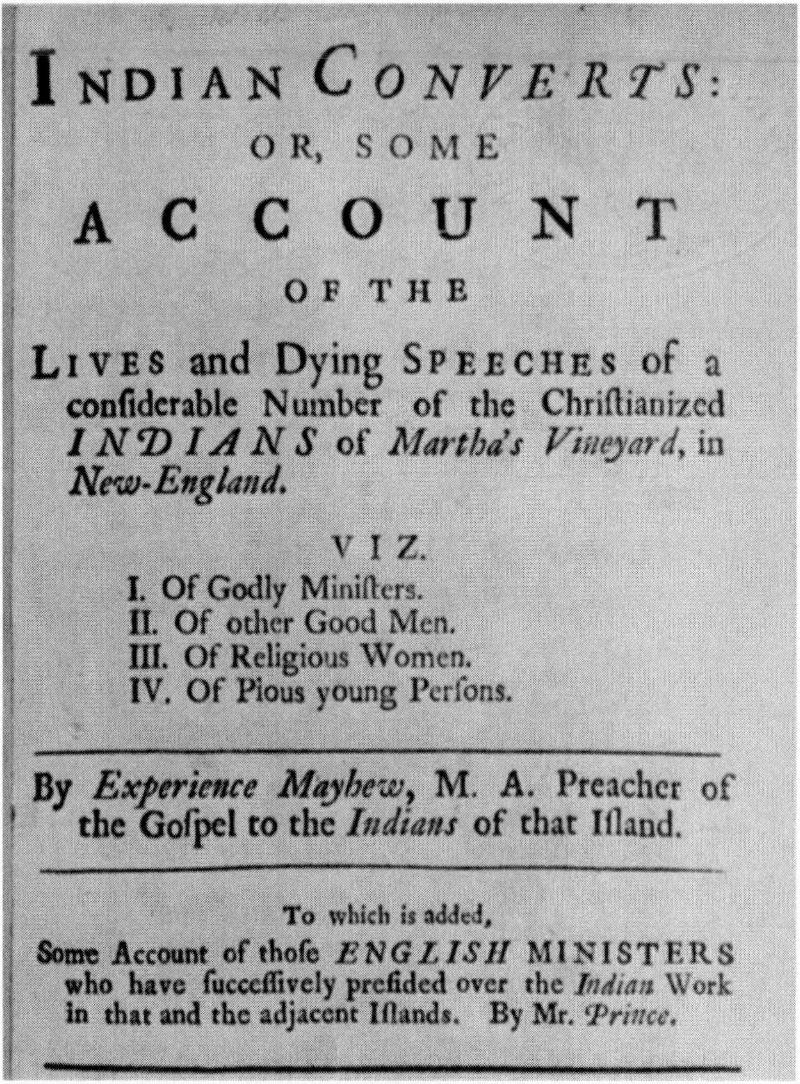

INDIAN CONVERTS:

OR, SOME

ACCOUNT

OF THE

LIVES and Dying SPEECHES of a confiderable Number of the Chriftianized *INDIANS* of *Martha's Vineyard*, in *New-England.*

VIZ.

I. Of Godly Minifters.
II. Of other Good Men.
III. Of Religious Women.
IV. Of Pious young Perfons.

By *Experience Mayhew*, M. A. Preacher of the Gofpel to the *Indians* of that Ifland.

To which is added,
Some Account of thofe *ENGLISH* MINISTERS who have fucceffively prefided over the *Indian* Work in that and the adjacent Iflands. By Mr. *Prince.*

FIGURE 5. Title Page of Experience Mayhew, *Indian Converts, or Some Account of the Lives and Dying Speeches of a Considerable Number of the Christianized Indians of Martha's Vineyard, in New-England* (London, 1727). The Wampanoags refused to appoint Experience Mayhew as their minister in the early eighteenth century, more because of a determination to maintain full control of their church than out of any antipathy toward him. Indeed, Mayhew was the Wampanoags' greatest advocate during a period of tremendous need. Among his legacies is this publication, *Indian Converts*, which contains scores of Christian Wampanoag biographies drawn from Mayhew's personal knowledge, his family's missionary writings, and not least of all, Wampanoag oral histories. It is the only source of its kind from this period and it allows the lives of figures like Zachariah Hossueit to be told with a level of detail that would otherwise be impossible.

Englishmen – "for their Pastors."[27] By the mid–eighteenth century the
Wampanoag church was almost a century old, which made churchgoing
a traditional activity. Church was the one place where the community gathered together to hear the people's own language as a sacred language, and
where Wampanoags held all the positions of respect.[28] Unwilling to risk this
sanctity, some Indians left for the Baptist meeting, where they continued to
receive financial support from the New England Company while keeping it
at safe a distance.[29]

Mayhew downplayed the Baptist schism, claiming that "the number
of people belonging unto this is very inconsiderable," but once again
he stretched the truth.[30] By 1702, the Aquinnah Baptist Church boasted
30 members (10 male and 20 female), and by 1739 Chappaquiddick and
Nantucket Wampanoags had formed their own Baptist meetings.[31] Certainly
the Baptists were a minority of the Native population, at most twenty percent, but they counted several prominent community members and their
ranks were growing by the year . . . that is, until Zachariah Hossueit left
them.

Zachariah Hossueit's move in 1740 from Baptist assistant to Congregationalist preacher stemmed the tide. His motivation might have been a larger
flock with a bigger salary and stronger ties to colonial elites, all to better serve
his political ambitions.[32] At the same time, one cannot rule out that his shift
was a matter of the heart, for his leadership clearly inspired Aquinnah's
Congregationalists. What is certain is that Baptist growth stagnated with
Hossueit at the orthodox helm, even though the denomination was explod-
ing among colonists and mainland Indians caught up in the enthusiasm of
the Great Awakening.[33]

In an age of corroding public institutions, Zachariah Hossueit's status
as magistrate, teacher, and minister, his written command of Wampanoag
and English, and his descent from a sachem merely served as qualifications
for leadership, not as a mandate. He had to prove his mettle against the

---

[27] *Indian Converts*, 112.

[28] On some of these themes, see Kathleen Bragdon, "Native Christiantiy in 18th Century
Massachusetts: Ritual as Cultural Reaffirmation," in *New Dimensions in Ethnohistory:
Papers of the Second Laurier Conference on Ethnohistory and Ethnology* (Hull, Quebec:
Canadian Museum of Civilization, 1991), 119–26.

[29] For similar conclusions about Narragansett Baptists, see Simmons, "Red Yankees."

[30] E. Mayhew, *A Brief Account of the State of the Indians on Martha's Vineyard*, 3.

[31] *Diary of Samuel Sewall*, 1:465; CPGNE, Recs., Box 1, December entries and Nov. 22,
1738; Nathaniel Philbrick, *Abram's Eyes: The Native American Legacy of Nantucket Island*
(Nantucket, Mass.: Mill Hill Press, 1998), 277.

[32] CPGNE, Box 1, December 13, 1740.

[33] Edwin Scott Gaustad, *The Great Awakening in New England* (New York: Harper and
Brothers, 1957), esp. chap. 7; Simmons, "The Great Awakening and Indian Conversion in
Southern New England," in William Cowan, ed., *Papers of the 10th Algonquian Conference*
(Ottawa: Carleton University Press, 1979), 25–36; Simmons, "Red Yankees."

Wampanoags' enemies before he could expect his neighbors' full support. There was ample opportunity for him to do so, since cooperation between three types of foes – Native profit-seekers, corrupt colony guardians, and encroaching Englishmen – plagued virtually every Wampanoag village during his lifetime. Aquinnah would emerge from the fray intact owing largely to his efforts.

III

Unseating the sachems did not purge the Wampanoags of rapacious community members, and in some ways the Indians' poverty and the reach of their creditors left them more vulnerable than ever to inside jobs. The growing trend of Indians leasing out land to colonists brought in much needed capital, but it gave outsiders footholds from which they could make more permanent claims to Native territory, particularly when they had an Indian collaborator. The constant coming and going of Indians who labored for the English as whalers, house servants, and farm hands made it difficult for them to participate in what was now the community's collective responsibility to monitor its lands. In any case, with so many Indians losing the battle to make ends meet, a number of them were tempted to sell off the communal resources they were supposed to defend. The conditions were ripe for graft and the brothers Elisha and Israel Amos (or Ianoxso) were ready to exploit them to the fullest.

Although the Amos brothers were the paternal great-grandsons of Ompohhunnut, who challenged Mittark for the Aquinnah sachemship during the opening salvos of King Philip's War, there was little else in their history to suggest these men would cause their neighbors trouble. Their family had moved back and forth between Nashuakemuck and Takemmy for three generations until the 1720s, when their father, Amos Ianoxso Sr., finally settled them in Christiantown, where he became a pillar of the community. Before long he had served as deacon, ruling elder, magistrate, meeting moderator, and courtroom "agent." He had opposed English encroachment at every turn, and put up bail for neighbors in trouble with the law.[34] Israel and Elisha Amos did not lack for good examples.

Yet Elisha was an enigmatic figure, who in one breath cared for the sick and indigent, and in the next connived against his love interests and relatives.[35] Between 1727 and 1731, both Ruth Charles and Sarah Quenue

---

[34] Testimony of Bethia Escohommon and Experience Mayhew in Suffolk Files, #43637; DCD, 6:97, 374; CPGNE, Recs., Box 1, December entries 1729–31, November 29, 1732, December entries 1732–37, November 22, 1738, December entries 1739–40; DCCP, 1722–36, 692, 701, 703, 825; DCCP, 1722–62, 872; DCGSP, 1730–52, 746, 746b, 836; Force Papers, October 24, 1735, November 21, 1736; Box 174A, File 42, November 21, 1736, MVHS; Box 5S, Envelope 3, MVHS.

[35] *Native Writings*, 1:151–7.

charged him with fathering their children, but failing to pay support in violation of rulings by justices Zaccheus Mayhew and John Allen.[36] In 1736, one of Amos's own brothers testified that Elisha "had burnt Ruth Charleses house...& that the said Elisha also towld him he would Burn Coll: Mayhews howse & Majr Allen's house...because they had bin Sevear with him when he had bin brought before them."[37] That same year, Amos's wife Rebecca abandoned him, and his father-in-law, Daniel Suncosoh of Mashpee, sued him for the costs of maintaining her.[38] It is uncertain who won this case, but clearly Amos fell on hard times, for in 1745 he sued his own father for debt.[39] Then, two years later, somehow he convinced Esther Nunnamuck to engage to marry him, but within months the wedding was off and Nunnumuck was in court seeking damages.[40] It was not easy to love Elisha Amos.

The land market was the ideal place for Elisha Amos to express his antisocial tendencies. Christiantown was supposed to remain an exclusively Indian place, but once the town meeting had distributed family plots there was nothing to obstruct Indians from bargaining with other Indians and no reason to think that there should be. As such, beginning in the mid-1730s and stretching well into the 1740s, Amos used money advanced to him by Simeon Butler, the corrupt former agent of Jacob Seeknout, to buy up one tract of land after another from his neighbors – fifteen acres from Solomon Ned, eight acres from Hosea Manhut, seven acres from William Charles, the "Great Field" from William Soquin.[41] Amos's elite ancestry and a few provisions allowing Native grantors to remain on the deeded land made it appear that he aspired to become a sachem.[42] If so, his model was Keteanummin rather than the respected leaders of memory. In crass violation of Christiantown's long struggle to survive as an Indian haven within Tisbury, Amos leased and illegally sold his new holdings to Englishmen, including the hated Ebenezer Rogers.[43] Yet for the moment no one was willing to challenge these deals. Amos had the backing of several powerful Englishmen, so a fair hearing was unlikely in any Vineyard court. Moreover, it was impossible not to be intimidated by Amos's record of violent retribution against anyone who

[36] DCGSP, 1722–62, 872; DCCP, 1722–36, 692; DCGSP, 1730–57, 733.

[37] Suffolk Files, #43282.

[38] Suffolk Files, #43638.

[39] DCCP, 1730–55, 786.

[40] DCD, 7:238; DCCP, 1730–55, 787.

[41] DCD, 7:28, 140–41, 239–43, 292, 330, 340, 467; 8:71.

[42] This interpretation is put forth by Daniel R. Mandell, *Behind the Frontier: Indians in Eighteenth-Century Eastern Massachusetts* (Lincoln: University of Nebraska Press, 1996), 103, 222 n. 96. For clauses allowing Indian grantors to stay on the land, see *Native Writings*, 1:158–61; DCD, 7:53.

[43] DCD, 8:122, 138. DCD, 7:140–1, and 8:135, mention Elisha Amos's lease to Englishman Jacob Clifford in passing.

crossed him. Not only had he bullied former lovers, but he went so far as to torch his own family's house, nearly killing his father, to coerce the old man into naming him heir over his older brother Israel. According to another brother, Jacob, a year earlier Elisha had said "he was determined to burn it, but was lo[a]th he should loose by it & therefore admonished [Jacob] to sell it & take a bond for the Money & then he would burn it down & towld him that his brother [Israel] amos would not be able to build another house & then they two would enjoy the land."[44] The scheme worked to perfection; in 1742 the shaken father deeded his estate to the family arsonist.[45]

It took awhile, but by 1747 these abuses had convinced Christiantown to complain straight to the Massachusetts legislature. Amos Ianoxso Sr. told of his very son "conveying away his Estate under Pretence of its being an Instrument of another Nature," and the town as a whole accused him of "using divers fraudulent Practices for alienating their Estates from them: Praying that no Deed or Instrument thus obtained by him should be good in Law unless it be acknowledged before Justices of the Peace nominated by this Court for that Service."[46] Boston ordered Amos and Butler to explain themselves, which was enough to drive their crooked operation elsewhere.

Pushed out of Christiantown by public opinion and the gaze of mainland authorities, Amos picked the small Nashuakemuck village of Roaring Brook as his next target. This time he drew on Butler's funds, not only to buy land, but to extend generous loans to Indians who would put up land as collateral. When they proved unable to pay, he foreclosed upon their plots, pulled down their houses, and sued everyone who got in his way.[47] Shortly, he was in sole possession of some one hundred acres at this isolated location and looking for a new place to con. A disturbance his brother had stirred up at Aquinnah provided the opportunity.

After moving to Aquinnah in the late 1730s, Israel Amos led a protest against the Wampanoag sheep-right committee, accusing it of extending colonists' grazing rights "over and above what the Indians['] stock shall require."[48] On the surface this was a matter of principle about whether the Indians' lessees or the Indians themselves would control Aquinnah's resources. The petitioners also might have been concerned about the grazing rights of John Allen. Ever since the creation of the English town of Chilmark in 1714 on the site of the former Manor of Tisbury, Allen had used his

---

[44] Suffolk Files, #43282.

[45] DCD, 7:53, 239–42.

[46] *Mass. Acts and Resolves*, 14:31.

[47] On loans, see DCD, 8:295. On purchases, see DCD, 7:330, 543; 8:165, 181, 183, 290, 429, 431. On pulling down houses, see DCGSP, 1730–52, 768; Dukes County Records, SL DUK 1N, NEHGS. On lawsuits, see DCCP, 1730–55, 784–5; DCD, 8:151; Force Papers, February 3, 1748; Suffolk Files, # 29779, 64989, 64994, 66753, 65383, 98783. On the connection between Amos and Butler, see *Mass. House Journals*, 23:253.

[48] CPGNE, Box 2, March 17, 1739 (quote) and May 5, 1740.

power as town sheriff and county justice to abuse the Wampanoags almost without compunction, including clasping Abigail Wompas in chains and selling her into indentured servitude in Rhode Island, and conspiring to get Jane Nahoman drunk so she would sign a fraudulent deed.[49] Nevertheless, Israel's main purpose in this affair was to loosen the committee's authority over land he coveted for himself. In 1740, his father granted him the family claim to one-quarter of Aquinnah descended from Ompohhunnut's 1675 settlement with Mittark.[50] Months later, Israel purchased an overlapping one-eighth of the neck from Job Paaonut (or Pawhonet), the grandson of Ompohhunnut.[51] The family's title had remained dormant for sixty-five years, but Israel meant to resuscitate it. As the New England Company learned, Amos "lays claim to some land at Gayhead & threatens to sue."[52]

It was Zachariah Hossueit who rose up to confront Israel Amos, buttressed by a large Aquinnah family and a constituency amassed through years of public service. Yet as he prepared for what became a court battle of nearly twenty years' duration, Elisha Amos stepped into the fray, joining his brother to enclose part of the Aquinnah commons and buy up the land rights of at least ten Wampanoag families with the intent of bringing in colonial renters.[53] Aquinnah tolerated short-term leases of family land when work pulled the owners away from home, but seizing new acreage specifically for that purpose was unacceptable.[54] The plot thickened as Aquinnah's newly appointed guardian – none other than John Allen – conveniently overlooked Elisha's long arrest record and asked Boston to appoint him as a magistrate. Hossueit wasted no time penning a forceful response, knowing that an Amos magistracy and Allen guardianship would throw open his people's lands to the market. "We say truly we need a judge," he explained to the New England Company, but if Elisha Amos was that judge "we shall be much more miserable. This Elisha Amos has robbed us of our gardens and also of our fresh meadows and our land . . . we would be much more miserable because of this Elisha Amos, just as the word of God says in Job 34:30," a passage that reads, "Let not the hypocrite rule."[55] With the attention of

---

[49] On the Wompas case, see DCCP, 1722–36, 688, 694. On the Nahoman case, see DCCP, 1736–42, 710 verso. Allen's troubled history with the Indians can be also be traced in *Mass. House Journals*, 13:64; DCR, 1:225; DCCP, 1730–55, 708, 785–7, 811–12, 819; DCGSP, 1722–62, 872; DCGSP, 1730–57, 741 verso; Force Papers, October 24, 1735, April [ ], 1737, and October 10, 1745; Suffolk Files, # 31091, 31240, 31279. On his land purchases, see DCD, 2:304; 3:151; 4:236, 237, 241; 5:17, 90, 324; 6:2.

[50] DCD, 6:374.

[51] DCD, 6:405.

[52] NE Co. MSS, 7953, 106 (quote); CPGNE, Box 2, February 9, 1741, August 19, 1742; DCCP, 1730–55, 793, 797.

[53] DCD, 6:10; 8:148, 191, 203, 354, 429–30, 460, 552, 574; ZHP, Ag. 19 #33060–7; Suffolk Files, #144020; RSCJ, Barnstable, January 1755, 9.

[54] DCD, 8:574.

[55] *Native Writings*, 1:224–5.

some of Boston's most powerful men now trained upon him, Allen suddenly lost his enthusiasm for Amos's candidacy.

Although few details survive of Hossueit's struggle with Israel Amos, by the late 1750s clearly he had triumphed and consolidated his status as Aquinnah's leader.[56] In 1746, in the middle of the court battles, Aquinnah placed new restrictions on taking in colonial livestock, but allowed Hossueit, "Liberty to hire out his write [right] or part of them to the Mantors," a Chilmark family, "as he shall see fit."[57] Nineteen years later, it gifted Hossueit one hundred sheep-rights in acknowledgment of how he "stood by us and bore the big[g]est part of the Charge" in fending off the Amos brothers.[58] Reciprocity had returned to Aquinnah government. The people were generous to Hossueit because he showed that he would use these resources to defend the community in the traditional spirit of Wampanoag leadership.

Bitterness ran deep between the Amoses and their neighbors, yet this was the last time they faced off. Strikingly, Hossueit presided over the wedding of Israel Amos to Abigail Abel in 1757.[59] Elisha's purchases of Native land ended in 1758 and he died nine years later.[60] Then in 1776, Israel sold the Aquinnah Proprietors (the organization comprising all Aquinnah adults with rights to the land) a tract called "Elisha's Farm," which he had been renting out to colonist Josiah Tilton.[61] Perhaps Israel's sale was a mere business transaction rather than a symbol of reconciliation. However, one detail suggests something more. Some time just before 1763, Elisha Amos married a woman named Rebecca, a slave of colonist Cornelius Bassett. After Elisha's death, she remarried and went by the name Rebecca Hossueit.[62] This chronology bears all the signs of old-style Indian politics, in which a wedding between antagonistic families signals a new era of peace.

Hossueit could not have defeated the Amoses if he had not solved the sachem's quandary about how to fund his political activities without selling the land. Hossueit met his legal costs partially through his combined salaries as minister, schoolteacher, magistrate, and clerk. By 1771 he took in at least £100 Massachusetts currency a year for his efforts, most of it paid by the New England Company.[63] Channeling this money to public interests led

---

[56] CPGNE, Box 2, June 22, 1757.

[57] Mass. Archives, 31:523.

[58] ZHP, 1763 Mr 24-N28, #33060–8.

[59] *Native Writings*, 1:66–9

[60] DCP, 5:50, 53.

[61] DCD, 10:349.

[62] DCD, 14:2; DCP, 5:50. The marriage of Amos and Rebecca is detailed in Barnstable Superior Court of Judicature, #6563, Inhabitants of Edgartown vs. Inhabitants of Tisbury, Segel, Pierce, Montorosso Collection: Wampanoag Genealogy and Related Documents, Box 2, MVHS.

[63] CPGNE, Box 1, December entries, Box 2, October 8, 1757; "Memorial of Zachariah Mayhew, October 1, 1759," Misc. Bound MSS, MHS; "Indian Accounts at Martha's Vineyard for the year 1771," Misc. Bound MSS, MHS.

his neighbors to extend him special grazing privileges, which, in turn, gave him more resources for good works. When he was not in court, he drafted his people's wills and petitions, took down meeting minutes, interpreted documents, preached God's word, and conducted wedding ceremonies. He drew on long credit lines at colonial stores to support charitable causes, for instance, buying hundreds of pounds of beef and mutton from Peter Norton in a single year, presumably for poor relief.[64] He even served as point man for the New England Company, distributing its annual shipments of school supplies and religious tracts, and its donations of emergency food during a famine in 1762.[65] Hossueit made himself valuable to his neighbors in almost every conceivable capacity and received their strong support in return.[66]

Hossueit was hardly less valuable to the English. His disproportionate share of Aquinnah grazing rights and sway over community affairs gave him influence with powerful colonists such as John Allen who wanted Wampanoag pasture for their livestock and Wampanoag customers for their stores. In 1735, Hossueit purchased two thousand shingles and nails from Allen toward the repair of the Gay Head meeting house, while in other years he grazed and tended to Allen's herds.[67] Thereafter, when Allen as a creditor pressed charges against an Indian debtor, or as the county sheriff arrested an Aquinnah resident, or as the Gay Head guardian made underhanded decisions, Hossueit could personally appeal to the man for moderation by reminding him of their shared interests. Hossueit was coveted by mainland colonists as well. Visitors from Boston often lodged at his home, and when they wanted to meet with the Native community or to have their speeches and letters translated from English into Wampanoag, they went to Hossueit first.[68] As Samuel Sewall wrote, "such of them as can speak English, find themselves vastly accommodated for the entertaining and communicating of Knowledge, beyond what they were before."[69]

In many ways, Hossueit was a classic cultural broker. His uncommon skills and leadership among the Indians brought him to the attention of colonists, who then recognized him as the community representative and reinforced that role by extending him special privileges such as official lines

---

[64] Loose document, Box 2S, Env. 9, MVHS.

[65] CPGNE, Recs., Box 2, October 9, 1762.

[66] My thinking in this and the following paragraph has been particularly influenced by Timothy Earle, ed., *Chiefdoms: Power, Economy, and Ideology* (New York: Cambridge University Press, 1991); Earle, *How Chiefs Come to Power: The Political Economy of Prehistory* (Stanford, Cal.: Stanford University Press, 1997); Marc J. Swartz, ed., *Local-Level Politics: Social and Cultural Perspectives* (Chicago: Aldine Publishing, 1969); Myron J. Aronoff, ed., *Ideology and Interest: The Dialectics of Politics*, Political Anthropology Yearbook 1 (New Brunswick, N.J.: Transaction Books, 1980).

[67] John Allen Account Book, 1780–1820 [the actual dates are 1730–59], 20, 21, 32–3, MVHS.

[68] Josiah Tilton to Zachary Horsut, March 28, 1766, ZHP.

[69] "Samuel Sewall Letter Book," *MHSC* 1st ser. 1 (1886), 602.

of communication, material resources, and titles with real authority. But Hossueit, unlike many other go-betweens, was not a man of two separate worlds. The Wampanoags were indelibly a part of a colonial New England, or rather, colonial New England was a part of them despite the cultural and racial boundaries that continued to distance them from their English neighbors. As such, Hossueit's influence flowed from holding multiple offices in institutions that Wampanoags and Englishmen shared and from his ability to read and write the documents that shaped both their lives and mediated their relations. The irony was that even as Hossueit drew on English resources to defeat local rivals, he was also learning to apply them within circumscribed limits to fend off the colonial state.

IV

The 1746 Massachusetts law authorizing three guardians for every recognized Indian plantation was conceived as an act of benevolence.[70] It was plain to see that earlier regulations had failed to ease the Natives' struggles with debt and land loss, so legislators concluded that the Indians needed well-heeled, reputable overseers to tend to their daily affairs. These men would keep order as Justices of the Peace, channel legitimate Indian complaints to Boston, prevent Indian land from being sold without approval, and manage Indian resources by allotting planting grounds, renting out the surplus, and applying the proceeds to schools and poor relief. This well-intentioned system met its goals when its appointees were devoted to their task. Unfortunately, too often the guardianship was a means for avaricious men to line their own pockets.

Chappaquiddick was particularly victimized by this legislation. Whereas in the fifteen years before the guardian act there were only five recorded sales of Wampanoag land, in the next fifteen years there were thirty.[71] Eventually the Indians convinced Boston to launch an investigation, which revealed conditions to be even worse than the public record indicated. Mainland officials discovered:

[The colonists have] erected nine Houses upon the Indians Lands there; have made upwards of sixty Purchases of Land, containing by Estimation two thousand acres or more of great Value, and for very trifling inconsiderable considerations; have cut and carried off more than five hundred Cords of Wood; put on by far more Cattle than by [the 1715 grazing] agreement they were allowed to do, and kept them on much

[70] On the guardian system, see Kawashima, *Puritan Justice and the Indian: White Man's Law in Massachusetts, 1630–1763* (Middletown, Conn.: Wesleyan University Press, 1986), 32–3, 55–6, 103–6.

[71] DCD, 5:196, 429–30; 6:49, 195, 269, 468, 531; 7:14–15, 348, 525; 8:69, 158, 194, 203, 220, 308, 351, 361, 449, 453, 484, 486, 489, 536, 555, 559, 572, 610; 9:63, 154; 10:60; 11:158–9; 12:23.

longer; have not paid them [the Indians] the [rent]...and that even [the Indians']
planting rights which their Ancestors held and possessed beyond the memory of man
are taken from them; and that when they looked for Judgement they found no Relief;
two of their Guardians [John Sumner and Jonathan Newman] being Purchasers or
Possessors which your Committee apprehend belongs to the Indians.

It was bad enough that the guardians allowed conflicts of interest to interfere with their legal judgments, yet they also duped the Wampanoags into
thinking they would receive justice to get them to run up "Large Bills of
Cost...paid either by more Lands being sold, or the Indians bound out to
go on Whaling Voyages or other Services."[72] This racket was an open secret
on the Vineyard. Everyone knew that the Chappaquiddick guardian John
Sumner was at once a merchant who extended poor Indians generous credit
for liquor, food, and tools; an owner of livestock that trampled over the
Indians' lands; and a Dukes County judge who ruled on the Indians' cases
for debt and trespass. His appointment as guardian meant nothing more to
him than an opportunity to swindle the Wampanoags further.[73]

Massachusetts responded to this blatant graft, not with swift action, but
discussion and delay. Two years later legislators were still talking over the
matter. In the end, they sympathized more with English trespassers, who
claimed to have acted in ignorance of the law and pleaded that taking away
their illegally held lands would "render them and their Families miserable
the Remainder of their days," than with the Indians whose actual misery
extended from the colony's failure to enforce its own rules.[74] Ultimately,
Boston allowed the colonists to stay in exchange for funding a survey of
other contested tracts.[75] Yet, as late as 1762, the committee authorized to
conduct this study still had not filed a report. Obviously it would never
be done, so in a clever maneuver designed to challenge the government's
missionary commitment, the Wampanoags proposed that the disputed land
could be used for a new Indian meeting house.[76] But their strategy was to no
avail. Five years later they wondered that "no Relief is yet granted" despite
their assertions that "nothing would Satisfie the Inhabitants of Edgartown
Short of our Entire & Speedy Extirpation." After years of being fleeced, the
Indians lacked tillage, firewood, fencing material, and pasture, which led
them to conclude, "we shall be Slaves to the s^d [English Chappaquiddick]

---

[72] *Mass. Acts and Resolves*, 17:81–4.

[73] On Sumner's activities as guardian, see *Mass. Acts and Resolves*, 15:110; 16:241; *Mass. House Journals*, 35:91; as proprietor, see Edgartown Records, 1:220; as store owner, John Sumner Account Book, 1749–1752, MVHS; as grantee, DCD, 8:536, 537, 559, 560. Sumner declined to rule on the highly publicized grazing dispute. See Kawashima, *Puritan Justice*, 106.

[74] Mass. Archives, 33:231.

[75] *Mass. Acts and Resolves*, 17;480, 522, 542; FNPR, 2:394, 396.

[76] Mass. Archives, 33:187.

Proprietors or must leave our Lands."[77] Similar petitions followed in 1768 and 1773, claiming that every passing day "Seem[s] to Double [the colonists'] Diligence to our Disadvantage." Boston might have seen Chappaquiddick's affairs as a minor nuisance, but the Wampanoags of Chappaqquiddick felt surrounded by "Destroyers."[78]

Desperate, the Indians dipped into their meager funds to hand-deliver their grievances to King George, a timely decision given that he had already lost patience with Massachusetts because of the spiraling revolutionary crisis.[79] The crown ordered the unruly colony to redress the Wampanoags' grievances, but unfortunately for the Indians, the white democratic rule that was proving so troublesome for them on the island had also weakened the king's voice in Boston. Officials complied with the letter but not the spirit of the directive by appointing yet another spineless committee, which judged that giving back the Wampanoags' lands would create too many "inconveniences" for the English and that the issue of more recent sales should be taken up by another committee.[80] Unsurprisingly, the flow of Indian petitions ground to a temporary end. The paper and ink were not worth the price.

Things were no better in Christiantown. Poverty had weakened Christiantown's consensus against land sales and in less than ten years more than one hundred acres of the mile-square village had been bargained away.[81] In 1760 the New England Company received word that "much land given to the Christian Indians, forever, by their sachems has been alienated to the English," and asked Massachusetts to investigate.[82] But once again the colony proved unwilling to uphold its own laws that protected Indians. It decided that the lands in question were "so much better by the improvements [the colonists] have made upon them," that justice was served by confirming the illegal deeds and having the English grantees pay to have the bounds

---

[77] Mass. Archives, 33:444–6. The Indians' pleas were not mere rhetoric. In Samson Coquit's 1777 account with colonist Sarah Shaw, £5 of his £11 5s. 9d. overdue bill was for wood. See DCCF, Indian Papers, Box 4.

[78] Mass. Archives, 33:470–1, 586–7.

[79] Public Records Office, CO 5/762, petition copy in Segel, Pierce, Montorosso Collection: Wampanoag Genealogy and Related Documents, Box 3, MVHS; *Boston Gazette*, No. 982, January 31, 1774.

[80] Mass. Archives, 33:586–7.

[81] DCD, 8:131, 332, 387, 389, 390, 441, 476, 480, 500, 597. A list of Indians receiving poor relief in "Disbursements to the Indian Poor," Experience Mayhew Papers, MHS, suggests that Christiantown had a higher rate of poverty than other Wampanoag villages on the island. This source does not list the recipients' places of residence, but I have determined hometowns based on appearances in the public record and on surname clusters in certain villages. The breakdown by village was as follows: Christiantown ($n = 14$); Gay Head ($n = 8$); Chappaquiddick ($n = 7$); Chilmark ($n = 5$); Sengekontacket ($n = 4$); Nunnepog ($n = 3$); unknown ($n = 27$).

[82] CPGNE, Recs., Box 2, November 11, 1760.

run.[83] Englishmen believed that land existed to be turned into profit. From the colony's viewpoint, Indians simply did not maximize the potential of their lands and therefore had to make way for a people who would. After all, what was the point of unused land?[84] Nobody asked the Wampanoags.

Christiantown and Chappaquiddick suffered quietly before bringing their guardians' corruption to public view and then prayed in vain that Boston would provide them with some relief. By contrast, when Gay Head's new guardians, Pain Mayhew and William Hunt, earmarked 900 acres for leasing and ordered the Native inhabitants to vacate, the Indians immediately scribbled off a flurry of angry petitions to the legislature.[85] In 1749 twenty-three men and nine women calling themselves "The Poor Indian Proprietors of Gayhead" declared that they had "met together and by a vote" and agreed that "we would plant our gardens on (the land) that the Guardians have leased out," because without that land, in "another year the poor Indians (will) not have gardens." And not only gardens, but grazing land as well: "The number of our Cretures are about 400 (we know not the number of sheep)," they wrote, and since "no longer do we have pasturage freely where our animals can feed," they wondered, "what shall these Cretures do for Pasture."[86] The guardians were either ignorant of, or disdainful toward, the Wampanoags' need for land, for they counted only 112 Indians at Gay Head whereas the petitioners reckoned 165.

The Aquinnah Wampanoags tailored their words to their audience more carefully than the Indians of Chappaquiddick or Christiantown. As "poor" Indians making a "humble petition" to "honorable" men, they played upon English expectations of deference from social and racial inferiors. They appealed for justice as fellow subjects of the crown, asking that "this new law may be taken away from us, because before this new law came those Englishmen were unable to treat us as they pleased. Therefore we say (we) would (have) only the law of our King George on this land of ours at Gayhead." As "Proprietors," they claimed the right to manage their village lands – *their property* – no less than the proprietors of any other New England town, and they were explicit that they would "use" the land for farming and pasture, not hunting and gathering.[87] The Indians' message, then, was that they were

[83] *Mass. Acts and Resolves*, 4:619 (quote); DCD, 9:196–8.

[84] On this theme, see William Cronon, *Changes in the Land: Indians, Colonists, and the Ecology of New England* (New York: Hill and Wang, 1983); Carolyn Merchant, *Ecological Revolutions: Nature, Gender, and Science in New England* (Chapel Hill: University of North Carolina Press, 1989).

[85] *Mass. House Journals*, 22:106; 24:200; 26:117, 234; 30:22; 31:277; 45:28. Generally on Indian troubles with guardians, see Mandell, *Behind the Frontier*, 143–58.

[86] Mass. Archives, 31:643–5; *Native Writings*, 1:170–5.

[87] On the values Englishmen attached to pasture, see Patricia Seed, *Ceremonies of Possession in Europe's Conquest of the New World, 1492–1640* (New York: Cambridge University Press, 1995), 25–31. On livestock, see Cronon, *Changes in the Land*, 141, 143–4; Virginia

about to fulfill the New England founders' expectation of transforming savages into Christians, and the "howling wilderness" into a civilized world of
fields, fences, property, and law. Was it not appalling, they implied, that the
guardians obstructed such a divine experiment?

In case these arguments failed, the Wampanoags added one more detail
that was sure to raise eyebrows, namely that they were "De[c]eived for the
money" from Aquinnah leases. Massachusetts bit at this charge if none else,
ordering Mayhew and Hunt to answer the Indians in full. The guardians'
justification for evicting Wampanoags from the leased land was that "it is
no more than [the Indians] practice themselves," which ignored the Indians'
point that there was a difference between moving of one's own accord and
someone else's orders. Moreover, the guardians contended, the Wampanoags
already had enough grazing land for their meager herds. Massachusetts
appears to have accepted these explanations, but it was less convinced of
the guardians' financial integrity. A "very extraordinary" invoice exposed
the guardians for hiring English pasture for Indian livestock at high rates
while simultaneously leasing Indian pasture out to English husbandmen –
including several of the guardians' relatives – at reduced rates. Suspiciously,
the guardians lacked receipts for disbursements and seemed to have taken
an inordinate number of unreasonably costly trips to Aquinnah. Excuses
met every charge, but Boston found them "very imperfect" and therefore
subtracted £210 17s. 6d. from the guardians' accounts, leaving a balance of
only £24 18s. 3d.[88] By acting quickly, the Aquinnah Wampanoags had successfully used Boston to rein in their overseers. They had also posted notice
that they intended to defend their lands.

It was Zachariah Hossueit who coordinated the petition campaign.
Theophilus Mayhew testified "that he Saw several of the Indian whose names
were to the said Petition. I heard them say th[a]t they did not put their names
to said Petition but that they liked well what Zachary done, & some of the
Indians said th[a]t they were not at the Meeting & knew nothing about it."[89]
Indeed, every signature on the petition was in Hossueit's hand. Was this an
act of chicanery, an attempt to deceive Boston authorities? Perhaps, but there
is other evidence to suggest legitimate Wampanoag political procedures generated the petition. Wampanoags say that in historic times their votes were
cast by family representatives based on careful consultation with relatives.
Positions were widely known before any tally was made. Possibly Hossueit
wrote down the names of family heads only after speaking with them directly

---

DeJohn Anderson, "King Philip's Herds: Indians, Colonists and the Problem of Livestock
in Early New England," *WMQ* 51 (1994), 601–24; and David J. Silverman, "'We chuse to
be bounded': Native American Animal Husbandry in Colonial New England," *WMQ* 60
(2003), 511–48.

[88] Mass. Archives, 32:597–9.

[89] Mass. Archives, 31:500.

or with their kin. Hossueit's petition stated that there were 165 Indians at Gay Head; the number of petitioners was thirty-five, which if they spoke for separate houses would make for a reasonable 5.2 persons per family.[90] Hossueit's drafting of a petition that reflected public opinion and then listing the names of his supporters might have been deceitful from an English perspective, but among the Indians it was not. Hossueit had already established himself as the bridge between the Native community, whose command of the written word was shaky at best and largely limited to Wampanoag, and a colonial state that insisted on precise, legalistic English-language documents. He had a proven track record of defending Aquinnah against its enemies, including the guardian Pain Mayhew, who he had once sued for trespass or unpaid rent.[91] Hossueit was now his people's leader. He had a mandate to act.

This is not to say that Hossueit enjoyed unanimous, unequivocal support. Boston decided not to appoint guardians for Aquinnah between 1758 and 1773, during which time Hossueit filled the vacuum as pastor, schoolmaster, and clerk. But at least twenty-three Wampanoag neighbors resented his rule. In 1767 they asked Boston to reinstate the guardians, because, they said, under their tenure the Indians had enjoyed order, an equal distribution of lease profits, and a cedar rail fence around the commons. Now, "the Fencing Afor[e]said is taken away from us and kept by some among us and we Denyd," and some "Designing men" and "Dishonest persons" had begun to "take in so many Creatures as makes the feed so poor that we cannot hire our Rights out and are Deprived altogether of our Interest [in] the Profits of the whole neck."[92]

There is evidence to suggest this protest was as much about Zachariah Hossueit's power as the absence of "order." There was bad blood between the Hossueit family, Zachariah in particular, and a handful of the signatories. In 1726, Joseph Pomet and several others were charged with breaking into Jonas Hossueit's house and carrying away his goods.[93] While Zachariah was magistrate, he had Old Barnabus arrested for stealing livestock from Abel and Joseph Hossueit, Jonathan Ocusha fined £15 for poisoning Deborah Hossueit, and Alice [Els] Harry arrested for assaulting another Indian.[94] Hossueit's opponents also might have resented his crackdown on Elisha Amos. Seven of the petitioners had either sold Amos land or were closely related to people who had. They may well have begrudged Hossueit obstructing the sale of land for which they had no immediate use. Colonial and

---

[90] Meeting with Aquinnah Wampanoag tribal members Ryan Malonson, June Manning, Tobias Vanderhoop, William Derwood Vanderhoop, Gladys Widdiss, and Beverly Wright, February 14, 2000.

[91] DCCP, 1730–55, 792.

[92] Mass. Archives, 33:416.

[93] DCGSP, 1722–62, 870.

[94] DCGSP, 1722–62, 872; DCGSP, 1730–57, 756–7 (verso), 760 (verso).

community law kept Gay Headers from selling to non-Indians, and Amos was the most active Indian land trader on the island. Hossueit had closed off a prime market opportunity to needy families who might have otherwise unloaded their claims at Aquinnah and moved to another Wampanoag community, a fairly common practice elsewhere on the island.[95]

The Baptist church was a final though less measurable cord between the proguardian petitioners. In 1774, the signatory Silas Paul would become the first ordained Baptist minister at Gay Head since the death of Jonah Hossueit.[96] His congregation boasted only thirteen full members, so it is possible that most, if not all, of the petitioners in 1767 were Baptists who resented the Congregationalist minister who had quit their ranks. Like most historical issues in local Indian politics, there is no way to know for sure. What is clear, though, is that Hossueit had his enemies and that the 1767 petition and subsequent documents requesting colonial intervention had as much to do with unspoken, internal rivalries as the issues set forth in writing.

Nevertheless, Hossueit's performance, first against the Amos brothers, then against the guardians, established him as Aquinnah's preeminent public figure, a position he did not forfeit until his death in 1772. In the early 1760s, he went all the way to the Superior Court in Barnstable to defend his rights to Pechacah's Neck in Chilmark, just outside of Gay Head, against the rival claim of colonists Benjamin and Nathan Skiff. His victory there proved that he could beat the English in the same courts that regularly

---

[95] Several Indians sold Amos land at places other than where they lived. In the 1750s, Joseph Amos, Henry Amos, and Jemimiah Almick of Christiantown, and Isabel Ohhomon of Edgartown deeded Elisha Amos rights at Gay Head (DCD, 8:148, 191, 552). A number of families at Aquinnah made similar grants, as when James Talman sold part of Sengekontacket in 1753 and 1759, or Judah Pocknet and Bethia Tockanot sold their Roaring Brook land in 1756 (DCD, 8:267, 431, 9:82).

Shared surnames between island and mainland Wampanoag communities suggest the opportunities for Indians to sell land in one place and move to another. The Vineyard Indians and the Wampanoags of Sandwich held in common the names Job (which clustered at Sengekontacket), Sampson (Chappaquiddick), Robin (Chappaquiddick), Chamuck (Christiantown), Francis (Gay Head), Joel (Chappaquiddick and Gay Head), Amos (Vineyard-wide), Coomes (Nashuakemuck), Cagenhew (Chappaquiddick), Webquish (Chapppaquiddick), and Moses (Chappaquiddick). Sandwich residents Joshua Coomes and Jesse Webquish were likely former residents of the Vineyard. See "Votes at an Indian Meeting, Sandwich, October 1761," Misc. Bound MSS, MHS.

Shared surnames with the Dartmouth Wampanoags included Simon (clustered at Chappaquiddick), Sampson (Chappaquiddick), Amos, Joel (Chappaquiddick and Gay Head), Abel (Nashuakemuck), Jeffery (Chappaquiddick), and Job. Rachel Amos had moved from the Vineyard to Dartmouth in the late seventeenth century, Jeremy Joel in the mid–eighteenth century. See "List of Indians at Dartmouth, Aug. 25, 1763," Misc. Bound MSS, MHS. On the Amos connection with Dartmouth, see E. Mayhew, *Indian Converts*, 38. On Joel, DCD, 9:42.

[96] Backus, *History of New England*, 1:438–9.

victimized Native litigants.[97] Then in 1767, he called the guardians to task again. At an ordination in Mashpee drawing together high-ranking Indians and Englishmen from all over the region, Hossueit represented the Vineyard's Natives and gave the cornerstone sermon, then took the opportunity to inform the New England Company officials in attendance, "that to this day some English people hold lands at a place called Deep Bottom," in southern Tisbury, "which were formerly leased to them by Mess'rs Hunt and Sumner and Major Mayhew when they were guardians to the Indians although the leases have been expired some time."[98] This event also enabled Hossueit to showcase his skills and strengthen his base of support. Several former Gay Headers had recently moved to Mashpee, including Hossueit's sister Hepzibah Akoochuck, plus Isaac Hossueit, Joseph Mittark, Eli Moses, Peter Job, "Old Zephariah," and "Widow Amos."[99] Word of his performance was sure to reach home. Certainly Hossueit swapped stories and strategies with other Wampanoag leaders like Mashpee's Reuben Cagenhew, who in 1760 had carried a petition against trespassers and the guardians all the way to the King's Royal Council in London.[100] Indians did not take these relationships lightly. They knew that Hossueit's voice carried great distances through his wide association of church contacts, kin, and friends. He had beaten the odds using a variety of strategies and resources, a mix of tradition and innovation, and become a force to be reckoned with.

V

At first it appeared that the career of Zachariah Howwoswee Jr. was modeled after his father's. Born in 1738, at age twenty-two he married sixteen-year-old Sarah Talman of a distinguished Sengekontacket family, and shortly found employment as pastor and one of three colony-appointed guardians at Chappaquiddick.[101] Then in 1772, Howwoswee returned to Gay Head to fill his deceased father's pulpit while also preaching circuit to other Native congregations.[102] He reflected his father's determination to protect Aquinnah's morals by accumulating evidence that colonist Beriah Luce permitted bawdy socializing at a house he rented from the Indians, which convinced

---

[97] Suffolk Files, #144134, 144206, and 44298; DCCP, 1730–55, 811; DCCP, 1736–42, 711 (verso); DCD, 9:194, 199; DCP, 1:66; RSCJ, May 1760, 44, May 1763, 48.

[98] "Report of the Committee on the State of the Indians," 13–14, 17; CPGNE, Box 2, October 27, 1767. For more on the annual gathering of Cape and island Indians, see Gideon Hawley Diary, August 28, 1757, and September 11, 1757, MHS.

[99] "Mashpee Births, Deaths, and Marriages," Hawley Journal.

[100] Mandell, *Behind the Frontier*, 157.

[101] *Native Writings*, 1:66–9; CPGNE, Box 2, October 27, 1767; Mass. Archives, 33:615.

[102] NE Co. MSS, 7956/2, 21–6.

the county court to revoke Luce's inn-holding license.[103] Howwoswee's father would have been impressed, perhaps all the more so when in 1784 Zachariah Jr. was appointed one of Aquinnah's guardians, the only Indian among them.[104]

After the American Revolution came to Martha's Vineyard, Howwoswee showed he was his own man with his own character. In September of 1778, a dozen British ships descended on Vineyard Haven Harbor as one of a series of strikes to divert American attention from a massive transfer of royal troops toward the South. Terrified islanders scrambled to meet British General Grey's orders to deliver him 10,000 sheep, 300 cattle, and all of the militia's arms, lest the redcoats help themselves to more. When the fleet raised anchor it left the Vineyard with only 802 cattle and 2,702 sheep; it would be twenty years before the herds reached prewar levels.[105] For the Indians of Chappaquiddick, who had suffered endlessly from encroaching livestock, "Grey's Raid" was a positive event. It was less so for the Aquinnahs, for although they managed to keep their own livestock out of British hands, their lessees did not. The Wampanoags' crop yields plummeted without manure fertilizer, their cattle nearly starved from the subsequent lack of winter feed, and they were left to seek "recourse to the whites on the east end of the Island for a supply of bread corn."[106] In all likelihood, income from sheep-right rents took a similar plunge since pasture was now open elsewhere on the island. The Wampanoags had retained their animals during the British raid because they were not full members of the society Grey warred against, but the reality was that their economy was inseparable from that of their white neighbors.

Aquinnah needed every resource it could find, and to this end, in 1787 Howwoswee moved to recover the 800-acre "Farm" the New England Company had managed since the 1720s.[107] He already knew that American independence would make it difficult for the English organization to pursue him through the courts, but what finally convinced him to lead Aquinnah's own rebellion was an investigation into the Company's title, which found

---

[103] The evidence is in ZHP, 1782 F6-Mr 7. The petition is in "1782 Protest against Beriah Luce to Innhold," among a bundle of papers listed as "Titles," in a metal file listed as "Petitions: Common Pleas," Dukes County Superior Court.

[104] *Mass. Acts and Resolves*, Resolves 1784/85, Chap. 4.

[105] James Freeman, "A Description of Dukes County, Aug. 13th 1807," *MHSC* 2d ser., 3 (1815), 89; Banks Papers, Vol:Rev., 1775–81, unpaginated, MHS; Charles Edward Banks, *The History of Martha's Vineyard, Dukes County Massachusetts*, 3 vols. (Boston: George H. Dean, 1911) vol. 1, chap. 24; Daniel Ricketson, *The History of New Bedford, Bristol County, Massachusetts* (New Bedford, 1858), 72, 280–3.

[106] Box 6S, Env. 4, MVHS; William Baylies to James Bowdoin, July 1, 1786, Banks Papers, Vol:Gay Head, MHS (quote).

[107] NE Co. MSS, 7956/2, 73; Joseph Thaxter to John Lathrop, September 30, 1808, Misc. Bound MSS, MHS.

"there was not deed on Record."[108] As such, one April morning, missionary Zachariah Mayhew, to whom the Company had granted the Farm's rent in lieu of a salary, awoke to discover that the Wampanoags had torn down a mile-long fence surrounding the estate. In the days following the Wampanoags "violently opposed my tenant driving our cattles to the farm for pasture, and openly turned off some that I had there before." They proceeded to "set up an Indian house and placed a family in it on the farm, with the view of getting possession," posted that any outsider "was not permitted to keep so much as a pig or to have any enclosure on it," and barred Mayhew's tenants from crossing into Aquinnah altogether.[109] Unlike earlier contests for the Farm, this time the Indians would brook no compromise. A startled Mayhew wrote, "they declare that I have no right to possess the farm under the Commissioners or the Company in England, that it is their property, and that they are resolved to defend their title by law, as I am informed, have engaged attornies for that purpose."[110] Howwoswee had indeed obtained the support of some "busy lawyers" and other "principal men then in power" by promising them lease privileges if they helped win back the acreage. These men outmaneuvered Mayhew at the bench, leaving him little choice but to concede the Indians victory.[111] In 1789, for the first time since 1687 when Josiah Mittark had sold the sachemship to Thomas Dongan, the Wampanoags were back in full possession of Aquinnah.

To this point, Howwoswee's campaign seemed entirely consistent with his father's defense of Wampanoag communal values, but after securing the Farm he engrossed its profits for himself. Jabez Athearn understood that Howwoswee moved into the Farm's house and seized one-third of the land as private compensation for his ministerial and guardian duties, which the New England Company no longer paid.[112] Then in 1790 Howwoswee and his fellow guardian, Simon Mayhew, increased the number of sheep rights from 200 to 711, with Howwoswee taking a disproportionate share. Aquinnah was deeply indebted to Howwoswee and his father. It had watched these men fend off one community threat after another and rewarded them with sheep-right privileges, public offices, and deference. However, Howwoswee's recent behavior recalled the Keteanummins and Elisha Amoses of memory who sold out their own kind under the corrupting influence of power and profits. Grateful as the people were, history taught them never to yield to leaders "persuing their own advantage in opposition to ours."

[108] Report of Joseph Thaxter on the State of the Indians, SPGNA, Box 6, File 4.

[109] NE Co. MSS, 7956/2, 63–4. See also "Memorial of Zachariah Mayhew, June 25, 1787," Misc. Bound MSS, MHS; DCCF, Box 4, File 2; Justice of the Peace/Circuit Court of Common Pleas, Warrants, 1782–1839, Singles, DCCF, Box 1.

[110] NE Co. MSS, 7956/2, 21–6.

[111] NE Co. MSS, 7956/2, 21–6; Report of Joseph Thaxter, SPGNA, Box 6, File 4.

[112] NE Co. MSS, 7956/2, 85–6. On the issue of salaries, see, NE Co. MSS, 7956/2, 21–6.

Fifty-two Wampanoags accused Howwoswee and Mayhew of conspiring to rent "to a few white people about one half of Gay Head to be pastured with sheep," including the guardians' own. The Indians "likewise suppose our pay is handed to us at an Advanced price and we are not allowed to receive any profit for the herbage of a considerable part of Gayhead. The Profits whereof is claimed and taken by one of our Guardians [Howwoswee] for his own use. Our Guardians not settling their Accounts gives us good reason to think their conduct is not good."[113] The state agreed and promptly removed the men.

Howwoswee never enjoyed the full support of his people again. In 1801, the Wampanoag Baptist preacher Thomas Jeffers moved to Gay Head from the mainland and quickly won over the people, leaving Howwoswee to face half-empty pews every Sunday.[114] Embittered by this fall from power and increasingly in debt to white creditors, Howwoswee refused to share the Farm's parsonage with Jeffers and instead began selling and leasing its lands to outsiders.[115] But Howwoswee had taught his people all too well. They prevented his tenants and grantees from driving cattle onto the peninsula, and contested his bargains all the way to Massachusetts Supreme Court, where they won.[116] The Indians were willing to honor leaders who earned their respect, but never again were they going to allow anyone to become bigger than the group.

VI

The fall of Zachariah Howwoswee casts into relief the issues of structure and personality as components of Indian leadership. Howwoswee possessed all the tools to succeed as a leader. He boasted an honorable name, the offices of minister, clerk, and guardian, excess grazing privileges, and an impressive education, plus he had the benefit of his father's stellar example. His reclamation of the Farm suggested he was worthy of these gifts, and that

[113] Passed Legislation Packet, Resolves 1789, Chap. 57 (quotes) and Resolves 1791, Chap. 76, Mass. State Archives.

[114] Isaac Backus to John Rippon, November 10, 1798, Houghton Library, Harvard University, Cambridge, Mass.; Zachariah Mayhew to Peter Thatcher, July 28, 1801, SPGNA, Box 3, File 11; Joseph Thaxter to John Lathrop, September 30, 1808, Misc. Bound MSS, MHS; Gideon Hawley to Rev. Jedidah Morse, Undated, Hawley Journal; Edward Augustus Kendall, *Travels Through the Northern Part of the United States in the Years 1807 and 1808*, 3 vols. (New York: I. Riley 1809), 2:196–7.

[115] DCD, 13:127; 15:230, 231; 16:54–5; 21:131–2. Howwoswee's debts are addressed in DCCP, 1807–1809, entry for November 1807; DCD, 16:367–9.

[116] "Petition of the Proprietors, Nation, and Tribe of Gayhead," Unpassed Legislation, Box 2, File-House Unpassed 8029–1816 (4), Mass. State Archives; Gay Head Petition of April 1, 1815, in "Report on Complaint of the Gay Head Indians, 10 June 1815," Governor's Council Files, Box June 1815–July 1816, Mass. State Archives; Edward S. Burgess, "The Old South Road of Gay Head," *Dukes County Intelligencer*, v. 12, no. 1 (1970), 22–3.

the craftiness for which Anglo-Americans criticized him would be a source of Wampanoag pride. He was minister of the Wampanoag's community church and a student of scripture, having by his own count read the entire Bible fifty times by 1813.[117] But like the sachems of old, Howwoswee bowed to the temptation to use his power and the people's trust for his own selfish gain.

Zachariah Hossueit Sr. could have taken a similar path, but instead he resolutely defended the Wampanoags' communal lands and values by innovatively melding customary modes of authority with new sources of power. In many ways his leadership style was strikingly similar to historic sachems: he acquired wealth for public purposes, dazzled with the spoken word, orchestrated consensus, arbitrated differences, and consolidated ties to outside communities – he was in every way the man who goes in front. But Hossueit was more than an old sachem in new clothes. He could not have been so effective without a church to put him in the pulpit, without the title of magistrate to advertise his backing by colonial authorities, without the literacy skills and command of English he learned in mission schools, without salaries paid by the New England Company, without credit lines at English stores, and without sometimes compromising Aquinnah's autonomy by inviting English authorities to act against wayward Indians. Hossueit was a great leader because he recognized that the defense of Aquinnah's communal lands and communal values required concessions to the realities of colonial power.

The Wampanoags' communal ethic had been a part of their culture well before the onset of colonial settlement, but probably as something taken for granted rather than as a part of their conscious identity. It took exposure to English private-property ways, missionaries, and especially threats against the Native land base for Wampanoags to see communalism as the core of their peoplehood in the colonial world.[118] When Indians cooperated to defend the commons, they dramatized the idea that "us" no longer referred to the followers of a particular sachem but to the Native people of a particular place who shared resources, a church, governing, and the responsibility to keep "them" – whites – outside of the community's boundaries. Facing down selfish men such as Elisha Amos or Howwoswee

[117] ZHP, F 1809 N11–1813 Ag 2.

[118] The literature on the construction of ethnic identity is immense. My thinking has been shaped primarily by the seminal Frederick Barth, ed., *Ethnic Groups and Boundaries: The Social Organization of Culture Difference* (Bergen-Oslo: Universitets Forlaget, 1969); Richard Thompson, *Theories of Ethnicity: A Critical Appraisal* (New York: Greenwood Press, 1989); Anya Peterson Royce, *Ethnic Identity: Strategies of Diversity* (Bloomington: Indiana University Press, 1982); James Clifford, *The Predicament of Culture: Twentieth-Century Ethnography, Literature, and Art* (Cambridge, Mass.: Harvard University Press, 1988); Joanne Nagel, "Constructing Ethnicity: Creating and Recreating Ethnic Identity and Culture," *Social Problems* 41 (1994), 152–76; Jean Comaroff and John Comaroff, *Ethnography and the Historical Imagination* (Boulder, Co.: Westview Press, 1992).

reinforced that the community came first and that among the most pertinent community values was corporate ownership and management of the land. Mashpee Wampanoags drove home this point in 1757 when they insisted to Massachusetts "*our Land is not to be sold or given with out the Consent of all.*"[119] Aquinnahs made the same statement in softer tones when they shifted en masse from Howwoswee's Congregationalist Church to the Baptist congregation. Wampanoag communalism was at once a moral principle and an essential element in the struggle to preserve an Indian homeland in colonial New England.

The Aquinnahs' defense of their communal territory and values put them in rare company. At mainland Indian places such as Mohegan, Stonington, and Charlestown, and even within the island villages of Chappaquiddick and Christiantown, every time individuals got away with selling community resources to outsiders, they shrank the stage on which communal values could be enacted. Aquinnah stood out because it had a leader to translate the people's values into successful action, thus proving the enduring practical worth, not just the morality, of such principles. Every victory made the people of Aquinnah ever more committed to their distinct ways, place, social system, and kind. Even outsiders took notice. In 1816 Chilmark's Ebenezar Skiff marveled at the ability of the "the Gayhead tribe" to persevere, "their having so often lost and as often regained the possession of their lands being always defendants."[120] In the future, the Wampanoags would continue to be defendants, whether the issue was territorial boundaries, the peoples' claim to a distinct Indian identity, or their right to enforce communal norms among their own kind. But they would do so with an intact land base and a firm sense of who they were.

---

[119] Petition of Mashpee to the Commissioners, August 4, 1757, Gideon Hawley Letters, MHS. Emphasis in original.

[120] Ebenezar Skiff to Paul Cuffee, October [ ], 1816, Paul Cuffee Papers, Microfilm Roll 2, NBFPL.

6

The Costs of Debt

Tobit Potter's life was never easy. Born in 1709 as the illegitimate son of the Vineyard Wampanoag Elizabeth Uhquat, Potter appears to have spent most of his childhood shuttling back and forth from the mainland colonial household where his mother was an indentured servant, to other English homes where he himself worked. Uhquat finally gained her release some time after Potter's ninth birthday, but that brought no end to her son's troubles. She could not bear the cost of supporting him and therefore committed the boy to serve Edward and Mary Milton of Tisbury while she returned to her natal village of Christiantown. The Miltons, exceptionally good employers, instructed Tobit in reading and Christianity, and he proved receptive. The missionary Experience Mayhew wrote of Potter, "he said once when he came from Meeting that hearing the Minister mention those Words, *If my Father and Mother forsake me, the Lord will take me up*; he was glad to hear this, for that he thought he had no body to take care of him."

Doubtless there were many times when Potter invoked the comfort of this passage. He fell ill after four years with the Miltons, prompting his masters to transfer him to yet another English family. However, the change of environment did nothing to improve the boy's health, so he was sent to Christiantown to be nursed by his impoverished mother. In theory the event was a homecoming but in practice it was awkward, for this was Potter's first extended stay in an Indian village. Having spent most of his childhood among colonists he could not speak Wampanoag to other Indians – his only language was English. Riddled with disease and oppressed by feelings of abandonment and isolation, Potter died at age thirteen. His mother passed away months later from what neighbors said was guilt over her son's premature end.[1]

Tobit Potter's ordeal with poverty, sickness, indentured servitude, and ultimately, forced acculturation, foreshadowed the next hundred years of Indian life on Martha's Vineyard, and, indeed, throughout southern New England

---

[1] *Indian Converts*, 194–6, 257–60.

and probably most of the Atlantic coast under English control. Changes in the environment, Native economy, and fashion, along with the debilitating effects of disease, meant that virtually all Natives had become dependent upon store credit for clothing and sustenance. Wampanoags hauled before the bench for criminal behavior suffered the added burden of court fines bloated with racial bias. Whether their creditors were merchants or the courts, increasingly the Wampanoags had little choice but to sell colonists their labor, and not only of adults but of children as well, or else sever indispensable credit lines and face lengthy jail terms. This pattern gave Englishmen disproportionate influence over the socialization of Indian young people and therefore over the direction of Indian cultural patterns. Every passing generation heightened the number of Wampanoags raised predominantly by colonists until many of them no longer adhered to what previous generations considered basic Indian behaviors, including most conspicuously use of Wampanoag as a first language. What began as a creeping cultural shift emerged as a Wampanoag identity crisis when Englishmen and even some Indians began to question whether there was any basis left for the Natives to be considered a distinct people.

The painful irony was that just when the Wampanoags became most like their English neighbors outwardly, a rising swell of racism pushed the bar of civilization separating the two groups to its highest point. The Indians' acculturation did not change that they were trapped near the bottom of New England's hierarchy by a cycle of debt peonage, poor education, white prejudice, and persistent schemes to bilk them of their land and labor. Thus, the Indians who New England colonists tended to see were servants performing menial jobs, often alongside black slaves, the most degraded segment of colonial society. This uninspiring image was reinforced by colonial newspapers, which tended to cast Indians in two crass stereotypes, one an impoverished drunken sociopath from a nearby "remnant tribe" who had absorbed all the worst qualities whites had to offer, and the other a vicious woodland savage who massacred and mutilated backcountry settlers irrespective of age or sex.[2] Colonists did not need to have any direct contact with Indians to get the message that the Natives were an inferior sort of people. After the Revolution, some whites, particularly evangelicals and politicians concerned about the United States' international reputation, advocated renewed missionary commitment to the Indians, but a less prominent majority had concluded after generations of forest warfare and failed missions that reform was hopeless, that Indians were more wolves than men, roving a broad underused country and terrorizing the edges of civilization. Like wolves, the

---

[2] Impression garnered from a systematic reading of stories relating to Indians in the following New England newspapers: *Boston News-Letter* (1704–1776); *Boston Gazette* (1722–1747); *Boston Evening-Post* (1735–1775); *Connecticut Courant* (1764–1773); *New-London Summary* (1758–1763); *Connecticut Gazette* (1763–1771); *Newport Mercury* (1759–1775).

Indians had to be driven out or exterminated to make way for a superior and divinely sanctioned yeoman society, since, the thinking went, if Indians were tamed they would wither and die, and if they were left wild they would soak their teeth in whites' blood. For generations colonists had expressed nascent racial ideas about Indians when contrasting savagery and civility, blustering against wartime Indian enemies, or denying the authenticity of Indian Christians, but this perspective was different in asserting the irreconcilability of the two peoples and the inevitability of Indian decline. Rejecting the Indians' capacity to change was full-fledged racism.

Although Wampanoag spokesmen readily acknowledged their communities' troubles, they were not about to resign themselves to extinction, as some whites would have it. More than a century of contact with the English, accompanied by disease, missionization, warfare, and land loss, taught that they could sustain their peoplehood in the midst of unrelenting change because of the integrity of their communal lands and customs and their sense of history and place. But the seizure of Indian children was unprecedented in its invasiveness and the extent of its cultural fallout. Indentured servitude stretched the Wampanoags' capacity to turn collective adaptation into community strength to its utter limits.

I

Seventeenth-century New Englanders found it difficult to secure Indian labor. Although by 1675, Wampanoags from as far away as the Vineyard traveled to the Boston area for seasonal work clearing stumps, building fences, and harvesting crops, they were independent and, thus, unpredictable employees.[3] Indians earned enough through short employment stints to meet their limited demand for manufactured goods, particularly when they could supplement their wages by selling the products of their traditional economy such as fish, meat, feathers, corn, baskets, and wild fruit.[4] A minority among the Wampanoags, Massachusetts, and Narragansetts even raised domestic animals for sale.[5] Colonial farmers could only hope that Indian laborers would

---

[3] "Historical Collections," 207, 210; Daniel Gookin, "An Historical Account of the Doings and Sufferings of the Christian Indians in New England in the Years, 1675, 1676, 1677," *Archaeologia Americana*, Transactions and Collections of the American Antiquarian Society, 2 (1836), 434; Thomas Shepard, *The Clear Sun-shine of the Gospel Breaking Forth upon the Indians in New England* [1648], MHSC 3d ser., 4 (1834), 59; Joshua Micah Marshall, "'A Melancholy People': Anglo–Indian Relations in Early Warwick, Rhode Island," *NEQ* 68 (1995), 411–12.

[4] "Historical Collections," 185; Elizabeth A. Little, "Index to Mary Starbuck's Account Book with the Indians," *Nantucket Algonquian Studies* 8 (Nantucket, Mass., 1981).

[5] "Historical Collections," 184; John Josselyn, "The Second Voyage," in Paul J. Lindholdt, ed., *John Josselyn, Colonial Traveler: A Critical Edition of "Two Voyages to New-England"*

show up at the proper time of year, in sufficient numbers, and stay on until the job was finished. Hundreds of Indian slaves and bonded servants taken as prisoners of war or purchased from Carolina were hardly enough to exhaust the colonists' labor needs. In any case, authorities eventually discouraged the importation of Indian slaves because they were justifiably wary about having such a dangerous population in their midst.[6] Indentured servitude was another matter, however.

Beginning in the 1690s, colonial whaling and military campaigns substantially raised the demand for Indian workers. Whaling started as a small local Nantucket business, with a handful of crews scurrying from beachfront launches to hunt near the shore. But growing profits expanded this operation while the search for fresh whale herds pushed it further out to sea. By the 1720s, whalers hunted forty to fifty miles offshore, and in 1730 Nantucket alone boasted twenty-five vessels and produced 3,700 barrels of oil. The true windfall came after 1750 with the development of shipboard tryworks, which by enabling blubber to be processed on deck encouraged captains to remain at sea for a year or more until their hulls were full. By the early 1770s, Nantucket boasted more than eighty ships employing over 1,000 laborers, and Massachusetts as a whole, including the Vineyard port of Edgartown, required more than 4,000.[7]

Manpower was also at a premium in the armed forces that battled New France and its Indian allies as well as on farms that had lost men temporarily,

---

(1674; Hanover, N.H.: University Press of New England, 1988), 105; Experience Mayhew, *A Brief Account of the State of the Indians on Martha's Vineyard*, app. to his *Discourse Shewing that God Dealeth with Men as with Reasonable Creatures* (Boston, 1720), 11–12; M. Halsey Thomas, ed., *The Diary of Samuel Sewall, 1674–1729*, 2 vols. (New York, 1973), 1:465; Little, "Indian Horse Commons at Nantucket Island, 1660–1760," Paper presented at the 1986 meeting of the American Society for Ethnohistory at Charleston, S.C., 1–24; Virginia DeJohn Anderson, "King Philip's Herds: Indians, Colonists, and the Problem of Livestock in Early New England," *WMQ* 51 (1994), 601–24; Marshall, "A Melancholy People," 411, 420.

[6] Michael L. Fickes, "'They Could Not Endure That Yoke': The Captivity of Pequot Women and Children After the War of 1637," *NEQ* 73 (2000), 58–81; Margaret Ellen Newall, "The Changing Nature of Indian Slavery in New England, 1670–1720," in Colin G. Calloway and Neal Salisbury, eds., *Reinterpreting New England Indians and the Colonial Experience* (Boston: Colonial Society of Massachusetts, 2003), 106–36; Jill Lepore, *The Name of War: King Philip's War and the Origins of American Identity* (New York: Alfred A. Knopf, 1994), chap. 6.

[7] Zaccheus Macy, "A Short Journal of the First Settlement of the Island of Nantucket," *MHSC* 1st ser., 3 (1794), 161; Daniel F. Vickers, "Maritime Labor in Colonial Massachusetts: A Case Study of the Essex Cod Fishery and the Whaling Industry of Nantucket, 1630–1775" (Ph.D. diss., Princeton University, 1981), 150–7; Richard C. Kugler, "The Whale Oil Trade, 1750–1775," in Philip Chadwick Foster Smith, ed., *Seafaring in Colonial Massachusetts* (Boston: Colonial Society of Massachusetts, 1980), 153–73; Edward Byers, *The Nation of Nantucket: Society and Politics in an Early American Commercial Center, 1660–1820* (Boston: Northeastern University Press, 1987), chaps. 4 and 7; Alexander Starbuck, *History of the American Whale Fishery: From Its Earliest Inception to the Year 1876*, 2 vols. (1878; New York, 1964), 1:1–42.

and sometimes permanently, to military service. Despite woefully incomplete records, it is clear that Wampanoags fought alongside Englishmen in most, if not all, of New England's eighteenth-century wars. In 1710 during Queen Anne's War, Massachusetts and New Hampshire governor Joseph Dudley pledged to reinforce flagging colonial troops by obtaining "some Martha's Vineyard Indians at small hire."[8] Fourteen years later, in campaigns against the Micmac and Wabenaki Indians of Nova Scotia and Maine, five likely island Wampanoags – Ephraim, Sam Simpson, Isaac Francis, Titus Moses, and Jeremy Quanch – were shot down in ambush, while another, William Jeffers (probably of Aquinnah), barely escaped with his life.[9] In July of 1756 amid the Seven Years' War, a group of Wampanoag soldiers gathering wood near Annapolis Royal in Canada fell under attack, leading to the deaths of Solomon Ned of Christiantown, Pilot Sowomog of Aquinnah, and James Horn of Sengekontacket, and to the wounding of Joseph David of Aquinnah.[10] A number of these men took up arms either as substitutes for white masters or under pressure from creditors who wanted their signing bonuses and salaries. Experience Mayhew wrote of the Wampanoag Samuel James who "being pressed to go as a Soldier into the War, he was most grievously distressed on that account, and came weeping to me, praying me, if it were possible to get him released; telling me, that his leaving of his wife would be a greater Grief to her than she was able to endure."[11] In 1757, colonists James Allen and Cornelius Bassett sued one another over who had first rights to garner James Tockanot's (or Tackanash's) earnings from service on the New York front.[12] In lockstep with the market for whalers, English demands for Indians soldiers and replacement agricultural workers mounted with each succeeding clash between France and England, until, according to historian Richard Johnson, Indians "were bearing at least twice the proportionate defense burden of their white counterparts."[13]

As colonists knew from their efforts to part Indians from their land, the best way to force Indians into service was to run them into debt, demand the balance, and take them to court when they could not pay.[14] This strategy

---

[8] Nathaniel Bouton, D. D., *Documents and Records Relating to the Province of New-Hampshire, from 1692 to 1722* (Manchester, 1869), 440–1.

[9] *Boston News-Letter*, Nos. 1064 (June 18, 1724), and 1074 (August 20, 1724).

[10] Letter of David Major, August 29, 1759, Box 3, Folder 3, Curwen Family Papers, AAS; *Boston News-Letter*, 2038 (September 20, 1759).

[11] *Indian Converts*, 107.

[12] Suffolk Files #144098. Citation courtesy of Andrew Pierce.

[13] Richard Johnson, "The Search for a Usable Indian: An Aspect of the Defense of Colonial New England," *JAH* 64 (1977), 631.

[14] Harry Andrew Wright, "The Technique of Seventeenth Century Indian-Land Purchases," *Essex Institute Historical Collections* 77 (1941), 185–97. The best study of this practice in relation to service is Daniel Vickers, "The First Whalemen of Nantucket," *WMQ* 40 (1983), 560–83. Cf. Little, "Nantucket Whaling in the Early 18th Century," in William Cowan, ed., *Papers of the 19th Algonquian Conference* (Ottawa: Carleton University Press, 1988), 111–31.

TABLE 2. *Martha's Vineyard Indian Credit Purchases in Colonial Stores, 1732–1804*

Merchant (Years)	Money[a] (%)	Cloth & Clothing (%)	Food (%)	Legal Costs[b] (%)	Livestock (%)	Tools (%)	Building Materials (%)	Domestic Items[c] (%)	Services[d] (%)	Liquor (%)	Tobacco & Pipes (%)
J. Allen (1732–52)	28	16	25	9	0.05	4	7	3	5	0.05	0
J. Sumner (1749–52)	6	63	4	5	0	9	0	12	1	1	0
P. Norton (1759–65)	4	86	0	0	10	0	0	0	0	0	0
B. Norton (1768–69)	23	13	7	0	0	6	3	4	43	1	0.05
M. Mayhew (1781–84)	22	13	26	22	0	0	0	3	9	3	0
W. Mayhew (1793–1801)	24	22	10	0	0	3	0	18	3	17	3
D. Look (1799–1804)	27	46	9	6	0	1	0	1	0	6	3

[a] Includes money borrowed and forwarded to other individual accounts.
[b] Includes drawing up writs and deeds as well as payment of fines.
[c] Includes bottles, earthenware, jugs, etc.
[d] Includes medical care, shoe repair, agricultural jobs like plowing, and transportation costs such as ferry tolls.

Sources: Account Books of John Allen (1732–52), John Sumner (1749–52), Peter Norton (1759–65), Beriah Norton (1768–69), Matthew Mayhew (1781–84), William Mayhew (1793–1801), and David Look (1799–1803, 1800–04), located at the MVHS; DCCF, B4.

became especially effective after the turn of the seventeenth century as Indians grew dependent upon store credit for clothing and sustenance. By 1700, it was unfashionable and unchristian for Indians to dress in skins, reed-woven clothes, or just shirts with leggings, as they did in the seventeenth century. Indians either had to purchase spinning wheels and procure wool to manufacture their own cloth, which a slim minority did, or buy finished material or clothing from local merchants.[15] Cloth, clothing, and sewing items constituted sixteen percent of the value of Wampanoag charges at John Allen's store between 1732 and 1752, sixty-three percent at John Sumner's between 1749 and 1752, and eighty-six percent at Peter Norton's between 1759 and 1765 (see Table 2).[16] Even among merchants who did not specialize in fabric, like Beriah Norton, cloth and clothing sales made up no less than thirteen percent of the value of Indian transactions. Food purchases, particularly corn, meat, and sweeteners, were also significant, running as high as twenty-six percent at some stores (Tables 2 and 3). English land encroachment had severely restricted the Wampanoags' movement and thus compromised their mixed subsistence base of corn–beans–squash horticulture, hunting, fishing, shellfishing, and wild-food gathering.[17] Fences crisscrossing the landscape served as boundaries not to be breached. Dams prevented fish from migrating along streams.[18] Farms displaced forested game habitat and livestock rooted out deer herds until Indians were forced to raise their own livestock or buy meat, even during the traditional hunting season of late fall and winter.[19] Traditional economic activities were further undermined when Indians went to work for colonists during planting and harvest seasons in order to pay off their store accounts. Unable to raise their own crops, laborers turned to purchased corn to carry them through the lean winter months until April's fish runs and the first harvest at midsummer (see Figure 6). Thus a cycle began: a family relied upon credit for a season or two; then, with creditors calling, adults found themselves forced to go back to work for Englishmen and once again neglect their own subsistence activities; the next cold season,

---

[15] *Diary of Samuell Sewall*, 1:465.
[16] These numbers are comparable to those presented by Vickers, "First Whalemen," 572, for Nantucket.
[17] Peter Thomas, "Contrastive Subsistence Strategies and Land Use as Factors for Understanding Indian–White Relations in New England," *Ethnohistory* 23 (1976), 1–18.
[18] *Mass. House Journals*, 16:49.
[19] William Cronon, *Changes in the Land: Indians, Colonists, and the Ecology of New England* (New York: Hill and Wang, 1983), 101; Kathleen J. Bragdon, "Native Economy on Eighteenth-Century Martha's Vineyard and Nantucket," in William Cowan, ed., *Actes du Dix-Septième Congrès des Algonquinistes* (Ottawa: Carleton University Press, 1986), 31; Lorraine E. Williams, "Ft. Shantok and Ft. Corchaug: A Comparative Study of Seventeenth-Century Culture Contact in the Long Island Sound Area" (Ph.D. diss., New York University, 1971), 180, 199; Kevin McBride, "'Ancient and Crazie': Pequot Lifeways during the Historic Period," in Peter Benes, ed., *Algonkians of New England: Past and Present* (Boston: Boston University Press, 1993), 66.

TABLE 3. *Martha's Vineyard Indian Food Purchases by Credit from Anglo Stores, 1730–1809*
(each item as % of total for that time period)

Date	Vegetables (%)			Grains (%)			Meat (%)				Drinks (%)		Sweeteners (%)			Fruit[a] (%)	Starches[b] (%)	Spice[c] (%)	Biscuit (%)	Cheese (%)
	Beans	Corn	Peas	Barley	Flour	Rye	Fish	Beef	Mutton	Pork	Coffee	Tea	Honey	Molasses	Sugar					
1730–39	0	59	0	1	0	1	2	8	10	0	0	0	0	11	2	5	0	0	0	2
1740–59	0	16	0	2	1	2	2	5	44	0	0	0	0	17	2	2	1	1	0	2
1760–79	3	33	2	0	5	0	0	0	0	3	3	4	3	22	17	1	2	0	0	0
1780–99	0	21	0	0	1	1	1	8	1	6	4	18	0	25	7	0	1	3	0	1
1800–09	0	15	0	0	2	9	0	18	1	2	0	16	0	20	7	0	0	6	1	2

Note: No data for 1730–31, 1753–58, 1766–67, 1770–80, 1785–92, or 1805–9.
[a] Includes apples and pumpkins.
[b] Includes potatoes and rice.
[c] Includes ginger, pepper and salt.

Sources: Account Books of John Allen (1732–52), John Sumner (1749–52), Peter Norton (1759–65), Beriah Norton (1768–69), Matthew Mayhew (1781–84), William Mayhew (1793–1801), John Look (1793–1801), and David Look (1799–1803, 1800–04), located at the MVHS; DCCF, B4.

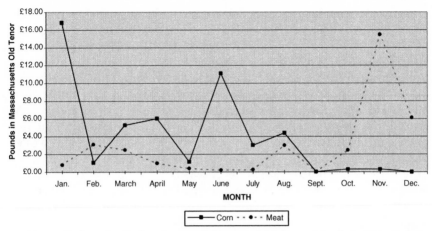

FIGURE 6. Indian Credit Purchases of Corn and Meat on Martha's Vineyard, by Month, 1730–1749. *Sources:* Account Books of John Allen (1732–52) and John Sumner (1749–52), MVHS. *Note:* No data for 1730–1, 1742–3, or 1746–8.

they returned to the store, debts mounted, and the pattern repeated itself.[20]

Some merchants tapped their casks to put the Indians into further arrears. It was expressly illegal throughout southern New England to sell Indians liquor, so merchants either had to veil these transactions in their account books or else avoid documenting them altogether.[21] Paying Native laborers under the table in alcohol was one way to beat the system. In 1741, Jonathan Dellano of Rochester, Massachusetts, gave Indian Peter Daniel nine gills of rum in exchange for farm work, a deal that came to light only because Daniel was arrested "for breaking up a Bedroom" of Dellano's "and then getting to bed w[h]ere [Dellano's] Children were" after drinking his pay.[22] Straight-up swaps involving liquor was another way to keep alcohol purchases off the books. But the most obvious means of skirting the law was

---

[20] Bragdon, "Native Economy," 32–3; Daniel Mandell, "'To Live More Like My Christian English Neighbors': Natick Indians in the Eighteenth Century," *WMQ* 48 (1997), 566–7. See also Richard White, *The Roots of Dependency: Subsistence, Environment, and Social Change among the Choctaws, Pawnees, and Navajos* (Lincoln: University of Nebraska Press, 1983).

[21] This legislation is conveniently gathered in *Laws of the Colonial and State Governments Relating to Indians and Indian Affairs from 1633 to 1831 Inclusive* (1832; Standfordville, N.Y.: E. M. Coleman, 1979), 12–14, 38, 42–3, 46–7. See also Peter Mancall, *Deadly Medicine: Indians and Alcohol in Early America* (Ithaca, N.Y.: Cornell University Press, 1995), esp. 103–06, and Yasuhide Kawashima, *Puritan Justice and the Indian: White Man's Law in Massachusetts, 1630–1763* (Middletown, Conn.: Wesleyan University Press, 1986), 79–81, 82–5.

[22] David Thomas Konig, ed., *Plymouth Court Records, 1686–1859*, 16 vols. (Wilmington, Del.: Michael Glazier, Inc., 1978), 2:211.

to conduct transactions in cash. Experience Mayhew related that William Taphaus of Nashuakemuck, "was given to labour with his Hands, and did by working among the English, frequently get money and bring it home, giving the same to his Wife to lay up for him, yet he would in a short time demand it again of her, and spend it all in Drunkenness."[23] Indians also had the option of borrowing money on credit, then handing that money back for alcohol. This gave Indians the product they wanted and colonists a legal record of the Indians' debts. Borrowed money typically made up a quarter of the value of Indian store accounts (see Table 2). Since most alcohol sales took place off the books and because colonists were able to clear themselves merely by taking an oath of innocence, generally officials were unwilling to prosecute the matter. Only on Nantucket, where Quaker beliefs precluded most colonists from taking oaths, were rum peddlers convicted with any frequency.[24]

The connection between liquor and debt is clear despite merchant efforts to disguise account book evidence. Tisbury tavern owner Robert Cathcart faced repeated accusations of selling alcohol to Indians. Not coincidentally, he also sued numerous Wampanoags for unpaid debts, bought several parcels of Indian land at low rates, and died in 1718 with 117 Natives owing him a total of £168 8d.[25] So too Samuel Athearn, who was one of the few colonists to be formally charged with selling Wampanoags drink during the 1720s, and to have filed as many as seventeen suits of his own to collect outstanding Indian debts.[26] With the high fixed expenses of clothing and provisions, alcohol was something most Indians could ill afford.

The Indians' vulnerability to debilitating illnesses compounded their struggles with debt. The massive epidemics that tore through Native New England in the early seventeenth century never struck again with such fury, but localized outbreaks persisted throughout the colonial period. In Josiah Cotton's "Indian Vocabulary," designed to instruct colonists in the Wampanoag language, the author sets up a mock dialogue between an Englishman and an Indian. The colonist asks, "Why do you remove from Natick? You will get more money there than at Sandwich." The Indian answers, "My family is sickly there." "And they were healthy at Sandwich?" "Yes." "Don't you owe a great deal of money there?" "Yes," the Indian

[23] *Indian Converts*, 95.
[24] NCD, 3:157, 163, 171, 178, 179, 186–7, 189; NCCR, 1:59, 62, 66, 70, 72, 78, 79, 83, 107, 112, 113, 148, 149, 152, 161, 165, 185, 187.
[25] On charges of liquor peddling against Cathcart, see DCCR, 1:107, 114, 143, 236; Scrapbook of Deeds, 17, MVHS. On Cathcart's land purchases from Indians, see DCD, 1:9, 53; 2:49, 60, 218, 303, 355. On Cathcart's suits for debt, see DCCR, 1:183, 195, 206; Force Papers, January 16, 1722. On the total of his Indian accounts, see DCP, 1:102–7.
[26] Dukes County Court of Common Pleas, Records, 1724–1725, unpaginated, NEHGS; Charles Banks, *Martha's Vineyard Court Records*, 54, 56, NEHGS.

responds, "but I hope to clear it quickly."[27] Realistically, this Wampanoag's chances would have been slim. Although they continued to use herbal remedies prescribed by Native doctresses, desperate Indians turned to expensive English doctors. Writing from Mashpee in the late eighteenth century, missionary Gideon Hawley observed that "one week's sickness will impoverish the greatest part of them, and exhaust their stores so as to render them destitute of every comfort."[28] Not surprisingly, in petitions to colonial authorities, Indians frequently cited medical costs as their primary impetus to sell land.[29]

Christian rites of passage, particularly funerals, were another significant burden. In 1736, for instance, John Allen's store charged David Demos of Aquinnah for "a sheet to Beury your brother in," twenty-seven feet of boards, and dozens of nails, presumably for a coffin. The total expense was £1 5s. 6d., or about five days' worth of work.[30] If Demos's brother had suffered a long decline, this charge went into a pile of bills accumulated by the family to feed, clothe, and doctor the sick man during his ordeal.

Above all, sheer poverty precluded most Indians from ever satisfying their creditors. As several recent studies of Indian wills demonstrate, most Natives were poor even by the standards of New England's lower ranks.[31] One factor restricting Indian accumulation of wealth was the cultural responsibility to share their earnings. By all appearances, island Wampanoags maintained their long-standing custom of providing lodging and hospitality to needy kinfolk and visitors, even though nearly everyone was pinched.[32] Wealthier Indians had the additional responsibilities of hosting foreign visitors and generously donating to holiday feasts.[33] Experience Mayhew was surprised by

[27] Josiah Cotton, "Indian Vocabulary," *MHSC* 3d ser., 2 (1830), 239. This dialogue might have been based on an actual conversation between Cotton and John Neesnuman of Natick, known in 1719 as "the most accomplished person possibly, in the province, for understanding the English and Indian Languages, and Speaking them." That year, Neesnuman did indeed travel from Natick to Sandwich "upon a visit," but fell sick at Braintree during his return and died. See NE Co. MSS, 7955/1, 101.

[28] Gideon Hawley to Governor John Hancock, July 8, 1791, Gideon Hawley Letters, MHS. See also Konig, *Plymouth Court Records*, 5:301.

[29] Konig, ed., *Plymouth Court Records*, 2:133, 143, 147; Mandell, "'To Live Like My Christian English Neighbors,'" 572; Mandell, *Behind the Frontier: Indians in Eighteenth Century Massachusetts* (Lincoln: University of Nebraska Press, 1996), 87, 131; Jean M. O'Brien, *Dispossession by Degrees: Indian Land and Identity in Natick, Massachusetts, 1650–1790* (New York: Cambridge University Press, 1997), 110. On Indian doctresses, see *Indian Converts*, 140–1, 165.

[30] John Allen Account Book, April 16, 1736, 14, MVHS.

[31] Vickers, "Maritime Labor," 160; Mandell, "'To Live More Like My English Neighbors,'" 568–71. See also accounts of the Native poor in Ruth Wallis Herndon, *Unwelcome Americans: Living on the Margin in Early New England* (Philadelphia: University of Pennsylvania Press, 2001), 60–6, 91–4, 132–4.

[32] *Indian Converts*, 85, 92, 102–3, 110, 138–9, 142, 171, 185, 231, 235, 263.

[33] *Indian Converts*, 89, 90, 93, 101.

Nashuakemuck's William Taphaus, who during the late seventeenth century "fell into another Extreme rarely to be found among our Indians, viz. that of being too sparing . . . and was not at all forward to give good Entertainment to such as came to visit him."[34] As historian James Axtell explains, "unless everyone in the community could shift at the same time to an individualistic, every-man-for himself philosophy of accumulation, the provident exemplar of the 'civilized' way would lose all incentive by being eaten out of house and home by his improvident friends and relatives."[35]

Indians also realized that any property they might accrue was at risk of being appropriated in lawsuits filed by Englishmen. Most Indians in southeastern New England, particularly those on the islands and Cape Cod, lived in jurisdictions controlled by a small number of colonial families, which meant that Indians could find themselves saddled with steep fines for trivial, even baseless, charges, like taking horses on joy rides.[36] Nantucket Wampanoags protested that they could not have justice at home, "both Judges and Jurors, being all parties in the cause."[37] To appeal local cases to the mainland Superior Court, Indians had to put down a surety of £40, something they were understandably reluctant to do given their perpetual struggles with debt.[38] Better to spend money in hand than wait for the sheriff to seize one's riches.

Overextended as they were, a disproportionate number of Indians fell into arrears. In 1718, Wampanoags represented just 62 of tavern keeper Robert Cathcart's 172 "good accounts" (or thirty-six percent), but 60 of his 106 "desperate debts" (fifty-seven percent). Five years later, Indians accounted for six of nine "bad debts" claimed by Benjamin Hawes, lawyer to Chappaquiddick sachem, Jacob Seeknout. In 1732, even with their population in steep decline, Vineyard Indians owned 4 of John Worth's 48 "good debts" (eight percent), yet 13 of his 33 "bad debts" (thirty-nine percent).[39]

---

34 *Indian Converts*, 96. See also 167, 170–71.

35 James Axtell, *The Invasion Within: The Contest of Cultures in Colonial North America* (New York: Oxford University Press, 1985), 166.

36 Konig, ed., *Plymouth Court Records*, 1:262; 2:87; DCCR, 1:5, 12, 15, 22, 118.

37 NCD, 1:110. On the Mayhews' domination of the Martha's Vineyard courts, see Mass. Archives, 41:132; and Charles Edward Banks, *The History of Martha's Vineyard, Dukes County, Massachusetts*, 3 vols. (Boston: George H. Dean, 1911), 1:164–212. On Barnstable County, see John J. Waters Jr., *The Otis Family in Provincial and Revolutionary Massachusetts* (Chapel Hill: University of North Carolina Press for the Institute of Early American History and Culture, 1968), chap. 4. On suppression of Indian rights within the court system, see Mass. Archives, 31:249–52; *Mass. Acts and Resolves*, 12:599.

38 Kawashima, *Puritan Justice and the Indian*, 139–40; David Grayson Allen, *In English Ways: The Movement and Transfer of English Local Law and Custom to Massachusetts Bay in the Seventeenth Century* (Chapel Hill: University of North Carolina Press for the Institute of Early American History and Culture, 1981), 237–8.

39 DCP, 1:107, 148–9, 3:28–31.

By the early eighteenth century, New England courts were busy with colonists' suits against Indian debtors, usually for sums that were minor by English standards. If the accused could not post bond, he or she waited for trial in jail, where charges for imprisonment might double or triple the final cost of the judgment.[40] Indians who lived outside communities designated as protected "Indian plantations," like the Wampanoags of Sengekontacket and Nashuakemuck, or on plantations with lackadaisical or corrupt guardians, like those of Chappaquiddick, often met these debts by taking out mortgages, selling land, or, in the end, having their territory seized and auctioned off by the probate court.[41] Experience Job, for example, not only appeared as a "desperate" debtor in the estates of colonists in 1718 and 1732, but in 1723 also granted tracts stretching across Sengekontacket neck to colonists Thomas Norton and John Butler Jr.[42]

Yet most Indians, both on the Vineyard and the mainland, lived in protected zones, and therefore could not use their land to pay off debts unless they received permission from Boston.[43] Instead the courts seized the only capital these Indians possessed – their labor. In 1693 a £25 debt led a Vineyard judge to bind Wampanoags James Covell and Keape to Matthew Mayhew, who immediately sold the two Indians off-island to work for Jacob Mayee of Southold, Long Island, for the term.[44] Often considerably smaller debts led to court action (see Tables 4 and 5). Bethia Joel of Mashpee was bound to Silvaneus Gibbs of the Cape Cod town of Sandwich for fourteen months in order to discharge £7 5s.[45] If these Indians had been allowed to sell their land they might have been able to pay off their debts and fend off indenture, at least temporarily. The price Indians paid for the special laws designed to protect their territory, was lost control over their labor.

Binding out Indian debtors began in earnest in the late seventeenth century and quickly became standard practice. Recognizing their fate, many Indians signed indenture contracts before proceedings even began to avoid court costs that sometimes ran as high as half the original debt

---

[40] William Towner, *A Good Master Well Served: Masters and Servants in Colonial Massachusetts, 1620–1750* (New York: Garland Publishing, 1998), 78.

[41] DCD, 3:140–1, 293, 7:125–6; DCP, 12:58, 3:146–7, I/493a, I/612a. See also the debt of £396 8d. that Benjamin Natick ran up with Beriah Norton in 1769, and his subsequent land sales, in Beriah Norton Account Book, 1768–1769, Box 9S, MVHS; and DCD, 9:154; 10:591; 11:178, 348, 351–2, 515.

[42] DCP, 1:107, 3:28–31; DCD, 3:500; "Scrapbook of Deeds," 39, MVHS.

[43] Kawashima, "Legal Origins of the Indian Reservation in Colonial Massachusetts," *American Journal of Legal History* 13 (1969), 42–56; Charles J. Hoadly, ed., *The Public Records of the Colony of Connecticut*, 15 vols. (Hartford, 1850–1890), 6:13–14, 402.

[44] Southhold Records, 2:74–5, cited in Charles Banks Papers, "Unbound Documents," 42, MHS.

[45] Otis Family Papers 1701–1800, January 8, 1736, MHS. See also DCCR, 1:30, 64.

TABLE 4. *Court Cases in Which Indians Were Sued for Book Debt, 1700–1755*

County	Number of Cases	Average Debt Awarded to Creditor	Average Court Cost to Indian Debtor	Court Costs as % of Debt
Dukes (MV)[a]	35	£4.04	£2.03	51
Nantucket	67	£16.03	£1.13	7
Plymouth	44	£8.17	£2.12	29

[a]*Note:* Dukes County Court Records are woefully incomplete for this period. Therefore the figure of thirty-five cases probably underrepresents the number of debt suits against Martha's Vineyard and Elizabeth Island Wampanoags.

Sources: DCCR, Vol. 1; Force MS; "Proceedings of the Inferior Court of Common Pleas, October, 1747," Box 5S, Env. 8, MVHS; Dukes County Court of Common Pleas and General Sessions of the Peace, Records, 1725–25, and Dukes County Records, NEHGS; Suffolk Files #14041 and 144652, Massachusetts State Archives, Boston, Mass.; Box 174A, Env. 33, MVHS; NCR, vol. 1; David Thomas Konig, ed., *Plymouth Court Records, 1686–1859*, 16 vols. (Wilmington, Del.: Michael Glazier, Inc. for the Pilgrim Society, 1978).

TABLE 5. *"Desperate" Debts Owed by Martha's Vineyard Indians to Colonial Estates*

	Year and Number of Cases		
Debt Range[a]	1718	1723	1732
£0–2.0	47	5	5
£2.01–4.0	12	1	1
£4.01–6.0	1	0	1
£6.01–8.0	1	0	2
£8.01–10.0	0	0	0
£10.01+	0	0	4
Ave. Debt	£1.08	£1.16	£4.12

[a] In Massachusetts Old Tenor
Source: DCP, 1:107, 148–9; 2:28–31; 3:28–31.

(see Table 4).[46] Indians who did not reach out-of-court settlements often failed to appear in court, thereby conceding the verdict and saving themselves the price of an attorney; standard legal work, such as drawing up a writ and having it served cost more than Indian laborers could make in a week.[47] But the system's machinations did not end once Indians were bound

[46] Vickers, "First Whalemen," 580.
[47] Suffolk Files, #14041; Otis Family Papers (1701–1800), January 8, 1736, and January 6, 1743/44, MHS; "Indenture of Simon Porrage," April 10, 1738, Misc. Bound MSS, MHS; Eunice Barney Swain Collection, 113 Nantucket Historical Association. On trials conceded by default, see all twelve cases of Indian debt in Dukes County Court of Common Pleas, Records, 1724–1725, NEHGS, as well as NCCR 1:22, 35, 36, 54, 63, 64, 65, 71, 124, 125,

to their creditors; their indenture contracts were yet another commodity that could be sold to whaling merchants or farmers.[48] The double-sale of labor gave New Englanders far from Indian settlements an abiding interest in maintaining the supply of Indian bonds.

A lack of popular support undercut official efforts to ease the Indians' burden. In 1709, Massachusetts prohibited suing Indians for overdue debts because those "unable to pay are brought further in debt by imprisonment, charge of law-suits, and a rigorous pursuit, and finally made servants."[49] Yet it backed off from this bold measure in 1718, 1725, and 1746, in favor of guidelines for Indian indenture contracts and limits on the amount of debt for which Indians were liable. But even watered-down laws were rarely enforced, and when they were invoked, seem only to have increased out-of-court arrangements between Natives and their creditors.[50] The Indians' collusion with Englishmen to bypass laws protecting them against forced labor reflected just how dependent they had become upon credit lines to feed and clothe themselves.

Debt was not the only road to indenture; large numbers of Indians also fell into bonded labor as a result of criminal prosecution. Usually Indians convicted of theft were unable to pay compensation running as high as treble the value of the missing objects. The lucky ones found Englishmen to meet their charges at the bittersweet cost of having to repay yet more creditors.[51] The less fortunate worked off their fines as indentured servants. In 1716, Indians Jo Skinny and John Moab of Nantucket received eight years of labor each, on top of thirty stripes from the whip, for stealing £80 from Stephen Coffin Jr.[52] Back on the Vineyard, in October 1734, Dinah Sissetom

141, 146, 150, 151, 160, 167, 175; Konig, ed., *Plymouth Court Records*, 5:46, 56, 57, 66, 82, 86, 105, 134, 138, 165, 202, 259–60, 285, 290, 376, 406, 514, 559. In John Allen's Account Book, MVHS, Indians during the 1750s typically received 2s. per day for their labor (pp. 11, 12). Native Abel George had to pay 4s. for a writ to be drawn when he sued Samuel Look. James Talman Jr. owed 17s. 6d. for having Anglo James Milton serve a writ (p. 44). Having a deed drawn and acknowledged cost Elisha Amos £1 10s. (p. 48).

[48] Mass. Archives 31:138, 140, 141, 148; Konig, ed., *Plymouth Court Records*, 5:293; *Boston Gazette*, No. 513, Sept. 15, 1729 (ad selling three years' service of a "Lusty Indian Woman"); *Boston News Letter*, Nos. 746, July 28, 1718(ad selling "a very likely Indian Woman's time"), 831, March 17, 1720 (ad selling "a very likely Indian Woman's Time for Eleven Years and Five Months"), 40 [under brief run as *Weekly News-Letter*], Sept. 28, 1727 ("likely Indian Woman . . . for Four Years"); Vickers, "Nantucket Whalemen in the Deep-Sea Fishery: The Changing Anatomy of an Early American Labor Force," *JAH* 72 (1985), 291; John Strong, *The Algonquian Peoples of Long Island from Earliest Times to 1700* (Interlaken, N.Y.: Empire State Books, 1997), 279.

[49] Kawashima, *Puritan Justice and the Indian*, 183.

[50] Mass. *Acts and Resolves*, 1:640–1, 2:104, 363–5; Kawashima, *Puritan Justice and the Indian*, 183–7, 219; Kawashima, "Jurisdiction of the Colonial Courts over the Indians in Massachusetts, 1689–1763," *NEQ* 42 (1962), 545.

[51] Kawashima, *Puritan Justice and the Indian*, 136–7.

[52] NCD 3:171.

of Sengekontacket was found guilty of stealing three bedsheets from the
house of John Daggett. Sissetom had no money to compensate Daggett, so
the court bound her out for a full three years.[53] Martha Job received two
years of service in 1747 for her inability to pay 45 shillings' damage after
stealing a silver shoe buckle from Simeon Butler of Edgartown.[54] Terms of
such length were standard penalties for New England Indians throughout
the eighteenth century.[55]

Courts also sentenced impoverished colonial lawbreakers to bondage,
but their low valuation of Indian labor meant that Natives spent more time
than Englishmen working off their bills. Between 1700 and 1748, Plymouth
County's General Sessions of the Peace forced fifteen Indian men, nine Indian women, and seven colonial men into service to answer unpaid damages, fines, and fees. The court assigned a wide range of values to the labor
of Indian males, from a low of 12s. 1d. per year to a high £9 per year
(Massachusetts Old Tenor). The average stood at £4 9s. 3d. The appraisal
of Native women's work was more consistent. All females were credited between £2 1s. and £5 per year, with most between £3 1s. and £4, for an average
assessment of £3 9s. 3d. per year. The court was considerably more generous
toward Englishmen. The court rated four of the seven indentured colonists at
more than £11 per year, with two receiving over £30; the overall average for
colonists was £12 4s. 8d. per year. The three colonists whose labor was valued within the Indians' range hailed from the lower reaches of New England
society – they were a "transient person," a "laborer," and a "mariner" –
yet each of them was credited more per year for his work than the Native
average.[56]

No one bothered to justify this bias in sentencing, but Experience Mayhew
understood. Colonists scoffed when he told them about Wampanoags who
were "Israelites indeed, whose hearts are upright with the Lord their God."
Instead, "the Greatest number of our English neighbours are continually
observing how very wicked the Indians are, and exclaiming against them as
if all the sin of the world were got into them, and will hardly own that there
is one good among them, and to speak a word for them is made a matter

---

[53] DCCF, "Indian Papers," General Sessions of the Peace, October [ ], 1734, Box 4.

[54] Charles Banks Papers, "Unbound Documents," 49, MHS.

[55] NCCR 1:11, 48, 77, 87, 88, 95, 107, 113, 126, 141, 155, 171, 174; 2:40 (inverse and verso),
41 (inverse and verso), 43 (inverse); Konig, ed., *Plymouth Court Records*, 1:228, 247, 249,
254, 262, 268, 273, 294; 2:26, 31, 41–2, 79, 83, 87, 98–9, 155, 188, 189, 190, 208, 211;
DCCR 1:59, 61, 65, 68, 93, 99, 102, 103, 143, 225; John Noble, ed., *Records of the Court of
Assistants of Massachusetts Bay, 1630–1692* (Boston: Suffolk County, 1901–28), 1:296. For
the beginnings of this trend, see Lyle Koehler, "Red–White Power Relations in the Courts of
Seventeenth Century New England," *AICRJ* 3 (1979), 1–31, esp. 12–20; and James P. Ronda,
"Red and White at the Bench: Indians and the Law in Plymouth Colony, 1620–1691," *Essex
Institute Historical Collections* 110 (1974), 200–15.

[56] Konig, ed., *Plymouth Court Records*, 1:247, 262, 268, 294; 2:18, 26, 31, 32, 41–2, 44, 66,
79, 81, 86, 87, 98–9, 106, 118, 121, 155, 173, 188, 189, 208, 211, 217, 227, 240, 264.

of reproval unto any that shall be so bold as to venture to do it."[57] These people saw no virtue in Mayhew's evangelical work because they considered the Indians "so badd that they seem to think it best to give them whol[l]y up, and indeed there are too many of our English that seeme not to care how much worse they still make them...." The courts were no different. They issued such heavy penalties to Indians, less to discipline them, than to exploit their labor. As a weak, subjected, and hated population, the Natives were open game.

In theory, indenture was a time to work off unpaid bills or court fines. In practice, Native servants routinely had years tacked onto their terms, usually for minor criminal charges. In 1690, Matthew Mayhew caught his servants Hannah and Moab stealing corn, money, unwashed linen, rum, and molasses, for which they were sentenced to be sold "anywhere within the King's Dominions."[58] Three years later, a young servant named Keape pilfered money from Mayhew's trunk while two other Indians kept lookout on the street. The men were ordered to pay Mayhew £5 or else be sold into seven years of service.[59] In 1725, a Plymouth court charged Desire Pequin with running away as well as stealing several articles of clothing to the value of £8 from her master Captain Benjamin Warren and the missionary Josiah Cotton. Warren was unwilling to pay Pequin's fines, "and her said master chusing to Sell her," the court bound her for four years "after the term is fully completed that the said Captn. Warren has in her already by Indenture."[60]

Some Indians received added time for more overt resistance to their masters. In a 1702 Nantucket Sessions of the Peace, Peter Coffin charged his Wampanoag servant, Ned, with "abusing his [Coffin's] wife[,] knocking her down with an Iron wedge as also shooting at him and placing several shots in his head to the great endangering of his life and also for stealing several things out of his house and running away several times." Ned confessed and received an extra year of service plus a £5 17s. 6d. bill for the costs of court and prosecution, probably to be paid off with additional time.[61] The mainland Wampanoag David Chassuck received an additional five years of service for stealing and burning the record of his indenture.[62] Like these men, indentured Indians throughout New England stole, ran away, and sometimes assaulted their masters, to voice their grievances or gain their freedom. The usual effect, however, was to extend their period of suffering.[63]

---

[57] E. Mayhew to Cotton Mather, August 28, 1723, Misc. Bound MSS, MHS.
[58] DCCR, 1:69, 70.
[59] DCCR, 1:93. Keape is identified as Mayhew's servant in Southold Records, 2:74–5, Banks Papers, Unbound Docs. 42, MHS.
[60] Konig, ed., *Plymouth Court Records*, 2:66. For indentures extended for theft and/or running away, see also 1:247, 250, 254, 262, 294; 2:41–2, 81, 86, 88, 91; 5:208, 369, 462; 6:8.
[61] NCCR, 3:176.
[62] Konig, ed., *Plymouth Court Records*, 2:109. See 2:122 for a similar case.
[63] Suffolk Files #20203; NCD, 1:48, 62, 87, 88, 101, 203; 3:151 (inverse), 186–7.

Store debt and court fines produced indentured Indians at a steady rate, but colonists' heavy demand for labor inspired even more creative ways to secure Native workers. Some Englishmen were not above kidnapping Indians or drawing up false documents to claim service.[64] In 1710, Cape Cod Wampanoag Gershom Worsano agreed to run an errand to Boston for a colonist named Kukliart, to whom he owed £8. Yet when the Indian arrived in town, the constable quickly took hold of him for no apparent reason. "Finding he was like to be clapt onboard for a long voyage to Barbaadoes there to old Engl[an]d & thence to Salvadores befor he sh[ou]ld return home," Worsano escaped and sought out minister Samuel Danforth for help. According to Danforth, Worsano was "willing to pay [Kukliart] honestly in work at tilling time or in whaling in winter season," and only asked "not [to] be hindered from looking after his aged mother."[65] In a similar case twenty years later, a Vineyard court fined its own High Sheriff and later Indian guardian, John Allen, for seizing Chilmark's Abigail Wompas, throwing her in a Plymouth jail, and then carrying her in irons to Newport for sale into bondage.[66]

Occasionally, colonists and Indians collaborated to fool legal authority. In March 1701, a Vineyard Wampanoag named Toby, servant to Jacob Norton, admitted to torching the house of Benjamin Norton of Edgartown on a Sabbath evening. The rationale, Toby asserted, was "because Benjamin lent him a horse and then charged him with illegally riding it." Yet when the constable brought Toby in for sentencing, that same Benjamin Norton "with a Considerable Elevated voice" offered a bond for £100 to £200 to keep Toby out of jail. The matter "looked something strange to the court," which led a magistrate to dig deeper into the case and uncover a poorly veiled scheme. Benjamin had arranged with Toby to burn down his house and confess to the act, the idea being that after the court indicted Toby, Benjamin would waive the charge, pay the court costs, and then, according to their logic, wind up with Toby as a servant (hopefully to help build a new house). "This business is as a child," Benjamin was overheard boasting. Apparently the two had not counted on half a dozen people testifying that they had either been with or seen Toby far from Benjamin's home at the time of the blaze. Moreover, the Englishman had made little effort to conceal his intrigue. Two Indians, including Toby's mother, were present when Benjamin advised Toby, "say you burnt the house, you shall not be long there you shall be out, I will pay." After an Indian named Abigail pleaded with Toby "to remember God," he

---

[64] Banks, Dukes County Court Records, p. 16, NEHGS; Hawley to Anonymous, August 29, 1801, Hawley to Anonymous, December 22, 1801, and Hawley to Ephraim Spooner, December 2, 1801, Hawley Journal.

[65] Samuel Danforth to Samuel Sewall and Edward Bromfield, June 18, 1710, Misc. Unbound MSS, MHS.

[66] DCCP, 1722–36, 688, 694.

finally admitted that he had, in fact, concocted his story "upon Benjamin giving me expectation of being free from my master."[67]

II

Toby's desire to escape his master might have proceeded from long years of bondage, for many Indians began working for Englishmen as children. Some of them merely accompanied their indentured mothers into service.[68] Others were bound out by the probate court when both or even just one of their parents died, since officials generally preferred English masters to Indian guardians.[69] Yet most child servants were bound out not by court order or town statute, but because their parents sold them to fend off creditors and litigants. Joseph Quasson of Monomoy, near Plymouth, was born in 1698 and lived with his parents for his first six years. "Then," he recalled, "my Father died five Pounds in Debt to Mr. Samuel Sturges of Yarmouth. I was bound out to him by my Mother on that Account." Quasson did not taste his freedom until twelve years later.[70] Gershom Barnabus of Mashpee not only agreed to perform three years of whaling for John Otis beginning in 1728, but indentured "his two Children namely Moses Barnabus, a boy of about five years old Last August & a girl named Jerusha of about three years old. Moses to serve until age 21. Jerusha until 18," in exchange for £15 a year.[71] In 1737, Wampanoag Robin Meserick, with the consent of his wife, committed his sons John and David to serve Gideon Holloway until the boys reached the age of twenty-one. Meserick owed Holloway £56 and could void his sons' indenture only if he paid off his debt within three years.[72] In 1740, Anna Paul of Christiantown rented a boy to Joseph Gilbord in exchange

[67] Suffolk Files, #5300; DCCR, 1:118, 144.
[68] DCCR, 1:100; DCCR, 1:143, 144. See also "1723 Indenture, Alice Sachemus, Indian Woman" Pilgrim Hall, Plymouth, Mass., available online at http://www.pilgrimhall.org/natamdocs.htm.
[69] *Indian Converts*, 184; DCP, 5:65; 8:60; Doc. R13, Box 2S, Env. 4, MVHS; Herndon, "Racialization and Feminization of Poverty in Early America: Indian Women as 'the poor of the town' in Eighteenth-Century Rhode Island," in Martin Daunton and Rick Halpern, eds., *Empire and Others: British Encounters with Indigenous Peoples* (London: UCL Press, 1999), 186–203; Herndon, *Unwelcome Americans*.
[70] Samuel Moody, *Summary Account of the Life and Death of Joseph Quasson, Indian* (Boston, 1726).
[71] Covenant of Indenture, April 28, 1728, Misc. Bound MSS, MHS. For similar cases, see Konig, ed., *Plymouth Court Records*, 2:77; 6:8; Indentures of Samson Fuller (1747), Lydia Cottenham (1751), Abraham Cottenham (1752), and John Buck (1754), in Indentures of Apprenticeship of Norwich, Groton, and New London, 1719–1786, Connecticut State Archives, Hartford, Conn.; Tom's Indenture, April 3, 1727, Folder: Correspondence, 1727–1760, Samson Occum Papers, 1710–1792, Connecticut Historical Society, Hartford, Conn.; Strong, *Indian Peoples of Long Island*, 278.
[72] "Indenture of Robin Meserick," July 6, 1737, Misc. Bound MSS, MHS.

for 10 shillings per month.[73] Nine years later, Abel George of Aquinnah received £3 from John Allen "for which he promas his Sun to go a whaling for me next spring."[74] Christiantown's Elizabeth Pattompan was bound out in 1704 when her father Josias found himself overwhelmed with court fees.[75]

Masters were responsible for clothing and feeding their child servants and, technically, for teaching them how to read – something that Indian parents were frequently unable to do because of poverty and lack of education. In few cases, Indian parents actually paid for their children's room and board in expectation that they, like white apprentices, would learn valuable skills during their service.[76] However, it was debt that overwhelmingly drove the system – and the system soon overhauled Indian society. As early as 1716, Cotton Mather observed that Indian children "are now generally in English families."[77] Fifty-four years later, Mashpee minister Gideon Hawley surveyed the social landscape and noted:

There is scarcely an Indian Boy among us not indetted [indentured] to an English Master . . . their neighbors find means to involve the Indians so deeply in debt as they are obliged to make over their boys, if they have any, for security till payment. The case is thus, an Indian having got in debt (he hardly knows how) obliges himself to go a whaling till he answers it: and because life is uncertain, his master obliges him in his Covenant or Indenture to include his Boy, who is bound to serve in case he should die or should not take up the Indenture by such a term or should get farther in debt to him. The Indian faithfully serves his master, every season for whaling as long as he is fit for such a service (for the longer he serves, the more he is embarassed) till finally being worn out he is turned off and becomes an object of charity. As for the boy, he is forfeited, because his father, tho' he has earned his master thousands, never was out of debt.[78]

The Mashpees found the issue of children's service so vast and complicated that when they petitioned the Massachusetts legislature for assistance in 1761 they admitted "we can[']t at present think of any other method to prevent it."[79] Neither could the government. Laws that required guardian or magistrate approval of indenture contracts never considered how easy those signatures were to come by or how interested some officials were in

---

[73] Proceedings of the Inferior Court of Common Pleas, October 1743, Box 5S, Env. 8, MVHS.
[74] John Allen Account Book, 16, MVHS.
[75] *Indian Converts*, 238. See also 202, 203, 261.
[76] O'Brien, *Dispossession by Degrees*, 136.
[77] C. Mather to William Ashurst, January 5, 1716, Cotton and Increase Mather Letters, MHS.
[78] Gideon Hawley to Andrew Oliver, December 9, 1760, Hawley Journal. See also Hawley to Anonymous, June 1, 1794, Hawley Letters, MHS.
[79] Mashpee Indians to a Committee Appointed to Hear Indian Grievances, August 13, 1761, Hawley Letters, MHS.

maintaining the supply of Indian laborers.[80] In 1760, some Massachusetts legislators tried to go further by submitting a bill to cap Indian debt with any one merchant, outlaw the sale of Native children into service, and prohibit the fines and court charges officials used to force Natives into bondage.[81] Yet the proposal received little support, and so the system churned out one underage servant after another with marked consistency throughout the eighteenth century. Even as late as 1794, Hawley could still report "many" Mashpee children serving indentures, while thirteen years later James Freeman found 100 of 242 Aquinnah Indians absent from their homes, "being children put out to service in English families, and other whale men."[82]

Hearkening back to his childhood during the 1790s and early 1800s in Tisbury, author James Athearn Jones wrote "it was my grandfather's custom, and had been that of his ancestors... to take Indian boys at the age of four or five years until they had attained their majority... During my minority we had three of these little foresters in our house."[83] Yet the work was not over for Jones's childhood companions once they reached adulthood, for then "they usually left us to be sailors," both willingly and by court order.[84] This line of employment took Indian boys and men even further from their home villages. Indians working the coastwise trade during the 1730s traveled back and forth between Boston and Carolina, while whalers typically hunted the waters off Cape Breton, Newfoundland, and Labrador. By 1782 Hector St. John de Crèvecoeur could write of the Vineyard and Nantucket Wampanoags, "go where you will from Nova Scotia to the Mississippi, you will find almost every where some Natives of these two islands employed in seafaring occupations."[85] To that list he might have added the Brazilian coast, Falkland Islands, and eventually the Pacific Rim, for after the Revolution New England whalers coursed most of the world's oceans. The men of

---

[80] Kawashima, *Puritan Justice and the Indian*, 217–20; John A. Sainsbury, "Indian Labor in Early Rhode Island," *NEQ* 48 (1975), 384; Hoadly, ed., *Public Records of the Colony of Connecticut*, 6:184.

[81] Mandell, *Behind the Frontier*, 135.

[82] Gideon Halwey to Samuel P. Savage, July 31, 1794, Samuel P. Savage Papers, MHS; James Freeman, "A Description of Dukes County, August 13th 1807," *MHSC* 2d ser., 3 (1815), 94. See also "Visit to the Elizabeth Islands," *North American Review and Miscellaneous Journal* 5 (1817), 319.

[83] James Athearn Jones, *Traditions of the North American Indians: Being a Second and Revised Edition of "Tales of an Indian Camp,"* 3 vols. (London, 1830), 1:x. See also the case of the executed Indian, Julian, who lived with his master for twenty years: *The Last Speech and Dying Advice of poor Julian, who was executed the 22d of March 1733 for the Murder of Mr. John Rogers of Pembroke* (Boston, 1733).

[84] Jones, *Traditions of the North American Indians*, 1:x.

[85] J. Hector St. John de Crèvecoeur, *Letters from an American Farmer* (1782; New York: E. P. Dutton, 1957), 115. See also Paul Cuffee, *Narrative of the Life of Paul Cuffee, a Pequot Indian, during Thirty Years Spent at Sea, and in Travelling in Foreign Lands* (Vernon, Conn., 1839), 3–6; Vickers, "First Whalemen," 568.

the small Wampanoag tribe were perhaps the most widely traveled people of their era anywhere in the world, but it was rarely out of choice.

Despite the occasional financial windfall from a few years abroad, most Indian sailors struggled to break out of the pattern of service. Like mariners of all stripes, they had a tendency to spend their way out of the doldrums that set in amid the austere tedium of shipboard life, but Indian sailors were especially prone to splurge hard-earned wages because their relations expected presents and feasts.[86] In July 1797, Hezekiah Joel returned to Chappaquiddick from whaling with a pocketful of money. At William Mayhew's store alone he instantly received £30 credit. Yet one month later he had spent all the money – and more – on liquor, cloth, molasses, a teapot, coffee, tobacco, and tools.[87] Most whalemen never even saw this kind of cash because they received their wages in advance of shipping out. "Their employment operates as a disqualification to any industry while they are on shore," wrote the Christiantown guardian in 1817. "Having expended the profits of one Voyage around Cape Horn they engage again."[88]

One traveler noted that merchants recruited Indian whalemen through "a sort of crimping, in which liquor, goods, and fair words are plied, till the Indian gets into debt and gives his consent," although the negotiation may not have always been one-sided. Tourist David Kendall wrote:

On the one hand great advantages are taken of [the Indian's] folly, his credulity, and his ignorance; on the other, he torments the ship or share-owner with his indecision and demands, till the moment of sailing the ship. First he agrees to go, and accordingly receives some stipulated part of his outfit, then he 'thinks he won't go;' and then he is to be coaxed and made drunk. Again, he 'thinks he won't go,' unless such and such articles are supplied, and the articles he often names at random, and for the sake of inducing a refusal. One Indian was mentioned to me, that though he would not go, unless five pounds of soap were given him; and another, that though the same, unless he received seven hats."[89]

In most cases Indians were obligated to go, usually under unfavorable terms. "Our men are sent [on] Long voiages to sea by those who practice in a more soft manner that of Kidnapping," protested Christiantown, "and when they Return with ever so great success they are still in debt and have nothing

---

[86] Marcus Rediker, *Between the Devil and the Deep Blue Sea: Merchant Seamen, Pirates, and the Anglo-American Maritime World* (New York: Cambridge University Press, 1987), 147–9; W. Jeffrey Bolster, *Black Jacks: African American Seamen in the Age of Sail* (Cambridge, Mass.: Harvard University Press, 1997), 183–5.

[87] William Mayhew Account Book, July 1797, MVHS.

[88] PLP, Acts 1817, Chap. 99.

[89] Edward Augustus Kendall, *Travels through the Northern Part of the United States in the Years 1807 and 1808*, 3 vols. (New York, I. Riley 1809), 2:194–5. Such tactics were common in recruiting seamen. See Konig, ed., *Plymouth Court Records*, 7:42; Rediker, *Between the Devil and the Deep Blue Sea*, 81–2.

to receive."[90] Part of the problem was that whalers had fixed expenses far beyond those of landed wage earners. Before sailing from New Bedford in 1803, Aquinnah's Caleb Pond bought three pairs of stockings, two pairs of mittens, one short jacket, one waist coat, one pea coat, three pairs of thick trousers, boots, two pairs of shoes, three flannel shirts, a hat, tobacco, paper, a tin pail, a chest lock, as well as passage from Martha's Vineyard to dockside. Without anything extra, Pond already carried a debt of £25.[91]

Women, too, struggled to regain their independence. In 1725 Aquinnah's Abigail Joel contracted to work one year for Mary Clifton of Portsmouth, New Hampshire. Clifton pledged herself to provide Joel's food, drink, and lodging, plus £7 at the end of the term; Joel's only financial responsibility was to clothe herself with items purchased from Clifton. That requirement alone put her in debt over £30. Later, Joel incurred an £8 penalty for lost service when she bore an illegitimate child under Clifton's roof, and she further inflated her account by charging a wedding dress and shoes. Soon after her wedding, Joel ran away, only to be caught at dockside and have a £1 penalty added to her tab. Then a second child cost her another £5, bringing the total to £26 7d. after credit for work.[92] Unless they remained shoddily dressed and sexually inactive, the chances of bondwomen gaining their freedom were slim indeed.

Despite the odds, some Indians avoided illness, pregnancy, family crisis, and criminal mishap, and by frugally managing their scant resources, they escaped the cycle of debt and indenture. Josiah Hossueit left unpaid bills and court cases strewn through the records of Martha's Vineyard during the 1720s and early 1730s, but by 1736 he had discovered the resolve and means to change his life.[93] Over a span of three years, Hossueit whittled down his debt from a high of £21 17s. 5d. to just 10s. by combining steady farm work (£1 for a day of shearing and two days of unspecified labor; £4 2s. for several small jobs over the course of a year) and periodic sea wages (£10 for a whaling share; £4 fishing on Jacob Norton's sloop; £7 from Ben Coleman).[94] For Wampanoags like him who managed to escape the snare of credit, the ideal was to build an "English" house, and maintain independence by combining income from sheep-rights, men's wages for fishing and farm work, and

---

[90] PLP, Acts 1804, Chap. 84. See also, GIP, Box 3, Folder 15, September 22, 1818; William Comstock, *A Voyage to the Pacific: Descriptive of the Customs, Usages, and Sufferings On Board of Nantucket Whale-Ships* (Boston, 1838), back cover.

[91] Account of Caleb Pond, April 3, 1803, David Look Account Book, MVHS.

[92] New Hampshire Provincial Court Records, Case #18462, New Hampshire State Archives, Concord, N.H. I am grateful to Holly Mitchell for providing me with a copy of this manuscript. For a similar episode, see Herndon, "Racialization and Feminization of Poverty," 190–1.

[93] DCP 1:107, 148–9; Dukes County Court of Common Pleas, Records, 2, NEHGS.

[94] John Allen Account Book, 8, 9, 13, 14, 15, 22, 23, 38, 39, MVHS.

women's earnings for basket and broom sales and domestic service. Those who never paid off their bills or fell back into arrears worked backbreaking manual jobs into their forties and even fifties, and then set up *wetus* or shacks on the land of their creditors and continued to live informally in the servile status that consumed the earlier portion of their lives.[95]

Wampanoags were not the only New England Indians plagued by debt and indentured servitude. Mainland Natives were pursued only slightly less vigorously, both by local farmers and coastal ship merchants whose reach extended into the interior through their purchase of rural store debts.[96] In 1700, Indians near Massachusetts Bay protested the English "drawing them to consent to covenant or bind themselves or children Apprentices or Servants for an unreasonable Term in pretence of, or to make Satisfaction for some small debt contracted or damage done by them."[97] Thirteen years later, during one of Experience Mayhew's two missionary visits to Rhode Island and Connecticut, the Narragansett/Niantic sachem Ninigret complained, "that his people were many of them indebted to the English, & lived with them, and so did not care for him." At an unnamed Indian town just east of Narragansett Bay, Mayhew could not find an audience to proselytize because "the Indians were so scattered among the English, that I could not come at them."[98] In 1715, on Long Island, Native children were said to be "now generally in English families," and in 1729 one observer commented that the Narragansetts were "either all servants or labourers for the English."[99] Around the same time, nineteen of thirty-one Mashantucket Pequot males resided with colonists, and some forty years later, Connecticut reported of its Indians, "many of them dwell in English families."[100] Unfortunately, the only document that adds numerical specificity to these observations is a 1774 Rhode Island census, which found thirty-eight percent of Indian males under sixteen, thirty-nine percent of males over sixteen, thirty-two percent of females under sixteen, and thirty-six percent of females over sixteen residing

[95] Josiah Cotton Memoirs, MHS, 376; John Wood Sweet, *Bodies Politic: Negotiating Race in the American North* (Baltimore: The Johns Hopkins University Press, 2003), 36–8.

[96] Nathaniel Philbrick, *Abram's Eyes: The Native American Legacy of Nantucket Island* (Nantucket, Mass.: Mill Hill Press, 1998), 211.

[97] Mass. Archives, 30:458a.

[98] *Some Correspondence*, 110–11.

[99] William Ashhurst to Cotton Mather, January 5, 1716, Box 5, Folder 3, Mather Family Papers, AAS; William S. Simmons, "Red Yankees: Narragansett Conversion in the Great Awakening," *American Ethnologist* 10 (1983), 258.

[100] Connecticut Archives, "Indian Series," Series 1, Vol. 1, Doc. 151, Connecticut State Archives, Hartford, Conn. See also, Answer returned to the Queries sent the Governor and in Company of His Majesty's Colony of Connecticut, October 1762, Misc. Bound MS, MHS; Carl Bridenbaugh, ed., *Gentleman's Progress: The Itinerarium of Doctor Alexander Hamilton, 1744* (Chapel Hill: University of North Carolina Press for the Institute of Early American History and Culture, 1948), 98.

in colonial homes.[101] However, in light of observers' consistent assertion that "many" or nearly "all" Indians were servants, it is likely that the census merely hinted at the enormity of the Indians' struggle with debt peonage.

III

Bonded service affected the Indians of Martha's Vineyard and the rest of southern New England not only as individuals but as cultural groups. Inevitably, having so many Indians, children in particular, live among the English promoted the Natives' acculturation to colonial ways. Some acculturative changes proved empowering for Native communities, while other shifts were decidedly less welcome. In either case, Wampanoags, Narragansetts, and Pequots struggled with how to define themselves as they became more like their English neighbors.

Indentured Indian children had not only to cope with separation from their parents and relatives but to adjust to the colonists' strange customs, the most shocking of which was corporal punishment. Indians refused to strike or even directly scold their young for fear of wounding their self-confidence and, perhaps, out of a widely held Indian belief that negative thoughts diminished the life force of the person against whom they were directed; however, as servants to the English, young Natives met with very different treatment.[102] English masters typically applied physical abuse to "break the will" of stubborn subordinates.[103] In 1724, Barnabus of Aquinnah charged Samuel Bassett with beating him, which Bassett justified by identifying Barnabus as his servant.[104] Historian Lorenzo Greene's impression from the records is that "servants were often subjected to merciless whippings. In fact, they frequently appear to have been treated worse

---

[101] Sainsbury, "Indian Labor in Early Rhode Island," appendix, 392–3. See also, A. Holmes, "Additional Memoir of the Moheagans, and of Uncas, Their Ancient Sachem," *MHSC* 1st ser., 9 (1804), 78; Herndon and Ella Wilcox Sekatau, "The Right to a Name: The Narragansett People and Rhode Island Officials in the Revolutionary Era," *Ethnohistory* 44 (1997), 440–1.

[102] Roger Williams, *A Key into the Language of America*, eds. John J. Teunissen and Evelyn J. Hinz, (1643; Detroit: Wayne State University Press, 1973), 115–16; "Historical Collections," 149; Cotton Mather to Dr. John Woodward and Dr. James Jurin, October 1, 1724, in Kenneth Silverman, ed., *Selected Letters of Cotton Mather* (Baton Rogue, La.: Louisiana State Press, 1971), 398; Axtell, ed., *The Indian Peoples of America: A Documentary History of the Sexes* (New York: Oxford University Press, 1981), 31–43.

[103] Philip Greven, *The Protestant Temperament: Patterns of Child-Rearing, Religious Experience, and the Self in Early America* (Chicago: University of Chicago Press, 1977) 49–52; Towner, *A Good Master Well Served*, 104, 134–6, 168–9; Axtell, *The School upon a Hill: Education and Society in Colonial New England* (New Haven, Conn.: Yale University Press, 1974), 89–90.

[104] Dukes County Court of Common Pleas, Records, 24, NEHGS.

in this respect, than the slaves."[105] Indeed, the Mohegan Samson Occum related the story of "a poor Indian boy . . . who was bound out to an English Family, and he used to Drive Plow for a young man, and he whipt and Beat him allmost every Day . . . but Says he, 'I believe he Beats me for the most of the Time because I am an Indian.'"[106] Beating Indian servants was so common that it worked its way into colonial dark humor. In Cotton's "Indian Vocabulary," the reader is given only the colonist's lines in a mock dialogue with an Indian:

How many years old are you?
Eighteen; and how old is that boy or girl?
Why do boys of that age run about and do nothing?
You had better let me have him and I will learn him to write and read.
He shall want for nothing, neither meat, drink, cloathing, or drubbing.[107]

This was a laughing matter to colonists but to Indians it was not. Perhaps the most formative childhood memory of Pequot William Apess occurred when his grandmother returned home intoxicated and "fell to beating me most cruelly; calling for whips, at the same time, of unnatural size, to beat me with; and asking me at the same time, question after question, if I hated her."[108] Drunk or not, the whip and charged question begs the possibility that Apess' grandmother was reenacting episodes from a servant's past.

No doubt many beatings were completely unprovoked; others might have come in response to the Indians' unfamiliarity with assigned tasks or their resistance to labor they associated with the opposite sex. Although Cape and island Wampanoags were among the first Indians to adopt Christianity, there is little evidence to suggest they voluntarily embraced the colonists' gendered division of labor. Experience Mayhew's book, *Indian Converts*, which contained 126 biographical accounts of Christian Wampanoags, gives only a few examples of Indian men raising crops, which suggests that the majority still shunned "womanly" tasks.[109] As late as 1727, missionaries like Mayhew were still frustrated that "we cannot get the Indians to improve so far in English Ingenuity, and Industry, and Husbandry, as we could wish for."[110]

---

[105] Lorenzo J. Greene, *The Negro in Colonial New England* (New York: Columbia University Press, 1942), 231. See also Axtell, *School Upon a Hill*, 123–5.

[106] Harold Blodget, *Samson Occum* (Hanover, N.H.: Dartmouth College Publications, 1935), 42.

[107] Cotton, "Indian Vocabulary," 240.

[108] William Apess, *On Our Own Ground: The Complete Writings of William Apess, a Pequot*, ed. Barry O'Connell, (Amherst: University of Massachusetts Press, 1992), 120–1.

[109] *Indian Converts*, 89, 181. On the New England Indian gendered division of labor during the early seventeenth century, see Kathleen J. Bragdon, "Gender as a Category in Native Southern New England," *Ethnohistory* 43 (1996), 578; Cronon, *Changes in the Land*, 44–9.

[110] *Indian Converts*, xvii.

Whether debt pushed Indians into service or pulled them into wage work, growing numbers of Indian men swallowed their pride and took up a hoe. Richard Macy paid a Nantucket Wampanoag in 1714 for "tending one acre of corn and reaping one acor of wheat." In 1732, John Allen of Martha's Vineyard compensated Joshua Coomes for hoeing and mowing grass, while the Rev. Ebenezer Parkman of Worcester, Massachusetts employed Joshua Misco and wife to hoe corn *together* for two days.[111] Women also had adjustments to make. In Native villages, women worked mostly in the home or garden preparing or processing food and making clothing. As servants they performed similar tasks, but the technology of spinning wheels and particularly the care of domestic animals such as chickens and cows were decidedly novel at first.[112] As one newspaper ad for a runaway Indian woman servant said, the escapee was trained up to "Sew, Wash, Brew, Bake, Spin, and Milk Cows."[113]

Indentures played a key role in Native acculturation by making colonial agricultural and household tasks an accepted part of Indian life. Natick's Joseph Comech remarked in 1750 that "in his Minority [he] Served an Apprenticeship with an English man, and being well instructed in the art or calling of Husbandry, he intended to follow said Calling."[114] In 1767, a Narragansett father objected to schoolmaster Eleazor Wheelock putting his son to work in the fields when he should have been teaching him, arguing "I can as well learn him that myself... being myself bro't up with the best of Farmers."[115] Women rarely left such statements, but changes in their work patterns suggest that they, too, were adopting English ways. Nantucket Wampanoags Sarah Nobanash, Betty Ephraim, Patience Amos, and Experience Mamuck received credit from Richard Macy for spinning yarn and sewing, possibly on equipment that they owned themselves, given the presence of spinning wheels and looms in a few Native estate inventories.[116] In 1739, Hannah Hossueit dropped dead as she "went out to Milk a Cow or

[111] Richard Macy Account Book (1707–1760), 37–8, Nantucket Historical Association; John Allen Account Book, 12 (hoeing), 21, MVHS; Francis G. Walett, ed., *The Diary of Ebenezer Parkman, 1703–1782* (Worcester, Mass.: American Antiquarian Society, 1961), 150.

[112] On female labor in New England, see Laurel Thatcher Ulrich, *Good Wives: Image and Reality in the Lives of Women in Northern New England, 1650–1750* (New York: Vintage, 1980), chap. 1; Ulrich, *A Midwife's Tale: The Life of Martha Ballard, Based on Her Diary, 1785–1812* (New York: Vintage, 1991).

[113] *Boston News-Letter*, No. 820, December 28, 1719–January 4, 1720.

[114] Mass. Archives, 32:86.

[115] Sweet, *Bodies Politic*, 117.

[116] Macy Account Book, 30, 31, and two unnumbered pages with the accounts of Amos and Mamuck; DCP 3:158 (John Talman, 1743); Middlesex County Probate Records, Case #s 2411 (Ruth Thomas, 1758), 20489 (Joseph Sinee), 2845 (John Brooks), Mass. State Archives; Elizabeth A. Little, "Probate Records of Nantucket Indians," *Nantucket Algonquian Studies* 2 (Nantucket, Mass., 1980), 12.

Cows at the Gayhead."[117] By the mid–eighteenth century, the few Indians who bothered to leave wills generally bequeathed cows to women, who were obviously responsible for milking them, and horses and oxen to men, who used them for plowing, hauling, and travel.[118]

To be sure, the Indians' labor among the English was not the only factor that encouraged them to take up new tasks and technology. Missionaries continued to promote the benefits of colonial work ways, certainly persuading some listeners. Other Natives, distressed that their poverty left them vulnerable to exploitation by merchants and judges, carefully decided "to Live more like my Christian English neighbors."[119] Still, the enormity of servitude's impact on Indian culture becomes obvious if one considers the Rhode Island census figures. According to those statistics, at least one-third of Native children were living with the English at a given time, most under indentures that kept them in service until their late teens or early twenties. When these servants returned home as adults, they passed on what they learned to their children, some of whom were in turn bound out to colonists. By the second half of the eighteenth century, probably nearly all Native households included at least one person who had spent a significant portion of his or her childhood as a servant; thus, the cumulative influence of servitude on Indian work patterns was even greater than what the actual number of former servants would suggest.

The labor individual Indians performed eventually became a key part of their public identities, at least when dealing with the English. In the late seventeenth century, government documents would identify prominent Natives as "minister," "preacher," "magistrate," or "sachem," according to his or her standing, but reserved the catchall "Indian" for the masses. Things began to change in the era of indenture. A 1717 deed labeled Aquinnah's Abel Wauwompuhque Jr. a "planter."[120] By the 1720s and 30s, Wauwompuhque was joined by John Talman, "husbandman," and Abigail Silas, "spinster." Far more common, however, were the tags "Indian laborer," "Indian fisherman," "Indian whaleman," "Indian seafaring man," "Indian yeoman," or "Indian spinstress," that followed almost every Wampanoag figure in public documents from the mid–eighteenth century onward.[121] Vineyard deeds even referred to the Indians of Christiantown collectively as "labourers."[122] Surely it came as no surprise to the Natives that colonists judged their two

[117] Suffolk Files, #46669.
[118] DCP 3:116 (Nicodemos, 1736); 5:30 (Elisha Amos, 1763), 50 (Thomas Coomes, 1760).
[119] Mandell, "'To Live More Like my Christian English Neighbors'," 567.
[120] DCD 3:300.
[121] DCD 4:57–8, 112, 268, 283, 304, 345, 346; 5:40–1, 104–5, 288, 302, 323, 384, 433–4; 6:10, 49, 61, 82, 114, 168, 195, 240, 248, 252, 269, 318, 323, 359, 361, 382, 468, 488, 531; 7:14–15, 28, 66, 81, 124, 141, 340, 348, 393–4, 437, 530; 8:151, 159, 203, 274, 332, 351, 373, 449, 452, 486, 572, 610; 9:99.
[122] DCD 6:292–3; 7:85–6, 183.

most significant characteristics to be race and the low-skilled work they almost invariably performed. Significantly, though, Indians rarely identified themselves collectively as "labourers."[123] "Natives unto the Island of Chabbaquidick," "Indians of the Gay Head," or "Indian Inhabitants of said island," were the ways they wanted to be known.[124] Individuals might work on a whaling ship or in an English kitchen, but when they gathered together they were a people of a place to which they had rights.

The changes Indians experienced in their dress, at least partially as a result of poverty and widespread indentured servitude, were of equal importance to their public identity. Between the advent of English settlement and King Philip's War, praying Indians signaled their Christianity by cutting their hair and donning shirts, pants, shoes, hats, and cloaks.[125] However, many Christian Indians refused to abide by the English dictate that people dress according to their station in the colonists' social hierarchy. Indian women had a special liking for jewelry and clothes that colonists considered gaudy and ungodly. The rebellious servant Sarah Peag of Christiantown drew Experience Mayhew's ire because she was "much set upon for making her self fine with Ornaments."[126] By contrast, Jerusha Ompany "did not appear to affect gay and costly Clothing, as many of the Indian Maids do, yet always went clear and neat in her Apparel, still wearing such things as were suitable to her own Condition and Circumstances."[127] Yet the Indians' lack of funds, combined with their dependence upon masters for clothing, meant that by the mid–eighteenth century most appeared more like members of the lower rung of the colonial working class than a distinct ethnic group. Eleazor Wheelock refused to allow Indian students of his Connecticut boarding school to wear donated clothing he judged too elegant, and apparently his attitude was widespread.[128] Newspaper descriptions of runaway Indian servants commonly described them dressed raggedly in "an old grey Petticoat, very much patch'd," a "felt Hat about half worn," a "middle Jacket Kersey, the fore Skirts of which is worn off, torn down the back seam, and sewed," or in "no shoes or stockings."[129] William Apess recalled that as a servant his treatment "was not so bad as I have seen – I mean my table fare and lodgeing – but when we came to the clothing part, it was mean enough, I can assure you. I was not fit to be seen anywhere among decent folks."[130] Nor was he intended to be. It is not surprising, then, that when Gideon Hawley

---

[123] For exceptions, see *Native Writings in Massachusett*, 1:158–61.

[124] Mass. Archives 32:356; 33:73, 161, 187; 33:231–2, 368–9, 416, 470–1, 488.

[125] Axtell, *Invasion Within*, 172.

[126] *Indian Converts*, 204.

[127] *Indian Converts*, 175.

[128] Sweet, *Bodies Politic*, 118.

[129] *Boston News-Letter*, No. 2108, August 23, 1744, runaway ad for Indian Thomas Scoggens; Taylor, ed., *Runaways, Deserters, and Notorious Villains*, 3, 35, 97.

[130] Apess, *On Our Own Ground*, 124.

went to Mashpee in the mid–eighteenth century, he noticed that the Indians "were dresssed in English mode; but in old battered garments."[131]

Servitude also influenced the Indians' food ways. Throughout the early seventeenth century, the standard Indian dish was a corn mash that included some mix of vegetables, fish, shellfish, or game. Water was the Natives' sole drink. But as merchants stocked alternative foods and extended Indians credit, as traditional sources of protein became less accessible and as Native tastes became accustomed to the food provided by colonial masters, the Indian diet began to change. Indians continued to consume traditional foods such as corn stews and roasted fish, but account books show that by the early eighteenth century they also ate mutton, beef, cheese, and potatoes, massive quantities of molasses and sugar, and smaller amounts of peas, biscuits, and apples, all of which were common to English tables (see Table 3). By the early nineteenth century, Gay Head's Esther Howwoswee was known for her meals of salt mutton, potatoes, and short cake, the latter cooked "with butter but no other relish; she baked it round [in a pot covered with coals], like our [English] spider cake."[132] Indian purchases of tea and coffee lagged some ten years behind colonists', but Indians were avid consumers of those popular drinks by the 1760s – probably just as young servants brought up with these drinks were coming of age.

Thus, by the end of the eighteenth century, several of the characteristics that had previously distinguished Natives from their colonial neighbors were no longer a part of Indian life. Indians became more like Englishmen in their gendered division of labor, in their food and dress ways, and perhaps even in their propensity to beat children. This is not to say, however, that the Natives either fully acculturated or that they assimilated. Ironically, in some ways debt peonage thwarted such convergence. By relegating Indians to lower caste status as "laborers" and handicapping their ability to maintain stable mother–child relationships, servitude promoted the idea that Indians were incapable of living "ordered" English lives and belonged at the periphery of colonial society.[133] At the same time, a few skills learned in the context of service empowered the Indians to assert their distinctiveness. Spinning and weaving promoted the Indians' self-sufficiency by enabling them to produce their own clothing from their own wool. Livestock provided meat and raw materials and doubled as a usufruct claim to the people's common lands. The Indians were fortunate in this respect, for acculturation shifted

---

[131] Hawley to Anonymous, 1 June 1794, Hawley Letters, MHS. See also Moody, *Summary Account of . . . Joseph Quasson*, 3–4; Linda Welters, "From Moccasins to Frock Coats and Back Again: Ethnic Identity and Native American Dress in Southern New England," in Patricia A. Cunningham and Susan Voso Lab, eds., *Dress in American Culture* (Bowling Green, Oh.: Bowling Green State University Press, 1993), 6–41.

[132] Edward S. Burgess, "The Old South Road of Gay Head," *Dukes County Intelligencer* 12 (1970), 26.

[133] Ann Marie Plane, *Colonial Intimacies: Indian Marriage in Early New England* (Ithaca, N.Y.: Cornell University Press, 2000), esp. chap. 4; Herndon, *Unwelcome Americans*.

more of the symbolic weight of their peoplehood onto the reservation itself. It was the place where their boundaries were clearly marked, where their communal values were shared, where their ancient stories took place and their ghosts haunted.[134] Yet these fringe benefits of indentured servitude must have been cold comfort to people who barely had time to enjoy the surroundings of home and whose family members had been torn away from them.

IV

Food, labor, dress, child rearing: these are major elements of any people's cultural life. But indentured servitude's impact on Indian culture was even greater, its reach even longer. It struck much nearer to the foundations of Indian identity when it began to interfere with the people's ability to pass on Native languages through word of mouth and print. Gradually, Indians became English-only speakers, and this change more than any other threatened Indian claims to distinctiveness.

During the first two-thirds of the eighteenth century, as more and more Natives served indentures, Indian literacy rates stagnated or declined. This lack of progress is remarkable given that Native parents sometimes bound out their children with the intention of providing for their education, and because it contrasts the steady rise of Indian literacy during the seventeenth century when the Natives often taught their own schools.[135] During a 1698 survey of Indian towns in Massachusetts, Grindal Rawson and Samuel Danforth found Indians, particularly children, making rapid progress in reading at almost every stop.[136] Twelve years later, Josiah Cotton reported that over a third of the Monument Pond Wampanoags near Plymouth could read, with the skill widely shared among men and women.[137] E. Jennifer Monaghan notes that in Mayhew's *Indian Converts*, thirty-seven percent of the adult male characters were mentioned as being able to read, and seven percent as

[134] William S. Simmons, *Spirit of the New England Tribes: Indian History and Folklore, 1620–1984* (Hanover, N.H.: University Press of New England, 1985); Kathleen J. Bragdon, "Language, Folk History, and Identity on Martha's Vineyard," in Anne Elizabeth Yentsch and Marcy C. Beaudry, eds., *The Art and Mystery of Historical Archaeology: Essays in Honor of James Deetz* (Boca Raton, Fla.: CRC Press, 1992), 331–42; Mandell, *Behind the Frontier*, chap. 6.

[135] The best study of Native literacy in southern New England is Kathleen Joan Bragdon, "'Another Tongue Brought In': An Ethnohistorical Study of Native Writings in Massachusett" (Ph.D. diss., Brown University, 1981), chaps. 3–4. On the Indians sending their children to live with Englishmen in order to secure their education, see *Indian Converts*, 115, 261; Axtell, *Invasion Within*, 187–9; Margaret Connell Szasz, *Indian Education in the American Colonies, 1607–1783* (Albuquerque: University of New Mexico Press), chap. 8.

[136] "Indian Visitation," 129–34.

[137] An Account of Monument Ponds taken by Josiah Cotton their Minister in the year 1710, Curwen Family Papers, Box 2, Folder 1, AAS.

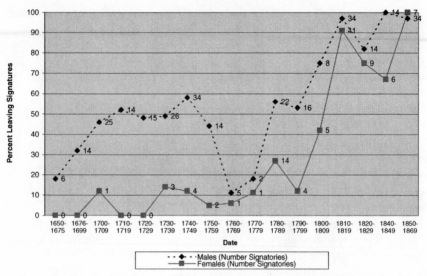

FIGURE 7. Indian Signature Rates on Martha's Vineyard, by Sex, Per Decade (number leaving signatures on deeds, wills, and petitions, and that number as % of total). *Sources: Native Writings;* DCD; DCP; Mass. Archives vols. 31–3; PLP-Resolves 1785, chap. 4; Resolves 1789, chap. 57; Resolves 1790, chap. 106; Resolves 1796, chap. 46; Acts 1804, chap. 84; Acts 1811, chap. 78; Resolves 1820, chap. 46; Resolves 1822, chap. 22; Acts 1827, chap. 114; Acts 1838, chap. 101; Acts 1870, chap. 213; ULRIA, 2 Boxes; GIP; Box 174A, Env. 34, and "Scrap Book of Deeds," MVHS. *Note:* These figures should be seen as correlating only roughly to the actual rate of full literacy among the Vineyard Indian population. As Ives Goddard and Kathleen Bragdon note, literate Indians often had others write documents and their signatures for them. Later they would add a mark validating what had been written (*Native Writings,* 1:22). It is also likely that some Indians without writing skills had their signatures written for them, and then neglected to add their marks, thus making it appear that they were capable of signing their names.

possessing writing skills. Among women and children, Mayhew identified forty-nine and seventy-three percent, respectively, as readers, and three and fourteen percent as writers.[138] Certainly Mayhew focused disproportionately on the most literate Indians. Nevertheless, these figures are supported by the percentage of Vineyard Wampanoags who fixed their signatures to deeds, wills, and petitions (though here again, formally educated Indians were probably overrepresented). Measured on a decade-by-decade basis, between 1700 and 1740 the percentage of Indian males who closed their official documents with a signature rather than a mark fluctuated between forty-seven and fifty-seven percent, while the number of female signatories always hovered below twenty percent (see Figure 7).

[138] Monaghan, "She loved to read in good Books": Literacy and the Indians of Martha's Vineyard, 1643–1725," *History of Education Quarterly* 30 (1990), 502–3, n. 18.

At midcentury, these percentages took a precipitous fall, with males at eleven percent for the 1760s and females at seven percent. A loss of missionary fervor and the cessation of Indian-language publications contributed to this decline, but another factor seems to have been the coming of age of large numbers of Indian children who had grown up in English homes rather than in their Native villages where they could attend Indian schools.[139] In the late seventeenth century Hannah Sissetom boarded with a religious English family who taught her to read, "tho not very well."[140] Hepzibath Assaquanhut was sent to live in a Tisbury home for seven years "until she was a Woman grown," but left service with a similarly poor command of the written word.[141] Assaquanhut's experience was so common that in 1708 the commissioners of the New England Company issued a circular letter asking authorities to ensure that Indian indentured servants were taught reading and the catechism.[142] However, their prodding was to little end. Years later a Connecticut report found that "many of the Indians in this Government put out theire Children to the English to be brought up by them, and yet sundry of the persons haveing such Children do Neglect to learn them to read, & to Instruct them in the principals of the Christian faith, so that such Children are in danger to continue heathen."[143] Whaling precluded access to schools and home training for adolescent Indian males. House servants were less mobile and therefore theoretically subject to more regular lessons. Most of them, however, had to wait until the winter months for tutoring, if they received it at all.[144]

Not until the late eighteenth century, when Indian servants began to receive regular instruction from white women – who were themselves in the process of gaining full literacy – did Indian signature rates start to climb, particularly among females working within the home.[145] In 1802 James Freeman hinted at the superior education of house servants when he observed at Mashpee "the females are in general better taught then the males."[146] Rising Indian literacy might also have reflected, as Gideon Hawley put it,

---

[139] On waning missionary enthusiasm, see Jean Fitzz Hankins, "Bringing the Good News: Protestant Missions to the Indians of New England and New York," (Ph.D. diss., University of Connecticut, 1993).

[140] *Indian Converts*, 184.

[141] *Indian Converts*, 202.

[142] NE Co. MSS, 7953, 20.

[143] "Indian Series," Series 1, Vol. 1, Doc. 131, Connecticut State Archives, Hartford, Conn.

[144] Apess, *On Our Own Ground*, 7. Axtell, *School Upon a Hill*, 129, points out that after 1695 masters were not bound by the law to instruct their servants.

[145] Kenneth A. Lockridge, *Literacy in Colonial New England: An Enquiry into the Social Context of Literacy in the Early Modern West* (New York: W.W. Norton, 1974); Gloria L. Main, "An Inquiry into When and Why Women Learned to Write in Colonial New England," *Journal of Social History* 24 (1990–91), 579–89; Joel Perlmann and Dennis Shirley, "When Did New England Women Acquire Literacy?" *WMQ* 48 (1991), 50–67; Axtell, *School Upon a Hill*, 178.

[146] James Freeman, "A Description of Mashpee," *MHSC* 2d ser., 3 (1815), 5.

that Indian children "are now put out in good families and brot up pretty well," whereas earlier their masters had neglected their education.[147] Despite this progress, Indian signature rates would not catch up to those of whites until the Vineyard's Frederick Baylies began an extensive schooling movement among Wampanoags and Narragansetts in the early nineteenth century. Rather than producing a more literate Indian population, servitude appears to have had quite the opposite effect.

Even though indentured Indians did not learn to write English at a high rate, they certainly learned to speak it, some to the exclusion of their natal language. In the early eighteenth century, Wampanoag was the dominant tongue at Aquinnah. Experience Mayhew had to serve as an interpreter when Samuel Sewall met with the Natives there in 1714, even though two colonists had spent the last six years teaching English to island Wampanoags.[148] The only Indians who could be called truly bilingual were those who grew up in English homes, attended colonial boarding schools, or spent considerable time with English ministers. Well into the 1720s, the vast majority of Indians understood their own tongue "much better" than English, and even as late as the 1760s, one could find individuals like Thomas Tackanash (or Tocknot) who spoke "very bad English."[149]

But change was at hand. In the early eighteenth century, the New England Company ceased its Native-language publications.[150] Thereafter, every torn page of an Indian version of the *New England Confession of Faith*, or waterlogged chapter of the *Practice of Piety*, or burnt copy of *Call to the Unconverted*, represented a blow to the future of traditional speech. The lack of such texts would have posed little danger to the Wampanoags' language if their young people regularly interacted with Indian adults, but in fact Indian communities in eighteenth- and early-nineteenth-century New England struggled to foster such relationships. Military service and whaling devastated Indian males, while disease carried off the adults of both sexes.[151] In 1730, smallpox decimated the Indians of Chatham on Cape Cod "so that there is scarce any grown person of the Indians left in this Town."[152] Six years later, a smallpox epidemic that appears to have been especially lethal to adults killed off perhaps half of the Yarmouth Wampanoags, and in 1763–64 yellow fever

---

[147] Letter of Gideon Hawley, Letter IV, ca. July 1794, Samuel P. Savage Papers, MHS

[148] NE Co. MSS, 7955/1, 56–7, MSS, 7953, 23, 24. See also *Sewall Diary*, 2:751.

[149] E. Mayhew, *A Brief Account*, 9–10 Boston *News-Letter*, No. 2684, September 10, 1761, account of Fort Frederick deserters.

[150] William Kellaway, *The New England Company, 1649–1776* (New York: Barnes and Noble, 1961), chap. 6; Bragdon, "'Another Tongue Brought In,'" 46.

[151] Jack Campisi, *The Mashpee Indians: Tribe on Trial* (Syracuse, N.Y.: Syracuse University Press, 1991), 88; Mandell, *Behind the Frontier*, 128–32; "Memoir of the Nyhantic Tribe of Indians," *MHSC* 1st ser., 10 (1809), 104; Connecticut State Archives, "Indian Series," Series 1, Vol. 2, Doc. 239a.

[152] *Boston News-Letter*, No. 1400, November 19, 1730.

carried off almost all of the grown-ups on Nantucket – those most fluent in the Native language – plus some 39 Vineyard Wampanoags, mostly at Chappaquiddick.[153] In 1790, the Chappaquddicks pleaded for Massachusetts to assist with their legal debts because "the greatest part of the Natives are Female, some of them very old and helpless."[154] Similarly, in 1807, David Kendall found Mohegan in Connecticut populated "for the most part [by] very aged persons, widows, and fatherless children. The young men go to sea and die." At Gay Head he discovered that "the women and children make more than the due proportion. On the soil, there were not at this time more than fifteen or sixteen men and boys."[155] Women of these communities spent long stretches of time performing wage work off the reservations, and children were often quite young when they left home as bondservants, thereby obstructing Native-language conversation.

Linguist Joshua Fishman explains that a language shift "implies the breakdown of a previously established societal allocation of functions, the alteration of previously recognized role relationships, situations, and domains, so that these no longer imply or call for the language with which they were previously associated."[156] No description better captures social life in Indian villages that were beginning to serve as way stations for able-bodied laborers, leaving only the very young and the old and used-up. The language shift came in stages. First, a few members of the community – then most, then essentially all – became bilingual in varying degrees, with some probably handicapped by a frustratingly imperfect command of either language. A 1707 newspaper advertisement calling for the return of a runaway Wampanoag servant named Hannah Wapuck, aged twenty, noted, "she speaks good English, not very perfect of the Indian Language."[157] By 1732, Josiah Cotton

---

[153] On smallpox in Yarmouth, see *Boston News-Letter*, No. 1763, January 2, 1738. Note that issue no. 1766 from January 23, reports that in Edgartown 11 of 12 deaths from the same smallpox outbreak were adults. On the yellow fever epidemic that struck Nantucket and Martha's Vineyard, see Letter of Jasper Manduit, January 5, 1765, Box 1, CPGNA; *Boston News-Letter*, No. 3127, January 26, 1764; *Newport Mercury*, No. 283, February 6, 1764; *Boston Evening Post*, No. 1482, January 30, 1764; Elizabeth A. Little, "The Nantucket Indian Sickness," in William Cowan, ed., *Papers of the 21st Algonquian Conference* (Ottawa: Carleton University, 1990), 181–96; Edouard A. Stackpole, "The Fatal Indian Sickness of Nantucket That Decimated the Island Aborigines" *Historic Nantucket* 23 (1975), 8–13; Donald Pelrine, "The Indian Sickness in the Town of Miacomet," *Historic Nantucket* 39 (1991), 67–9

[154] PLP, Resolves 1790, Chap. 106.

[155] Kendall, *Travels*, 1:201–2, 2:194–5. See also Freeman, "Description of Dukes County," 93–4; "D. Wrighte to Alden Bradford, 9 April 1839," Eliot-Andrews Collection, MHS.

[156] Fishman, *Language and Ethnicity in Minority Sociolinguistic Perspective* (Clevedon/Philadelphia, 1989), 22. Also informing this discussion is William L. Leap, *American Indian English* (Salt Lake City: University of Utah Press, 1993); and A. Richard Diebold Jr., "Incipient Bilingualism," in Dell Hymes, ed., *Language in Culture and Society: A Reader in Linguistics and Anthropology* (New York: Harper and Row, 1964), 495–506.

[157] *Boston News-Letter*, No. 149, February 17, 1706/1707.

found that four of five Indian families on the Plymouth side of Eel River "understand English pretty well."[158] In 1754, the Mashpees invited colonist Gideon Hawley to preach alongside Native minister Solomon Briant because "some of us did not understand the Indian dialect fully."[159] In 1767, a Boston newspaper reported of the Vineyard Wampanoags that "the Indians are fond of retaining their own Language...they generally however understand English, especially the younger ones among them."[160] To accommodate the uneven language skills of community members, that same year a joint communion service between the Natives of Cape Cod and Martha's Vineyard included a morning service in Wampanoag and afternoon worship in English.[161] A generation later, in 1802, Gideon Hawley determined that at Mashpee "the English language is now more copious perhaps than any of the old language, and is eno' [enough] for an Indian to know."[162]

For a time, bilingualism appeared to be on the rise, but in the end what was really ascendant was English. When a child, like Tobit Potter, returned home unable to speak Wampanoag, his relatives would have to speak to him in the colonists' language.[163] Certainly they would also try to teach him the Indian language, but time worked against them. Young men who promptly left their villages again to go whaling, or young women who entered domestic service in distant towns and cities, could not immerse themselves in the Native tongue until middle or old age. By then it was too late. Not only is language acquisition more difficult for adults than children but, as anthropologist Anya Peterson Royce notes, learning the behaviors of one's ethnic group after maturity is "laden with stress" because one is not given much latitude for mistake. An adult starting down this path "can be easily discouraged unless the rewards are sufficiently tempting or the first identity is particularly negative."[164] Given a shrinking base of Native speakers and no economic incentives, pride of identity became the only reason to learn Wampanoag. For most people the pull was not strong enough. Consequently, the number of English-only speakers grew steadily over the course of the eighteenth century until they formed a majority by its end. The death of New England's Algonquian tongues would not come until some time after

---

[158] Josiah Cotton Memoirs, unpaginated, MHS.

[159] "At a Meeting of the Indians in Mashpee, July 28, 1754," Hawley Letters, MHS.

[160] *Boston News-Letter*, No. 3351, December 24, 1767.

[161] "Report of a Committee on the State of the Indians in Mashpee," *MHSC* 1st ser., 10 (1815), 13.

[162] Hawley to R.D.S, August 1802, Savage Papers, MHS.

[163] See, for example, the account of Joseph Quasson of Monomoy near Plymouth. Quasson was put out by his mother in 1703 at six to pay off a £5 debt. He gained his release at age 18 and returned to the Native community. Owing to his poor wardrobe, he shifted his attendance from the English to the Indian church, where, he admitted, "I understood nothing." Moody, *Summary Account of . . . Joseph Quasson*, 4.

[164] Royce, *Ethnic Identity: Strategies of Diversity* (Bloomington: Indiana University Press, 1982), 188.

Indian women began marrying non-Indians in large numbers, but exogamous marriage was just the last blow to languages that had already been severely weakened by indenture.

V

In the late nineteenth century, botanist Edward Burgess visited the Wampanoag community of Aquinnah where elders told him stories about Zachariah Howwoswee, who was the last Indian minister to preach in the Wampanoag language until his death in 1821 at age 83. Aquinnahs remembered that whenever Howwoswee switched the language of his sermons from English to Wampanoag, "there were but few of them could know what he meant . . . and they would cry and he would cry." Howwoswee knew his listeners could not understand his words, but they could share a sense of their collective history, loss, and perseverance. As Howwoswee put it, speaking his ancestral tongue was a way "to keep up my nation."[165]

Much about Wampanoag society and culture had changed during Howwoswee's lifetime. Beginning in the late seventeenth century and through the early 1800s, English merchants exploited the Indians' dependence upon store credit to coerce men, women, and children alike into bonded service. Judges and guardians colluded in this effort by binding out Indians who could not pay off their store accounts or court costs. Meanwhile, colonial officials made only token gestures to end this abuse, even though they were fully aware of it.

Under such circumstances, Natives lost control not only over their workaday lives but the very upbringing of their young people. Large numbers of children and young adults spent most of their developmental years working in the colonists' homes and on their farms and ships, where they heard and spoke English, performed English work ways, wore English clothing, and ate English foods. Over time, they could not help but become more like their masters. Not all of the resulting changes were negative. After all, it was essential for people who wanted to persist in a colonial-dominated region to learn how to run an English-style farm and speak English. But as Burgess's account of Howwoswee illustrates, other developments, particularly the decline of the ancestral tongue, felt like loss, not just change. Indians mourned their increasing inability to speak Wampanoag, Narragansett, or Pequot. They knew a precious tie with their past was fraying.

Their white neighbors did too, and they cited the Natives' language loss as evidence that New England Indians were "disappearing" or "becoming extinct." The Indians, of course, did not accept this view. They placed a new cultural emphasis on old traditions like folklore, communal values, and land, and their distinctive brand of Christianity, while developing new expressions

[165] Burgess, "Old South Road," 22.

of their peoplehood such as pride in race, pageants of pan-Indian dress and dance, and sprinkling English-language conversations with the Native words they still knew. In short, no less than Wampanoags seventeenth century, who used Christianity to adapt their communities and customs to a rapidly changing world, Natives who experienced the deep change brought on by indentured servitude discovered new expressions of old identities.[166]

The ability of some Indians to adjust to changing circumstances should not obscure that after King Philip's War Englishmen confronted them with a formidable and in some cases overwhelming set of challenges; indentured servitude should rank with land encroachment as the most significant of them. It pulled apart Indian families, radically influenced Indian behavior, and initiated the loss of the Indians' ancestral languages. It forced Indians to occupy one of the lowest rungs of the New England social ladder, just a step above African American slaves and several steps below everyone else. In the next century, as African Americans began marrying into Native communities, it would be all the Indians could do just to defend the third-class status promoted by the colonists' exploitation of their debt.

---

[166] On the discourse of the "disappearing Indian," see Roy Harvey Pearce: *Savagism and Civilization: A Study of the Indian and the American Mind* (1953; Berkeley: University of California Press, 1988), chaps. 2–5; Robert F. Berkhofer Jr., *The White Man's Indian: Images of the American Indian from Columbus to the Present* (New York: Vintage Books, 1979), 157–66; Brian W. Dippie, *The Vanishing American: White Attitudes and U.S. Indian Policy* (Lawrence: University of Kansas Press, 1982); Jeffery Steele, "Reduced to Images: American Indians in Nineteenth-Century Advertising," in S. Elizabeth Bird, ed., *Dressing in Feathers: The Construction of the Indian in American Popular Culture* (Boulder, Col.: Westview Press, 1996), 45–64; Jean O'Brien, "'They are so Frequently Shifting Their Place of Residence': Land and the Construction of Social Place of Indians in Colonial Massachusetts," in Daunton and Halpern, eds., *Empire and Others*, 204–16. Among many strong studies on the Indians' ethnic markers in the nineteenth and twentieth centuries, see Simmons, *Spirit of the New England Tribes*; Bragdon, "Language, Folk History, and Indian Identity"; and Gloria Levitas, "No Boundary is a Boundary: Conflict and Change in a New England Indian Community" (Ph.D. diss., Rutgers University, 1980).

7

"Newcomers and Strangers"

Blood boiled at Aquinnah in 1812 when news broke that Zachariah Howwoswee Jr. and Simon Mayhew had submitted a petition to Boston claiming to represent the ten so-called "few remaining Indians of Gayhead." In it they asserted that the Wampanoags "used to get along quite peaceably and well... [but] now there are so many Negroes and Molattoes got in among us, who are proud, lazy, and do not do right, and hurt us very much, & we cannot help ourselves." The only way to protect the besieged Natives, Howwoswee and Mayhew contended, was for Massachusetts to place Aquinnah under new guardians, namely themselves.[1] These underhanded men had attempted several land grabs over the last twenty years, only to be defeated at every turn.[2] Now, with Howwoswee sunken in debt and Mayhew overconfident following his election as Chilmark's representative to the state legislature, they hatched this new scheme with the obvious purpose of engrossing Wampanoag territory.

Aquinnah professed shock at the petition's "absurditites," but no one could have been surprised that race had finally entered the community's politics. Recently, a stark shortage of Indian men had forced growing numbers of Indian women to marry outsiders, a disproportionate number of whom were "blacks" and "mulattoes" since segregationist workplace conditions, laws, and customs grouped Natives with other "people of color." Although there were scattered examples of Wampanoags pairing with African American slaves stretching back several years, this was the first time open marriages took places in such large numbers, thereby presenting the Indian

---

[1] The petition can be found in PLP, Acts 1811, Chap. 78. For documents that uncover the plan, see ULRIA, House Unpassed 8029–1816 (4); "Report on Complaint of the Gay Head Indians, June 10, 1815," Governor's Council Files, Box, June 1815–July 1816, Mass. State Archives; Ebenezer Skiff to Paul Cuffee, October [], 1816, Paul Cuffee Letterbook, NBFPL.

[2] DCD, 15:231; ULRIA, House Unpassed 8029–1816 (4); *Mass. Acts and Resolves, 1809–1812*, Acts 1811, chap. 78.

communities in which the "mixed" couples lived with a host of formidable challenges: Could a non-Indian participate in local government? Could he retain Wampanoag land if his Indian wife died? How would the children of mixed marriages learn the people's language and customs?[3] These questions, loaded with implications for the future of Indian society, tended to bring out the ugliest in people who debated them. Over the course of the nineteenth century, the Indians' fear of being invaded from within made race baiting a signature of their public life.

"Mixed" families and their Indian neighbors also contended with white New Englanders' sharpened sense of hierarchical racial difference between themselves, "Indians," and "blacks." Such thought grew ever more virulent and widespread over the late eighteenth century as a backlash against the Revolution's egalitarian rhetoric and the emancipation of northern slaves, and in response to the ongoing terror of frontier warfare, until by the nineteenth century it was basic to the nation's public discussions: Euro-Americans facing lifelong status as wage laborers claimed equal political privileges and social respectability by heralding their "whiteness" and degrading fellow workers of color; white frontiersmen and their advocates justified the country's appropriation of Indian territory by fire, sword, and the pen with claims that "whites" had a divine right to "improve" land wasted by "savages," even when that "improvement" entailed expanding the slave regime; white politicians used racial demagoguery to build national coalitions across sectional and class lines that otherwise threatened to confirm the Founders' nightmares that the republic was doomed to failure.[4] And the list could go on. The various strands of American racism that wove through these debates defy categorization as a single ideology, but there was a certain amount of consensus that when a person was born with almost any quantity of "black blood," he or she was infested with debased "black" characteristics: servility, stupidity, childishness, laziness, fetidness, and a host of others. "Indianness," by comparison, referred to transience, cunning, pride, lawlessness, blood thirst, and a propensity toward alcohol abuse. These "Indian" qualities, unlike "black" ones, were for individuals to lose rather than acquire, whether by "extinction," as degraded Native peoples withered away

---

[3] DCGSP, October 1730–October 1757, 739, 750.

[4] This scholarship on these themes is vast and growing exponentially. The most useful works for this study include, Joanne Pope Melish, *Disowning Slavery: Gradual Emancipation and 'Race' in New England, 1680–1860* (Ithaca, N.Y.: Cornell University Press, 1998); David R. Roediger, *The Wages of Whiteness: Race and the Making of the American Working Class* (New York: Verso, 1991); Alexander Saxton, *Rise and Fall of the White Republic: Class Politics and Mass Culture in Nineteenth-Century America* (New York: Verso, 1990); Reginald Horsman, *Race and Manifest Destiny: The Origins of American Racial Anglo-Saxonism* (Cambridge, Mass.: Harvard University Press, 1981); Richard White, *The Middle Ground: Indians, Empires, and Republics in the Great Lakes Region, 1650–1815* (New York: Cambridge University Press, 1991), 339–523; Colin Calloway, *The American Revolution in Indian Country: Crisis and Diversity in Native American Communities* (New York: Cambridge University Press, 1995), 272–301.

or were overrun by American expansion, or by dilution, as Indians "mixed" with other peoples, especially blacks. Thus, an Indian community that adopted racial others forfeited its claim to be "Indian." Blackness trumped Indianness, and racial identity trumped community or tribal identity – a racial construction that conveniently enlarged the servile black labor pool while shrinking the number of Indians on the land. Such ideas, combined with the Wampanoags' high degree of acculturation, encouraged whites to redefine the inhabitants of Aquinnah, Chappaquiddick, Christiantown, and other Native places as "people of color," which northerners typically conflated with "black."

This semantic shift obfuscated the complex adaptations of Native peoples to their new in-laws and neighbors, and vice versa, as well as threatened to erode white support for laws that protected "Indian" territory from division and sale. Howwoswee and Mayhew crafted their petition to appropriate a small tract of land at the margins of New England, but their strategy conjured up ideas powerful enough to overhaul Indian lives throughout the eastern seaboard. The document was an omen that the Indians' struggle to integrate "strangers" and their children would also involve grappling with the racial perceptions and policies of outsiders.

I

For all of their sinister intent, Howwoswee and Mayhew referred to an actual trend of Indian–black marriages taking place at Gay Head and throughout the East, driven by the deaths of Indian men in military service and on the high seas.[5] Twenty-five of twenty-six Cape Wampanoags who marched in one of Barnstable County's regiments during the War for Independence never returned home and the fortunate soul who did probably introduced a camp disease that in 1778 killed seventy people in Mashpee out of a population of

[5] For a sampling of important studies on Indian–black relationships focused outside of New England, see Karen I. Blu, *The Lumbee Problem: The Making of an American Indian People* (New York: Cambridge University Press, 1980); Gerald M. Sider, *Lumbee Indian Histories: Race, Ethnicity, and Indian Identity in the Southern United States* (New York: Cambridge University Press, 1993); Theda Perdue, *"Mixed Blood" Indians: Racial Construction in the Early South* (Athens: University of Georgia Press, 2002); Jack D. Forbes, *Africans and Native Americans: The Language of Race and the Evolution of Red–Black Peoples*, 2d ed. (Urbana: University of Illinois Press, 1993); Claudio Saunt, *A New Order of Things: Property, Power, and the Transformation of the Creek Indians, 1733–1816* (New York: Cambridge University Press, 1999); James H. Merrell, "The Racial Education of the Catawba Indians," *Journal of Southern History* 50 (1984), 363–84; Helen C. Rountree, *Pocahontas's People: The Powhatan Indians of Virginia through Four Centuries* (Norman: University of Oklahoma Press, 1990), esp. chaps. 7–9; J. Leitch Wright Jr., *The Only Land They Knew: The Tragic Story of the American Indians in the Old South* (New York: Free Press, 1981), chap. 11; Daniel F. Littlefield, *Africans and Creeks: From the Colonial Period to the Civil War* (Westport, Ct.: Greenwood Press, 1979).

just 300.[6] Wampanoag sailors fared no better, subject as they were to privateers, violent weather, and workaday accidents, particularly when battling
whales. Between 1750 and 1779, Nantucket lost thirty-eight ships and 494
men, which, given one historian's estimate that five of thirteen whalemen
were Native, would put the number of Indian dead from that port alone at
about 190.[7] Casualties of this sort devastated Indian villages already reeling
from the effects of indentured servitude. In his 1792 census of Aquinnah,
Moses Howwoswee counted fifty-five adult women and only twenty-seven
adult males.[8] Even the younger generations were imbalanced, since boys
shipped out to sea as early as age thirteen.[9] In 1798, females outnumbered
males sixty-five to fifty-one among Gay Headers under the age of eighteen.[10]
Native women with an interest in marrying sometimes had little choice but
to look outside the community.

They found a prime market for husbands among the free men of color
who labored as sea hands, longshoremen, cooks, and caulkers in the whaling towns that dotted the Wampanoags' ancient territory. Most of these
workers were former slaves freed by recent northern emancipation laws,

[6] Jack Campisi, *The Mashpee Indians: Tribe on Trial* (Syracuse, N.Y.: Syracuse University Press, 1991), 88; Mashpee Births and Deaths for 1778, Hawley Journal. On Indian military service, see Richard R. Johnson, "The Search for a Usable Indian: An Aspect of the Defense of Colonial New England," *JAH* 64 (1977), 622–51; Russel Lawrence Barsh, "Native American Loyalists and Patriots: Reflections on the American Revolution in Native American History," *Indian Historian* 10 (1977), 9–19; Francis G. Hutchins, *Mashpee: The Story of Cape Cod's Indian Town* (West Franklin, N.H.: Amarta Press, 1979), chap. 4; Calloway, *American Revolution in Indian Country*, chap. 3; Daniel R. Mandell, *Behind the Frontier: Indians in Eighteenth Century Eastern Massachusetts* (Lincoln: University of Nebraska Press, 1996), chaps. 5–6; Mandell, "Shifting Boundaries of Race and Ethnicity: Indian–Black Intermarriage in Southern New England, 1760–1880," *JAH* 85 (1998–99), 468–9; Jean M. O'Brien, *Dispossession by Degrees: Indian Land and Identity in Natick, Massachusetts, 1650–1790* (Cambridge: Cambridge University Press, 1997), chap. 5.

[7] "List of Vessels Lost," Notebook A, File 18, Macy Family Papers, Nantucket Historical Association, Nantucket, Mass.; J. Hector St. John de Crèvecour, *Letters from an American Farmer* (1782; New York, 1967), 175–6. On losses to privateers, see Alexander Starbuck, *History of the American Whaling Fishery from Its Earliest Inception to the Year 1876*, 2 vols. (1878; New York: Argosy-Antiquarian, Ltd., 1964), 1:33, 34, 77, 170, 171.

[8] Moses Howwoswee, "Account of the Indians Resident at Gay Head, March 19, 1792," Misc. Unbound MSS, MHS.

[9] Crew Lists and Seamen's Protection Papers from NBFPL provide the following age data for identifiable Vineyard Wampanoag sailors during the first three-quarters of the nineteenth century: Ages 10–14 ($n = 2$); 15–19 ($n = 23$); 20–4 ($n = 51$); 25–9 ($n = 28$); 30–4 ($n = 7$); 35–9 ($n = 8$); 40–4 ($n = 2$); 45–9 ($n = 1$); 50–4 ($n = 2$); 55–9 ($n = 0$). $N = 124$. Median age = 24.

[10] "A List of Children under Eighteen Years of Age, the 14th Day of May, 1798, at Gayhead, Dukes County," Misc. Bound MSS, MHS. Narragansett oral tradition holds that until recently female infants had a higher survival rate than males, but offers no explanation. See Ruth Wallis Herndon and Ella Wilcox Sekatau, "The Right to a Name: The Narragansett People and Rhode Island Officials in the Revolutionary Era," *Ethnohistory* 44 (1997), 440.

manumission, or running away, while others were sailors from all corners of the globe whose travels had landed them in America.[11] The side streets of New Bedford, which by the early nineteenth century had superceded Nantucket to become the busiest whaling port in the world, contained what one magazine reporter described as "a greater variety of human species than is elsewhere to be found under the bright sun of Christian civilization. Europeans there are of every flag and language; Native Yankees...Gay Headers and negroes; aboriginals and Africans; Island Portuguese as plenty as whales'-teeth; with an occasional sprinkling of Chinese, Luscars, Australians, and Polynesians, cannibals and vegetarians."[12] Sometimes a certain racial egalitarianism emerged from the rowdiness of dockside watering holes and the working solidarity of the ship, but it was equally common for off-duty sailors to separate into gangs of "whites" and "non-whites," for captains to insist on segregating their crew's lodgings, and for certain taverns and boardinghouses to cater to "whites only."[13] Thus, regardless of their separate origins, "people of color" in New England port towns tended to form their own neighborhoods, like the heterogeneous "New Guinea" district of Nantucket, and webs of sociability that ultimately introduced working men of color and Native women.[14] And aside from mutual attraction and affection, these groups had good practical reasons to consider one another as mates, with Indian women lacking a sufficient pool of courtiers at home, and colored seamen often starved of female company and

[11] William Dillon Pierson, *Black Yankees: The Development of an Afro-American Subculture in Eighteenth-Century New England* (Amherst: University of Massachusetts Press, 1988), chap. 2; James Oliver Horton, *Free People of Color: Inside the African American Community* (Washington, D.C.: Smithsonian Institution Press, 1993), 26, 30–1, 34.

[12] "A Summer in New England: Paper One," *Harper's New Monthly Magazine* 124 (June, 1860), 9. On New Bedford's growth see Daniel Ricketson, *The History of New Bedford, Bristol County, Massachusetts* (New Bedford, 1858), 58, 59, 72, 300–302; James Freeman, "Notes on New Bedford," *MHSC* 2d ser., 3 (1815), 18.

[13] On at-sea racial segregation and inequality, see Margaret S. Creighton, *Rites and Passages: The Experience of American Whaling, 1830–1870* (New York: Cambridge University Press, 1995), 31, 146, 156–7; Daniel Vickers, "Nantucket Whalemen and the Deep-Sea Fishery: The Changing Anatomy of an Early American Labor Force," *JAH* 72 (1985), 289–90. Emphasizing relative tolerance onboard is Jeffery Bolster, *Black Jacks: African American Seamen in the Age of Sail* (Cambridge, Mass.: Harvard University Press, 1997), chap. 2, esp. 176–7, and with a class emphasis, Marcus Rediker, *Between the Devil and the Deep Blue Sea: Merchant Seamen, Pirates, and the Anglo-American Maritime World, 1700–1750* (New York: Cambridge University Press, 1987); Peter Linebaugh and Rediker, *The Many-Headed Hydra: Sailors, Slaves, Commoners, and the Hidden History of the Revolutionary Atlantic* (Boston: Beacon Press, 2000).

[14] Nathaniel Philbrick, *Abram's Eyes: The Native American Legacy of Nantucket Island* (Nantucket: Mill Hill Press, 1997), 197. Russel Lawrence Barsh, "'Colored' Seamen in the New England Whaling Industry: An Afro-Indian Consortium," in James F. Brooks, ed., *Confounding the Color Line: The Indian–Black Experience in North America* (Lincoln: University of Nebraska Press, 2002), 76–107.

enticed by the rare opportunity to partner with someone who enjoyed access to land.

Consistent with the international flavor of the whaling trade, a number of these men hailed from foreign climes. Joseph DeGrasse grew up on the Cape Verde Islands before marrying into Gay Head sometime before 1792, where he helped raise three children on a small farm.[15] William Vanderhoop, the son of a Surinamese mother and Dutch father, came to the Vineyard in the early nineteenth century by wedding Beulah Salisbury of Aquinnah, with whom he sired several children.[16] Portuguese John Anthony worked on a New Bedford whaler between 1840 and 1843, then married Betsy Mingo of Christiantown and raised two children upon five acres of land, then finally moved with his family to Gay Head in 1856.[17] Yet most of the outsiders who joined Native communities were black or mulatto men from the United States. Before marrying Mehitable Ames and settling down in a cottage at Aquinnah, James Bowyer called Alexandria, Virginia, his home.[18] William Matthews, who wed Margaret Prince of Chappaquiddick, was originally from Maryland.[19] All of these men saw in Native women and the Indian places of New England the possibility for love, family, and economic stability, something that was all too rare for free people of color in the young republic.

Howwoswee's and Mayhew's condemnation of Gay Head's "Negroes and Molattoes" ignored that most of the community's marriages were between Indians. Of twenty-nine Aquinnah weddings recorded in Chilmark between 1800 and 1838 (which is an incomplete record), only eight (twenty-eight percent) were between Vineyarders and mainlanders, some of whom were from other Indian villages like Mashpee or Narragansett. Not only were most nuptials between islanders, but eleven of twenty-nine (thirty-nine percent) were between members of the same village.[20] Similar numbers emerge from Mashpee, despite its missionary's characterization of the community as "greatly and variously mixed." In 1793, just sixteen of eighty-three Mashpee homes (twenty percent) contained male "outsiders," although this number would double by 1800.[21]

---

[15] Moses Howwoswee, "Account of the Indians Resident at Gay Head, March 19, 1792"; "A List of Children under Eighteen Years of Age, the 14th Day of May, 1798"; PLP, Resolves 1789, chap. 57.

[16] *Gay Head Report*, 37, 39; *Report of the Commissioners*, 62.

[17] Crew Lists, NBFPL; *Report of the Commissioners*, pp. 42, 61; DCD, 29:203–4, 37:457–8; Box 174B, Env. 11, MVHS.

[18] *Report of the Commissioners*, p. 62; Suzanne Glover and Kevin McBride, *Old Ways and New Ways: 7,000 Years along the Old South Road: An Archaeological Study* (Pawtucket, R.I.: Public Archaeology Laboratory, 1994), 15; Indian Collection, Box B, Env. 17, MVHS.

[19] *Vineyard Gazette*, May 13, 1881.

[20] Chilmark Town Records, 1:341, 347, 348, 350; 2:94, 95, 139, 405, 407, 434, Chilmark Town Hall, Chilmark, Mass.

[21] Mandell, "Shifting Boundaries," 471 (quote); Gideon Hawley, "An Account of the Number of Indian Houses at Mashpee, 1 July 1793," Houghton Library, Harvard University, Cambridge, Mass.; Hawley to Thatcher, August 5, 1800, SPGNA, Box 2, File 16.

However limited their number, exogamous marriages had a dramatic demographic impact on Indian villages, as illustrated in one rare document: an 1823 census of the Vineyard Wampanoags compiled by schoolteacher Frederick Baylies, a man who knew the Natives as well as anyone and who worked tirelessly among them for very little profit.[22] In this census, Baylies listed every individual's "blood quantum," a breakdown of racial inheritance into halves, quarters, eighths, and even sixteenths. These kinds of statistics produce widespread revulsion today since they suggest a relationship between the figures and a person's qualities and character. Nevertheless, blood quantums were of supreme importance to many antebellum New Englanders and therefore are critical to understanding constructions of racial identity during the period.[23]

The accuracy of the data is also problematic, even within the logic of the time. Among white record keepers, one clerk's "Indian" was often another's "man of color" or "black."[24] With this warning in mind, Baylies' numbers appear as precise as one can reasonably expect on an unavoidable scale of imperfection. In several cases, his quantums approximate less detailed descriptions of the same individuals in records such as New Bedford ship crew lists. For instance, Baylies described James Francis as a "full blood" Indian, while Francis's crew papers characterized him as an "Indian" with "black" hair. Along similar lines, Baylies submitted that Elemoth Howwoswee was a full Indian, while three sets of crew papers entered him as "Indian," "Native," and "Dark." Descriptions for "mixed" persons also are telling. Elijah Cooper, whom Baylies identified as three-fourths Indian, one-eighth black, and one-eighth white, appeared in various crew lists as "copper," "light," and "Indian," with hair three times described as "black," once as "wooley," and once as "brown." John Devine Sr. was "fully black" according to Baylies. His crew papers entered him as "black" with "wooley" hair. Other apparent matches abound (see Appendix B).

Of course, Baylies' quantums are not definitive and the crew lists are not independently reliable. Several cases exist in which different vessels labeled the same person as "Indian" and "black," as in the case of Philip Dodge, whom Baylies listed as three-fourths Indian, one-eighth black, and one-eighth

---

[22] Frederick Baylies, "The Names & Ages of the Indians on Martha's Vineyard, taken about the 1st of Jan., 1823," MSS A, S 53, File 1HA, NEHGS.

[23] Such measurements continue to influence Indian affairs, particularly the extension of federal recognition to communities petitioning for "tribal" status. See Terry P. Wilson, "Blood Quantum: Native American Mixed Bloods," in Maria P. Root, ed., *Racially Mixed People in America* (Newbury Park, Cal.: Sage Publications, 1992), 108–25.

[24] Herdon and Sekatau, "Right to a Name," 433–62. See also Donna Keith Baron, J. Edward Hood, and Holly V. Izard, "They Were Here All Along: The Native American Presence in Lower-Central New England in the Eighteenth and Nineteenth Centuries," *WMQ* 53 (1996), 566–73. Generally on colonial terminology for "mixed race" peoples, see Jack D. Forbes, *Africans and Native Americans: The Language of Race and the Evolution of Red–Black Peoples*, 2d ed. (Urbana, Ill.: University of Illinois Press, 1993).

TABLE 6. *Frederick Baylies' "Blood Quantums" for the Indians of Martha's Vineyard, 1823*

Age	Full Indian		>1/2 Indian; Not Full		Mixed; <1/2 Indian		Black/White; No Indian		Full Black		Full White		Total	
	Male	Female	M	F	M	F	M	F	M	F	M	F	M	F
Gay Head														
Over 40	3	24	7	10	1	0	4	0	2	1	0	0	17	35
20–39	7	12	29	29	0	0	3	0	5	0	0	0	44	41
0–19	2	5	39	62	4	1	0	0	0	0	0	0	45	68
Totals	12	41	75	101	5	1	7	0	7	1	0	0	106	144
% of Sex	11	28	71	70	5	1	7	0	7	1	0	0	42	58
Christiantown														
Over 40	0	2	3	0	1	1	0	0	1	0	0	0	5	3
20–39	0	2	4	7	0	0	0	0	1	0	0	0	5	9
0–19	0	0	18	10	0	1	0	0	0	0	0	0	18	11
Totals	0	4	25	17	1	2	0	0	2	0	0	0	28	23
% of Sex	0	17	89	74	4	9	0	0	7	0	0	0	55	45
Chappaquiddick														
Over 40	0	0	1	12	0	1	1	0	1	0	1	0	4	13
20–39	0	0	4	7	5	6	1	0	3	0	0	0	13	13
0–19	0	0	6	9	26	15	1	0	0	0	0	0	33	24
Totals	0	0	11	28	31	22	3	0	4	0	1	0	50	50
% of Sex	0	0	22	56	62	44	6	0	8	0	2	0	50	50

Sources: Frederick Baylies, "The Names and Ages of the Indians on Martha's Vineyard, taken about the 1st of Jan, 1823," MSSA/S53/Folder 1HA, NEHGS

white. Nor can one extrapolate from Baylies' figures to determine the racial quantum of a person's parents. Was someone described as half Indian, half black the product of an "Indian" mother and a "black" father, or of two "half Indian, half black" people? To be sure, the document raises as many questions as it answers, yet the impression left by cross comparison is that Baylies tried to be accurate and that his figures provide the best means to judge those who commented on the racial makeup of Vineyard Indian communities.

When Howwoswee and Mayhew wrote their petition, "mixed" children already formed a majority of their cohort at Gay Head. Of the Aquinnah residents included in Baylies' census who were alive in 1811, only five percent of males and forty percent of females, or twenty-nine percent of the total population, were listed as "full blood" Indians. Most people were of mixed Indian and black and/or white ancestry (sixty-four percent of males and sixty percent of females) with almost all of them of "half" Indian ancestry or greater. Those with no Indian ancestry included seven "full" black males (nine percent of the male population), one "full black" female (less than one percent of the females), and nine "half black, half white" males (eleven percent of the male population). Using Baylies' numbers, one would have been equally correct to assert that in 1811, ninety-four percent of the Aquinnah population was of Indian ancestry, as to emphasize that seventy-one percent were not of "full blood." These contending perspectives and their political implications shaped a century of racial conflict within the Indian community and between the community and outsiders.

Exogamous marriages made Indian politics more turbulent but it is equally clear that they helped stabilize the Natives' unbalanced population. An overview of Aquinnah, Christiantown, and Chappaquiddick in 1823 shows the ratio of males to females was evening out despite continued losses from whaling. Whereas females outnumbered males by fifty-one to twenty-six among those over age forty, among ages twenty to thirty-nine the gap dropped to near parity, sixty-three to sixty-two. The isolated two-family village of Deep Bottom probably would have disintegrated were it not for the marriages of African Americans Turner and John Saunders to Native women and the subsequent growth of their families. Furthermore, even though the number of "full blooded" Indians was in decline everywhere, at Aquinnah and Christiantown the "quantum" of Indian "blood" was on the rise. Aquinnah males of "half Indian" ancestry or more climbed from forty-two percent among those over forty, to seventy-four percent among those twenty to thirty-nine, to ninety-eight percent for those nineteen and under. At Christiantown the leap was equally dramatic. Whereas only forty percent of males and sixty-six percent of females over forty were "half Indian" or more, the numbers for those under age nineteen were a hundred percent for males and eighty-three percent for females (see Table 6). Migrations and marriages that followed old tribal paths partially explain this climb. Working backwards from an 1861 census, it appears that only twenty-six percent of adults in Vineyard Indian villages were from outside communities, and of those outsiders, seventy-nine percent were from other Wampanoag communities on the island or mainland. Similarly, although sixty-seven percent of the Indians' marriages were between people from different communities, in forty-eight percent of those nuptials both spouses were from recognized Indian places.[25]

If Howwoswee truly viewed the demographic changes of his community through the prejudice-laden blood-quantum filter, he possessed legitimate cause for concern. Some Indian communities on the Vineyard, particularly those near the whaling port of Edgartown, seemed less to have adopted outsiders than been overrun by them. None of the Chappaquiddicks on the 1823 census who were alive in 1811 were of "full" Indian blood. Twenty-five of thirty-one males were "mixed," of whom only six were "half" Indian or more. Chappaquiddick also had four "full" black men and one "full" white. Newcomers made an even greater impact at Sengkontacket or Farm Neck, which appears to have been abandoned by all those interested in living in an "Indian" community, since only one family with scant Native ancestry was left.

Perhaps Howwoswee's use of blood-quantum language was a cynical manipulation of whites' racial attitudes. Even before Indians began outmarrying at such a high rate, the prevalence of Indian indentured labor and the growing numbers of homeless Indians joining other indigent people on the road led many New Englanders to associate Natives as a whole with servile black laborers. Legislators made this association over and over again in statutes that placed special restrictions on "Indian, Mulatto, and negro Servants and Slaves."[26] The *Newport Mercury* newspaper did its part in 1772 when it took a graphic of a dark-complexioned man that for decades had been used only in ads for runaway black slaves and suddenly began applying it to ads for fugitive Indian servants.[27] Thus, when Indians and blacks married one another, it was merely a step in the lengthy process by which the majority imagined them as a single "people of color."[28] It was "customary,"

---

[25] Earle Report, Appendix B.

[26] *Mass. Acts and Resolves*, 1:535–36; John Russell Bartlett, ed., *Records of the Colony of Rhode Island and Providence Plantations in New England* (1636–1792), 10 vols. (Providence, 1856–65), 6:320; Melish, *Disowning Slavery*, 96.

[27] *Newport Mercury*, No. 742, September 23, 1772, No. 734, September 28, 1772, and No. 778, August 2, 1773.

[28] This paragraph draws heavily from Melish, *Disowning Slavery*; O'Brien, *Dispossession by Degrees*, chap. 6; John Wood Sweet, *Bodies Politic: Negotiating Race in the American North* (Baltimore: The Johns Hopkins University Press, 2003); Alden T. Vaughan, "From White Man to Redskin: Changing Anglo-American Perceptions of the American Indian," in his *Roots of American Racism: Essays on the Colonial Experience* (New York: Oxford

RAN away from the subscriber, in Dartmouth, on the second instant, an Indian boy, called Nathaniel Johnson, about 5 feet 4 inches high, wears his own hair, and had on a felt hat, a blue duffil outside jacket, a checked flannel shirt, a pair of striped flannel trowsers, old shoes and stockings, and carried with him two white Holland shirts, one pair of newly footed, gray yarn stockings, a white tow and linen pillow case, and a pair of dun-coloured trowsers: Whoever will return said Indian Boy to the subscriber a Dartmouth, or secure him in any of his Majesty's jails and give notice thereof, shall have three dollars reward, and all necessary charges, paid by

PHILIP SHERMAN.

FIGURE 8. Runaway Ad for Nathaniel Johnson, 1772. For decades, the *Newport Mercury* had attached the accompanying graphic of a dark-complexioned man only to its ads asking for the return of fugitive slaves, but in the 1770s it began to use the same image to represent escaped Indian servants. The timing coincided with a rise in Indian–black intermarriage, and a tendency among whites to refer to Indians as "people of color" or "blacks."

acknowledged a white Rhode Island sailor in 1823, "to call Indians colored men."[29]

The children of exogamous Indian marriages drew widespread commentary. After touring Gay Head in 1807, James Freeman believed, "of the Indians nine men are pure, and still more of the women; the rest are intermixed, chiefly with negroes."[30] An 1827 Massachusetts investigative committee found only a hundred "pure" Indians statewide, while another committee twenty years later concluded that "the admixture of African

University Press, 1995), 3–33; Ruth Wallis Herndon, "Racialization and Feminization of Poverty in Early America: Indian Women as 'the poor of the town' in Eighteenth-Century Rhode Island," in Martin Daunton and Rick Halpern, eds., *Empire and Others: British Encounters with Indigenous Peoples* (London: UCL Press, 1999), 186–203; Herndon and Sekatau, "Right to a Name."

[29] "Free Colored Seamen," *House Report*, 27th United States Congress, 3d Session, No. 80 (1843), 18–21.

[30] James Freeman, "A Description of Dukes County, August 13th 1807," *MHSC* 2d ser., 3 (1815), 94.

blood" was "the only one common to all the different tribes."[31] Francis Parkman was disappointed by his 1835 visit with the people of Aquinnah because "not more than half looked like Indians – the others negro or mulatto," while at Christiantown "I could find no real Indians, with one exception. They are for the most part decidedly African."[32] Some New Englanders doubted there were any "Indians" left at all. William Tudor argued in 1820 that the Wampanoag communities of Martha's Vineyard, Mashpee, and Herring Pond (near Plymouth) contained no one "of pure Indian blood. They are all of mixed blood, some crossed with the white, and some with the African races."[33] Edward Everett agreed, remarking, "of the tribes that inhabited New England, not an individual of unmixed blood and speaking the language of his fathers, remains."[34] *Harper's New Monthly* magazine brought this idiom to new heights in 1860 when it reported that the Gay Head school contained an "amalgamation of "races... [that have] never shown much aptitude for book learning" with "that brow-beaten and jaded appearance that we observe in educated quadrapeds."[35] Less verbose contemporaries had blunter ways of expressing the same idea. According to the *Atlantic Monthly*, the Wampaoags' white neighbors used "nigger" to refer to "these half-breeds."[36]

One of the exceptions among those neighbors, an advocate of the Wampanoags named Joseph Thaxter, emphasized in 1808 that outsiders who married into the island's Wampanoag communities were eventually "by us considered Natives" and that Indians in general were "healthy and are fast increasing," but most white New Englanders dissented and even Thaxter hedged in 1823 that the Natives "by mixture with the Blacks have lost I believe much of the Fox & acquired none of the Bear & Wolf."[37] Consistent with popular notions of immutable racial qualities, whites judged local Indians to be lacking authenticity when they did not conform to stereotypes of "savages" beyond the frontier. They expected Indians to be proud stoic hunter-warriors and eloquent chieftains with long straight hair and marvelous costumes compiled from nature's bounty. Instead they found laborers dressed like laborers with "mixed" physical characteristics and ordinary

[31] *Report of the Commissioners*, 6 (quote); "Report of a Committee Appointed to Investigate the Condition of the Indians, 1 March 1827," PLP, Acts 1827, chap. 114.
[32] "Report of a Visit of Enquiry at Nantucket, Martha's Vineyard, and to the Narragansett Indians... October 29, 1835," Andrews-Eliot Coll., MHS.
[33] William Tudor, *Letters on the Eastern States* (New York, 1820), 244.
[34] Edward Everett, *An Address Delivered at Bloody Brook, in South Deerfield, September 30, 1835* (Boston, 1835), 6–7.
[35] "A Summer in New England: Second Paper," *Harper's New Monthly Magazine* 124 (September 1860), 452.
[36] "A Visit to Martha's Vineyard," *Atlantic Monthly* 4 (1859), 292.
[37] Joseph Thaxter to John Lathrop, September 30, 1808, and Thaxter to Rev. James E. Freeman, March 1, 1832, Misc. Bound MSS, MHS.

GAY HEAD SCHOOL.

FIGURE 9. Inside the Gay Head Schoolhouse, 1860. Along with the church, the Gay Head school was the primary institution for socializing children to the people's distinct ways, even as it gave them skills to manage the outside world. Loss of outside funding for the school was one of the main concerns of Wampanoag opponents to Indian enfranchisement. Consistent with Americans' insistence that eastern Indians were "disappearing," *Harper's New Monthly* went out of its way in this image to downplay the Indian ancestry and cultural upbringing of the Gay Head school's students. In an accompanying article, it reported that the school contained an "amalgamation of races ... [that have] never shown much aptitude for book learning" with "that brow-beaten and jaded appearance that we observe in educated quadrapeds."

surnames like Cooper, Rodman, Salisbury, and Vanderhoop. New England Indians seemed to "exhibit little characteristics of their race, except the power of patient and silent sufferance."[38] Even the few remaining "pure bloods" had become "ignorant and degraded," in one writer's opinion, "mean and depressed" in another's, and "miserable" in yet another's.[39] *Harper's* mused that the face of Aquinnah's Deacon Simon Johnson showed "scarcely a trace of the Indian visible. The stolid, inscrutable countenance of wild man, the snaky subtlety that peers from his restless and glittering eye, have given

[38] "Report of a Committee Appointed to Investigate the Condition of the Indians, March 1, 1827," PLP, Acts 1827, Chap. 114.
[39] "Visit to the Elizabeth Islands," *North American Review and Miscellaneous Journal* 5 (1817), 319; Freeman, "Description of Dukes County," 92; Tudor, *Letters on the Eastern States*, 244.

place ... to the mild and peaceful light of Christian civilization," which most whites had concluded was antithetical to true "Indianness."[40]

Not that retention of those supposed "Indian" characteristics would have done Johnson any good. By the early nineteenth century many Americans agreed that they were justified in clearing Indians from east of the Mississippi rather than attempting to assimilate them because Indians were so innately suited to the ways of the woods that they could not transition to the Euro-American order. The thinking went that Natives who tried to adapt merely absorbed the worst qualities of white society and sank into alcoholic depression, laziness, and abject poverty.[41] As one tourist wrote after visiting Aquinnah, "the Indian" was incapable "of exchanging his own purely physical ambitions and pursuits for the intellectual and cultivated life belonging to the better class of his conquerors, while his wild and sensuous nature grasps eagerly at new forms of vice which follow in their train."[42] Edward Everett agreed. "We cannot perceive," he wrote, " ... in what way the meadows could be drained and the beaver dams broken down without expelling their industrious little builders; – nor in what way the uncivilized man, living from the chase ... destitute of arts and letters, – belonging to a different variety of species, speaking a different tongue, suffering all the disadvantages of social and intellectual inferiority, could maintain his place."[43] The island Wampanoags' Christianity, livestock, fences, European dress, and wage work failed to impress these white naysayers. William Tudor cited the Wampanoags as evidence that it was "hopeless" to civilize Indians and that the "unfortunate race" faced "inevitable destruction."[44]

Several pundits believed the time was at hand, evidence to the contrary. Cape Cod was home to Mashpee, the largest Indian community in Massachusetts, but after journeying through the area in 1802, a contributor to the Massachusetts Historical Society's journal wrote, "at this time a traveler might pass through the country, and he will as seldom meet with an Indian as with a rattlesnake. Before another century is

[40] "Summer in New England: Second Paper," 452.

[41] Brian W. Dippie, *The Vanishing Indian: White Attitudes and U.S. Indian Policy* (Lawrence: University of Kansas Press, 1982), 25; Robert F. Berkhofer Jr., *The White Man's Indian: Images of the American Indian from Columbus to the Present* (New York: Vintage Books, 1978), 28–30; Roy Harvey Pearce, *Savagism and Civilization: A Study of the Indian and the American Mind* (1953; Berkeley: University of California Press, 1988); Sweet, *Bodies Politic*; Philip Deloria, *Playing Indian* (New Haven, Conn.: Yale University Press, 1998), chap. 3; James P. Ronda, "'We Have a Country': Race, Geography, and the Invention of Indian Territory," *JER* 19 (1999), 745–6; Ronald Takaki, *Iron Cages: Race and Culture in Nineteenth-Century America*, 2nd ed. (New York: Oxford University Press, 1990), chap. 5.

[42] "A Visit to Martha's Vineyard," 292. Along similar lines, see James Sullivan, *The History of Land Titles in Massachusetts* (1801; New York: Arno Press, 1972), 29–30.

[43] Everett, "An Address Delivered at Bloody Brook," 6–7.

[44] Tudor, *Letters on the Eastern States*, 236, 244.

completed, the red man will probably become as rare as the beaver."[45] "Massachusetts, Shawmut, Samoset, Squantum, Nantasket, Narragansett, Assabet, Musketaquid," chimed in Ralph Waldo Emerson decades later, "but where are the men?"[46] And despite the constant presence of Native whalers in his city, New Bedford's Daniel Ricketson imagined in 1858 that the Indian "is now known but by a few mouldering bones turned up by the plough-share, and we daily tread above the graves of this once mighty race."[47] Standouts like Joseph Thaxter aside, most of the Indians' white neighbors were loath to speak up in their defense even when they knew better, particularly when they sought to end the state's protection of Indian land. In 1827, Edgartown dismissed the Chappaquiddick Wampanoags' ongoing complaints about trespass by calling the petitioners "blacks."[48]

These comments reflected American racial attitudes as much as Indian outmarriage, for Indians had been "mixing" with outsiders for well over a century without drawing much comment. In 1792, Gay Head's Moses Howwoswee compiled an account "of how much we are mixed," probably to answer white critics of his people's couplings with African Americans.[49] Howwoswee's agenda was to dispute the "blackening" of Aquinnah, so his figures are suspect, but it is suggestive that he counted more than twenty-four Aquinnah proprietors, excluding "strangers," who were of Indian–white ancestry, most of whom were "eight part" or "sixteen part" white. A blood-quantum census taken at Mashpee eight years later produced similar results.[50] Clearly Wampanoags and Englishmen had been sleeping together all along. The very faces of Indian–white offspring testified to these relationships, but their parents rarely faced public charges of fornication or adultery because the stigma was too great, at least for the English.[51] It is equally conspicuous that no one challenged the "purity" of Wampanoag communities on the basis of the presence of these children. Indeed, it took until the 1840s for someone to record, and then in passing, that the Wampanoags of Yarmouth on Cape Cod were "generally intermarried with the whites" and that "practically, they are a part of the general community."[52] Whites found sex between Indians and

---

45 Anonymous, "Description and History of Eastham," *MHSC* 1st ser. 8 (1802), 175.

46 Dippie, *Vanishing Indian*, 32.

47 Ricketson, *History of New Bedford*, vi–vii.

48 Mass. House Rept. No. 68, 2.

49 Howwoswee, "Account of the Indians Resident at Gay Head, March 19, 1792"; Mandell, "Shifting Boundaries," 477.

50 Hawley to Thatcher, August 5, 1800, Box 2, File 16, SPGNA.

51 David D. Smits, "'We are not to Grow Wild': Seventeenth-Century New England's Repudiation of Anglo-Indian Intermarriage," *AICRJ* 11 (1987), 1–32. For later views, see Smits, "'Squaw men,' 'Half-Breeds,' and Amalgamators: Late Nineteenth-Century Anglo-American Attitudes Toward Indian–White Race Mixing," *AICRJ* 15 (1991), 29–61.

52 *Report of the Commissioners*, p. 46 (quote); Earle Rept., p. 109.

whites embarrassing, even immoral, and therefore the children of these relationships passed without commentary so long as they were born of Indian rather than white women. In the negrophobic environment of the early republic, whites showed little inclination to overlook Indian–black relationships too.

Zachariah Howwoswee's bitterness about the decline of the Wampanoag language and his community's traditional church suggests that land greed and defense of "racial purity" were not the only motivations behind the 1811 petition. By the late eighteenth century, the people's command of Wampanoag was already hobbled by the cessation of Native-language publications and the binding out of Indian children to English homes. Children born to a non-Indian parent were even less likely to learn the ancestral tongue, and their children still less so, and thus exogamous marriage served as the deathblow to southeastern New England's Indian languages. By 1823, Baylies could find only "six Indians who can talk Indian" and, with Howwoswee's death, "not one who can read Indian."[53] Some twenty years later, a visitor to Gay Head claimed "only two of them are still living who can speak their mother tongue; all the rest speak only English."[54] Similar conditions existed throughout the rest of New England. In 1827, a Massachusetts state committee surveyed the Native population and determined, "so far from needing instruction in English they have nearly lost their mother tongue & your Committee found some difficulty in finding an individual who still retained it."[55] By the same token, in 1838 Samuel Davis went to Mashpee to compile a Wampanoag vocabulary. Speaking with a "half blood," aged forty, Davis found, "in his infancy he learned the English tongue. These specimens there, of the Aboriginal, he has acquired, from the Old Natives of whom scarcely any more remain that speak it."[56] Doubtless there were some Indians who kept their knowledge to themselves, but by midcentury there were few people left in southeastern New England who spoke fluent Wampanoag, Narragansett, or Mohegan publicly anymore.

Most Aquinnahs switched their allegiance from Howwoswee to the Baptist preacher Thomas Jeffers in response to Howwoswee's land schemes, leaving only a few orthodox holdouts, but it was the people's loss of the Wampanoag language that finally emptied the Congregationalist pews.

---

[53] Baylies, "Names and Ages."

[54] Dr. Albert C. Koch, *Journey Through a Part of the United States*, trans. and ed. Ernst A. Stadler (Carbondale and Edwardsville, Ill.: Southern Illinois Press, 1972), 23.

[55] Mass. House Rept. No. 68.

[56] Samuel Davis Papers, Uncatalogued, May 1841, MHS. See also Jedidiah Morse, *A Report to the Secretary of War of the United States on Indian Affairs, Comprising a Narrative of a Tour Performed in the Summer of 1820, under a Commission of the President of the United States, for the Purpose of Ascertaining, the Use of the Government, the Actual State of the Indian Tribes in Our Country* (New Haven, 1822), 70; Elisha Clap to Jedidah Morse, July 22, 1808, Misc. Bound MSS, MHS.

Howwoswee was unwilling to conduct his services in English even though the children and grandchildren of his loyalists could not understand him. Whatever ethnic pride they felt from hearing spoken Wampanoag, their main purpose in attending church was to be inspired by the scriptures preached, and thus they began to drift out of Howwoswee's fold. Elisha Clap was right when he predicted in 1808 that Howwoswee's stubbornness meant the "Congregational order would soon become extinct. Only a few aged Indians, who do not understand English, attend his meeting, as he preaches in the Native language solely."[57]

While Howwoswee drove his parishioners away, the Baptists led by Thomas Jeffers pulled them in with egalitarian principles and the English language, capping off a decades' long process by which blacks and Indians found a common home in evangelical churches. Baptists had attracted scores of mainland Indians and blacks over the previous half century with their plain speech, encouragement of religious ecstasy, and democratic themes, including their radical claims that slavery and discrimination were sinful because all people stood equal before God.[58] Eventually, "respectable" whites put an end to this racial leveling, but blacks responded by forming their own congregations, where preachers thundered from the pulpit that justice, including revenge, awaited America's downtrodden in the afterlife.[59] Such churches could be found in whaling centers like New Bedford and Nantucket and probably served as another place for Wampanoags and colored sailors to bond.

Black and mixed-race Baptists brought new energy and direction to Wampanoag religious life. In 1793, Gideon Hawley railed that the Herring Creek Wampanoags followed "a Negroe man fanatick, who can neither read nor write, Scolds at a few, who are his attendants every Lord's day."[60] Jeffers moved to the Vineyard a few years later accompanied by his wife, Sarah, a woman Baylies and Hawley described as being of "mixt" Indian, white, and black descent.[61] Jeffers' replacement at Mashpee was a circuit rider named William Apess, a man of Pequot and African American

[57] Elisha Clapp to Jedidah Morse, July 22, 1808, Misc. Bound MSS, MHS.

[58] Pierson, *Black Yankees*, chap. 6; William S. Simmons, "Red Yankees: Narragansett Conversion in the Great Awakening," *American Ethnologist* 10 (1983), 253–71; Simmons, "The Great Awakening and Indian Conversion in Southern New England," in William Cowan, ed., *Papers of the Tenth Algonquian Conference* (Ottawa: Carleton University, 1979), 25–36; Erik R. Seeman, "'Justice Must Take Plase': Three African Americans Speak of Religion in Eighteenth-Century New England," *WMQ* 56 (1999), 393–414.

[59] Sylvia R. Frey, *Water from the Rock: Black Resistance in a Revolutionary Age* (Princeton: Princeton University Press, 1991), chaps. 8–9; Nathan O. Hatch, *The Democratization of American Christianity* (New Haven, Conn.: Yale University Press, 1989), 102–13; Gary B. Nash, *Forging Freedom: The Creation of Philadelphia's Black Community, 1720–1840* (Cambridge, Mass.: Harvard University Press, 1988).

[60] Hawley, "Account of the Number of Indian Houses, July 1, 1793," Houghton Library.

[61] Baylies, "Names and Ages"; Hawley to Jedidah Morse, Undated, Hawley Journal.

ancestry who preached the very themes that one would have expected to hear in the black Baptist churches of the day. "Assemble all nations to-gether in your imagination," he wrote, "and then let the whites be seated among them... Now suppose these skins were put together, and each skin had its national crimes written upon it – which skin do you think would have the greatest?"[62] Indians, their non-Indian spouses, and their offspring knew the answer, and it strengthened their sense of belonging together within the Baptist church. They also prayed in unison for the day when their oppressors would join hands in Christ to transcend this sinful history.[63] This vision was so popular that Christiantown's guardians felt compelled to pull down the Indians' meeting house to keep it from being used by "secteries & itiner-ants."[64] Despite their efforts, the Baptist faith took hold throughout Indian New England, becoming the first religion to cross virtually all of the region's tribal boundaries and, for that matter, the racial divisions within them.

Several decades after Howwoswee's death, Gay Headers still talked about how deeply sad and resentful he had been about the decline of his language and congregation. Although island Wampanoags had changed many aspects of their lives since the onset of European colonization, they had always gath-ered together in the Congregational church to hear the people's own language preached, thus linking the living to one another and the ancestors. In the early nineteenth century this ritual of identity was dying, and to Howwoswee it felt like the community was dying too.[65]

Whether Howwoswee liked it or not, the "Negroes and Molattoes" he derided in his petition were his neighbors and kin. They were not going to learn fluent Wampanoag. They were not going to worship in his church. Nor were most whites going to acknowledge them or their children as Indians. But with so many Indian men resting in watery graves or distant battlefields, the "strangers" represented the best chance for Howwoswee and his people to persist on territory that generations of Wampanoags had struggled to retain. If the people wanted their communities to remain Indian places, they had to redefine, once again, what "Indian" meant at home and abroad. This meant publicly defending the people's Indian identity, imbuing multiracial

---

[62] William Apess, *On Our Own Ground: The Complete Writings of William Apess, A Pequot*, ed. Barry O'Connell (Amherst: University of Massachusetts Press, 1992), 157. For more on Indians using Christianity to critique American society, see Bernd C. Peyer, *The Tutor'd Mind: Indian Missionary Writers in Antebellum America* (Amherst: University of Massachusetts Press, 1997); Laura K. Arnold, "Crossing Cultures: Algonquian Indians and the Invention of New England" (Ph.D. diss., University of California, Los Angeles, 1995), chaps. 4–5; David Murray, *Forked Tongues: Speech, Writing, and Representation in North American Indian Texts* (Bloomington: Indiana University Press, 1991), chap. 4.

[63] Apess, *On Our Own Ground*, 5–7, 120–1, 129–30, 147, 155–61, 212.

[64] Elisha Clapp to Jedidah Morse, July 22, 1808, Misc. Bound MS, MHS.

[65] Edward S. Burgess, "The Old South Road of Gay Head," *Dukes County Intelligencer* 12 (August 1970), 21–2.

children with a sense of Wampanoag cultural heritage, and discouraging the newcomers from violating the reserve's communal standards. These were among the last obstacles that some communities faced as intact units, but others emerged from the fray with newfound strength.

II

Vineyard Wampanoags were fully aware that public opinion placed them on the cusp of oblivion or denied that they were truly Indians, but they were not about to submit meekly to their doomsayers. Presenting themselves to Boston as "the Indian Natives of the Island Chapequiddick," "the Christiantown Tribe of Indians," or the "Gay Head Indians" subtly answered the critics, while adding "and people of colour" acknowledged the reality of intermarriage. In less diplomatic contexts they asserted their identity in even stronger terms, as Edward Kendall learned on a trip through Wampanoag country in the early nineteenth century. Kendall had been told that New England Indians were *"mixed,* that is, to have the children of Europeans and Africans among them," and indeed, just outside of Herring Pond he "met several of these Indians, answering this description, particularly women, half Indian and half negro," including one who appeared "almost more negress than Indian." To Kendall's surprise, this woman spoke of Herring Pond as "her *nation* (for it is thus the Indians always denominate their communities)" and "proclaimed herself an Indian."[66] Aquinnah had a similar answer to Howwoswee's charge that only a handful of Indians remained in their community. His opponents called themselves the "proprietors, nation and tribe of Gayhead," and advised Massachusetts not to appoint guardians unless they were "tender hearted brethren to the Gayhead Indians."[67] Even Nantucket Wampanoags proverbially rose from the dead to defend their Indian heritage. In 1823, four men from the island's New Guinea village told the Society for the Propagation of the Gospel, "there are among the coloured people of this place remains of the Nantucket Indians, & that nearly every family in our village are partly des[c]ended from the original inhabitants of this & neighboring places," contrary to the popular yarn that they had all but disappeared after the 1763–64 yellow fever epidemic.[68] Then, some twenty years later, Edgartown's *Vineyard Gazette* ran a three-part series entitled, "Visit to Gay Head," in which the anonymous author referred to the Aquinnahs as "our colored brethren – colored I call them for so they called themselves, no one that I saw using the term *Indian* . . . I was told that,

---

[66] Edward Augustus Kendall, *Travels Through the Northern Part of the United States in the Years 1807 and 1808*, 2 vols. (New York, 1809), 2:47–8. Emphasis in original.

[67] ULRIA, 8029–1816 (4).

[68] SPGNA, Box 1, File 8. On the postepidemic history of Nantucket's Indians, see Philbrick, *Abram's Eyes*, chap. 11.

probably, no case of pure Indian blood remained on the island." As if to rub salt in the wound, he criticized his "coloured" hostess for serving him a cold dinner. A few weeks later, someone from Gay Head published a retort. "We don't think its' best to be cooking great dinners on Lord's day," the writer explained, "no matter who comes... Indians tho' we be. We don't expect great men visiting us that day, and then going away and printing the account." The respondent suggested that next time the white author approached Aquinnah he should "turn Indian" and rough it back home, "though we hope that in that case he will not come to Gay Head to Live!"[69]

Lyrical prophets of Indian extinction might have been dumbfounded that people of mixed-race heritage who did not appear and act in accordance with popular stereotypes of Indians should classify themselves so. But people from historically "Indian" places with intact geographical boundaries and sizable populations – such as Aquinnah, Christiantown, Chappaquiddick, Mashpee, and Herring Pond – had been raised with a distinctly Indian cultural tradition and sense of identity. Only a few matched the standard of elders such as Zachariah Howwoswee and later Tamson Weeks, who still spoke fluent Wampanoag, or of others who continued to live in *wetus* into the mid–nineteenth century, but from these stalwarts younger people learned Wampanoag words and phrases.[70] Boys picked up the unique Wampanoag cattle call that rang throughout Aquinnah pastures.[71] Male relatives taught them where to find the best fishing spots – Wampanoag fishing spots – like the shoals of Devil's Bridge or the waters just off Noman's Land island, the most reliable deer runs, and the strategies to catch elusive prey. Matrons instructed girls how to make pottery from the clay of the Aquinnah cliffs, pack baskets from twined shoreline grasses, and, if a girl was especially bright, herbal medicine from plants at hiddenspots throughout the people's territory. They passed down the preparation of parched corn, which in the early twentieth century was eaten at Gay Head as a "ceremonial dish: a delicacy to be served on special occasions or when one's 'aboriginal nature or constitution' demands 'pure' food, sacred through being made from corn by an ancient process."[72] Some women's crafts, such as woodsplint basketry, were of recent origin for sale to whites, but they too became customs that supported the Wampanoags' sense of peoplehood. The significance of these acts

---

[69] *The Vineyard Gazette*, May 26, 1848, vol. 3, no. 3; June 1, 1848, vol. 3, no. 14; June 8, 1848, vol. 3, no. 5; June 22, 1848, vol. 3, no. 7. Microfilm Copy at the Edgartown Public Library, Edgartown Mass.

[70] James Freeman, "A Description of Mashpee in the County of Barnstable. September 16th, 1802," *MHSC* 2nd ser., 3 (1815), 4–5; Freeman, "Description of Dukes County," 93–4; Kendall, *Travels Through the Northern Part of the United States*, 2:179–80, 193; D. W. Stevens to Rufus Ellis, January 29, 1879, Andrews-Eliot Coll., MHS.

[71] Bugress, "Old South Road," 13.

[72] Gladys Tantaquidgeon, "Notes on the Gay Head Indians of Massachusetts," *Indian Notes* 7 (1930), 7.

rested in elders bequeathing to younger generations specialized knowledge about living off Wampanoag land.[73] Moreover, sometimes the Wampanoags' special ways forced outsiders to concede that they retained some "aboriginal traits." White Vineyarders noticed that the Wampanoags had distinct "sports and pastimes," that they curtseyed to other Indians and referred to all elders as "Auntie" or "Uncle," and that Indian women wore "only a handkerchief or a small blanket on the head" instead of bonnets.[74] They bristled when Wampanoags greeted them with "cold civility" as a gesture of contempt for innumerable schemes to "abridge their liberty."[75] Leavitt Thaxter devoted long hours to recruiting a missionary for the Indians, only to lose one candidate after another who found that the Wampanoags' "strange manners are not easy to deal with."[76] The people of Aquinnah, especially, could be "peculiar in their manners and customs."[77]

Stories about ancient Indian spirits, ceremonies, and culture heroes were among the Wampanoags' most important traditions.[78] In 1792, Thomas Cooper, a sixty-year-old Wampanoag from Aquinnah, shared with Benjamin Basset, a selectman from the Vineyard town of Chilmark, an oral tradition about how his people warded off yellow fever (a postcontact disease) "before the English came among the Indians." "After it had raged and swept off a number," Cooper explained, healthy people would gather together to conduct a two-part ritual. First, the rich would form a circle and toss up miniatures representing their most valued possessions for the poor to seize as

---

[73] Tantaquidgeon, "Notes on the Gay Head Indians of Massachusetts," 12–19; William Turnbaugh and Sarah Peabody Turnbaugh, "Weaving the Woods: Tradition and Response in Southern New England Splint Basketry," and Ann McMullen, "Looking for People in Woodsplint Basketry Decoration," in Ann McMullen and Russell G. Handsman, eds. *A Key into the Language of Woodsplint Baskets* (Washington, Conn.: American Indian Archaeological Institute, 1987), 77–94, 103–23; McMullen, "Native Basketry, Basketry Styles, and Changing Group Identity in Southern New England," in Peter Benes, ed., *Algonkians of the Northeast: Past and Present* (Boston: Boston University Press, 1993), 76–88; Laurel Thatcher Ulrich, *The Age of Homespun: Objects and Stories in the Creation of an American Myth* (New York: Alfred A. Knopf, 2001), chaps. 1 and 7.

[74] James Athearn Jones, *Traditions of the North American Indians: Being a Second and Revised Edition of "Tales of an Indian Camp,"* 3 vols. (London, 1830), 1:x, xii; Burgess, "Old South Road," 27; D. Wrighte to Alden Bradford, April 9, 1839, Andrews-Eliot Coll., MHS.

[75] Kendall, *Travels through the Northern Part of the United States,* 1:195–6; "Summer in New England: Second Paper," 451.

[76] Thaxter to Samuel K. Lothrop, April 19, 1853, Box 5, File 7, SPGNA.

[77] *Report of the Commissioners,* p. 76.

[78] The following two paragraphs rely heavily on William S. Simmons, *Spirit of the New England Tribes: Indian History and Folklore, 1620–1984* (Hanover, N.H.: University Press of New England, 1985), esp. chap. 7; Kathleen J. Bragdon, "Language, Folk History, and Identity on Martha's Vineyard," in Anne Elizabeth Yentsch and Marcy C. Beaudry, eds., *The Art and Mystery of Historical Archaeology: Essays in Honor of James Deetz* (Boca Raton, Fla.: CRC Press, 1992), 331–42; and my personal conversations with Tobias Vanderhoop of Aquinnah.

claims to that wealth. Next, the community would place the "most sprightly young man in the assembly" in a new *wetu*, and then set the structure ablaze while the people outside sang and danced in two columns. "The youth would leap out of the flames and fall down to appearance dead," Cooper continued. "Him they committed to the care of five virgins." Eventually the boy would awaken and recount a trance in which he traveled high up into the air "where he came to a great company of white people, with whom he had interceded hard to have the distemper layed; and generally after much persuasion, would obtain a promise, or answer of peace, which never failed of laying the distemper."[79] Bassett intended this story to be read as a quaint curiosity from New England's supposedly disappearing Indian remnant, but for Wampanoag audiences it contained powerful lessons about values and spiritual relationships that stretched back from the present to at least the early 1600s. With the Indians under intense pressure to divide their common lands and enter the individualistic competition of Yankee society, this oral tradition reinforced the ethic of sharing wealth with the ill and needy, both as a means to ease suffering, and to alleviate social tensions (symbolized by exclusion of the poor from the circle) that produced witchcraft, sickness, and community dissolution. It drew upon ancient Indian motifs, such as renewal by fire, social solidarity by dance, and truth by vision. And it acknowledged the historic connection between Wampanoag Christianity, prophesy, disease, and colonialism, in which precontact Wampanoag visions told that newcomers would possess the spiritual keys to future health and peace. Other stories, such as the giant culture hero Moshup abandoning the Vineyard because of impending white encroachment, or of an Indian mother and child freezing outdoors when no whites would take them in, reinforced that whites were "others" and the moral superiority of the Indian community.[80] Still other tales, several of which remain in circulation among Wampanoag people, emphasized the importance of kinship, generosity, and honoring spirits by interring the dead with grave goods or refraining from speaking their names. Storytelling, in other words, was a vehicle for transmitting the values, rules, and history of the people, as well as an opportunity for the young and old to reaffirm their connections to one another and the past.

Mnemonic devices for Wampanoag lore covered the landscape. Gay Head's Black Brook was (and is) a place of lurking ghosts, and walking (or rather sprinting) past sparked tales of former encounters with its spirits.[81] Children strolling along Aquinnah's cliffs learned to call a spot where

---

[79] Benjamin Bassett, "Fabulous Traditions and Customs of the Indians of Martha's Vineyard," *MHSC* 1st ser. 1 (1792), 139–40.

[80] "Journal of a Journey by Sea from Philadelphia to Boston, by William Wood Thackara, 1791–1839," *Old Time New England* 50 (1960), 61.

[81] Burgess, "Old South Road," 10–11.

Moshup once lived "Devil's Den," and to refer to the clay's gypsum veins as "Moshup's needles."[82] A fishing trip to Noman's Land might segue into an account of how Moshup separated the tiny island from the Vineyard by dragging his giant toe through the sand. In a cold wind or deep fog, parents evoked Moshup's disfigured wife, "Auntie Squant," or the ancient evil one, Cheepi, to frighten children into proper behavior. And then there were the "sacrifice rocks," really piles of sticks and stones, that endlessly fascinated whites. Wampanoags added to these mounds whenever they passed by as reminders of the people's history. Generally, Indians tried to hide these monuments from whites, even going so far as to blaze alternative paths because they resented being "ridiculed" as "idolatrous."[83] Whenever whites did catch a glimpse, the Indians played dumb, saying only "that they do so because they have been taught that it is right to do it, or because their fathers did so before them."[84] Allowing whites to know that a special tradition existed while protecting its details was a particularly effective way of fostering Indian group identity.

Imbuing children of mixed marriages with a sense of the sacred Wampanoag-landscape was hardly limited to folklore. Indian Christianity was itself a traditional practice, with its own cast of heroes and holy places. Its ancient presence at Gay Head was evident in cemetery headstones with Wampanoag language epitaphs.[85] Oral histories about the "Old Presbyterian Church" or "Church of the Standing Order" were peopled by leaders with names like Mittark, Wauwompuque, and Howwoswee. A sacrifice rock on the road between Edgartown and Tisbury marked the spot where missionary Thomas Mayhew Jr. last addressed the Indians before he was lost at sea.

Furthermore, the people's Christian history was still being written in a Wampanoag vernacular. In the early nineteenth century, the spirit moved

---

[82] *Gay Head Report,* 5.

[83] Franklin Bowditch Dexter, ed., *The Literary Diary of Ezra Stiles, D.D., LL.D.,* 3 vols. (New York: Charles Scribner's Sons, 1901), 3:76–7.

[84] Kendall, *Travels through the Northern Part of the United States,* 2:49–50 (quote). For other accounts of these mounds, see Cotton Mather, *Triumphs of the Reformed Religion in America: The Life of the Renowned John Eliot* (Boston, 1691), dedication; Freeman, "A Description of Mashpee," 7–8; "Visit to the Elizabeth Islands," 323. More generally on the sacred homeland, see Constance A. Crosby, "The Algonkian Spiritual Landscape," in Benes, ed., *Algonkians of New England,* 35–41. On Natives' secrecy about their traditions, see Ann McMullen, "What's Wrong with This Picture? Context Conversion, Survival, and the Development of Regional Native Cultures and Pan-Indianism in Southeastern New England," in Laurie Weinstein, ed. *Enduring Traditions: The Native Peoples of New England* (Westport, Conn.: Bergin & Garvey, 1994), 135–6.

[85] On cemeteries as part of the Indians' sacred landscape, see Patricia E. Rubertone, *Grave Undertakings: An Archaeology of Roger Williams and the Narragansett Indians* (Washington, D.C.: Smithsonian Institution Press, 2002), 165–6.

Aquinnah's Jane Wamsley to become the Indians' first female preacher – that is, until outraged whites threatened repercussions.[86] Blind Joe Amos from Mashpee replaced her and gained a devoted following by adorning his services with accordion music, an innovation that tended to raise white eyebrows even as it lifted Wampanoag spirits. He was equally at home presiding over baptisms that dramatized the historic depth of Wampanoag Christianity and its continuity with ancient traditions. On such occasions, the Aquinnah congregation would file out of Sunday meeting to the beach at the base of Moshup's cliffs, the centerpiece of the Wampanoags' creation stories. Then they filled the air with song as Amos led his disciple into the surf to be cleansed by waters that Wampanoags had traversed and harvested since time out of mind.[87] The candidate emerged from the bath born again onto land the people had been fighting to enjoy collectively for more than 150 years. And the community was there, together, to bear witness to this rite of passage just as they had done for countless others over the past two centuries. The ancient spirits of place and the Holy Spirit were familiar acquaintances in the Wampanoag homeland.

The physical boundaries and idiosyncrasies of Wampanoag territory reinforced the Natives' sense of distinctiveness and proprietorship in the land, while forcing whites to take heed. The Wampanoags cordoned off Chappaquiddick's North Neck with a dilapidated enclosure commonly known as the "Indian Line Fence." Travelers to Christiantown passed through the Wampanoags' clearly marked boundary lines before ascending "Indian Hill." The county road "died a natural death" at the peninsular entrance to Gay Head, and riders had to dismount and remove two sets of fence bars before continuing along a "faint track in the grass" that served as the Natives' main avenue. Inside whites found little sign of property and order as they knew it. Aquinnah was "not generally divided by fences," one curious visitor remarked, "the cattle of the whole tribe grazing together in amicable companionship."[88] Narrow footpaths crisscrossing through tangled scrub trees were the only ways to the Natives' "scattered" houses.[89] Outsiders got lost and felt like "strangers"; insiders knew they were home.

[86] Burgess, "South Road," 25; "A Summer in New England: Second Paper," 454.
[87] Koch, *Journey through a Part of the United States*, 20. See also Francis Parkman, "Report of a Visit of Enquiry at Nantucket, Martha's Vineyard & to the Narragansett Indians," October 29, 1835, Andrews-Eliot, Coll., MHS.
[88] "A Visit to Martha's Vineyard," 292. See also John Langdon Sibley: Private Journal, entry for August 9, 1852, Harvard University Archives, Pursey Library, Cambridge, Mass.
[89] *The Vineyard Gazette*, August 19, 1847, vol. 2, no. 15, and May 26, 1848, vol. 3, no. 3; "A Summer in New England; Second Paper," 448–51; Koch, *Journey through a Part of the United States*, 15; Freeman, "Description of Dukes County," 53; "A Visit to Martha's Vineyard," 285; *Report of the Commissioners*, 19; Sibley Private Journal, August 9, 1852.

Communal norms emphasized that the reserve was the people's homeland. "They are kind and considerate to one another," wrote Leavitt Thaxter, "and especially to the poor," a custom that never failed to amaze whites steeped in the ethic of individual self-sufficiency.[90] Families could enclose as much of the commons as they needed for as long as they wanted, but they could not sell any of that land to outsiders.[91] Whites were also struck that "while one proprietor has but half an acre, and another has over a hundred acres, there is no heart-burning, no feeling that the latter has more than his share."[92] A committee from Boston that investigated Mashpee in 1843 found the Wampanoags so inattentive to personal property markers that it was nearly impossible to tell just whose land was whose.[93]

The Wampanoags held all other natural resources collectively as well, including pasture, reed grass, wood, peat moss, wild fruit, and fishing stations. Aquinnah's stinting committee managed the people's lands by fixing the number of livestock each tribal member could graze on the commons and assigning spaces in a "general planting field" that was plowed at public expense.[94] Rather than compete against one another for wild cranberries, the people specified a time for communal harvesting and turned the occasion into a holiday. When ships anchored offshore to buy clay from the Gay Head cliffs, anyone who helped dig received a share of the profits, with a portion going toward support of the poor.[95] At the turn of the century Christiantown and Chappaquiddick functioned differently only in that state-appointed guardians periodically allotted new planting lands to correspond to each family's increase or decline in numbers.[96] But in the 1820s these places switched to the Gay Head model, believing it would promote "improvements" and prevent guardians from abusing their power to lease out "excess" territory. They also wanted to guarantee "that when a

[90] Thaxter to Earle, 3 February 1860, JMEP, Box 2, File 3. See also, *Report of the Commissioners*, p. 8; Earle Report, 22–3, 34, 41.

[91] ULRIA, Box 2, File 9419–1824.

[92] *Report of the Commissioners*, pp. 20–1 (quote); Tudor, *Letters on the Eastern States*, 243–4; Earle Report, pp. 33, 42.

[93] "Report on the Rects. [sic.] and doings of the Commissioners under the act of March 3, 1842, for the partition of lands in the District of Mashpee, February 9, 1843," in Governor's Council Files Box, July 1842–April 1843, Mass. State Archives.

[94] Freeman, "Description of Dukes County," 94; D. Wrighte to Alden Bradford, April 9, 1839, Andrews-Eliot Coll., MHS; Burgess, "Old South Road," 3–4.

[95] *Mass. Acts and Resolves, 1845*, chap. 22, 522–3; Box 4S, Env. 25, MVHS; "Visit to the Elizabeth Islands," 318; Ebenezer Skiff to Frederick Baylies, May 3, 1823, Misc. Bound MSS, MHS; Leavitt Thaxter to John Milton Earle, Febuary 3, 1860, JMEP, Box 2, File 2.

[96] *Mass. Acts and Resolves*, Acts 1809/10, chap. 69, pp. 104–5; "Commissioners Respecting Chappaquiddick Island, March 8, 1810," in a bundle marked "Titles" contained in metal file marked "Petitions," Dukes County Superior Court.

foreign[e]r shall marry and settle among us, he shall be subjected to the same law to which we are," namely, Wampanoag custom.[97]

Non-Indians who married into Wampanoag communities, particularly former slaves, had been raised to associate male freedom with independent decision making. They found the Wampanoags' communalism stifling, even emasculating, which prompted some of them to chafe at it. In 1784, accumulating Wampanoag complaints about "the new comers the strangers" led Gay Head to appoint a committee to determine just who the "Proper Proprietors" were.[98] Across Vineyard Sound, in the late 1780s several Mashpee Wampanoags denounced the "Negroes and English who have happily planted themselves here," charging, "they and their children unless they are removed will get away our Lands & all our Privileges in a short time."[99] These concerns were warranted. Some thirty years later, Christiantown was mired in two lawsuits which, the guardian explained, "arose in consequence of Negro men marrying Native Women amongst them and many other difficulties."[100] Indian hostility toward blacks reached such a pitch that when a "negro" named Richard Johnson stood trial in 1823 for murdering Wampanoag Mary Cuff (or Cuffee), his lawyer based the defense on the Natives' prejudice. "These Indians are a peculiar set of people," the argument went. "They have land and rights which they enjoy as a tribe. A stranger who comes among them participates and lessens those rights – he is an object of suspicion; he is viewed with a jaundiced eye and is made a scapegoat to bear the sins of others. Being at sea the greater part of his time, and a foreigner to them, they have no community of interest or affection with them, his existence to them is an evil."[101] Outsiders who had not grown up with the people's values and a sense of historic responsibility to preserve the commons could not be trusted to act in accord with the Native community. Free black men wanted the same privileges whites enjoyed, including the right to own, manage, and sell land. They understood liberty as the pursuit of one's self-interest, an idea that clashed with Indians who sought the freedom to maintain the distinctive communal practices that kept

---

97 "Petition of the Indians of Chappaquiddic[k]," May 22, 1826, PLP, Acts 1827, chap. 114 (quote); Chappaquddick Indians to Joseph Thaxter, April 1826, Edgartown Congregational Church Records, MVHS; Act for the Better Regulation, Instruction, and Government of the Indians and People of Colour in the County of Dukes County, *Mass. Acts and Resolves 1825–1828*, Acts 1828, chap. 114; Christiantown Land Ownership in 1828, Box 174B, Env. 11, MVHS; DCD, 23:292–316, 34:390–417; "Petition of the Indians of Christiantown," December 30, 1828, GIP, Box 3, File 15; *Report of the Commissioners*, 15; Earle Report, 18–19.

98 ZHP, File 1777 My 12-Ag 28, File 1784 Ap. 16–22.

99 "Petition and Address of the Indians of Mashpee [undated]," Hawley Journal.

100 ULRIA, Box 2, File SU 13034–1850 (4). See also DCD, 15:153; 20:88–9.

101 Gloria Levitas, "No Boundary is a Boundary: Conflict and Change in a New England Indian Community" (Ph.D. diss., Rutgers University, 1980), 184. For more on this case, see *New Bedford Mercury*, July 18, 1823.

their people together in an otherwise fiercely competitive and individualistic Yankee world.

Disputes over the community's responsibility to care for the indigent wives and children of mixed marriages magnified these tensions. In 1804, Christiantown complained about "white people & Black people who come from other parts & bring their wives & Children and Leave them Amongst the Original Inhabitants," based on the women's ancestral but not personal connections to the community.[102] Usually the men promptly shipped out, leaving their wives to "scrabb as well as they can to support themselves & children."[103] More often than not the women came up short and then expected public charity. Aquinnah, like most Indian communities, judged this to be "not right," adding, "we are willing to do all we can for Gay Head poor; but we are not willing to maintain people that do not rightly belong on Gay Head, for we have no means of supporting them."[104]

The Wampanoags extended their own women greater political and economic power to guard against the newcomers. Mashpee ruled that only the Indian wives and children of mixed marriages, not the husbands, could demand house and garden plots, stinting rights, and a say in town meeting.[105] Aquinnah followed suit, for as Zacheus Howwoswee explained in 1860, "we the proprietors on gayhead wish to conduct our own business separate from the foreigners & strangers[.] we never have al[l]owed them any pole right on gayhead therefore they have not any in our Land but work on their wife's portion of land."[106] The number of female signatures on Indian petitions rose dramatically between 1750 and 1850, sometimes to an even greater degree than their proportion of the total adult population (see Table 7). For the first time, whites began to notice Indian women speaking in public, which suggests that this was a recent development. Women's new role was not simply a response to men's absences at sea, for in historic times men had retained control of public business even though they were often away to hunt, war, trade, and conduct diplomacy. Instead, it was aimed to counter the "strangers." Non-Indian men in the community must have found this development deeply humiliating since most of them had been raised in settings in which the eldest (white) male served as the "head of household." Once again, the Indians had denied them the exercise of Anglo-America's manly prerogatives.

---

[102] PLP, Acts 1804, chap. 84.

[103] Joseph Thaxter to James Freeman, March 1, 1823, Misc. Bound MSS, MHS.

[104] *Report of the Commissioners*, 88 (quote); Zacheus Howwoswee to John Milton Earle, August 25, 1859, JMEP, Box 2, File 3; Earle Report, 44–5. See also Daniel Mandell, "The Saga of Sarah Muckamugg: Indian–African American Intermarriage in Colonial New England," in Martha Hodes, ed., *Sex, Love, Race: Crossing Boundaries in North American History* (New York: New York University Press, 1999), 84.

[105] *Report of the Commissioners*, 26, and GIP, Box 2, File 13.

[106] Howwoswee to John Milton Earle, January 27, 1860," JMEP, Box 2, File 3.

TABLE 7. *Female Signatories to Indian Petitions, 1746–1838*

Community	Year	# Female Signatories	% of Signatories
Gay Head	1746	0	0
Gay Head	1747	15	40
Gay Head	1749	10	32
Gay Head	1753	17	32
Gay Head	1767	11	46
Gay Head	1785	21	62
Gay Head	1789	28	54
Gay Head	1790	0	0
Gay Head	1811	7	78
Gay Head	1815	32	60
Gay Head	1820	0	0
Gay Head	1838	36	77
Christiantown	1741	7	32
Christiantown	1804	5	45
Christiantown	1817	8	50
Christiantown	1824	7	41
Chappaquiddick	1762	0	0
Chappaquiddick	1767	6	26
Chappaquiddick	1768	4	33
Chappaquiddick	1773	3	43
Chappaquiddick	1790	0	0
Chappaquiddick	1799	4	44
Chappaquiddick	1810	27	61
Chappaquiddick	1811	24	51
Chappaquiddick	1812	15	45
Chappaquiddick	1818	7	50
Chappaquiddick	1824	11	79
Chappaquiddick	1826	15	88
Chappaquiddick	1827	7	70

Sources: Mass. Archives, 31:187, 315, 523–4, 551, 643; 32:356; 33:416, 470, 488, 583. PLP, Resolves 1785, chap. 4; Resolves 1789, chap. 57; Resolves 1790, chap. 46; Resolves 1790, chap. 106; Acts 1804, chap. 84; Acts 1811, chap. 78; Acts 1817, chap. 99; Resolves 1820, chap. 46; Acts 1827, chap. 114; Acts 1838, chap. 101. ULRIA, SU 2532–1799; SU 4093–1810; SU 9419–1824. GIP, Box 3, File 15. In the Massachusetts Governor's Council Files, Massachusetts State Archives: Chappaquiddick Petition of May 18, 1807 in "Report on petition of the people of colour on Chappaquiddick....," Box January 1806–July 1807; Chappaquiddick petition of 1811 in "Report on Complaint of Chappequiddick Indians...June 10, 1811," Box, Febuary–December 1811; Gay Head petition of April 1, 1815, in "Report on a Complaint of Gay Head Indians, June 10, 1815," Box, June 1815–July 1816; "Petition of Indians of Chippaaquiddic for Guardians, Sept. 19, 1818," Box, May 1818–Febuary 18, 1819; Chappaquiddick petition in "Report on Compt. of Chippaquiddick [sic.] Indians, Feb. 12th, 1824," Box, January 1824–January 1825

In 1860, Zacheus Howwoswee, Zachariah's grandson, emphasized that his people wanted "our voters [proprietors] to be the Native indians of the soil not foreigners[.] You will understand what I mean by Native Indian of the soil if any come from another indian settlement we do not call them foreigners."[107] Joel Rogers appears to have been one of these other Indians. In 1792 Moses Howwoswee listed him as "part white" and a "stranger," but fourteen years later Rogers spoke of "*we* the tribe," "the Gayhead people," who were under siege by "the white people" of "a connected gang which extends throughout the Vineyard whose interest it would be to impoverish *us* and get *our* land sold out of *our* possession."[108] Rogers had become a "stranger" only in name after living at Aquinnah for several years, applying his literacy skills to neighbors' causes, and assuming public duties like field driver.[109] As a person of Indian and white descent, he did not "blacken" Aquinnah's public image, and probably he shared the Wampanoags' commitment to a communal land base. It was easier than ever for Indians coming to the Vineyard from the mainland, to become members of the Wampanoag community.

Non-Indian outsiders were free to participate in Wampanoag political life only if they went along with the Indians' consensus. In 1824, "full blacks" William Mingo and Thomas James signed a Christiantown petition against land sales, and in 1838 John Salisbury leant his support to a ban on liquor peddling. But even then, the Indians earmarked these men as "nonproprietors."[110] It was out of the question for an outsider to express open dissent. In 1860, Howwoswee complained, "the foreigners makes the most disterbence among us" because "the strangers got the vote" on clay sales, despite not having "any pole right."[111] Aquinnah's proprietors found this development so unnerving that they asked Massachusetts to make their meetings "legal" and ban outsiders from them. African American resistance to such indignities would shape relations with their Indian neighbors for years to come.

III

The Indians' restrictions on black strangers violated basic principles advocated by black leaders for their people's moral and economic uplift. In cities such as Boston, New Bedford, Providence, and Newport, African Americans

---

[107] Howwoswee to Earle, September 10, 1860, JMEP, Box 2, File 3 (quote); Earle Report, 32.
[108] Rogers to Paul Cuffee, Oct. 24, 1816, Cuffee Letterbook (my emphasis).
[109] ZHP, File 1773, Mr 29; UPLP, B2, 8029–1816 (4).
[110] ULRIA, Box 2, File 9419–1824; PLP, Acts 1838, chap. 101; Baylies, "Names and Ages"; DCD, 36:222–3.
[111] Howwoswee to Earle, January 27, 1860, JMEP, Box 2, File 3.

gathered their own churches rather than suffer the humiliation of segregated balconies that white parishioners called "nigger heaven."[112] They formed mutual aid societies to help members fund the cost of a spouse's funeral or illness. And they started newspapers and fraternal organizations that promoted education, sobriety, thrift, neatness, and chastity – in all, "elevation" toward "respectability," and, they hoped, social acceptance by whites. A special call went out to African American men to strive toward the middle-class convention of supporting a housewife through hard work and entrepreneurial drive, even though most whites refused to hire "coloreds" for well-paying jobs. If African American males walked a straight moral line and threw themselves into business, these reformers hoped, economic success and an amelioration of white bigotry would eventually follow.[113]

Certainly Indians empathized with African Americans yearning for respect, since often they suffered from the same discrimination. Natick minister Stephen Badger wrote in 1798 that Indians "are generally considered by white people, and placed as if by common consent, in an inferiour and degraded situation, and treated accordingly. Of this they themselves seem to be not a little sensible. This sinks and cramps their spirits, and prevents those manly exertions which an equal rank with others has a tendency to call forth."[114] Shipmasters clamored after Indians at hiring time in the belief that they could spy whales at greater distances than other sailors, but on social occasions they shunned the Natives along with other "coloreds."[115] In 1849, a Christiantown whaler lamented that although he had risen to the rank of second mate, "the moment we fall in company with other vessels, or arrive in port, and our captain invites other captains and mates to dine, I am banished from the forecastle."[116] One of the reasons the Chappaquiddick Wampanoags refused to attend church in Edgartown was the whites'

---

[112] William J. Brown, *The Life of William J. Brown of Providence, R.I., with Personal Recollections of Incidents in Rhode Island* (1833; Freeport, N.Y.: Books for Libraries Press, 1971), 46.

[113] Melish, *Disowning Slavery*, chap. 4; Horton, *Free People of Color*, chap. 5; Robert J. Cottrol, *The Afro-Yankees: Providence's Black Community in the Antebellum Era* (Westport, Conn.: Greenwood Press, 1982), chap. 2.; James Brewer Stewart, "The Emergence of Racial Modernity and the Rise of the White North, 1790–1840," *JER* 18 (1998), 186, 188–9. For the origins of this thinking among whites, see Richard L. Bushman, *The Refinement of America: Persons, Houses, and Cities* (New York: Alfred A. Knopf, 1992). For one of its antebellum political incarnations, see Daniel Walker Howe, *The Political Culture of the American Whigs* (Chicago: University of Chicago Press, 1979).

[114] Badger, "Historical and Characteristic Traits of the American Indians," *MHSC* 1st ser., 5 (1798), 38.

[115] Earle Report, 27; William Comstock, *A Voyage to the Pacific: Descriptive of the Customs, Usages, and Sufferings On Board of Nantucket Whale-Ships* (Boston, 1838), 17.

[116] *Report of the Commissioners*, 14–15.

insistence that they assume a "respectful" position, clearly referring to the balcony or the back of the room.[117] White treatment of Indians as "coloreds" was not only demeaning but potentially dangerous. While visiting southern ports, sailors of "mixed" ancestry had to prove they were Indians to avoid imprisonment, since after 1822 South Carolina, Alabama, and Louisiana required the incarceration of black seamen for fear they incited slave rebellions. Narragansett Amos Daley escaped confinement in South Carolina only after his mates testified that his mother was indeed an "Indian" and, unlike Daley himself, possessed "straight black hair," a critical measure of Indianness for many whites.[118] The Indians' future was indelibly wrapped up in the fate of African Americans.

Indians had ample opportunity to discuss white racism and its solutions with black advocates of the uplift agenda. In harbor towns, Native men and women received their warmest welcome in "colored" taverns, boarding houses, barbershops, and churches, where reform was a central topic of conversation. Native whalers traversed much of the known world swapping opinions with black sailors, whom some historians see as wellsprings for the era's radical egalitarian movements.[119] Almost every Indian had friends and relatives living in an urban "colored" community. Some of these contacts still called the reservation "home," made occasional visits, and intended to return permanently as soon as they steadied their finances.[120] Others, however, had been born off-island or spent years in the city without fostering an Indian identity and considered themselves members of the black community.

The best-documented example of this sort of self-fashioning is Paul Cuffee, the son of an emancipated slave named Cuffee (or Kofi) Slocum and an Indian woman from Harwich on Cape Cod named Ruth Moses. Paul Cuffee made his home in the mainland town of Dartmouth, and there managed to turn his business sense and drive into a lucrative maritime trading operation. Although his mother was a Wampanoag and his wife was a Pequot, Cuffee proudly declared himself an "African" and promoted a "back-to-Africa" colonization movement for American freedmen. By contrast, his brother Jonathan lived at Aquinnah as part of the Indian community,

---

[117] Joseph Thaxter to John Lathrop, September 30, 1808, Misc. Bound MSS, MHS.

[118] "Free Colored Seamen," 18–21; Bolster, *Black Jacks*, chap. 7; Horton, *Free People of Color*, 152; Leon F. Litwack, *North of Slavery: The Negro in the Free States, 1790–1860* (Chicago: University of Chicago Press, 1961), 51–3.

[119] Bolster, *Black Jacks*; Linebaugh and Rediker, *Many-Headed Hydra*.

[120] For a look at this phenomenon among modern Indians, see Jeanne Guillemin, *Urban Renegades: The Cultural Strategy of American Indians* (New York: Columbia University Press, 1975). Morris W. Foster, *Being Comanche: A Social History of American Indian Community* (Tuscon: University of Arizona Press, 1991), calls attention to the importance of face-to-face interaction as a component of Indian tribal identity.

enjoying a modest and safe tenure on the land in exchange for sacrificing the entrepreneurial opportunities that Paul had exploited so effectively. It was Paul Cuffee's opinion that bans on Gay Headers selling territory to outsiders "renders them miserabil" and "in an Infant State for Self Government," and that the only way to ameliorate this condition was for Aquinnah to adopt white private-property and bourgeois ethics. He lectured Joel Rogers about the need for "a Reformation amonge you as a moral People...you are not able to obtain enough for your families through the Summer – what is more Destructive in a Society of people than excessive drinking & Idleness."[121] It was maddening for Cuffee to think of his relatives trapped in a net woven of Indian custom and protective legislation that discouraged individual enterprise, civic participation, and community "progress," while he did everything he could to walk upright, garner wealth, and squeeze past racist obstacles. Doubtless many blacks living on Indian reservations concurred.

Vineyard Wampanoags were not adverse to "improvement" per se, but they were determined to have everyone in the community proceed together rather than conform to the individualistic ethos that had become a hallmark of the industrializing North. They clamored for school funds because education benefited the people as a whole, and by 1817 they had convinced the Society for the Propagation of the Gospel in North America to sponsor Frederick Baylies as their teacher. Baylies became that and more. He not only taught Wampanoag children, but encouraged Indian self-sufficiency by training and supervising Native instructors. As was the case in the late seventeenth century, this approach led to a dramatic rise in the Indians' literacy and math skills, reversing several generations of decline. Then Baylies expanded his rounds to include the Wampanoags of Nantucket and the mainland, and the Narragansetts of Rhode Island, with similarly positive results.[122] As the

[121] Paul Cuffee to Pearson Freeman, October 19, 1816 ("miserabil"), and Cuffee to Rogers, December 3, 1816 (all other quotes), Cuffee Letterbook.

[122] Letters in the files "Frederick Baylies, June–July 1810," and "Chappaquiddick Indians," in Records of Harvard Grants for Work among the Indians, Papers, 1720–1810, 1 Box, Harvard University Archives, Pursey Library, Cambridge, Mass.; John Foster, *A Sermon...Preached before the Society for Propagating the Gospel* (Cambride, Mass., 1817), 41; *Report of the Society for Propagating the Gospel among the Indians and Others in North America* (Cambridge, Mass., reports for 1819, 1820, 1822, 1824, 1826); *Discourse Preached before the Society for the Propagation of the Gospel...with the Report of the Select Committee* (Cambridge, Mass., 1821); Thaddeus Mason Harris, *A Discourse Delivered Before the Society for Propagating the Gospel...with the Report of the Select Committee* (Cambridge, Mass., 1823), 43–4; John Codman, *Importance of Spiritual Knowledge: A Sermon Delivered Before the Society for Propagating the Gospel...with the Report of the Select Committee* (Cambridge, Mass., 1825); Ebenezer Porter, *The Duty of Christians to Pray for the Missionary Cause: A Sermon...with the Report of the Select Committee* (Cambridge, Mass., 1828), 39; Benjamin Wisner, *The Proper Mode of Conducting Missions to the Heathen: A Sermon Delivered before the Society for Propagating the Gospel* (Boston,

Wampanoags' literacy rose, so did the number of families subscribing to reform-minded newspapers filled with advice columns on sobriety, religiosity, industriousness, and morality. It was no coincidence that in 1831 Gay Head's Deacon Simon Johnson and Thomas Cooper reported "an interesting revival in religion" among their people.[123] Within a decade, dozens of Aquinnahs had formed a "temperance society" that petitioned Boston to ban liquor sales on the reservation because excessive drinking promoted "dissolute habits" and kept them "backward."[124] Another motivation, as expressed by the Wampanoags of Mashpee, was that "if we say one word we are then called poor drunken Indians, when in fact we are not, that we have joined the temperance cause and wish to be counted so and heard to by your honors."[125] The Indians took pride in their reforms and considered themselves inferior to no one, as Aquinnah's proprietors broadcasted when they voted to bestow the honorific "Esquire" upon their own office holder, mariner, and farmer, George Belain.[126] However, their goal was not to reshape their lives according to a totalizing "civilization" program but to gain a modicum of public respect and thus greater collective security.

The Wampanoags' historic balancing act of acculturating without assimilating grew precarious as embarrassed officials in Boston took note of the state's disenfranchised Indian population. Particularly after 1830, Massachusetts was the nation's center for antislavery sentiment and organizations. The pages of William Lloyd Garrison's newspaper, *The Liberator*, the legislation of Massachusetts senators Charles Sumner and Henry Wilson, and speakers at the lectern of the Massachusetts Antislavery Society, launched one moral barrage after another against the South's social system and political agenda.[127] Both notable and notorious for their Brahmin

1829), 37; Alden Bradford, *A Discourse Delivered before the Society for Propagating the Gospel* (Boston, 1830); *Report of the Select Committee of the Society for Propagating the Gospel* (Boston, reports for 1831–1833, and 1840); SPGNA, File 8; Journal of Frederick Baylies, entries for January 10, 1827, and January 1, 1828, Box 3, and entries for January 1, 1829, and January 1, 1830, Box 4, Andrews-Eliot Coll, MHS.; Parkman, "Report of Enquiry," October 29, 1835, Andrews-Eliot Coll., MHS; Frederick Baylies, Letters, Box 26, MVHS.

[123] Simon Johnson and Thomas Cooper, Indians, to Alden Bradford, Esqr., November 12, 1831, Andrews-Eliot, Collection, MHS.

[124] Wrighte to Bradford, May 28, 1838, Misc. Bound MSS, MHS; *Report of the Commissioners*, 79; PLP, Acts 1838, chap. 101. For more on the era's temperance movement, see Paul E. Johnson, *A Shopkeeper's Millenium: Society and Revivals in Rochester, New York, 1815–1837* (New York: Hill and Wang, 1978); W. J. Rorabaugh, *The Alcoholic Republic: An American Tradition* (New York: Oxford University Press, 1979); and Ian Tyrrell, *Sobering Up: From Temperance to Prohibition in Antebellum America, 1800–1860* (Westport, Conn.: Greenwood Press, 1979).

[125] Memorial of the Mashpee Indians, May 21, 1833, GIP, Box 2, File 3.

[126] Gay Head Town Records, Box 174A, Env. S1, MVHS.

[127] James M. McPherson, *The Struggle for Equality: Abolitionists and the Negro in the Civil War and Reconstruction* (1964; Princeton, N.J.: Princeton University Press, 1995).

self-righteousness, the Bay Staters' pontifical air found justification in that the commonwealth had achieved the highest degree of civic equality for blacks of any state in the country. Massachusetts stood with Maine, New Hampshire, Vermont, and Rhode Island as the only antebellum states that allowed black males to vote on the same basis as whites. While other states found new ways to obstruct black public life, New Englanders began to desegregate day schools, colleges, and trains, and to open lecture halls to speakers and audiences of all complexions. Bigotry and discrimination prevailed, but Massachusetts seemed closer than any of its peers to achieving antislavery activist Wendell Phillip's vision of a country made up of "only American citizens."[128]

Yet Massachusetts had to endure stinging charges of hypocrisy for its Indian affairs. In 1807, the state codified a long-standing custom by ruling that inhabitants of incorporated plantations (meaning Indians) were ineligible for the franchise, based on the idea that Indians' communal holdings made them unsuited to a political system premised on one man–one vote and the sanctity of private property.[129] The tiny size of the commonwealth's Indian population and the Indians' desire to remain inconspicuous allowed this law to stand despite the elimination of property-holding requirements for white and black voters in 1821. However, in 1838 Mashpee forced its anomalous status into the public eye when it protested against the paternalism of the Indian guardianship system. Echoing the controversy over Andrew Jackson's determination to remove the southeastern tribes to Oklahoma even after the Supreme Court had defended their sovereignty, the Mashpees, led by William Apess, announced their determination to "rule our selves" because "all men are born free and Equal says the Constitution of the Country."[130] Accordingly, the Mashpees elected a new government to replace a string of incompetent guardians, fired their Harvard-funded minister, took possession of their meetinghouse, and put an end to the rampant white encroachment on their woodland.[131] Apess's arrest and a compromise

---

[128] Cited in McPherson, *Struggle for Equality*, 221 (quote), 223–9; Litwack, *North of Slavery*, 105–12.

[129] James H. Kettner, *The Development of American Citizenship, 1608–1870* (Chapel Hill: University of North Carolina Press for the Institute of Early American History and Culture, 1978), 287–300; Alexander Keyssar, *The Right to Vote: The Contested History of Democracy in the United States* (New York: Basic Books, 2000), 59, 164–5.

[130] Jill Lepore, *Name of War: King Philip's War and the Origins of American Identity* (New York: Alfred A. Knopf, 1998), 209. On the connection between opposition to removal and later abolitionist activity, see Mary Hershberger, "Mobilizing Women, Anticipating Abolition: The Struggle against Indian Removal in the 1830s," *JAH* 86 (June 1999), 15–40.

[131] *Rights of the Mashpee Indians: Argument of Benjamin H. Hallett, Counsel for the Memorialists of the Marshpee Tribe, Before a Joint Committee of the Legislature of*

granting the Mashpees greater self-government broke the "insurrection," but not before media coverage forced Massachusetts to acknowledge that Christiantown, Chappaquiddick, Gay Head, Mashpee, and Herring Pond were "five communities within the state, but not of it, subject to its laws, but having no part in their enactment; within the limits of local municipalities, yet not subject to their jurisdiction; and holding real estate in their own right, yet not suffered to dispose of it except to each other."[132] Massachusetts abolitionists, who often lambasted southerners for neglecting the religious condition of their slaves, were equally distressed to learn that Indians in their own backyard had not received regular missionary attention for almost fifty years. Reformers knew they could not hope to change the South without attempting to perfect their own society, so they launched a series of investigations to determine if the Indians were ready for Massachusetts citizenship. Their main object was to measure the Indians' conformity to white definitions of respectability.

An isolated few had entertained the idea of Indian citizenship as early as the 1790s, but rarely in the context of serious debate, because it was widely held that Indians were so naturally prodigal that if they divided their territory and accepted the vote they would soon squander all their resources and join the region's wandering poor.[133] Such concerns rang through the Indian Commissioners' reports of 1849 and 1861, which argued that grinding poverty and ignorance left most Natives unsuited for the franchise.[134] However, investigators were surprised to find Wampanoags at the Vineyard and Herring Pond earning comfortable livings through a combination of wage work, animal husbandry, farming, fishing, and the sale of common resources like berries, wood, shellfish, and pasture.[135] The Natives, with a few exceptions, had decent framed houses, sometimes with multiple

Massacusetts...Published at the Request of Isaac Coombs, Daniel Amos, and William Apes (Boston, 1834); Donald M. Nielsen, "The Mashpee Indian Revolt of 1833," *NEQ* 58 (1985), 400–20; Campisi, *The Mashpee Indians*, 101–9; Barry O'Connell, "Introduction," to Apess, *On Our Own Ground*, xxxv–xxxviii.

[132] Earle Report, p. 121.

[133] "Letter from Gideon Hawley...30 July 1794," *MHSC* 1st ser. 4 (1795), 66; "Visit to the Elizabeth Islands," 320; Tudor, *Letters on the Eastern States*, 244; Ebenezar Skiff to Frederick Baylies, May 3, 1823, and Joseph Thaxter to James Freeman, March 1, 1823, Misc. Bound MSS, MHS; Jean O'Brien, "Divorced from the Land: Accommodation Strategies of Indian Women in Eighteenth-Century New England," in Mary Jo Maynes, Ann Waltner, Brigette Soland, and Ulrike Strasser, eds., *Gender Kinship, Power: A Comparative and Interdisciplinary History* (New York: Routledge, 1996), 319–33.

[134] *Report of the Commissioners*, 25, 38, 41, 43; Earle Report, 63, 83–4.

[135] Morse, *Report to the Secretary of War*, 69; Wrighte to Bradford, April 9, 1839, Andrews-Eliot Coll., MHS; *Report of the Commissioners*, 7, 18–19, 20–1; B. G. Marchant to J. M. Earle, August 27, 1859, JMEP, Box 2, File 3; Earle Report, 17, 26–7, 36.

rooms, decorated "with pictures and curiosities collected in the eastern and southern seas."[136] The Indians' churches and schools lacked polished leadership, but the community's dedication made these institutions viable and relevant.[137] Contrary to white stereotypes, the vast majority of Natives appeared "temperate and chaste."[138] The Commissioners were struck most of all by the effectiveness of the Indians' town meeting government, the infrequency of litigation, and the people's generous support of the poor.[139] The whole scene was "almost realizing the wildest dreams of the communists."[140]

These observations suggest that the Commissioners' initial recommendation against extending the Indians citizenship had less to do with the Natives' socioeconomic condition than the Indians' almost unanimous sentiment against change.[141] Earlier in the century, Gay Headers would literally hide upon the approach of white strangers for fear they came from the state to impinge on the community's autonomy.[142] Gay Head even arranged to have a Boston watchmaker sound the alarm if any petition regarding their affairs went before the legislature.[143] They "do not know, and they do not want to know, under what law they live," wrote the Commissioners in 1849, "they only ask to be let alone, and not, by ill-advised legislation, to be constantly reminded of their vassalage."[144] A decade later the Wampanoags' opinions remained unwavering despite continual outside pressure to aspire to civic equality. Massachusetts officials were surprised that Aquinnah remained "strong and decided against a change, all the most intelligent and respectable portion of the residents concurring therein."[145] The Wampanoags' alternative proposal was "to have the doings of our meetings legal," which was to say, recognized by the state, binding on the inhabitants, and "separate from the foreigners & strangers."

---

[136] *Report of the Commissioners*, 7 (quote), 13, 19; Earle Report, 18, 27, 36; Koch, *Journey through a Part of the United States*, 16; Glover and McBride, "Old Ways and New Ways," 15.

[137] B. G. Marchant to J. M. Earle, September 17, 1859, JMEP, Box 2, File 3; *Report of the Select Committee of the Society for the Propagation of the Gospel in North America* (Cambridge, Mass., 1861), 21, 24; *Vineyard Gazette*, June 1, 1848, vol. 3, no. 4.

[138] Leavitt Thaxter to John Milton Earle, 3 Febuary 1860, JMEP, Box 2, File 3.

[139] *Report of the Commissioners*, 9–10, 14, 15–16, 20–1; Thaxter to Earle, Feb. 3, 1860, JMEP, Box 2, File 3; Gay Head Town Records, 1858–1866, Box 174, Env. S1, MVHS.

[140] *Report of the Commissioners*, 21.

[141] Ann Marie Plane and Gregory Button, "The Massachusetts Indian Enfranchisement Act: Ethnic Contest in Historical Context, 1849–1869," *Ethnohistory* 40 (1993), 611, n. 38.

[142] Kendall, *Travels*, 2:195–6.

[143] ULRIA, Box 2, File 8029–1816 (4).

[144] *Report of the Commissioners*, 23.

[145] Earle Report, 37, 43 (quote).

FIGURE 10. Deacon Simon Johnson (1794–1875). This image of Deacon Simon Johnson is an ambrotype taken in the 1860s, about a decade before he died. Johnson was Aquinnah's political and religious leader throughout the mid–nineteenth century. *Harper's New Monthly* described him as "tall, and of the most chieftan-like appearance," and strikingly intelligent. Reportedly, he only left the island three times in his life, twice to go to Boston and once to Salem. Along with Zacheus Howwoswee and Jane Wamsley, Johnson stood as one of the most outspoken opponents of Indian enfranchisement and division of the commons. Courtesy of the Martha's Vineyard Historical Society.

Faced with a united front, Massachusetts relented, and in 1862 made Gay Head an official self-governing "district."[146]

Other Indian communities rejected the franchise because it would rob them of special state protections and render them "the prey of shrewder and

---

[146] Howwoswee to Earle, August 25, 1859, and January 27, 1860, JMEP, Box 2, File 3.

JANE WORMLEY.

FIGURE 11. Sketch of Jane Wamsley. *Harper's New Monthly* published this drawing of Jane Wamsley and an unidentified child in 1860 when Wamsley was about 62 years old. Earlier in life, she made a name for herself as a Baptist preacher. Around the time of the *Harper's* article, she was noted for her steadfast defense of Gay Head's protected status as an Indian reservation despite pressure from outside the community and within to divide collectively held lands and accept the franchise.

sharper men outside, that the little property they possess would be wrested from them, and that . . . the community would be consequently broken up, and scattered among those who would have no particular sympathy with them, and would not render them the aid which they now receive, in time of trial and need."[147] Paying taxes would be no tonic for this loss. "They do

---

[147] Earle Report, 24–5.

not wish to be taxed in any shape," wrote Charles Marston of the Mashpees. "They are bitterly opposed to it."[148] The Natives felt no shame having Boston fund their schools and infrastructure because of "a vague idea that the State has large funds drawn from the sale of lands which would have been theirs, and that this belongs to them as a portion of the interest of the proceeds... so that whatever they receive is but a just due."[149] Aid was not charity, but justice.

The Commissioners' tendency to think of "people of color" as a single entity made it difficult for them to understand the Indians' complacency, particularly in light of the immense risks undertaken by black political activists during the buildup to the Civil War. They could only deduce that the Natives rejected citizenship because white prejudice made them feel depressed and inferior, even though they conceded that the Gay Head Indians' "unwritten law" was "probably as well adapted to their condition as any that can be devised."[150] The Commissioners' solutions to this "problem" were, first, to have the Indians "trained to habits of patient, persevering, earnest, hopeful, and systematic industry," which would boost their supposed lost confidence, and second, to double the campaign against racism.[151] The program for black uplift and abolition, in other words, was the best way to address Massachusetts' "Indian problem."

Beneath the veneer of unanimous Indian conservatism was a dissident faction comprising mostly "strangers" and their near relatives that yearned for full American rights but struggled to make its voice heard. In 1860, Leavitt Thaxter wrote to Boston on behalf of Aquinnah's main spokesman, Deacon Simon Johnson, to express Johnson's concern "that some one has written you to the purpose that the people of Gay Head desire a division of lands." "A division of the land," he stressed, "will not promote the best interests of the tribe... and this I think is the opinion of most of the people there who are *not* foreigners."[152] The following year, Gay Headers spoke out overwhelmingly against reform, "except a very few, whose bad character and vicious habits have rendered them a nuisance to the place."[153] When

---

[148] C. Marston to John Milton Earle, October 14, 1859, JMEP, Box 2, File 2.
[149] Earle Report, p. 13.
[150] Earle Report, 33 (quote), 34.
[151] Earle Report, 129–30. My emphasis here differs somewhat from that of Plane and Button, in "The Massachusetts Indian Enfranchisement Act," who submit that the 1849 and 1861 committees recommended against Indian enfranchisement because they believed that social conditions rendered the Indians economically and intellectually unfit for the responsibility. My reading is that the Commissioners were impressed with conditions on several Indian reserves, particularly on the Vineyard, but that they determined the Indians' unwillingness to embrace citizenship in and of itself made them unfit to participate in a voluntary democracy.
[152] Leavitt Thaxter to John Milton Earle, January 28, 1860, JMEP, Box 2, File 3.
[153] Earle Report, 43.

the Commissioners visited Chappaquiddick, two unnamed men complained privately about restrictions on Indians signing private contracts or using land as collateral, since they believed "equal privileges were the natural right of all, and they did not choose to be deprived of them." In all likelihood, these men were Isaac Joab and David Belain, who lived profitably on the "white side of the line," paying property taxes, poll taxes, and voting.[154] Yet in public meetings they deferred to the majority who had "no desire to enjoy the privileges of citizenship" and no "inclination to enjoy the privilege of voting and incur the liability of taxation."[155] According to Commissioner John Milton Earle, "the individual, who at first, was most earnest for a change, on taking a more enlarged and comprehensive view of the matter, was satisfied that it was best the change should not be made," calling it "best for the tribe."[156]

As long as the opponents of the franchise could successfully discourage public disagreement and convince state officials that citizenship in a voluntary democracy would have to be imposed upon them, the status quo appeared safe. However, the forces unleashed by the Civil War and Reconstruction changed everything. The war's mounting losses convinced President Abraham Lincoln and a reluctant northern public that "military necessity" required the abolition of slavery, first in the unconquered Confederate states, then in the nation as a whole, thus leading to the 1862 Emancipation Proclamation and the Thirteenth Amendment of 1865. These were revolutionary measures by most Americans' standards, but the woeful failures of postwar Reconstruction demonstrated that they were not enough. Northerners saw that unless freed men gained the vote, Lincoln's Republicans would never compete below the Mason–Dixon Line, and, with Democrats in power, unrepentant rebels would retake southern state governments, institute race codes to reduce blacks to serfdom, and smash the dream of opening the South to free labor. The North, Radical Republicans argued, had to lead the way to a constitutional guarantee of black voting rights by enfranchising its own "colored" population. Several Union states resisted, but after Iowa and Minnesota adopted black suffrage in 1868 and Congress reached a compromise to permit states to erect wealth and literacy restrictions at the polls, the stage was set for the Fifteenth Amendment of 1870. It proclaimed, "the right of citizens of the United States to vote shall not be denied or abridged by the United States or by any State on account of race, color, or previous condition of servitude."[157] In theory, Vineyard Wampanoags were unaffected,

---

[154] B. G. Marchant to John Milton Earle, September 17, 1859, December 31, 1859, JMEP, Box 2, File 3; Earle Report, 19.

[155] *Report of the Commissioners*, 12 ("taxation"), 14 ("citizenship"); Earle Report, 129.

[156] Earle Report, 25.

[157] McPherson, *The Struggle for Equality*, 377–82, chap. 18.

since the Fourteenth Amendment's extension of national citizenship to "all persons born or naturalized in the United States," excluded "Indians not taxed." But in practice, this legislation was the deathblow to the Indians' separate legal status.

One of the most dramatic effects of the Reconstruction era was that, for at least a few years, time seemed suspended, and the opportunity to recast society based on ideals rather than inherited structures appeared to be at hand.[158] Abolitionists who campaigned for a color-blind society had once been reviled as political lepers in the North and South alike, but now they held leadership in the country's ruling party. Millions of African Americans who had toiled under the whip and been told by the Supreme Court they had no rights that whites were bound to respect, now had their freedom guaranteed by the Constitution. Laws banning them from testifying in court and serving on juries or placing them in inferior public accommodations were falling across the nation. African American men, so often stereotyped as childlike, ignorant, and untrustworthy, had asserted their dignity in the Union's armed forces and now anticipated political equality. The United States was making giant strides toward living up to its own founding principles during these years and the end was not yet in sight.

New England Indians had fought alongside blacks in the "colored" ranks, and yet there was no franchise or elevated status for them at the war's end.[159] Gay Head, in particular, had contributed generously to the campaign. Alfred P. Rose died at age sixteen at the Battle of Petersburg among the "colored troops" of Massachusetts. James Diamond, Peter Johnson, and Daniel Nevers had marched with the blue-coated army, and Edwin D. Vanderhoop, Joseph P. Anthony, Sidney Johnson, Nathan Johnson, Lewis Attaquin, and William Morton had sailed with the Union navy.[160] The experience of risking their lives and watching men die for profound civic principles purged them of any trace of political apathy.[161] They could no longer tolerate Massachusetts categorizing them as permanent wards, as children, along with "lunatics" and "idiots" in the asylums. Caught up in nation's whirlwind of reinvention, they were ready to demand the same political rights their sacrifice had afforded African Americans.

[158] Eric Foner, *Reconstruction: America's Unfinished Revolution, 1863–1877* (New York: Harper and Row, 1988), 26–9.
[159] For a look at Pequots among the "colored" troops, see Laurence M. Hauptman, *Between Two Fires: American Indians in the Civil War* (New York: Free Press, 1995), chap. 8.
[160] Gorham Hatch to S. K. Lothrop, October 1, 1863, and October 1, 1864, SPGNA, Box 2, File 15; Thomas Minnis, *Sketches of Edgartown, Tisbury, and Chilmark, Martha's Vineyard* (n.p., 1877), MHS; Burgess, "Old South Road," 16.
[161] On the range of ideas animating both Union and Confederate soldiers over the course of the war, see James M. McPherson, *What They Fought For, 1861–1865* (Baton Rouge: Louisiana State University Press, 1994).

With veterans like these reinvigorating the dormant question of Indian citizenship, factions from each of the island's Wampanoag communities successfully applied to have the state prepare to partition their remaining common lands and distribute the franchise.[162] "We do not see a good reason why such of us as are willing to work and take care of ourselves should not be allowed to do so," one group of petitioners explained. "We take in some of our families three Newspapers per week and they all go to show that if a man would be useful he should be free to act when opportunity offers."[163] In Aquinnah, this pro-suffrage party was an alliance of "strangers," veterans, and the comparatively well-to-do: it included Abram Rodman, a carpenter of Narragansett descent, and his wife Hosanna, who worked twenty-five acres with twelve cattle; James Diamond, a "foreign" seaman and veteran, and his wife Abiah; Haitian John Randolph and his wife, Serena; Isaiah Jerod, the son of a Cape Cod Wampanoag; and Samuel J. Haskins, an Aquinnah man "of no particular family."[164] These people were unaccustomed to lead yet determined in their course, as they proved in a meeting to discuss their petition with the state's representative, Rodney French. Deacon Simon Johnson and his supporters, Zacheus Howwoswee and Jane Wamsley, tried to speak for the entire community, as they always had, by politely asking Massachusetts to "let alone" their people, but John Anthony, a Portuguese man, would give them the last word, elders or not. Anthony said he "considered himself a man among men as good as 'any other man,'" and wished for a chance to prove it."[165] Others did too. In its coverage of this event, the *Vineyard Gazette* counted three votes against enfranchisement and nine in favor, leading it to conclude, "the sentiment of the people, generally, seems to be in favor of enfranchisement and the establishment of a separate town."[166] Later events proved Gay Headers were less sure than the vote indicated.

Opponents of the franchise had a legitimate fear that "by being incorporated as a town we shall soon lose our identity as Indians."[167] Indeed, since the late seventeenth century, Wampanoag history and culture had revolved around the defense of shared resources against intense pressure to divide and

---

[162] DI/235, DCP.

[163] "Petition of Abraham and Hosanna G. Rodman and six others of the Gay Head Tribe of Indians, Asking to be Enfranchized, May 11, 1869," PLP, Acts 1870, chap. 213.

[164] Earle Report, Appendix B; Minnis, *Sketches of Edgartown*, 146.

[165] Besides those who had signed May's pro-suffrage petition, the Aquinnahs voting for the franchise at this meeting included: Leander Bassett, originally of Farm Neck (Sengekontacket), and the child of a "full black" father and a "3/4" black mother, according to Baylies' census; Alvin Manning, who was married to a woman from Vermont and whose brother-in-law was the foreigner and veteran James Diamond; Samuel Peters, whose wife, Francis Rose, hailed from Taunton; and Thomas Jeffers, the brother-in-law of Leander Bassett. See Levitas, "No Boundary is a Boundary," 218.

[166] *Vineyard Gazette*, June 4, 1869, vol. 24, no. 8.

[167] "Petition of Aaron Cooper, Thomas Jeffers, and Isaac D. Rose, Selectmen and Treasurer of the Gay Head Indians . . . Feb. 4, 1869," PLP, Acts 1870, chap. 213.

sell. The communities of Nunnepog, Sengekontacket, and Nashuakemuck no longer existed because the people had exposed themselves to the merciless competition of the market. Aquinnah, and to a lesser extent, Christiantown and Chappaquiddick, lived to tell the tale because they had discovered innovative ways to sustain the commons, ranging from unseating the sachem and establishing corporate government, to adopting livestock, leases, lawsuits, and more. Common land was more than real estate to them. It kept the people together despite the pull of the outside world and provided a stage on which to play out their communal values and tell their people's stories. How could anyone expect individual landowners to uphold a community without fences in which nobody was allowed to fall behind? How would parents pass on their oral traditions if outsiders cordoned off places for the telling? And once these things were lost, how would the people distinguish themselves from other "people of color"? For elders such as Johnson, Howwoswee, and Wamsley, the new proposals tore at the very heart of who they were.

Those in favor of citizenship did not reject their people's history and culture. However, they were insistent that they were capable as other Americans of recognizing their economic interests and casting their votes intelligently. Their men had lived and worked in the rough-and-tumble neighborhoods of mainland cities, fought monstrous whales on open seas, and stared down the barrels of Confederate guns. What need did they have of protection? Some of their women, having raised families almost single-handedly and served in local government, wanted suffrage for the males as a first step to their own enfranchisement, and therefore joined women across racial lines to petition for this right.[168] If losing their special legal status as Indians led whites to deny their identity, so be it. Off-island experiences taught them that nobody could rob them of their peoplehood because they knew who their relatives were, they knew their history, and they knew where to find their homeland.

A month after Gay Head's meeting with Rodney French, Massachusetts passed its "Act to Enfranchise the Indians." This legislation declared the state's Natives "citizens of the Commonwealth" with all the inherent "rights, privileges, and immunities, and subject to all the duties and liabilities, including "the same rights as other citizens to take, hold, convey, and transmit real estate." However, it also required a petition by any single reservation member to launch a county review of whether the common lands should be divided. And so the threat loomed for a little while longer.

---

[168] "Petition of Cynthia Attaquin, Betsey J. Ockery, Sarah Brown, et al., Febuary 20, 1869," Unpassed Legislation, Mass. State Archives; "Petition of Tristram Freeman & others, the only male inhabitants of the Deep Bottom Tribe of Indians on Martha's Vineyard, Asking to be restored to citizenship & that Females in this State be Enfranchised, March 1869," Mass. State Archives. Copies courtesy of Ann Marie Plane.

FIGURE 12. Images of Martha's Vineyard Wampanoags in the Late Nineteenth Century. In order: Deacon Thomas Jeffers of Aquinnah (b. 1826); "Mrs. George Belain," probably Sophia Belain (maiden name Peters) of Aquinnah (b. 1817); Frank Peters and Alonzo Belain of Aquinnah, ca. 1880; Samuel and Lucinda Mingo, probably of Christiantown, ca. 1880. Marriages with "outsiders" during the late eighteenth and nineteenth centuries meant that every Wampanoag community included some people with physical characteristics that challenged dominant notions of what "Indians" were supposed to look like. Whites used these appearances to justify redefining the Indians as "people of color" and withdrawing state protection of their common lands. The Wampanoags dissented since they knew their peoplehood was defined by more than just "race." Nevertheless, some "strangers" joined whites in calling for a division of the Wampanoags' common lands, and that was indeed a formidable challenge to the core of Indian identity. Courtesy of the Martha's Vineyard Historical Society.

The Fifteenth Amendment and the Wampanoags' pro-suffrage lobby drove this legislation, but the decades-old argument that the Indians were not Indians in the first place was an underlying force.[169] Before passage of the Enfranchisement Act, Massachusetts Governor William Claflin told the Legislature that the Natives' protective status "should exist no longer. These persons are not Indians in any sense of the word. It is doubtful that there is a pure-blooded Indian in the State... A majority have more or less of the marked characteristics of the aboriginal race, but there are many without a drop of Indian blood in their veins... the characteristics of the white and negro races have already nearly obliterated all traces of the

[169] Plane and Button, "Massachusetts Indian Enfranchisement Act," 588.

FIGURE 12 (*continued*)

Indian."[170] The New Bedford *Mercury* agreed in its story about the citizenship debate at Aquinnah, writing "there is little or no pure aboriginal blood among these people, who partake of the African race with which they are largely mixed."[171] Ironically, some people used the same argument to oppose enfranchisement, since in the case of Gay Head and Mashpee it would lead the state "to incorporate a whole town of negroes." Nevertheless, most others believed that Massachusetts was now required by the Constitution to extend citizenship to all its "people of color," even if they claimed to be Indians.[172]

[170] Cited in *Gay Head Report*, 28.
[171] Reprinted in *Vineyard Gazette*, August 20, 1869, vol. 24, no. 19.
[172] Senate Doc. No. 14, 10.

FIGURE 12 *(continued)*

For the Wampanoags of Christiantown and Chappaquiddick there was
little left to do. Their small villages became parts of Tisbury and Edgartown,
respectively, they divided what remained of their commons, and their legal status as "Indians" ceased. But the transition to citizenship was more
complicated at Aquinnah. Neither Indians nor whites wanted the district
annexed to Chilmark, so on April 30, 1870, Massachusetts passed its "Act
to Incorporate the Town of Gay Head," which transferred the Wampanoags'
commons from the tribal proprietors to a town meeting (essentially the same
body) and placed the new polity in Chilmark's congressional district. This
legislation also ruled that upon application by the Gay Head selectmen or any
ten resident land owners, the Dukes County Judge of Probate could arrange
to have two commissioners divide the commons.[173] The act took effect after
an August ceremony at Gay Head in which J. J. Smith, "a colored gentleman
from the 6th ward in Boston," lectured the Indians about what they "might
reasonably and proudly strive to attain and arrive at, by determination and
perseverance." This must have struck some elders as odd, given that their

[173] *Mass. Acts and Resolves, 1870,* chap. 213, 140–42.

FIGURE 12 (*continued*)

common lands were on the verge of being parceled out after two centuries of struggle. Either way, the Indians proceeded to elect a town clerk, treasurer, selectmen, tax collector, overseers of the poor, school committee, and constable. Gay Head was now officially a town of the commonwealth and its people were full citizens. The *Vineyard Gazette* reported that the day ended with "hearty handshaking, friendly smiles, and a cordial good affection."[174]

If this was in fact the case, the collegiality did not last. Within months, twenty-three Gay Headers had requested partition to begin despite objections by the Gay Head selectmen that such action would be "premature and unsafe, and, as we believe, must be attended with disastrous consequences

[174] *Vineyard Gazette*, August 26, 1870, vol. 25, no. 20.

to us, as a people."[175] The probate court scheduled a hearing on the issue at a site more than ten miles from Aquinnah, as if to announce that its decision was a *fait accompli*, as indeed it was. The following year Richard L. Pease completed a survey of the Wampanoags' territory, including a chart of individual land claims determined through extensive genealogical interviews.[176] For the first time since Englishmen had arrived on the island, officials possessed a numbered grid with which they could try to force the Natives to adhere to a private-property regime. And try they did: between 1871 and 1878, the state divided 2,350 acres of land among the 227 Aquinnah proprietors, and then left them to confront a marketplace they had defined themselves against for generations.[177]

Almost at soon as this was done, Wampanoags began to complain that enfranchisement was "an unwelcome event to them, and so far, has not proved a blessing."[178] "Some have sold lands to the neighboring whites," Moses Brown explained, "most of them are getting into debt" and others were "becoming disheartened and reckless."[179] A year later, D. W. Stevens reported with no sense of wit about an "unhappy division" among the Indians.[180] Perhaps not coincidentally, while Pease added the final touches to his survey of Gay Head, Zacheus Howwoswee died at age 87 and Deacon Simon Johnson at age 80, heartbroken at the idea of property lines being run across their commons and terrified at what the future would hold for their people, who, in the words of one official, were "now no longer technically 'Indians.'"[181]

IV

Citizenship effectively served as the deathknell for Chappaquiddick and Christiantown, since most of the Natives lost their lands to creditors in a matter of years. Thereafter, some moved to Gay Head, others relocated to the outskirts of Edgartown or the burgeoning Methodist resort at Oak Bluffs (near Sengekontacket), and still others to mainland cities with little hope of ever reestablishing themselves on the island.[182] When Stevens went to

---

[175] DI/235, DCP.

[176] Pease's notes can be found in Indian Collection, Box B, Misc. Docs. File, MVHS.

[177] *Gay Head Report*; Kevin McBride and Suzanne G. Cherau, "Gay Head (Aquinnah) Wampanoag Community Structure and Land Use Patterns, *Northeast Anthropology* 51 (1996), 17.

[178] Moses Brown to Rufus Ellis, March 30, 1876, Andrews-Eliot Coll., MHS.

[179] Ibid.; Levitas, "No Boundary is a Boundary," 334–6, 351–6.

[180] D. W. Stevens to Rufus Ellis, October 31, 1877, Andrews-Eliot Collection, MHS.

[181] Richard Pease's Notes on Indian Genealogy, Indian Collection, Box B, Misc. Docs. MVHS; Senate Doc. No. 14, 7 (quote).

[182] Stevens to Ellis, October 31, 1881, Andrews-Eliot Collection, MHS. On Oak Bluffs, see Ellen Weiss, *City in the Woods: The Life and Design of an American Camp Meeting on Martha's Vineyard* (New York: Oxford University Press, 1987).

Christiantown in 1877, he found "only a few coloreds there and their meetings are small," while Chappaquiddick had shrunk to only "eight or nine colored families."[183] Just four years later the communities exhibited signs of further decay. The people of Christiantown, he learned, "have dwindled down to very small numbers. I was told by them a few weeks ago when there, that their whole number did not exceed sixteen, including men, women, and children." At Chappaquiddick, "one of the leading Indians told me that their whole number did not exceed twenty three."[184] These two communities were heading in the direction of Deep Bottom, which was already "wholly deserted of aboriginal owners or occupants."[185] A few families hung on, but by the end of the century Christiantown and Chappaquiddick had all but ceased to function as geographically distinct Indian communities.[186]

Gay Head's factionalism portended a similar decline, but after a few years the people closed ranks in a manner that signaled the continuing vitality of Wampanoag values. Selectmen still set off communal pasture even after that land had been officially divided. Abram Rodman built a local inn and restaurant, but most people refrained from any business that would cause them to "stand out." Most land "owners" refused to erect fences or file wills, and nearly everyone upheld the custom of allowing impoverished kin to move onto and work family grounds for as long as they pleased. As one twentieth-century informant put it, "I remember...if you didn't have no land and I didn't have no land and the other folks had land and if you wanted to plant in there, why you could go in there and get a piece from them. They'd let you have all that. That's the way we always done things around here. I don't know anything about this buyin' and sellin' a piece of land."[187] Under such circumstances, it only took a matter of years before Pease's grid system was yet again a knot of unofficial, overlapping claims.

Invariably, some Natives fell into debt and had to sell off their rights. Yet when this occurred, Gay Head's geographical isolation and reputation as a place teeming with "coloreds" served the people well. White landowners rarely moved into town, thereby conceding local government to the Indians, who then scheduled town meetings for winter, when strangers were least likely to attend. The Wampanoags' stranglehold on town policy allowed them to tax outsiders for the benefit of the group while often "forgetting"

[183] Stevens to Ellis, October 31, 1877, Andrews-Eliot Coll., MHS.

[184] D. W. Stevens to the Society for the Propagation of the Gospel, May 4, 1881, Andrews-Eliot Coll., MHS

[185] Stevens to SPG, October 31, 1881, Andrews-Eliot Coll., MHS.

[186] Eleanor Ransom Mayhew, "The Christiantown Story, 1659–1969," *Dukes County Intelligencer* 1 (1959), 9; Frank G. Speck, *Territorial Subdivisions and Boundaries of the Wampanoag, Massachusett, and Nauset Indians, Indian Notes and Monographs* 44 (New York: Museum of the American Indian, Heye Foundation, 1928), 110.

[187] Levitas, "No Boundary is a Boundary," 217, 283 (quote), 344–5.

to gather monies from relatives. For all intents and purposes, the tribe and the town were synonymous.[188]

Gay Head remained a Wampanoag place run by Wampanoag customs because the majority of its residents, including those who lobbied for the franchise, were committed to these things. Two possibilities account for this apparent contradiction. First, at least some members of the progressive faction wanted civic equality as a matter of pride, but did not want to see individual profiteering become a part of Gay Head life. Once they secured the rights to vote and sell land, they could rest assured that their communalism and their consensus government was a matter of choice, not of state charity. Ironically, withdrawal of state protection strengthened these customs by finally removing the threat of outside interference and allowing the Wampanoags to slip into anonymity. A second possibility is that aspiring entrepreneurs fell back on communal traditions after witnessing the breakup of Christiantown and Chappaquiddick and the first few foreclosures at Gay Head. Market opportunities now seemed more like traps than privileges. Instead of risking all for the possibility of only moderate gains, they returned to the values that had enabled their people to survive as a people.

Gay Headers never celebrated the anniversary of the Enfranchisement Act or their town's "Independence Day." The unleashing of political dissent, exposure of racial wounds, and government meddling was something to forget, not memorialize. As part of this collective amnesia, some people even tried to deny the existence of blacks among the people's ancestors. One story in circulation by the early twentieth century attributed African features at Gay Head to a curse rather than flesh and blood:

It seems that a hundred years or so ago the Indians were all straight haired, but a certain squaw got into bad company consorting much with witches and other adepts of the black art. Her curiosity however, finally led her too far, and there came a time when she saw more than her friends thought good, whereupon the witches clawed her hair over her eyes and snarled it all up, and ever after the race has been snarly haired.[189]

This narrative drew a subtle lesson from Wampanoag marriages with African Americans, even as it denied that those relationships had taken place. In the traditional Indian style of collapsing a long history into a single

---

[188] Gay Head's twentieth-century history has produced a rich body of scholarship. See Levitas, "No Boundary is a Boundary"; Jack Campisi, James D. Wherry, Christine Gabrowski, and Bettina Malonson, et al., "Submission of the Historical Narrative and Supportive Documentation in Support of a Petition Requesting the Acknowledgement of the Gay Head Wampanoag Tribe" (1983), MS in the possession of the Aquinnah Wampanoag Tribal Council, Aquinnah, Mass.; William A. Starna, "'We'll All Be Together Again': The Federal Acknowledgement of the Wampanoag Tribe of Gay Head," *Northeast Anthropology* 51 (1996), 3–12; Christine Tracey Gabroski, "Coiled Intentions: Federal Acknowledgement Policy and the Gay Head Wampanoags" (Ph.D. diss., City University of New York, 1994).

[189] Simmons, *Spirit of the New England Tribes*, 99–100.

"mythologized" event, it taught that Natives should remain wary of racial outsiders, who might initially appear as "friends," but whose "black art," or unfamiliar ways, risked turning the people into something unrecognizable. Tragically, this story also attempted to obliterate the memory of caring relationships between African American men and Native women and the demographic stability outsiders brought to the community. Perhaps the saddest theme of all was the choice this story posited between being "Indian" and "black." The Wampanoags of Martha's Vineyard might have been able to resist dispossession by some of the most potent forces of American history, but they could not deny the power of the idea of race.

Conclusion

Fencing In, Fencing Out

For centuries, the Wampanoags have related that in ancient days a giant named Moshup led their people to Noepe, or Martha's Vineyard, where he served as their benefactor. He provided them with gifts of whale meat, mediated their disputes, and instructed them on the importance of courtesy. But English colonization and the spread of Christianity brought Moshup's guardianship to an end. Unwilling to accept the waves of change washing over his island, the giant "retired in disgust," never to appear again.[1] The only sign of his lingering presence were deep fogs that supposedly rose from his pipe while he lay hidden in the cliffs of Aquinnah.

Moshup was a model for proper living, but Vineyard Wampanoags could hardly afford to mimic his retreat. The Indians, unlike their culture hero, were surrounded by the graves and spirits of ancestors, mnemonic devices for the people's stories, and familiar places for hunting, fishing, gathering, and planting that had fed countless generations. Martha's Vineyard was not just land but the homeland. Abandoning it would set the people adrift where, at best, they would suffer from cultural amnesia, and, at worst, risk starvation and vulnerability. Therefore, although Wampanoags often shared Moshup's revulsion for the English and suffered incredible pressure to follow him into exile, they made the hard compromises to persevere in their natal territory.

Moshup never taught the Wampanoags to build walls, but they took up the practice to stake their claim to the island and the integrity of their communities in the face of English expansion. Whether constructed from wood or rock, boundaries like rail bars across Aquinnah's entrance, the "Indian Line Fence" of Chappaquiddick, and the Middle Line between the Mayhews' manor and northern Nashuakemuck, made powerful statements.

---

[1] William S. Simmons, *Spirit of the New England Tribes: Indian History and Folkore, 1620–1984* (Hanover, N.H.: University Press of New England, 1986), 173–4; personal conversation with Tobias Vanderhoop, June 1, 2000.

They identified the Wampanoags inside as members of the community and collective owners of the enclosed land. They reminded Englishmen beyond the pale that Indians had rights they intended to defend. From either vantage, the "other" stood across the border. Yet Wampanoags had learned the act of fencing from colonists, which suggests that the two parties did indeed possess some common ground. There is the island tradition that they shared the task of constructing the Middle Line in the belief that a good wall would make good neighbors. And every barrier had a passage through which select Englishmen entered and Natives exited, leading them out of familiar settings into another world. Walls fenced in, yes, and certainly they fenced out, but sometimes they brought the two peoples together.[2]

Even if the run of stones extending from Waskosim's Rock really is the original Middle Line, its durability was not enough to protect Indian land. This irony leads to a greater truth – the most effective walls on Martha's Vineyard were built not of raw materials, but of institutions and ideas that brought order to the potential chaos of cross-cultural relations. The Mayhews' proprietorship and manor ranks among them. Thomas Mayhew Sr.'s proprietary rights and, later, his manor privileges and political prerogatives under New York, enabled his family to dominate the island's Indian affairs and provided them with ample incentives to keep the peace. Certainly altruism shaped the Mayhews' tolerant evangelicalism and diplomacy, but so did the chance that outside authorities would curtail their independence if cross-cultural hostilities erupted, and their recognition that Indian support kept English political rivals from becoming too assertive. The family's fifty-year rule brought continuity and a measure of trust to Wampanoag–English relations during a tense period. There were no sudden shifts in policy, changes in personnel were rare, and both sides had ample time to learn each other's ways. The death of Thomas Mayhew Sr., the sale of his manor to Thomas Dongan, and the Vineyard's annexation by Massachusetts, weakened the Mayhews' influence and put colonists hostile to Indian interests in power, but the New England Company's acquisition of the manorial title quickened its power to safeguard the Natives. Until the Revolution, the Company used its manor rights to quash sales of Aquinnah territory at a time when other Indian communities were disintegrating piece by piece. Furthermore, Company agents, sometimes inadvertently, encouraged the spread of Indian animal husbandry and fence building, which gave Wampanoags a stronger

---

[2] Informing this discussion is Frederick Barth, ed., *Ethnic Groups and Boundaries: The Social Organization of Culture Difference* (Bergen-Oslo: Universitets Forlaget, 1969); Joane Nagel, *American Indian Ethnic Renewal: Red Power and the Resurgence of Identity and Culture* (New York: Oxford University Press, 1996); Morris W. Foster, *Being Comanche: A Social History of an American Indian Community* (Tuscon: University of Arizona Press, 1991); and Alexandra Harmon, "Wanted: More Histories of Indian Identity," in Philip J. Deloria and Neal Salisbury, eds., *A Companion to American Indian History* (Malden, Mass.: Blackwell, 2002), 248–66.

usufruct claim to their territory. In short, centralized English power in the form of the Mayhew's proprietorship and manor, in all of its incarnations, was essential to peace on Martha's Vineyard and Aquinnah's maintenance of a geographic boundary.

Of all the institutions that influenced Wampanoag history, nothing performed the tripartite functions of fencing in, fencing out, and channeling contact between peoples as effectively as the church. Historians frequently use Christianity to stand for the evils of colonization, but on the Vineyard its role as a gateway between the Wampanoag and English communities was indispensable to their coexistence. It was Christianity that provided Wampanoags with access to English power brokers who at critical moments defended their interests in government and law. It was the Wampanoags' commitment to battle sin that led to the establishment of their own courts within the English judicial system. It was exemplary Indian Christians who became the Wampanoags' magistrates. And it was the Wampanoags' ability to employ the language of Christian morality that occasionally caught the attention of outside authorities when justice was in short supply locally. Colonial legislators would not have made even their half-hearted attempts to protect Aquinnah, Chappaquiddick, and Christiantown, if the residents had not been members of the de facto state church and showed an obvious commitment to Christian social order.

Christianity also served the Wampanoags' efforts to restructure their communities for the challenges of the colonial era. For over two hundred years, churches drew the people together when disease, poverty, land loss, and the sachem's decline, threatened to scatter them in all directions. Churches recruited the Wampanoags' candidates for leadership, developed their literacy and oratorical skills, and provided them with titles that commanded public respect. In courtrooms and on the ground, churchmen led the Indians' battles against English encroachment and the sachems' abuses of power. When the sachems fell, Wampanoag congregations supplied the prototype for the town meeting governments that replaced them. In the late eighteenth and early nineteenth centuries, when exogamous marriages were on the rise, churches helped introduce newcomers to Wampanoag ways. Christianity, in short, bound the Wampanoags together and helped sustain them as a people.

The Vineyard Indians' retention of certain distinct Indian values and customs, like the ethic of reciprocity, oral traditions, and the Wampanoag language, helped them sustain their local identities as Aquinnahs and Chappaquiddicks and their larger identity as Wampanoags. Since so many missionaries advocated stamping out "savage" culture, on the surface it might appear that these traditions survived *despite* Christianity. Yet missionaries did not dictate the terms of Wampanoag religious life. Indians were equal players, if not the dominant ones, from the very start, which enabled them to turn Christianity into an expression of their peoplehood. They transformed Sunday meeting into the local community's main gathering, and turned ordinations and celebrations of the Lord's Supper into Wampanoag tribal events. Well after most Indians had adopted English as their first language, they continued to attend church services where the minister preached in the Native language. The Wampanoags' Christian funerals included grave goods even though they had incorporated coffins, extended burials, and headstones. Wampanoags drew on the ideal of Christian charity to reinforce communal traditions, particularly their generous care of the poor, and they appealed to Christian fellowship to encourage political consensus. The Wampanoags understood that refusing to adapt to English rule was slow suicide, not cultural preservation, but they were not about to sever all ties to the past. That was inconceivable. Instead they appropriated the colonists' religion as their own and imbued it with their core values and community spirit.

Although Christianity helped the Wampanoags carve out space in a white-dominated society, it simultaneously contributed to the racial divisions that relegated them to third-class status, something no one could have foreseen when the mission began in the 1640s. The Indians who first hosted John Eliot told him Christianity would unite them with the English as a single people. As they put it, "in 40 yeers more, some Indians would all be one English, and in a hundred yeers, all Indians here about would so bee." Eliot responded approvingly, "that they and wee were already all one save in two things, which make the only difference betwixt them and us: First, we know, serve, and pray unto God, and they doe not: Secondly, we labour and work in building, planting, clothing our selves &c. and they doe not: and would they but doe as wee doe in these things, they would be all one with English men."[3] A certain naiveté fed this early optimism. Each side readily observed the other's differences in appearance and behavior but had little understanding of the cultural values beneath those forms. As Englishmen learned something about the Indians' communalism, and especially as Indians dealt with the colonists' acquisitiveness, they grew more skeptical about their peoples' compatibility. These differences in cultural values proved remarkably durable, and in many ways they grew more profound, but their outward expressions did not. By the mid– to late seventeenth century the Indians did indeed "know, serve, and pray unto God." They donned English clothes and eventually conformed to English work ways, although never with the urgency their missionaries or employers would have preferred. Yet the Indians' reforms were never enough. Every time they moved closer to the colonists' standard, the bar of civilization rose higher. Wapetunk of Takemmy saw the pattern emerging as early as 1667 when he asked John Cotton Jr., "Why doe not English church men let Indi[an] church men rest in

---

[3] Thomas Shepard, *The Clear Sun-shine of the Gospel Breaking forth upon the INDIANS in New-England* (London, 1648), MHSC 3d ser., 4 (1834), 50.

there houses seeing th[ey] must all rest with God?"⁴ Still, the Wampanoags continued to pursue Christian reforms. When war threatened in the 1670s, they submitted to the crown and established formal courts to enforce biblical law. Then they adopted livestock, erected fences, overthrew traditional leaders, and created town meeting governments. Yet still colonists refused to intermarry with them, to respect the integrity of their territories and jurisdictions, and, most tellingly, to concede that the Wampanoags, or any Indians for that matter, were bona fide Christians. The terror wrought by "friend Indians" during King Philip's War confirmed English suspicions that "civilized" praying Indians were "savages" beneath it all, potentially as treacherous, lazy, ungovernable, and bloodthirsty as Natives of the hinterland were supposed to be. The praying Indians' loyal service hardly mattered if it was only a matter of time before they were exposed as false friends too. For most colonists, the Wampanoags would never "all be one English" no matter what they did.

With wartime hatreds carrying into peacetime, Englishmen had clear consciences about reducing the praying Indians to impotence and poverty. Colonial authorities neutered the Wampanoags' Christian courts, then did away with them altogether, as if to force Natives to adhere to the stereotype that they were incapable of responsible self-government. Many Wampanoags were literate, and all of them were Christian, yet the English refused to sit them on juries, even in trials of their own people. English courts conspired with the Wampanoags' creditors and guardians to force Native people, including children, into bonded labor, even though English masters often neglected Indian children's education and spiritual state. All the while, Massachusetts ignored open violations of laws meant for protecting the Wampanoags' land and limiting their access to liquor. All this was enough to make the Wampanoags believe that Indians were the only true Christians in New England: charitable despite their poverty and faithful despite their trials. Ultimately, it was not religion or culture that made the bar of civilization unreachable for Indians, but white racism, in all of its evolving idioms. And nothing made that lesson so painfully clear to the Wampanoags as the limits of Christian fellowship and the breadth of the colonists' Christian hypocrisy.

The failures of Christianity were just the beginning of the Wampanoags' struggles with race. By the late eighteenth century, white Americans, particularly in the East, tended to think of race as a white–black issue, but the Wampanoags and many other Natives insisted it should be "triangulated" to include them as a distinct group. It was essential for them to do so, since their servile labor and mixed marriages put them at risk of being redefined as "people of color" and "blacks" and losing state protection of their common lands. Yet Indian status carried its own drawbacks in an era of changing American ideas about race and citizenship. Colonial Americans had long conceived

⁴ Cotton Journal, 80.

of male property ownership as the standard for full political participation. Unlike slaves, servants, and wage earners – who were prone to being manipulated by their employers or banding together to soak the rich – propertied men were trusted to exercise independent judgment at the polls and vote against irresponsible wealth redistribution. Yet as it grew clearer during the early nineteenth century that industrialization was accompanied by limited social mobility for wage laborers, Euro-American workers sought respect by demanding full political rights, which they saw as the birthright of America's "white men." They also called for the degradation of "coloreds," who, unlike themselves, supposedly lacked the discipline, morals, and judgment of true republicans, simply by virtue of not being white. At the same time, poor whites on the frontier justified their appropriation of Indian land and aggression against Native peoples by identifying themselves as carriers of the yeoman republic of virtue, hard work, opportunity, and Christianity, and castigating "savages" as the antithesis of these ideals. Andrew Jackson and his Democratic Party became the champion of these men during the 1830s by pursuing universal white male suffrage, heightening poll barriers to "colored" people, and forcing so-called civilized Indians like the Cherokees, Creeks, Choctaws, and Chickasaws from their homelands. In short, more than ever before, white Americans conflated citizenship with whiteness and contrasted it with blackness and Indianness, leading to the dramatic expansion of white opportunity at the expense of racial others. Protected "Indian" status on a small reservation was about the best Wampanoags could hope for under these circumstances, but even then they were dismissed as a disappearing or blackened remnant that did not belong in a modernizing, democratic, and "white" America.[5]

Americans gradually accepted the idea of propertyless white voters, but even after Reconstruction they continued to judge communal Indian landholding as fundamentally incompatible with a society premised on "getting ahead." It was for this reason that Massachusetts made the Wampanoags forfeit their special Indian status and divide their common lands as the cost of citizenship. In the parlance of the era, Indians had to "become white" before they could become citizens, an idea that was eventually writ large in the Dawes Allotment Act of 1887, which parceled out the lands of western Indian reservations and eventually granted individual recipients the vote. The Wampanoags knew better. Reluctantly, they conceded to partition, but

[5] For a handful of leading works on these themes, see David R. Roediger, *The Wages of Whiteness: Race and the Making of the American Working Class* (New York: Verso, 1991); Joanne Pope Melish, *Disowning Slavery: Gradual Emancipation and "Race" in New England, 1780–1860* (Ithaca: Cornell University Press, 1998); Alexander Saxton, *Rise and Fall of the White Republic: Class Politics and Mass Culture in Nineteenth-Century America* (New York: Verso, 1990); Sean Wilentz, *Chants Democratic: New York City and the Rise of the American Working Class, 1788–1850* (New York: Oxford University Press, 1984); and a special issue of *Journal of the Early Republic* 19 (Winter, 1999).

when outside attention finally drifted from them, they restored communal values to the center of their collective life. They have remained there to this day.

Two difficult questions naturally arise from the story of the Vineyard Wampanoags. The first, which is fraught with ambiguity, is whether the sea wall surrounding the island was, in the end, the most significant factor in the Wampanoag–English peace and the Natives' retention of part of their homeland. During the period of European exploration, water was less an impediment to cross-cultural contact than an artery, making the Vineyard one of the most dynamic sites of the Columbian exchange. However, the violence of early encounters convinced island Wampanoags to withdraw from European commerce and diplomacy and to greet those who sought them out with violence. It was this *human* decision to turn the island into a sanctuary that enabled offshore Wampanoags to avoid the mainland's fierce intertribal and intercultural rivalries during the early seventeenth century and to escape the horrific epidemics of 1616–1618 and 1633. Political and geographic isolation, then, contributed to the Wampanoags' long-standing population majority and, in turn, made the English more cautious in their dealings. Similarly, the island limits of Thomas Mayhew's political power encouraged Wampanoags and Englishmen to look within the shoreline for solutions to their problems and to reach an uncommon range of compromises. Probably the Vineyard's offshore location discouraged English migration, thereby ensuring that pressure on Indian land remained low, but so did its relatively poor agricultural potential (like Cape Cod's), lack of participatory government, undistinguished pastorate, and the Mayhews' lackluster effort to recruit settlers. The water insulated Vineyarders during King Philip's War by requiring any invading force to launch a highly coordinated amphibious assault. But then again, if Philip's men or the colonial mob believed they had support among their island counterparts, it is possible they would have tried. Peace on the Vineyard flowed from the accord struck by Wampanoag and English islanders as well as the waters that surrounded them.

The role of geography in community survival is no less opaque. Aquinnah's peninsular location on the least populated end of an island certainly worked in the Natives' favor. There was only one entrance to guard and few whites nearby to try to breach it. Yet those few did try over and over again. The Aquinnah Wampanoags' answer was to erect a fence across the peninsula, fill nearby pasture with livestock, and keep the road in disrepair. If only other communities had taken similar advantage of their locations. Chappaquiddick was an island. Sengekontacket, Deep Bottom, and parts of Nunnepog were bound on three sides by ponds and the sea. Yet all of these communities died. Geography was a tool, not a promise.

The Aquinnah Wampanoags' survival as a distinct group also sprung from their exceptionally talented leadership and determined collective action. Unlike several neighboring Indian communities, Gay Head unseated its sachem when he began eviscerating the people's land base and replaced him with a town meeting that has survived with nominal changes for 300 years. When the island's other Indian settlements were collapsing with barely a fight, Zachariah Howwoswee Sr. prosecuted his community's enemies through every available means. The Aquinnah Wampanoags even distinguished themselves after the Revolution in their reluctance to wed outsiders and their tendency to make "strangers" feel unwelcome. Thus, the people experienced less internal pressure to divide the land and adopt the franchise. Without these initiatives, the advantages of Aquinnah's location would have been wasted.

The second question raised by the Wampanoags' experience is whether the conditions that advanced Indian–colonial coexistence on Martha's Vineyard, such as Indian adaptability (particularly adoption of the colonists' state religion) and centralized colonial power, were present elsewhere in early America and, if so, why they were not more widely exploited. The most obvious parallels come from French Canada. Its leaders were crown-appointed military men whose tenure depended partially on their handling of Indian affairs because of the Natives' importance as fur trappers, military allies (and potential enemies), and souls for influential missionary societies. New France's leaders could not meet their economic and imperial goals by strong-arming the Indians. Thus, like the Mayhews, they had to foster mutual affection and respect to exercise indirect influence, even going so far as to mediate the Indians' intertribal disputes by distributing massive quantities of presents and sometimes forgiving Indians for violent crimes against French colonists. French Jesuits, like the Mayhews, learned the Indians' languages, lived in or near their communities, and made strident efforts to relate Catholicism to the Indians' existing beliefs, thereby enabling them to win scores of followers across the Canadian hinterland and to gather several mission communities, a number of which exist today in the St. Lawrence River Valley. Unlike Englishmen on the Vineyard, French fur traders commonly cohabitated with and married Indian women, which confirmed the metaphorical kin terms they used with one another and created offspring who became essential mediators between their peoples. It is telling, however, that even under these circumstances New France never reached a Vineyard-like peace, nor could it have, since it was not an island inhabited by a singe Indian nation without complicated commercial and military considerations. In Canada, an alliance with one Indian nation often meant war with that nation's enemies. Yet New France did build a remarkable record of peace with numerous tribes on the basis of common rituals, kin ties, and mutual interests. The accommodations reached by Indians and Frenchmen were analogous in many ways to the ones that shaped Martha's Vineyard and allowed them too to share America.[6]

---

[6] The literature on French–Indian relations in and around Canada is vast. Among many excellent works, see Kenneth M. Morrison, *The Embattled Northeast: The Elusive Ideal of Alliance*

Ironically, the English colonies compare less favorably with Martha's Vineyard. Particularly during the first two-thirds of the seventeenth century, centralized colonial political power was rare along the Atlantic coast. It did exist on paper in proprietary Maryland and Pennsylvania, but the leadership's early commitment to missionary work (as in Maryland) and strict oversight of land policy (as in Pennsylvania) became a casualty of power struggles in which unruly settlers forced democratic concessions.[7] No other area under English control matched the limited potential of these colonies.

in Abenaki–Euramerican Relations (Berkeley, Calif.: University of California Press, 1984); James Axtell, *The Invasion Within: The Contest of Cultures in Colonial North America* (New York: Oxford University Press, 1985); Bruce G. Trigger, *Natives and Newcomers: Canada's "Heroic Age" Reconsidered* (Kingston, Ont.: McGill-Queen's University Press, 1985); Trigger, *The Children of Aataentsic: A History of the Huron People to 1660*, 2 vols. (Montreal: McGill-Queen's University Press, 1976); Daniel K. Richter, *The Ordeal of the Longhouse: The Peoples of the Iroquois League in the Era of European Colonization* (Chapel Hill: University of North Carolina Press for the Institute of Early American History and Culture, 1992); Denys Delâge, *Bitter Feast: Amerindians and Europeans in Northeastern North America, 1600–1664*, Jane Brierley, trans. (Vancouver: University of British Columbia Press, 1993); Richard White, *The Middle Ground, Indians, Empire, and Republics in the Great Lakes Region, 1650–1815* (New York: Cambridge University Press, 1991); Eric Hinderaker, *Elusive Empires: Constructing Colonialism in the Ohio Valley, 1673–1800* (New York: Cambridge University Press, 1997), chaps. 1–2; Catherine M. Desbarats, "The Cost of Early Canada's Native Alliances: Reality and Scarcity's Rhetoric," *WMQ* 52 (1995), 609–30; James P. Ronda, "The Sillery Experiment: A Jesuit–Indian Village in New France, 1637–1663," *American Indian Culture and Research Journal* 3 (1979), 1–18; John Steckley, "The Warrior and the Lineage: Jesuit Use of Iroquoian Images to Communicate Christianity," *Ethnohistory* 39 (1992), 478–509; Jan Grabowski, "French Criminal Justice and Indians in Montreal, 1670–1760," *Ethnohistory* 43 (1996), 405–29.

7 On Maryland, see Wesley Frank Craven, *The Southern Colonies in the Seventeenth Century* (1949; Baton Rogue: Louisiana State University Press, 1970), 200–1, 300–7; Helen C. Rountree and Thomas E. Davidson, *Eastern Shore Indians of Virginia and Maryland* (Charlottesville: University of Virginia Press, 1997), chaps. 3–4; C. A. Weslager, *The Nanticoke Indians: Past and Present* (Newark: University of Delaware Press, 1983); James H. Merrell, "Cultural Continuity among the Piscataway Indians of Colonial Maryland," *WMQ* 36 (1979), 548–70; Axtell, "White Legend: The Jesuit Missions in Maryland," in his *After Columbus: Essays in the Ethnohistory of Colonial North America* (New York: Oxford University Press, 1988), 73–85; Francis Jennings, "Indians and Frontiers in Seventeenth-Century Maryland," in David B. Quinn, ed., *Early Maryland in a Wider World* (Detroit: Wayne State Press, 1982), 216–41. On Pennsylvania, see Alden T. Vaughan, "Frontier Banditti and the Indians: The Paxton Boys' Legacy," *Pennsylvania History* 51 (1984), 1–29; Jennings, "Brother Miquon: Good Lord!" in Richard S. Dunn and Mary Maples Dunn, eds., *The World of William Penn* (Philadelphia: University of Pennsylvania Press, 1986), 195–214; Jennings, "'Pennsylvania Indians' and the Iroquois," in Daniel K. Richter and James H. Merrell, eds., *Beyond the Covenant Chain: The Iroquois and Their Neighbors in Indian North America, 1600–1800* (Syracuse, N.Y.: Syracuse Univerrsity Press, 1987), 75–92; Jennings, *Empire of Fortune: Crowns, Colonies, and Tribes in the Seven Years War in America* (New York: W. W. Norton, 1988); Jane T. Merritt, "Dreaming of the Savior's Blood: Moravians and the Indian Great Awakening in Pennsylvania," *WMQ* 54 (1997), 723–46; Merrell, *Into the American Woods: Negotiators on the Pennsylvania Frontier* (New York: W. W. Norton, 1999).

With the exception of seventeenth-century Massachusetts, Plymouth, and Martha's Vineyard, and, to a lesser degree, eighteenth-century New York, every English colony failed to launch a missionary program of notable scale or duration, despite widespread acknowledgement that Jesuit efforts were at the root of New France's successful Indian diplomacy. Scholars have identified several reasons for the lifeless evangelicalism of the English: lack of sponsorship from a centralized church, married clergymen unwilling to expose their families to the dangers of life among the Indians, the colonists' headlong pursuit of landed wealth, English xenophobia, and religiously heterogeneous colonial populations unable to rally behind a single religious denomination.[8] Factors varied colony by colony, but the cumulative effect was that Englishmen lacked a shared ceremonial base, ideology, and population of trusted church figures with which to peaceably engage Native peoples. The rituals of political alliances such as the "Convenant Chain" between the Iroquois and New York or the "Chain of Friendship" between the Iroquois and Pennsylvania were imperfect substitutes.[9] The participants did not answer to a single god or moral standard, and diplomats from either side often worked at cross-purposes and deeply mistrusted one another, despite claims that they were linked as "fathers," "brothers," or "children." Englishmen involved in Native affairs more often than not lacked formal political power and high social standing, and thus could not guarantee that their promises would be kept. Most important, ritual diplomacy was limited to men of high status, with some exceptions among the Indians. To coexist, the two peoples needed something that transcended their many differences and reached into the common ranks. Without religion and blood, once the trade collapsed there was little else from which to choose. These shortcomings wrought bloody consequences across the early American frontier.

Even if the English had fulfilled their pledges to proselytize Native America, it is unlikely they could have produced a Christian Indian population as devout or acculturated as the Vineyard Wampanoags. Indeed, the Wampanoags showed a greater dedication to Christianity than most Catholic Indians in New France. Certainly the Wampanoags found creative ways to meld their traditional religious beliefs and customs with Christianity, and reconfigure their social hierarchy to church offices and courts, but the extent

---

[8] The best analysis of this issue is Axtell, *Invasion Within.* Also useful is Margaret Connel Szasz, *Indian Education in the American Colonies, 1607–1783* (Albuquerque: University of New Mexico Press, 1985).

[9] Jennings, *The Ambiguous Iroquois Empire: The Covenant Chain Confederation of Indian Tribes with the English Colonies* (New York: W. W. Norton, 1984); Jennings, *Empire of Fortune*; Richter, *Ordeal of the Longhouse*, chaps. 6, 10; Merrell, *Into the American Woods.* Especially insightful on the expectations Indians brought to their treaty alliances, but that Europeans generally did not reciprocate, is Robert A. Williams, *Linking Arms Together: American Indian Treaty Visions of Law and Peace, 1600–1800* (New York: Oxford University Press, 1997).

of their reforms was vast, from their abandonment of powwowing, to their active suppression of sin, to their changes in dress and burial ways, and far more. Generally Indians rejected such changes until they had been subjected to colonial rule and lost most of their lands. The Vineyard Wampanoags were different because the devastation of epidemic disease coupled with Thomas Mayhew Jr.'s skillfully crafted message convinced them of the power of the Christian God. It was the quest for his power that brought such energy to their Christianity and to the reforms that protected some of their autonomy and lands and underwrote the peace.

Martha's Vineyard's unique history emerged from favorable conditions for Indian–English coexistence and the bold, innovative people who capitalized on them. It might seem no surprise that its model for intercultural peace and Indian survival was not replicated elsewhere, given that model's contingence upon so many discrete events and personalities. However, this tiny eccentric island teaches a broad lesson about the meeting of peoples in early America by revealing the transcendent power of faith run aground the nefarious shoals of race. European settlers knew that Christianity could bring disparate human populations to terms with one another. They wrote of it in colony charters, spoke of it in sermons, and jotted it down in letters. What they did not know at the onset of their American venture were the limits of their Christian convictions when dealing with peoples of another complexion. Even on Martha's Vineyard, the legend of the Middle Line was more myth than history, since Englishmen ignored the wall to dispossess the praying Indians and relegate them to an abject status. It was the failure of Christian brotherhood that taught Wampanoags about the racial boundaries between them and neighboring whites. Fortunately, the faith also empowered the Wampanoags to write those boundaries onto the Vineyard landscape to safeguard parts of their culture and homeland.

Appendix A: The Population of Martha's Vineyard

Year	Indian Population								Non-Indian Population			
	Chappaquiddick	Nunnepog	Sengekontacket	Takemmy	Nashuakemuck	Deep Bottom	Aquinnah	Total	Edgartown	Tisbury	Chilmark	Total
ca. 1642								est. 3000				est. 85
1660												225
1675								approx. 1500				est. 350
1693									est. 125	est. 120		
1698	138	84	136	72	231	35	260	956	est. 200			est. 400
1705							Christians	approx. 900				
1714							248					
1720								est. 800				
1741												est. 1200
ca. 1747							112–165	est. 500–600				
1757									est. 900	est. 600	est. 455	1955
1765	86			39			188	>313	944	799	663	2406
1783									1220	1186	706	3112
1786								est. 400				
1790	75		25	40	24		276	440				3245
1792							251					
1798							est. 200					
1801			20	37	20		242	320				3118
1807	65–80						270					
1816												
1821	91		10	44		10	244	399				3292
1823	100		12	51		13	250	426				
1827	101		approx. 12	45		approx. 12	250	420				
1833								est. 400				
1839	70			<50			>200					3958
1849	85			49			174	408				4540
1861	74			53		13	204	>344				4403

SOURCES: APPENDIX A

S. F. Cook, *The Indian Population of New England in the Seventeenth Century* (Berkeley, 1976); "Historical Collections," 141–227; Charles Edward Banks, *The History of Martha's Vineyard*, 3 vols. (Boston, 1911); *Conquests and Triumphs;* "Indian Visitation"; *Some Correspondence;* NE Co. MSS 7955/1, 56; Experience Mayhew, *A Brief Account of the State of the Indians on Martha's Vineyard . . . 1694 to 1720*, appended to E. Mayhew, *A Discourse Shewing That God Dealeth with Men as Reasonable Creatures* (Boston, 1720); William Mayhew Memorandum Book, MVHS; Mass. Archives, 31:550, 643–5; Zachariah Mayhew to Richard Johnson, December 26, 1786, NE Co. MSS 7956/2, 21–26; Moses Howwoswee, Account of the Indians Resident at Gay Head, March 19, 1792, Misc. Unbound MSS, MHS; List of Children Under 18 at Gay Head, 1798, Misc. Unbound MSS, MHS; Zachariah Mayhew to Peter Thatcher, July 28, 1801, SPGNA, Records, Box 3, Folder 11; William Freeman, "A Description of Dukes County, Aug. 13th 1807," *MHSC* 2d ser., 3 (1815), 38–94; ULRIA, Box 2, File 8029–1816 (4); Massachusetts Governor's Council Files, "Report on Complaint of the Chappaquiddick Natives, &c., Box, June 1808–July 1809;" Ebenezer Skiff to Paul Cuffee, October 1816, Paul Cuffee Letterbook, NBFPL; Letter of Frederick Baylies, May 17, 1821, SPGNA, Recs., Box 1, File 5; Baylies, "The Names and Ages of the Indians on Martha's Vineyard . . . Jan. 1, 1823," NEHGS; Mass. House Document No. 68 (1827); Frederick Baylies, Letters, Box 26, Letter B, MVHS; D. Wrighte to Alden Bradford, April 9, 1839, Andrews-Eliot Coll., MHS; *Report of the Commissioners;* Earle Report.

APPENDIX A: EXPLANATION OF FIGURES

Figures for the Vineyard's Native population in the mid–seventeenth century are necessarily approximate. Contemporary writers made only general statements, such as that the Vineyard was a place "whereon many Indians live."[1] In 1674, Thomas Mayhew Sr. reported that the Vineyard and Nantucket each contained 300 Indian families, which given a low estimate of 5 persons per family would have put 1,500 natives on each island.[2] During King Philip's War, the Englishmen on Nantucket wrote to the governor of New York that their island had between 500 and 600 Indians capable of bearing arms and a total Indian population of 1,500. The Vineyard, they

---

[1] Samuel Maverick, "A Briefe Description of New England (1660)," Massachusetts Historical Society, *Proceedings*, 2d ser., 21 (1884–85), 243.
[2] "Historical Collections," 205.

asserted, had fewer native men of fighting age.[3] In 1694, Matthew Mayhew submitted that Martha's Vineyard and Nantucket collectively held "about" 3,000 adult Indians in the mid–seventeenth century.[4] Experience Mayhew obviously used these figures to posit that "1500 Souls" lived on the island in 1642.[5] Anthropologist S. F. Cook thought otherwise. He used the Mayhews' data to estimate a preepidemic population of 3,500 for the Vineyard and 2,500 for the smaller, less-forested Nantucket, numbers tacitly supported by historian Neal Salisbury.[6] David Henige includes Cook among Indian demographic history's chronic "High Counters," but I suspect he was close to the mark.[7] In 1698, following a vicious 1690 epidemic, Grindal Rawson and Samuel Danforth counted 955 Indians on the Vineyard with an average family size of 5.4.[8] Seven years later, Experience Mayhew reported 180 Indian families on the island, which by Rawson and Danforth's numbers would add up to a population of 972. Given what is known about the virulence of European disease among early American Indian populations, it is certainly possible that the Vineyard's Native population decreased by some two-thirds between 1642 and 1700, which would put the population at about 3,000 at the time of English settlement.

---

[3] Franklin B. Hough, *Papers Relating to the Island of Nantucket, with Documents relating to the Original Settlement of the Island, Martha's Vineyard and other Islands adjacent, known as Dukes County, While under the Colony of New York* (Albany, 1865), 84–5.

[4] *Conquests and Triumphs*, 30.

[5] Mayhew, *A Brief Account of the State of the Indians on Martha's Vineyard*, appendix to his *A Discourse Shewing That God Dealeth with Men as with Reasonable Creatures* (Boston, 1720), 2; "E. Mayhew to Anonymous, July 20, 1741," Mayhew Papers.

[6] Cook, *The Indian Population of New England in the Seventeenth Century*, University of California Publications in Anthropology 12 (Berkeley: University of California Press, 1976), 44; Salisbury, *Manitou and Providence: Indians, Europeans, and the Making of New England, 1500–1643* (New York: Oxford University Press, 1982), 29.

[7] Henige, *Numbers from Nowhere: The American Indian Contact Population Debate* (Norman: University of Oklahoma Press, 1998).

[8] "Indian Visitation," 131–2.

Appendix B

A Cross-Comparison of Official Descriptions of the Race/Complexion of Martha's Vineyard Indians

Name	1823 Census Description	Seaman's Protection Papers Description (Year)	Crew List Description (Year)
George Belain Sr.	1/4 Indian, 3/8 black, 5/8 white		"Yellow" with black hair (1832–36)
Aaron Cooper	3/4 Indian, 1/8 black, 1/8 white	"Copper" with black hair and eyes (1836)	"Mixed" (1829); "Black" with black hair (1833)
Coombs Cooper	3/4 Indian, 1/8 black, 1/8 white		"Indian" with black hair (1828) "Mulatto" with black hair (1831)
Elijah Cooper	3/4 Indian, 1/8 black, 1/8 white		"Md." with black hair (1818) "Copper" with "wooley" hair (1820) "Light Brown" (1824) "Indian" with black hair (1825)
Joseph C. Cooper	3/4 Indian, 1/8 black, 1/8 white		"Indian" with black hair (1824, 1828)
George David	3/4 Indian, 1/4 black		"Copper" with black hair (1831)

Name	1823 Census Description	Seaman's Protection Papers Description (Year)	Crew List Description (Year)
John Devine Sr.	Full black		"Black" with "wooley" hair (1832)
Philip Dodge	3/4 Indian, 1/8 black, 1/8 white	"Indian" (1842); "black" (1853)	"Yellow" with black hair (1834 and 1838)
Isaac Ephraim	1/2 Indian, 1/4 black, 1/4 white		"Black" with black hair (1820)
James Francis	Full Indian		"Indian" with black hair (1824–26, 1832) "Colored" with black hair (1831) "Wd." with black hair (1819–1821, 1836)
Thomas Francis	Full Indian		"Yellow" with black hair (1822, 1826) "Indian" with black hair (1825)
Francis Goodrich	1/4 Indian, 1/2 black, 1/4 white		"Mg." with black hair (1834) "Black" with black hair (1828) "Native" with black hair (1829)
Samuel P. Goodrich	1/4 Indian, 1/2 black, 1/4 white		"Yellow" with black hair (1831)
Isaac Johnson	1/2 Indian, 1/4 black, 1/4 white		"Colored" (1826) "Yellow" with "wooley" hair (1831)
Emanuel Joseph	1/2 Indian, 1/4 black, 1/4 white		"Black" with green eyes and "wooley" hair (1827)
Abel Manning	1/2 Indian, 1/4 black, 1/4 white	"Brown" (1845); "Indian" (1850)	

(continued)

(*continued*)

Name	1823 Census Description	Seaman's Protection Papers Description (Year)	Crew List Description (Year)
Thomas Manning	1/2 Indian, 1/4 black, 1/4 white		"Black" with "wooley" or "curly" hair (1832–33, 1835)
Andrew Nevers	3/4 Indian, 1/8 black, 1/8 white		"Black" with "wooley" hair (1830)
Simon Panu (II)	Full Indian		"Indian" with "straight black" hair (1826)
Asa Peters	5/8 Indian, 3/8 black		"Black" (1827)
Francis Peters	1/2 Indian, 1/4 black, 1/4 white		"Yellow" (1828)
George Peters	1/4 Indian, 3/4 black		"Black" with black or "wooley" hair (1828–33)
Johnson Simpson	2/6 Indian, 1/6 black, 3/6 white		"Black" with black hair (1826, 1832–33, 1835) "Light" with brown hair (1829)
Nathan S. Webquish	1/2 Indian, 1/4 black, 1/4 white		"Mulatto" with black hair (1829, 1834)

Index